The Last Dance

The Last Dance

Family Secrets and the Chicago Mob

James Jack and Eldon Ham

Copyright © 2011 by James Jack and Eldon Ham.

Library of Congress Control Number: 2010914277
ISBN: Hardcover   978-1-4535-8499-6
             Softcover   978-1-4535-8498-9
             Ebook   978-1-4535-8500-9

All rights reserved. No part of this book may be reproduced or transmitted in any form or by any means, electronic or mechanical, including photocopying, recording, or by any information storage and retrieval system, without permission in writing from the copyright owner.

This book was printed in the United States of America.

To order additional copies of this book, contact:
Xlibris Corporation
1-888-795-4274
www.Xlibris.com
Orders@Xlibris.com

Contents

Acknowledgments 9
Preface 13
Introduction 17

1 The Talking Dead 21
2 The Underworld 31
3 Family Secrets 47
4 The Night Chicago Died 65
5 Route 66 77
6 Plymouth Fucking Rock 91
7 Juice, Pizza & Vic Damone 109
8 Philly Beans and Me 121
9 Big Tuna, Little Jimmy 133
10 Tough Guys 146
11 Too Many Suspects 156
12 The Killer Breeze 183
13 Heavy Work 200
14 Strangers in the Night 214
15 The Godfather of Las Vegas 227
16 The Fateful Gloves of Nicky C. 245
17 My Name is Joey 261
18 The Last Supper 280
19 The Last Dance 302
20 Epilogue 310

Index 331

Dedication

To the Memory of James A. Jack

During the editing of this book my father passed away December 20th at the age of 82. My younger brother always said that dad was a "20th Century Dickens" and he would respond with a smile in his Scottish eyes followed by a subtle laugh and a short life story. Dad was the real deal, an original, a one of a kind, born, raised and mentored by the neighborhoods and streets of Chicago. He was not one to sit on the sidelines and watch life pass by, but would engage life no matter how it unfolded. Dad had a calling of sort, serve the neighborhoods for the betterment of the good and protect the streets from harm. Between these pages is a brief part of his life, dreams, nightmares and justice that shaped a small piece of Chicago's character. On behalf of my stepmom, brothers, sisters, grandchildren, great grandchildren, and all his friends that knew him as "Jimmy Jack," participate, embrace and enjoy life, and above all love the book.

Love you dad,
James R. Jack

and

Mitchell A. Mars, Chief, Organized Crime Section, Office of the United States Attorney, Chicago, Illinois (1952-2008) whose tireless work from 1992 to his untimely death led to the multiple convictions of the Family Secrets defendants, bringing justice for all, and a modicum of closure to many.

Acknowledgments

How do you thank so many for bringing my story to life, not to mention those who made a lifetime of work possible?

A special thank you goes to my co-author Eldon Ham for his continued support, respect, and faith in my project. I feel lucky to have his guidance, advice, and editorial ideas; working with him has been a pleasure. Our assistant Meghan, who contributed more effort to the manuscript than she may have expected, also deserves recognition for her enthusiastic contribution.

I will always be grateful to my dear friend David Uslan for all the time he devoted to helping me launch my book.

I would also like to acknowledge Det. Sgt. George Murphy, and my partner, mentor, and best friend Det. Frank Czech. Without their help, I feel I would have had no career on the Chicago Police force. I will forever be grateful to both.

How do you say "thank you" to so many who have helped so much in many large and small ways over the course of the Family Secrets trial? Their contributions have been invaluable and I am sincerely grateful for their help and support. I tried to include in the manuscript everyone who gave special attention to me and to my story; I sincerely regret if I omitted anyone.

Moreover, as a former law man myself, I would also like to acknowledge that neither this book nor the Family Secrets trial would have been possible without the contribution and cooperation of the Federal Bureau of Investigation, Internal Revenue Service, and the office of the United States Attorney for the Northern District of Illinois, especially U.S. Attorney Patrick J. Fitzgerald, First Assistant U.S. Attorney Gary Shapiro, Federal Bureau Special Agents Tracy Balinao, Dana DePooter, Mark Gutknecht, Andrew Hickey,

Christopher Mackey, Edward McNamara, Luigi Mondini, Christopher Smith, Anita Stamat, Michael W. Maseth, and John Mallul.

I wish also to acknowledge all the wonderful people I met daily at the Family Secrets trial, several of whom chose to share their personal thoughts with me, including a number of victim family members, law enforcement personnel, courtroom support staff, and others such as Michael J. Cain, author of the compelling book The Tangled Web; Al and Beryl Blitz; my dear friend Scott Cassidy, Assistant States Attorney from the Organized Crime Unit; Peter J. Wacks of Wacks Associates, a retires FBI agent; Dr. Patrick Spilotro and his wife Kathy; Chicago Sun-Times sports reporter Rick Telander; Crime of the Century author William J. Martin, whose book depicted the crime and trial of mass murderer Richard Speck who killed eight Chicago nurses in 1966; Chicago Sun-Times political columnist Carol Marin; widow Peggy Cagnoni (whose husband's car had been detonated by Frank Calabrese, Sr.); defendant Anthony "Twan" Doyle with whom I had many remarkable conversation during the course of the trial; the Ortiz family—Frank (brother of the victim), Ellen (widow), and Tony (son)—it was wonderful meeting and know all of them; Commander David G. Turnbaugh, Deerfield Police Dept.; attorney John S. Delnero of the Chicago firm Bell, Boyd & Lloyd; councilman Steve Bagbey from Evansville, IN.

I am especially grateful to my dear, dear friend and assistant Dawn Tremblay whose long hours, computer and email skills, and knowledge made this book happen. Jim Hub, general manager of Motor Werks, Barrington, IL helped me out in a pinch—thank you, Jim, for everything.

The labors of my book were partially in loving memory of my late dear friend and colleague Sgt. John A. DiMaggio (April 19, 1933 to February 8, 2008). I worked with John beginning with his first day on the job in 1957.

With great pleasure I acknowledge the help, understanding, and friendship of many, many law enforcement colleagues at the Federal Building in Chicago, all of whom did a first class job during the trial: Deputy U. S. Marshals John Glover, Mark Gunnoe, Jake Knight, Joe Manno, Curtis Blanc, Edward Gabes, and my special pal "Comet" who performs as Marshal Gabes' bomb sniffing dog.

Throughout the manuscript process I received much support from many service providers, for which I am very grateful: the eager staff and principals at K&M Printing Company in Schaumburg, Illinois, including Gary and Phil O'Brill; Rich, Mike, and Ken Stobart, and Christine Arendarczyk who helped me throughout the year [keep your chin up, Chris].

My favorite restaurants and their wonderful owners deserve a special thanks: for letting me occupy a table for hours on end as I worked and reworked my manuscript drafts: Joe & Giuseppe's Italian Restaurant in Arlington Heights, Illinois (and owner Pasquale Taibi; Christi's German Inn, Palatine, Illinois (and Olaf and Rosina); and Peter O'Brien's Restaurant & Bar on north Wells Street in Chicago's Old Town neighborhood.

No one deserves praise and extreme gratitude more than my long time friend and colleague Judge James Zagel who presided over the Family Secrets trial and welcomed me in his courtroom every day. I am eternally grateful for Judge Zagel's courtesy to me and his tireless efforts, devotion, and professionalism in conducting a long and arduous multiple murder trial. Judge Zagel's magnificent staff deserve a special mention: Anne M. Wolf, Steve Newman, Donald Walker, Ted Wiszowaty, and the delightful court reporter Blanca I. Lara. Thank you to all who made my project a little easier.

There is a special place in my heart for those in government service, so in addition to the others above, I would like to acknowledge William Paulin, Laura Shimkus, and Michael Walsch, all with the Internal Revenue Service, plus Randall A. Samborn from the Asst. U.S. Attorney Public Information Office who helped me almost every day during the trial, plus special agent Robert D. Grant, in charge of the FBI Chicago office.

Key members of the prosecution from the Office of the United States Attorney, including Denise Marie Belanger, T. Markus Funk, John Scully, Felice Weiler, and Mitchell A. Mars, deserve special acknowledgment and accolades. Without them, there would have been no Family Secrets justice.

My heartfelt thanks to all my friends of the news media in television, radio, and newspapers including Rummana Hussain, Chicago Sun-Times; Mike Robinson, reporter for the Associated Press; Steve Miller from WBBN news radio 780; Tom McNamee and Ron Theel, Chicago Sun-Times; and John "Bull Dog" Drummond, one of the best in the business.

I would be remiss not to acknowledge my wonderful physicians who do their best to keep me strong: Dr. Steven Leibach, Dr. Gilbert A. Sita, and Dr. Scott Glazer. Thank you for your unrelenting kindness.

Thank you to attorney Paul M. Brayman, counsel to Frank "the German" Schweihs, who kindly helped me where privilege and propriety would allow; and to Verna Sadock, the best sketch artist around, who provided the outstanding artist's courtroom scene for my book.

All the families of victims who I met at trial deserve to be acknowledged, especially Emma Seifert and her son Joey Seifert, who watched as Joey's father was gunned down in plain view. Thank you for all your time, and for the photos you kindly provided.

Finally, special thanks and acknowledgment to my dear friend Franchee Harmon who believed in me and published my first book Three Boys Missing—Franchee, you are strong and you will make it.

# # # #

Preface

When imprisoned and long established Chicago mob insider Frank Calabrese, Jr., typed and mailed a letter offering testimony and assistance against his own father, the feared patriarch and hit man Frank Calabrese, Sr., the fall of the Chicago mob as we once knew it was set into motion. Not many letters are disguised as a bullet, but this one was, eventually leading to the great Family Secrets multiple murder trial that brought down some of the most feared mob figures in the Chicago Syndicate history.

The Last Dance is a personal memoir of James A. Jack, a former homicide detective who began with the Chicago Police Department in 1954, then was thrust into one of the most famous Chicago murder cases of the 1950s when three young Chicago boys suddenly disappeared. That case endured a 40-year investigation of murder and intrigue, leading the author, known to many as Jimmy Jack, to write his first book *Three Boys Missing*, a true crime winner of three awards in non-fiction.

Fate brought Jimmy and me together. I agreed to help write this memoir that mostly takes place concurrently in multiple eras, mostly during the 1950s through 1980s, together with the modern day Family Secrets trial that unfolded in a Chicago federal courtroom during the summer of 2007. Jimmy Jack was there. He attended every day of the Family Secrets trial, recording key testimony of such mob luminaries as Joey Lombardo, Frank Calabrese, Sr., and Frank Calabrese, Jr., and multiple other accused mob insiders who were either defendants or prosecution witnesses. But that is not all; Jimmy's story is unique because Jimmy Jack was also present when many of these Mafia celebrities had first established themselves in the 1950s when Jimmy was on the ChPD force. Even his first true partner on the force, a cop called "Philly Beans" Tolomeo, turned out to be mob connected.

I got to know Jimmy Jack as both an icon of Chicago history and as a person, one of the sweetest guys around yet street-wise almost to a fault with a twinkle in his eye and a penetrating sense of humor. When I randomly asked one day if he had a personal opinion on what had happened to the mob-connected union leader Jimmy Hoffa, Jimmy Jack did not blink. "Look in the phone book under cement."

Jimmy Jack knows nearly everyone in Chicago law enforcement and the local judiciary from former governor and federal prosecutor James R. Thompson to James Zagel, the presiding Judge in the Family Secrets trial itself. Jimmy is even acquainted with Michael Uslan, who produced the latest round of spectacular *Batman* films in and around Chicago, and his son David Uslan, a rising filmmaker with a special interest in Mafia stories. Jimmy gets around. He once acted as body guard for the late Jackie Kennedy during one of her trips to Chicago, and he includes film star and former real-life Chicago cop Dennis Farina, Heisman Trophy winner Johnny Lattner, and football expert Tom Lemming, among his many friends.

Jimmy not only investigated and arrested many of the mob figures behind the Family Secrets investigation, he grew up with some of them in the neighborhoods, sometimes playing cards or dice with local tough guys when they were all of 14 years old. Later when he was on the police force, Jimmy was punched in the face by future mob hit man Frank Calabrese, and he even knew Bottles Capone, Ralph's bother.

The Last Dance covers Jimmy's life story, punctuated with additional Chicago mob history from the old Levy District days, where the term "underworld" was first coined, to such kingpins as Accardo and Giancana, not to mention the real story behind the slain Spilotro brothers, whose demise was depicted, somewhat erroneously, on the silver screen in the acclaimed film *Casino*. We tried to tell Jimmy's story not only from his perspective as a witness to the Family Secrets trial, but as a personal participant in Chicago mob history from five decades earlier, spicing his accounts of the trial testimony with Jimmy's own experience, observations, and mob stories. As it happens, Jimmy could just have easily grown up on the wrong side of the law like so many of the neighborhood gang. Jimmy's childhood was no picnic; he was actually kidnapped by his own father, ripped away from his mother to live secretly in another state. And he certainly could have joined any number of local street thugs when he returned to Chicago, still young and impressionable.

The mob—called The Outfit in Chicago—is an enigma. I learned from Jimmy that although its collective psyche is cold, distant, and detached, like the black eyes of a killer shark with no soul, the individual members can brim with personality, occasional humility, sometimes even warmth. In many ways some of them are wild but dangerous children at heart *a la* many of the figures portrayed in *The Soprano's* television show. Ultimately, though, most are desperate survivors entombed by a volatile underworld where death and destruction hold all the eventual trump cards.

It is no surprise that Jimmy is well liked by local law enforcement, the prosecutors, judges, victims, and a long line of celebrities with Chicago connections. Remarkably, though, he is also respected by many of the Outfit figures from the present and past, including alleged one-time boss Joey "the clown" Lombardo, who spoke to Jimmy often during the trial and later began writing Jimmy from prison.

James A. Jack is a genuine Chicago personality. His story is an insider's tale of hubris, power, murder, and self-destruction, a unique personal slant on the rise and fall of the Chicago mob as it once was from the Capone heydays to the reigns of Accardo and Giancana, then later Joey Lombardo, the Calabrese family, Frank "the German" Schweihs, and many more. In the end, *The Last Dance* is more than just a title, it is a euphemism for the breathtaking Family Secrets trial, the most significant mob prosecution since Al Capone himself, uniquely embellished by the gritty, personal back story told to me from Jimmy Jack's singular perspective.

Eldon L. Ham, co-author.

Introduction

The Family Secrets mob murder and conspiracy trial played out in a Chicago federal courtroom during the summer of 2007 was a crime family catharsis and a personal epilogue to my career that had begun five decades earlier as a young Chicago homicide detective.

My own ties to the Family Secrets trial began even earlier, though, on the streets of Chicago where many of the crime bosses got their start rolling dice, hustling, committing small capers and big crimes alike. My personal connection to notorious mob hit man Frank Calabrese, Sr. goes back to my first days on the police force, and throughout the trial I was reconnected with the past, my old friends, and my own youth.

Often during the many days of the trial during the summer of 2007, indicted co-conspirator Anthony "Twan" Doyle, a former Chicago cop discredited long ago by ties to the mob, would come over and sit next to me in the hall outside federal courtroom 2525. He wanted to chat, he just needed an ear to bend, a little companionship, a diversion from the dramatic, if not surreal, proceedings at hand. Doyle spoke of his job, the old days, his family, and even trips to Arizona. Sometimes his attorney Ralph Meczyh would join in.

Doyle was out on bond at the time. Unlike the defendants charged with murder, he was free to come and go. Although I was on the other side now, the side of the badge, Doyle did not hold that against me. For the most part, none of the defendants was hostile to me individually. Calabrese wanted nothing to do with me, but Joey Lombardo liked to make a connection once in awhile, mostly small talk, some wisecracks, sometimes a little humor, even though he was aging, on trial for his life, and struggling with health issues. We shared a common bond—not one of crime, per se, but one that evolved from the world of crime. It did not matter that we were on opposite sides, for we were permanently bonded by the past, by the common experience of a deadly game of cops, robbers, and murder that was played for real before, during, and after the days of Capone, continuing through the more contemporary mob figures like Accardo, Giancana, and even the crippled Joey Lombardo who spent three months at trial sitting directly before me.

Not everyone from the old neighborhoods went bad, of course. I found myself with a badge, some of the street kids became lawyers, even judges. My friend James R. Thompson, a former prosecutor who rode a string of headline convictions all the way to the Illinois governor's office, came from the neighborhoods like so many of the those who ended up behind bars. Now a super lawyer of the highest caliber, a virtual legend in Illinois law and politics, Jim Thompson still has time to say hello. One day during the trial he spotted me in the crowd, navigated his way to me, shook my hand, and congratulated me on my last book, *Three Boys Missing*, a 40-year odyssey of murder that began as one of my first cases as a detective. "It's a long way from Garfield Park," he said. Indeed it is, so far that none of us can really go home again, as novelist Thomas Wolfe observed, even though most of us can get still get a glimpse through the lens of history, family, or fading memories.

One day before court was in session, on August 22, 2007, a man approached me in the hall and introduced himself as Michael J. Cain, half-brother to Richard Cain who FBI agent Bill Roemer once called "the most corrupt police officer in the history of Chicago." When I told this man that I knew his brother, he seemed surprised. To my own surprise, he invited me to lunch where he produced a copy of *Three Boys Missing* and asked me to sign it. Better yet, Michael then gave me a signed copy of his own book *The Tangled Web*, written about the life and death of Richard Cain. We spoke of the old days, of course, especially Richard Cain's days on the Chicago Police force along with Gerry "Gene" Shallow—both of them mafia men. Cain's life of crime had come to an abrupt end, not an uncommon story. On December 20, 1973, he walked into Rose's Sandwich Shop on Grand Avenue. Cain was about to learn the hard way he had been set up. Two masked gunmen approached, shoved Cain into a wall where one of them placed a double-barreled shotgun under Cain's chin and proceeded to discharge both chambers. It was a messy end to a very messy life.

I grew up with many of the mob figures who rose to various ranks of power over the ensuing decades, I arrested some, I investigated the brutal murders of others, and then I found myself in court for the final chapters in the lives of some of the biggest Outfit figures in Chicago, names like Calabrese, Marcello, and even Joey Lombardo who not only befriended me during the proceedings, but actually asked if I would help write his own memoir. I haven't taking him up on it yet, but after the trial we became an unlikely pair of pen pals as Joey wrote dozens of letters to me from prison, some asserting his innocence, others recounting parts of the past, and others promoting the idea of his book. We were kindred spirits in a strange, pathetic way, connected by both the past and my own badge—albeit from opposite perspectives like flip sides to the same coin. The difference was that I would be walking out of courtroom 2525 and onto Dearborn Street. Joey would not.

1

The Talking Dead

"You're a fuckin' dead man."

Frank Calabrese was vocally defiant to the end. One of the last remaining significant Chicago crime figures, some with roots to Al Capone himself, Calabrese is a legendary mob hit man. But this day Calabrese was anything but invincible as he coldly lashed out against the civilized world with this one last threat. Seated at the defense table before federal trial Judge James B. Zagel, Calabrese was one of five defendants variously charged with a lifetime of mob mayhem including 18 alleged murders that were singled out among who-knows-how-many other misdeeds swept long ago under the gritty rug of mob secrecy.

Though barely audible, Frank's words were directed to federal prosecutor Markus Funk as he delivered closing arguments to an exhausted jury during the twilight moments of the front page "Family Secrets" murder, racketeering, and conspiracy trial. A three month Odyssey into the inner sanctum of the Chicago Syndicate, the trial was one of the most significant multiple mob prosecutions in Chicago history—and I was there.

Astonishingly, just six months after Frank's "you're a dead man" threat, the lead prosecutor on the case was, indeed, dead. Mitch Mars, chief of the organized crime division and lead prosecutor for the Family Secrets trial, suddenly succumbed to cancer in the prime of his career at age 55. Ironically, he had only learned of his cancer just after the trial and, hence, after Frank's promise of death. Even though Frank had directly threatened assistant prosecutor Markus

Funk and not Mars, the bizarre Karma of death is unmistakable. Though Frank Calabrese was indeed an agent of death during his hit man career, he was still mortal and, the last time I checked, mob voodoo was beyond his repertoire. Still, he must have smiled upon learning of Mars' stunning misfortune.

I heard every word of every day from every witness during the Family Secrets trial, but I was more than just another stiff with a pad and pencil. My story is real: I grew up with these guys. I knew many of them as kids, as street punks, as enforcers, and as "made" members of a world famous "family" that came to power when a young enforcer named Al Capone was first summoned from New York to Chicago in 1920. As the years wore on, I grew up with many of these family descendents; I befriended some, arrested others, and investigated many more. And so it was: I had been touched by the life and times of the Chicago mob, first as a discarded Chicago kid cut from the same cloth as the inner city fictional characters of James T. Farrell's *Studs Lonigan*, and then during my years on the Chicago police force, most of it as a detective in the one department than trumped all the rest: homicide.

The Family Secrets Trial was an especially emotional experience for me since I had walked and played and worked on many of the same streets as these mobsters, their friends and family, and even their victims. For all of us, this trial was a surreal journey through time and fate, for those same neighborhoods that produced them and me had also spawned a diverse cadre of future judges, police officers, detectives, some of the defense lawyers hired years later to work the system. Another neighbor became a bigger than life governor of Illinois, my friend James R. Thompson, who as a federal prosecutor would send many to prison, especially a cluster of crooked politicians including one-time Illinois governor Otto Kerner, as well as Thomas Keane, the influential aid to Chicago Mayor Richard J. Daley.

Some of the Family Secrets jurors had heard the muted Calabrese death threat, and that in itself would become an issue after the close of the trial. Calabrese, age 70 at the start of the proceedings, was weathered but still steady and even intent on reasserting the power he had first earned on the streets, bars, back alleys, and underworld joints a half century before, back when he and I were both in our 20's. Although menacing in tone, Frank's death threat was, in the end, mostly empty, for he was already a fallen mobster soon to hit bottom hard—and he knew it. Frank Calabrese, Sr. was about to finally confront a lifetime of truths including one last cruel but inevitable twist of fate: he would probably die in some distant matchbox cell far removed from the streets he once owned, and it was mostly his own family—his son Frank, Jr., and his brother Nick Calabrese—who had sealed his destiny with all the twist of a Shakespearean tragedy.

The Family Secrets Trial had been a marathon prosecution of five ruthless Syndicate figures accused of three decades of murder, racketeering, conspiracy, and related criminal mayhem. But now they were caught, finally nabbed by society and thrown into the grinding, sometimes idealistic but not always pristine wheels of civilization that we like to call justice. The trial was the beginning of the end—indeed the last dance for those who had shuffled their way to the top of the mob outfit.

Frank still managed to wear the sturdy presence of a tough guy, a ruthless man's man even as he awaited the final verdict. He knew I was there, because throughout the trial I had occupied my own front seat, a special chair near the jury that was assigned by Judge Zagel himself. Four of the defendants seemed, in some small degree, to actually enjoy my presence over those arduous months, and I appreciated their willingness to acknowledge me and engage in occasional small talk. Perhaps I was a welcome reminder of days long past, a strangely nostalgic era of crime and fury from as long as five decades before. Somehow I felt a kinship to them, for we all intuitively knew the bonds we had once shared for so long: the streets, the system, and now the inevitable twilight years that we wear on our faces. But the fifth defendant, Frank Calabrese, Sr. never said one word to me in over three months, even though he and the others had walked by me numerous times each day during the trial. I was seated near the jury and close to the marshals in charge of the courtroom, and whenever a defendant needed the washroom, the marshals would march him directly by. Frank never uttered a sound to me during or after the trial, even though we had become acquainted a half-century before.

I was 29 years old the very first time I ever spoke to Frank Calabrese, Sr., and at that moment he punched me square in the mouth and split my lip. I am sure Frank remembers that encounter, a fleeting moment that bonded us forever, rather like an ad hoc initiation into a fraternal underworld of cops, robbers, crime, corruption, and punishment comprising the esoteric world of law and order that we fool ourselves into calling "the system."

My first confrontation with Calabrese was on March 15, 1958, four years after I had started on the Chicago force as a motorcycle patrolman in February of 1954. Within a year I had been promoted to police detective in the district, a position I held for only about 3 years when my partner Frank Czech and I were working the neighborhoods with a little late-shift snooping around the local taverns including a mob hangout called "The Nest Lounge." Officially we were performing a routine neighborhood check, which means we were probing a bit as we often did, just to see what might turn up or crawl out. We didn't always pinch someone or scare up any criminal activity, but we liked to make sure the regulars knew we were watching. That was part of the job—and the fun—of being a young police detective on the streets of a city that swaggered from its swashbuckling past, a colorful history adorned with towering skyscrapers and sprawling rail yards, ubiquitous political bosses and robber barons, and of course gangsters. Those same streets of my own youth provided inspiration to the likes of Saul Bellow, Studs Terkel, and Ernest Hemingway, because this town gets into your blood and stays there. Perhaps the city is best described by the poets, for Carl Sandburg's "big shoulders" moniker has stuck like mortar and is still worn by every soul touched by the imposing town I call home: Chicago.

In the 1950s, as now, the Syndicate ran a number of joints in and around the city, many of which were called lounges. The Mob was partial to the word "lounge" because its members felt, perhaps somewhat pathetically, that it conveyed a sense of class that was missing from mere taverns. During Prohibition they were called "speak easies," then lounges, and now "clubs." The Nest Lounge was one such establishment, a two-story brick stand-alone at 3808 Central Avenue that featured a bar, a band, dancing, big crowds, and enough draping smoke to choke a city councilman. It was a store front with a canopy over its big sidewalk windows where there was a pitiable sign identifying the place, perhaps assuring that its many fine patrons might remember where they had been.

My partner Frank and I pushed our way through a dense weekend crowd of horny guys on the prowl and a generous helping of neighborhood babes, some classy, some brassy, and some just good girls feeling adventurous. As we walked in there was a long, long bar on the right with an elevated stage behind it where Tony Smith & His Band blasted a popular version of pop and jazz that kept the crowds rolling in. A packed dancing area was on the left, and cocktail tables were spread throughout—lounges had cocktail tables, taverns did not.

The crowd was jammed shoulder to shoulder, and the night looked promising when we noticed half the guys in the place were "milk bottles," our lingo for under-age minors. I didn't look so old myself, I suppose, and when I squeezed between a row of occupied stools to snoop behind the bar, I caught the attention of a solid, 200-pounder seated at the counter. He gave me the standard Chicago greeting: "What the fuck you lookin' at?"[1]

"Nothing much," I answered, which must have sounded like an invitation to punch me out, which he promptly did, busting my lip in the process. I didn't know who he was right away, nor did I give a particular damn at the time, so I grabbed the young hoodlum by the neck. That intimate moment is when I first became acquainted with the ruthless mob up-and-comer by the name of Frank Calabrese who one day would head the mob's south side crew. We struggled in front of the bar, banging into stools and patrons before waltzing our way into the crowd toward the door just as another thug jumped on my partner. I loved having my partner around, for he was not only a great companion, he was a rock-sturdy 6' 2" Polish guy who was quite a handful himself and, for that reason, was known to many simply as "Big Frank." By the time we had all wrestled ourselves outside, one back-up squad car was already there with three more on the way. I still had Calabrese by the neck, by then my lip was bloodied and sore, and I was partly out of breath and fully pissed off when he resumed our discussion.

"I didn't know you was coppers," explained Calabrese.

"We're not," I said, "we're policemen."

We ended up arresting Frank and wise guy Peter Rosa for battery on a police officer and disorderly conduct. We also nabbed future

---

[1] Versatile and ubiquitous, the phrase "What the fuck you lookin' at" conveys different meanings depending on which word is accented. Try it. The accent on "you" can prove especially volatile.

kingpin Carmen Caruso, plus the Iovinelli cousins, Cooney and Patrick, the latter for being the manager running things at The Nest. Both cousins were charged with serving booze to the milk bottle kids, two of whom we also pinched for good measure and charged with purchasing liquor as minors. Frank would later rise through the ranks as a mob hit man, and the Caruso family is now largely thought to be highly influential in the Chicago Syndicate. With links to Capone and Frank Nitti and more recently Sam Giancana, the Chicago Mob has always had its own unique identity, so around here they developed their own name, too. Sure, in Chicago the Mob is the Mob, sometimes the Syndicate, but never the Mafia—not here. The Chicago Mob is a singular amalgam of machine guns, booze, and history that adds up to an understated but deadly moniker: "The Outfit."

By the time the Family Secrets Trial was under way, the top Outfit Boss was considered to be No-Nose DiFronzo. He was not indicted at the time and therefore was not tried with the rest, but DiFronzo could be a target in the next go-round with the feds, who are patient to a fault and like to be sure they can get a conviction when they pull their figurative trigger. With the federal heat turned up on the front burners, No-Nose and many of the others kept a low profile during and after the Family Secrets case. Next time they might not have that luxury.

Since our bust of the two young Outfit soldiers at The Nest was on the weekend, we hauled everybody down to 11th and State for Holiday Court the next day. The city could have shut The Nest down altogether, but the place remained open for years. Who knows what happened after the arrest—that was out of my hands—but it was only a matter of time before everyone was back on the street.

The little capers never draw much attention, but major Mob prosecutions are big news and don't go down without a fight and a great deal of preparation, none of which is easy. Snitches are hard to recruit, witnesses can be intimidated or have a habit of disappearing altogether, and solid evidence can be difficult to come by. But the feds hit the jackpot with Frank Calabrese, Sr., and that made the Family Secrets prosecution something very special in the history of mob arrests nationwide. Calabrese was much different—he was nabbed at the hand of his son Frank, Jr., and his own brother Nick Calabrese.

Some fathers and sons share Sunday football, clean out the garage together, or perhaps share in the family business. The Calabrese duo did the latter, but their family business was jaded, to say the least. Frank Calabrese and son Frank, Jr., had been convicted in the late 1990s for loan sharking and racketeering together, and they were incarcerated at the same federal prison in Milan, Michigan. They also had their usual father-son issues, though these were much larger than most, especially considering that Junior was an unwilling participant in The Outfit. When Frank, Jr., agreed to wear a wire to secretly tape his father, the feds knew they had hit pay dirt.

According to yet another Frank, Junior's long time friend Frank Coconate, the junior Calabrese had long wanted to distance himself from The Outfit, but his father drafted him as a syndicate soldier anyway and he was trapped. Junior, says Coconate, was a regular guy who loved sports and wanted a normal life, but was abused by his father and dragged into The Outfit where he was forced to collect juice loans, among other God-knows-what misdeeds. Junior decided that the best way for him to achieve some semblance of normalcy was to go to the Feds, turn "states evidence," and keep his father in jail, perhaps forever—and that solitary goal would eventually become the beginning of the end for much of the crime family. So Junior agreed to wear the wire, taping his father during many intimate conversations together in prison. Remarkably, though, the "wire" was safely hidden in plain sight, for Junior always enjoyed listening to music through a pair of headphones, and so no one noticed or cared that he always had them on. It's a good thing no one else shared Junior's passion for music, for had Frank, Sr. or anyone else taken a "listen" for themselves, they would have been treated to quite a song and dance, for the headphones were, of course, a decoy. Frank, Jr., was listening all right: while appearing to enjoy his music, he was taping every word his father uttered about the crime laden past, the Mob capers, The Outfit. The psychiatrists could have a field day with such retribution by a son against the father, but as it happens it was the federal prosecutors who would celebrate the most.

Junior's uncle, who was Frank's brother Nick, would also become a key witness at trial, corroborating much of what Junior had to offer. Nick, though, was not very innocent himself. Nick had been charged with murder, and he admitted to 16 Mob hits at trial, many committed with his brother Frank, Sr., so he was giving himself up at the same time he was sinking his brother. We may weave many tangled webs, as they say, but when those strands finally unravel, it can be quite an Epiphany—if not one helluva mess.

As one might imagine, the Outfit does not like its laundry aired on the front page, so sensational trials like the Family Secrets case are not easily swallowed—a lesson experienced by yet another Calabrese in the family, a son named Kurt, who had been arrested and convicted of the same loan sharking enterprise that had landed Frank, Sr., and Frank, Jr. into prison together back in 1995. One day near the start of the Family Secrets marathon, Kurt came home to his upper crust suburban house in Kenilworth and found a bomb waiting, a not-too-subtle reminder for him to keep his distance from the case and his mouth shut—in and out of court. The bomb created quite a stir in Kenilworth, an exclusive village of lakefront mansions and one of the wealthiest communities, per capita, in the entire United States. But soon the bomb was discovered to be a fake, and was in fact a somewhat ridiculous Rube Goldberg collection of wires, pretend dynamite sticks, and a digital clock displayed in a plastic bag. But sometimes it's really the thought that counts, especially where The Outfit is concerned. No one was arrested, though, and there have never been any viable suspects, but it seems clear the message was not sent by the neighbors, the dry cleaners, or the UPS man.

The FBI, as it happens, could play mind games, too. As part of the Family Secrets investigation, it had embarked on a campaign of diversion, intentionally creating feelings of paranoia within The Outfit. The feds set James DiForti up as a snitch, making the Mob believe DiForti, a reputed Outfit killer, was ratting on them. Many members were convinced DiForti was selling out, including Calabrese, perhaps helping to distract Frank, Sr. from the real informant, his son Frank, Jr.

The Outfit is a structured organization that operates through designated crews. According to court records, augmented by an interview of FBI agent Kevin Blair conducted and reported by the *Chicago Sun-Times*, one such crew in Cicero, a Chicago suburb just over the city limits known for its embrace of Al Capone, had been infiltrated by two FBI informants in the 1990s. One of them was private investigator Sam Rovetuso, who was directed in 1998 to plant a false story with crew chief Michael Spano, Sr., the gist of which was that Rovetuso "had been visited by the FBI" who reported that they were issuing subpoenas in Cicero. Rovetuso even showed them a letter he got from his own attorney describing a list of topics, although the letter, the letterhead, the topics, and even the attorney were all complete fabrications.

At the same time DiForti had begun to look suspicious to the Cicero crew because he had been charged with a hit but had not gone to trial for two years. The Outfit could not help but wonder why. Then, through intermediaries, the feds planted the idea with Calabrese, in prison with his son, that the FBI was nosing around DiForti. Calabrese became obsessed with DiForti, who understandably did not crack, but the damage was done and Frank, Sr., never noticed that the true snitch was his music loving son.

Agent Kevin Blair, who provided that story, is credited with the "Family Secrets" name for the investigation that led to the trial of Calabrese and the others. But I always felt that the games between The Outfit and law enforcement, whether the feds or the Chicago police force detectives like me, were something of a long, long dance traced back for decades, all the way to the days of Prohibition in the 1930s. The bosses came and went, the crews were built and dismantled, the hit men, the soldiers, and the wise guys would come and go, all the while waltzing in and out of court or jail or prison, more like a giant game of musical chairs or a high school dance where everyone was climbing over each other to the top rung of the social ladder.

There will continue to be family secrets and there will still be new Outfit members and new underworld scams to run for many years, but for five of the most powerful, interesting, dangerous, and certainly colorful lynch pins of The Outfit, the Family Secrets trial was a clear turning point for the Mob as we know it in Chicago—and so for these five aging, proud, and once powerful crime figures, the game is finally over. With that wire worn by son Frank Calabrese, Jr., many family skeletons would be secret no more. For those five who ultimately stood trial—Frank Calabrese, "Little Jimmy" Marcello, Joey "The Clown" Lombardo, Paul "The Indian" Schiro, and discredited police officer Anthony "Twan" Doyle—this was indeed the end, their swan song, and I was there to witness this one last dance. I could have been one of them, one of many street kids, thugs, and hoodlums who would eventually become crew chiefs, assassins, and bosses. I took a slight turn, though, somewhere north of Al Capone and south of Tony Accardo, and I wound up with a badge and a lifetime of stories earned on the streets of Chicago—often at one end or the other of a loaded gun.

I am Detective James A. Jack, Chicago Homicide—Jimmy Jack to most. This is my story of neighborhoods, childhoods, mobsters, murder, mayhem, and of course the Family Secrets corruption trial, for some a last tango of cops, robbers, and lawyers that would fast become the mother of all Mob prosecutions in the last 50 years.

2

The Underworld

    In 1919 Congress passed a law that was destined to turn most Americans into criminals. The Volstead Act, the 18th Amendment to the Constitution, went into effect in 1920 and it criminalized the "manufacture, sale, or transportation of intoxicating liquors." Alcohol was suddenly contraband, every saloon a crime scene, and every citizen who took a drink was suddenly an outlaw. America was a Mad Hatter world where law was becoming the enemy of the people, and that became a windfall for organized crime.

    We all know the "Untouchables," that very descriptive familiar term from books and film depicting the role of Elliot Ness and the FBI in ridding Chicago of the gangster stranglehold which virtually defined the city during the 1920s and 1930s. Chicago in those days had fallen victim to the criminal underworld that controlled prostitution, gambling, drugs, alcohol—and even City Hall and the key political bosses of the day. Big Bill Thompson was a mayor who embraced the Chicago mobs, a kinship that must have been very lucrative, and the mobs were allowed to run wild with booze, machine guns, murder, and money—lots of it.

    The biggest, best and baddest of all was Alphonse Capone, a young New York gangster transplanted to Chicago in 1920. He was bigger than life, and his legacy remains as the number one gangster in the history of organized crime in America. I knew Al's brother Ralph in the 1950s, who was by then a broken down drunk everyone called "Bottles" for obvious reasons. But there was a time when Ralph had his own day in the sun, while running the Capone organization along with Frank Nitti and others when Al was eventually imprisoned for tax evasion.

Al himself never could have made it as a model for *Collier's* or the other top magazines in those days. He had a flat nose, thick lips, a bull neck, and a notorious scar from his left ear to his lip. Capone was fond of that scar—he enjoyed downplaying it as an old war wound, though of course he was never in the army or any wars other than the machine gun liquor wars in New York and Chicago. It really was a memento of a knife fight in a Brooklyn dance hall, but of course it would eventually help elevate his mysterious image as the ruthless "Scarface" Al Capone. This is the image that lingers today—the brutal scar-faced gangland boss of all bosses, impeccably dressed in well-tailored suits, a dress fedora, shined shoes and spats. Capone rose to power when he was in his late 20s, and he made hundreds of millions of dollars—billions in today's world—not just from crime, but from *organized* crime.

Frank Calabrese and the Outfit are an extension of those days gone by, and in many ways the criminals and gangs are much the same. Calabrese never made it past the fourth grade, same as Capone. And they both came through the ranks the hard way, street fights, petty thefts, warehouse heists, and murder. I know—Frank and his kind came from the same neighborhood streets of Chicago that I did. He went one way, I went the other—but my own boyhood was marred, too, mostly by an outcast father who actually kidnapped my brother and me, taking us out of state for years before we returned and I had a chance to settle in at age 14. Calabrese was inducted into the family business, so to speak, and he never really had a real chance in life except for organized crime. Today's mob, though organized, is not as powerful or lucrative as during the Prohibition era of Capone and the others who not only had ties to City Hall, they owned it. But over the years, the Outfit has still wielded plenty of power throughout the days of bosses like Tony Accardo, Sam Giancana, Joey "the Clown" Lombardo, and many others.

Thanks to the Outfit in Chicago, and the Mafia and other crime syndicates elsewhere, the criminal underworld is a faraway land to most of us, yet it operates right under our noses, sometimes just down the block or at a nearby street corner. But just what is crime, anyway? We know it when we see it, but where did it come from? Crime has existed for so long as there have been rules and someone willing to break them, but that just begs the question. In the stark philosophical sense, crime refers to all unsanctioned activity outside the rules and practices of society. Crime as we know it, therefore, most certainly began soon after early man began living, working, and hunting in groups, necessitating rules that were destined to be broken, thus invoking some form of retribution. Presto—we had outcasts, ne'r-do-wells, criminals.

"Crime," as it happens, is a term we borrowed from the Latin word *crimen* which itself had been a blend of Latin and Greek terms that meant to judge or to charge. Many early misfits were treated as outcasts; they were shunned—banned from their tribes or other communities. Social stigma is still an element of criminal justice and punishment, like forcing sex offenders to register or branding others with a metaphorical "scarlet letter." And when greater punishment was needed, criminals were imprisoned in hell-hole dungeons, impaled, beheaded, or crucified.

Criminal codes in their current form can be traced to a set of 50 articles constructed by the Sumerians over 4,000 years ago. The Romans subsequently developed an elaborate system of laws, while the Greeks were constructing a foundation of principles that soon led to the concept of democracy. The Roman influence made its way to England during the Roman occupation, but much of it remained even after the Romans left England circa 400 AD. After the Norman invasions, the King of England sought to unify control and installed a concept of laws that included acts against not just other citizens, but against the state as a group. Thus, the idea of a crime against "all" the people began to emerge.

Crime, politics, and fear would become entwined over the eons, leading to barbaric rituals, scapegoats, and power plays—like the Salem witch trials or even the symbolic witch hunts of the McCarthy era 1950s. But the state's right to proscribe unlawful activity in furtherance of itself and its citizens remains as the foundation for criminal law in the Western world.

Those who practice crime regularly today are generally known as members of society's underworld, while the rest of us operate, somewhat symbolically "above board." Although it is an aptly visual metaphor, the "underworld" description actually comes from the literal underground workings of Chicago's Levee districts in the early 1900s. These were low-lying areas near parts of downtown Chicago, essentially the First Ward and surrounding blocks, particularly the near west and south fringes of downtown. They attracted miscreants like flies—and certainly drew plenty of actual flies, squalor, and disease, especially the sexually transmitted kind. By 1910, a newly created Chicago Vice Commission concluded that there were over 1,000 "vice resorts" in Chicago employing over 4,000 prostitutes in these Levee districts.

Some of these locations were low lying and prone to flooding in the late 1800s, so these parts of the city were literally built up by raising Chicago's street levels by 10 or more feet. The effect was to create a more livable if not pristine ground level to the city's topography, but this elevated design also created a subterranean labyrinth of tunnels, cellars, and basements, the residue of which now constitutes Chicago's lower Wacker Drive and a variety of underground walkways and other passages, not to mention part of the subway and commuter train systems. Society operated above this level, while the dark shadows below hid the gamblers, hookers, drug purveyors, and other low-lifes who infested what became a literal and figurative Chicago "underworld." The descriptive term stuck and now is universally used to describe the seedy side to American crime everywhere, especially organized crime.

Evoking the dependable but unpredictable law of unintended consequences, crime in Chicago was boosted by the fall of the old South when the Civil War ended in 1865. After Robert E. Lee surrendered to General Grant, the decimated South remained crippled for many years causing a number of economic and social changes nationwide, some sweeping, some profound, and others more subtle yet nonetheless still significant. The South's old gentleman gamblers found themselves looking for action elsewhere, and they found it by heading north or west—either way they often landed in Chicago, a burgeoning prairie town of cattle butchers, railroads, merchants, industrialists, and criminals. Gambling flourished and the Chicago red-light district prospered. Legions of well-intentioned girls migrated to Chicago in search of fame, fortune, or husbands, many of whom sometimes turned to prostitution when other work proved scarce. Some of these new prostitutes were remarkable young, a tragedy in its own right. According to the federal White Slave Traffic Committee, in just one two-month period in 1907 authorities removed 278 girls from the Levee districts who were under the age of 15 years—and of course they were just the tip of the iceberg.

The Federal Mann Act raised the stakes against trafficking under-age girls across state lines for illicit purposes, and by 1914 federal law, combined with pressure from religious and other citizen groups, had forced a clean-up of the bordello districts. But the city found resistance to this purging from a surprising source: the new Mayor William Hale "Big Bill" Thompson, who gained office in 1915 and then took steps to actually discourage city efforts to eradicate prostitution and related criminal activity. Although he could not openly resurrect the Levee districts, he did oversee the systematic return of prostitution which was allowed to exist in more discreet forms under the Thompson administration. This afforded Big Bill a great deal of power over prostitution and related vice in Chicago, all of which led to a culture of brothels, kick-backs, bribery, and bag men greasing the hands of local politicians. During that time, needless to say, Chicago politics and crime became inextricably entwined, and that would very soon lead to some of the city's most colorful and storied history summed up by one world-wide name, Al Capone, who fueled his cold-blooded authority with violence and fear.

Only upon the arrival of superstar basketball player Michael Jordan in 1984 did Chicago begin to temper its international reputation for mobsters, crime, and the untouchable federal agents. For more than six decades before then, however, Chicago was already perceived as an unruly town of gambling, guns, booze, bordellos, and mayhem. Chicago's front page international reputation began soon after the arrival of Capone in 1920, and I remember some of these early days of mob warfare that carried into the 1930s when I was a very young boy. Local and national headlines during the Depression years were dominated by hard times, crime, and many storied criminal characters from Ma Barker and John Dilinger to Al Capone and his notorious henchman Frank Nitti. Over the ensuing years I would cross paths with the Capone clan myself, as well as the modern era Family Secrets Outfit and their own forefathers. Many members of the current Outfit are somehow tied to the Capone pedigree by blood or criminal lineage, or both, for all are simply the newest in a long progression of criminals nearly as old as Chicago itself, especially those of Italian descent who gained substantial notoriety and power from Capone himself. At one time the Irish and other groups vied for the criminal spoils, but Capone's staggering success tipped the balance of power to the Italian gangs.

A lot happened in 1920: Babe Ruth was shipped off to New York, Al Capone moved from New York to Chicago, Prohibition went into effect, and for the very first time the United States census found that more Americans were living in cities than in the rural countryside. Chicago itself would grow into a mammoth metropolis by the onset of the Roaring Twenties, and that unbridled growth had much to do with its criminal heritage. The city is still growing today, but cities are no longer defined so much by strict borders as the population sprawls far beyond the formal city limits. The Chicago Metropolitan area now has a population of over 9 million and it's beginning to reach Milwaukee where one day those two urban sprawls will likely meet and create a mega-metropolis along the western shores of Lake Michigan. As it happens, Chicago's size, growth spurts, and its very location would all influence its role as a haven for crime and the eventual stench of the Levee underworld.

Chicago, then, has quite the smelly heritage, but not all of it is symbolic. In the late 1600s French traders first settled the area that would later define today's Chicago along the southwest portion of Lake Michigan. One such trader, Pierre Moreau, erected a cabin in the low-lying bogs where the Chicago River poured into Lake Michigan. There is considerable debate over the meaning and origin of the word "Chicago," but the most credible accounts suggest it comes from an Indian term that referred either to onions in particular or just bad smells in general. One of the more plausible explanations credits the Pottawatomie Indian word "Chickagou" which meant "bad smell," since the swampy wet marshes along the river produced a number of foul odors, especially in the warm humid months, from such low lying fodder as local skunk cabbages, aptly named for their pungent odors. The descriptive symbolism is inescapable, for these are the very marshes that would later inspire the elevation of Chicago's downtown sections where the Levee districts sprang up in the late 19th Century, creating the "smelly" underworld of thieves, pick-pockets, gamblers, whores, and cut-throat murderers.

By 1803 the local Indian tribes had been pushed away and Fort Dearborn was constructed near today's draw bridges that span the Chicago River downtown at the consecutive north-south streets of Dearborn, State Street, and Michigan Avenue. In fact, the bridge at Michigan marks the southern tip of our world famous shopping Mecca, the "Magnificent Mile" of boutiques, hotels, and towering skyscrapers from the old Playboy Building (in earlier years called the Palmolive Building) and 100-story John Hancock Tower to the north and the Wrigley Building and looming Tribune Tower adjacent to the Chicago River at the south end. Today, this very site offers a breathtaking open expanse that shows off the river and the city's architectural breadth, including the gothic Tribune Tower just across the street from the sleek, spanking new 92-story Trump Tower. This panorama is frequently featured as the backdrop to scores of films shot in Chicago, specifically including the view from Tommy Lee Jones' window in "The Fugitive" starring Harrison Ford—a local Chicago area boy, by the way—that was filmed here and then won the Academy Award® in 1993.

The eventual settlements that sprang up around Fort Dearborn had swelled to 4,000 people by 1837 when Chicago was originally incorporated as a city. When the Illinois and Michigan canal was completed in 1848, Lake Michigan was connected to the Mississippi River via the Chicago and Illinois rivers, and the city immediately exploded in growth as a transportation hub. That same year the Galena & Chicago Union Railroad began operations, and soon Chicago became the rail hub for all of the central United States. Just after the Civil War, over 13,000 ships docked annually at the Chicago harbors, and by 1870 the city had grown to almost 300,000 transplanted people. We were sort of the original California in that respect: everyone was from somewhere else. Chicago had become a departure point for westward armies during and after the Civil War, and as a transportation center it attracted many westward souls who stopped off at Chicago before heading toward Nebraska, Colorado, and California—most of whom were ripe customers for gambling houses, saloons, and brothels, so soon Chicago would offer thousands of such establishments.

Only two blocks from the original Fort Dearborn site, an area of taverns and gambling houses sprang up along Clark Street between Monroe and Randolph during the 1870s. There were so many gamblers, drunks, and muggers that shootings become commonplace, dubbing the most dangerous section as "Hair Trigger Block." Clark Street would soon become world famous for the St. Valentines Day Massacre, where seven rival gang members would be gunned down by Capone enforcers about three miles north of the river on February 14, 1929. The "Gamblers Row" taverns produced their share of notoriety, too, including one such proprietor by the name of Mickey Finn who developed a mystery powder that could be slipped into a drink to render the patron unconscious and at the mercy of muggers and other various evildoers. Today, I suppose, it might be called the original date rape drug, but in any event, slipping someone a "Mickey" still means what it always did: knocking someone out by drugging his or her drink.

Chicago would receive an extremely rude makeover in 1871 when a fire broke out at Patrick O'Leary's barn on October 8. Whether Mrs. O'Leary's cow had knocked over a lantern is mostly the stuff of urban legend, but the fire itself was all too real. It killed over 300 people and destroyed almost 18,000 buildings. But it also inspired architects from around the world to pitch in and help rebuild the city, which is how Chicago first earned its reputation as an architectural wonder showcasing global styles that in turn attracted world students of architecture, a continuing cycle that has produced Louis Sullivan, Ludwig Mies van der Rohe, Daniel Burnham, Skidmore/Owens, including today's Helmut Jahn and others. Sullivan and others developed the vertical concepts of high rise architecture and eventually the "Chicago Style" of architecture followed.[2] Even Frank Lloyd Wright has roots here, in suburban Oak Park—a woodsy village that also produced a pretty good architect of words in Earnest Hemingway.

The massive reconstruction effort that followed Great Chicago Fire triggered a staggering flow of money that begat still more political graft complemented by both white collar and blue collar crime. Mayor Joseph Medill was elected as a reform candidate who would soon close many of the taverns and gambling houses, but those efforts simply forced crime in the city to become highly organized—ergo, the "organized crime" as we know it was born. Medill's chief nemesis in those days was a character by the name of Michael McDonald who owned the largest gambling and liquor establishment in the city. McDonald was the first to organize most

---

[2] In 1885 the world's first steel framed high rise building was constructed in Chicago and the skyscraper era was thus begun.

of Chicago's gambling and drinking house owners, who were soon labeled "McDonald Democrats" when they collectively got their own candidate Harvey Colvin elected mayor in 1873. McDonald himself, by the way, was also famous in his era as a big time boxing promoter who backed the first superstar champion John L. Sullivan, and he is also largely credited as the first to use the phrase "there's a sucker born every minute," even before showman P.T. Barnum supposedly coined it.

McDonald influenced Chicago politics until his death in 1907, after which unofficial control of organized vice was splintered among several factions of wards, politicians, and a host of unsavories who divvied the spoils usually by geography and often by ethnicity. Gambling got a huge boost when Cincinnatian John Payne developed a telegraph service that could convey race results all around the country. Monte Tennes, who took over McDonald's north side operations, bought the exclusive Chicago franchise for these race results and eventually became the reigning boss of all race track gambling in the country—even ousting Payne's group in the process.

A cast of colorful characters emerged from the underworld grime, including Hinky Dink Kenna and Bathhouse John Coughlin. John began in the message business and ended up a bathhouse entrepreneur, hence his descriptive moniker. Hinky Dink was supposedly named for a place where he swam as a kid. Who knows.

A series of political struggles caused the Levee Districts to move around a bit, pushing it several blocks south and out of the First Ward, leaving First Ward operatives Bathhouse John and Hinky Dink somewhat high and dry. Their solution was not to move the Levee again, but to move the First Ward with a little slight of hand redistricting. Not surprisingly, the new Levee area flourished, developing over 200 brothels. The Everleigh Club, located at 2131 S. Dearborn was the leader. The two Everleigh sisters ran the establishment so well that it became internationally known—and sometimes sought after by visiting dignitaries.

Rising political figure James "Big Jim" Colosimo was highly regarded in the surrounding Italian community, so he soon controlled the Italian vote in the Polk and Clark Street areas of the newly crafted First Ward. Eventually he married a local madam, then soon owned three brothels himself. Big Jim enhanced his power by acting as a prostitution bag man carrying illicit payoff cash from the red light districts to local politicians. A restaurateur as well, Big Jim operated Colosimo's Café at 2126 S. Wabash, just two blocks east of the Everleigh Club brothel. Colosimo's gained national fame and was at one time *the* place to be seen in and around Chicago. Patrons included a host of national celebrities of the day like Sophie Tucker and Enrico Caruso.

Big Jim's success and his Colosimo power base had much to do with the Italian influence over the First Ward politics and Chicago crime, a triumvirate that would dominate the city for many decades, even long past Colosimo's time. But his flashy success—he was also called Diamond Jim for reasons obvious to anyone he met—also had its detractors. An extortion group called "La Mano Nera" (the Black Hand) discovered the value of the "protection racket," prying money from nervous Italian business owners.

Between 1910 and 1915 there was a growing epidemic of Black Hand murders, and in the first few months of 1915 alone there were fifty-five bomb explosions in Chicago that were meant to intimidate Black Hand victims. Colosimo found himself as a crime chief turned victim, so he countered by summoning Johnny Torrio, one of his relatives, from New York. Torrio proved to be an astute businessman, for he decentralized the bordello business by spreading it to the suburbs just as the automobile was gaining in popularity. The Torrio-Colosimo organization would soon become the prototype for the modern crime syndicate.

Then organized crime received a monster boost. On January 29, 1919, the Eighteenth Amendment to the Constitution was ratified, and on January 16, 1920, it became effective. At that moment the infamous Prohibition era became official.

For all its good intentions—remember the law of unintended consequences—Prohibition would soon be the biggest boon to crime in the history of Chicago, not to mention the rest of the country. But "the rest of the country" was not a burgeoning transportation hub, centrally located with convenient rail and waterways, plus enough political graft to grease City Hall top to bottom. In true fashion, these guys Torrio and Colosimo were soon in conflict over how to exploit the new Prohibition windfall. Colosimo, a really big fish in a smaller neighborhood pond, was satisfied with his First Ward empire, but Torrio saw much bigger opportunities with Prohibition. He even tried to convince the local crime figures to dump their usual robberies, murder, and other violence to concentrate on pursuing the exploding market for illicit liquor. The customary mayhem was not abandoned, but the bootleg liquor business did take off in spectacular fashion.

Then Torrio would change Chicago and the entire history of American organized crime when he summoned his protégé, the stocky young enforcer named Al Capone, from New York to Chicago in 1920. Capone was to be Torrio's personal bodyguard, but Torrio also put him in charge of the Four Deuces Café, aptly named since it stood at 2222 S. Wabash, which was also Torrio's headquarters. Capone thrived and continued to impress Torrio, and soon Capone was decked out in cashmere overcoats and monogrammed shirts.

Tensions grew between Torrio and Diamond Jim Colosimo, and on May 11, 1920, Diamond Jim Colosimo was shot in the head while awaiting two truckloads of liquor to his own café. Capone was one of two main suspects. Some accounts, though, suggest that Frankie Yale from Brooklyn was the more likely perpetrator. Whether Capone did the murder or not, he no doubt learned from it, and in any event, both he and Yale would ultimately benefit. Yale would become Capone's first boss in organized crime, but with the sudden death of Colosimo, the 39-year-old Torrio would be in charge of both.

Torrio may have truly been the father of organized crime as we know it. He was an extraordinary businessman and entrepreneur who actually accomplished greater things along the lines of what he had hoped Colosimo would buy into. He understood principles of organization, distribution, and territorial rights. He also knew how to divide the spoils, doling out territories and generally keeping everyone happy—and in line. They all worked in relative harmony and were unimpeded by the authorities for about three years. Then Mayor Big Bill Thompson, a friend of graft and corruption, dropped out of the mayoral race, and in 1923 Chicago elected a new law-and-order mayor in William Dever, a reformer who through an immediate wrench into the well-oiled mob machinery.

Led by Dever, the Chicago police struck the mob hard, immediately shutting down 7,000 illicit speakeasies that were disguised as various restaurants, fountains, and soft-drink parlors. I am still shocked by the sheer numbers—imagine 7,000 underworld liquor joints, not to mention the massive effort to root them all out. Torrio's organization had been hit hard, and he felt enough heat to move his headquarters to the nearby Cicero, a suburban touching the west border of Chicago about nine miles due west of the Loop, the city's well known financial district aptly named for how the elevated trains circle the downtown area in a looping fashion.

Right-hand man Al Capone was in charge of the move, which he implemented while the "CEO" Torrio was on vacation in Italy. Capone chose the Hawthorne Inn, located at 4823 W. Twenty-Second Street on a virtual parallel to the Four Deuces Restaurant on Chicago's near south side. The value—and inherent risk—of these new high profile neighbors was not lost on the Cicero powerbrokers. The local Republicans were in charge, and although they welcomed this lucrative new enterprise in their midst, they also greatly feared the spread of Chicago's reform movement might eventually also root it—and them—out. So they cut a deal—why not?

Cicero politicians asked Capone for help with their 1924 re-election, and they offered free reign for Torrio's organization to produce and sell liquor—though they expressly excluded bordellos from the deal. Was that an immoral line that local Republicans were unwilling to cross, or were they reserving that lascivious slice of entrepreneurship for themselves? Regardless, Capone and Torrio were in the liquor business, and they were happy with the arrangement.

Capone, though, still had to deliver his end of the bargain, which he did in style. On Election Day in 1924, Capone dispatched an army of 200 gunmen to "encourage" locals to vote the right way—Torrio's way, of course—to keep the local political hacks in office. One problem: as an independent suburb, Cicero was not a part of Chicago, but it was still in Cook County, an urban sprawl dominated by Chicago but which also includes, as of today, nearly 200 suburban towns and small cities. The politics and power structure of Cook County and Chicago are often entwined, so it should have been no surprise when Cook County Judge Edmund Jarecki exercised his jurisdiction and countered Capone's gunmen with seventy Chicago police officers specially deputized with local power to engage the Capone thugs.

I suppose it was inevitable that a gun battle would break out—how do you throw all that firepower together in one small hotbed without somebody pulling a trigger? Soon bullets were flying everywhere with the police and Capone's gang in a full scale shoot-out at the intersection of 22nd Street and Cicero Avenue at the doorstep of a polling place. How appropriate. Today that scene seems very foreign—literally and figuratively—more like something that belongs in the streets of Baghdad instead of Cicero or Chicago. During the battle, Capone's life would be changed—it was there that his own brother Frank was killed by gunfire. But in the end, the gangs won and the Republicans maintained their hold on Cicero, as well as their alliance with the transplanted Chicago mob. To this day, Cicero is remembered for its ties to the Capone and Torrio empire, and it still has many well publicized ties to organized crime, all of which was boosted by the "Battle of 22nd Street."

The grateful Cicero politicians were quick to uphold their end of the Capone deal—it would be hard to imagine otherwise after just watching a battalion of gunmen take over the town and win an election. Soon the Torrio Syndicate owned or controlled over 160 local liquor and gambling houses within the Cicero borders.

Being displaced to Cicero had its drawbacks, though, for soon a number of other gangs were staking claims to new territories, police, and politicians, including the massive Chicago neighborhoods. The Terrible Genna Brothers, a consortium of six actual brothers, took over the near west side of Chicago in the Taylor Street vicinity—near the old Torrio and Capone and Colosimo hang-outs. But they weren't the only ones by any means. Klondike O'Donnell and his own brothers held a grip on Chicago's near northwest side, while Roger Touhy, a self-proclaimed bootlegger, controlled the far northwest side—this is the section of Chicago that visitors first pass during their trip downtown on the Eisenhower Expressway from O'Hare International, though in Capone's day trains dominated inter-city travel from Union Station and other hubs.[3] The near north

---

[3] O'Hare did not open until the late 1950s, then became an international behemoth when it expanded in 1962. Before then, Chicago's Midway Airport on the southwest side, close to Cicero as a matter of fact, had dominated the local air travel since 1931. Midway is still highly active. There were several major train stations in Chicago, including the LaSalle Station, Polk Street Station, the Northwestern Station, and the most

side, an area that includes Wrigley Field at Clark & Addison and the site of the nearby St. Valentine's Day Massacre a few blocks south on Clark Street, was run by the Dean O'Banion Gang. A variety of Italian and Irish gangs moved into the southwest side and far west where the Valley Gang of Frankie Lake and Terry Druggan operated dangerously close to the border with Torrio's Cicero territory.

The Genna Brothers and O'Banion's corps proved to be among the biggest and best. O'Banion's roots were deeply embedded in the near north side neighborhoods where he grew up in meager surroundings. His neighborhood ties and noticeably Irish heritage gave him an edge in controlling the local Irish vote and politicians, all of which came in handy when establishing a labyrinth of illegal liquor distributorships. Some of his gang became notorious in their own right, like Earl "Hymie" Weiss and Bugs Moran. Weiss, so they say, probably invented the oft-use theatrical invitation to take someone "for a ride," a Roaring Twenties death knell.

O'Banion was an especially effective vote getter, not only for his Irish charm, but the pistols he was known to carry on Election Day. They say he was prone to using them to shoot the knobs off tavern toilet doors as a subtle reminder for the occupants to vote, which presumably also meant voting the right way. Hardly surprising, the many powerful acquaintances of O'Banion included such local political scions as Chicago's chief of detectives and the commissioner of public works.

The Genna brothers were a particular thorn to O'Banion. With allegiances to Capone and Torrio, they had an especially nice set-up at 1022 W. Taylor Street where they operated a legitimately licensed factory to manufacture industrial alcohol. What better cover could there be for supplying a city-wide booze operation? O'Banion controlled the Irish, but the Genna's had substantial influence in the Italian community including close ties to the Unione Siciliana, a fraternal organization devoted to promoting the interests of Sicilians and Italian-Americans of Sicilian descent. The union was

---

famous of all, Union Station. Movie goers will recognize Union Station from the intense baby carriage scene wonderfully crafted inside the real Union Station by director Brian DePalma for the motion picture version of "The Untouchables" with Kevin Costner and Sean Connery.

actually based in New York, but wielded great power through the Italian vote in Chicago which had the largest Sicilian contingent in the country.

The Unione Siciliana was supported, among others, by a group called the White Hand Society, the color purity of its name intentionally meant to counter the extortionists of the Black Hand which had a stranglehold on Italian businesses and families, even the mobsters in some cases. When Mayor Dever's crack down program proved effective, the liquor business got a lot harder and that raised the stakes among competing gangs. The Genna's began to sell in O'Banion's territory, and O'Banion developed a proclivity for hijacking Genna's trucks. The rivalry became personal and sometime vicious. The Irish O'Banion is largely credited with some of the more colorful and demeaning terms for the Italians, like grease balls and "spic pimps."

The gang wars grew more personal, dangerous, and very distracting to the underworld businesses they fostered. O'Banion even sought out Torrio for help, hoping he could mediate gang tensions, but Torrio was not very enthusiastic. Perhaps O'Banion found this insulting, or maybe he just over-estimated his own power, but that led to his sale of a Larrabee Street brewery to Torrio—even though O'Banion knew the place would soon be raided by the authorities. The police came through with a raid that landed over 100,000 gallons of booze and nabbed over 30 gang members—including Torrio himself, who obviously was more than pissed off.

O'Banion owned a flower business—how fitting—that operated a number of delivery trucks from its main place of business at 738 N. State. In dramatic fashion at high noon on November 10, 1924, bullets rained down on O'Banion at his State Street shop. A lifelong Catholic who was even an alter boy at Chicago's majestic Holy Name Cathedral at State and Superior, O'Banion was denied burial at any of the Catholic cemeteries because of his notorious mob ties. The Genna Brothers probably orchestrated the hit for Capone and Torrio, but it was carried out by killers John Scalise and Albert Anselmi, prolific executioners who would also participate in the slaughter of seven ranking hoodlums at the St. Valentine's Day massacre five years later.

Two months later, on January 24, 1925, the Chicago crime landscape took an extraordinary turn. Crime boss Johnny Torrio himself was shot, probably by members of the O'Banion gang seeking retribution. He survived, though, but his reward was to finish a nine-month sentence in the Lake County Jail (north of Cook County and Chicago) that was lingering from the raided brewery incident. But Chicago would never be the same. When Torrio was released, he transferred his entire criminal empire to Al Capone, then Torrio left for New York. Sooner or later—probably sooner—Torrio would have met his demise in Chicago, so he virtually retired. Like an athlete in his prime, Torrio actually quit while he was ahead. In New York he still did a little bootlegging and even went into the bail bond business, but his days as the Chicago crime kingpin were over.

Capone was suddenly in charge of everything. The Torrio coalition of gangs weakened, though, so Capone faced a considerable task in holding the empire together, but also confronted a bigger challenge in fighting the infamous beer wars while more groups splintered as the Roaring Twenties drew to a close. Hymie Weiss succeeded O'Banion where long memories about the flower shop attack kept ill will running high. Then Weiss managed to align the various key Irish, Polish and Jewish gangsters, forming his own formidable coalition. The Sicilians, though, including the remaining terrible Genna brothers, and most of the Italian gangs, stuck with Capone. So the battle lines were clearly drawn along ethnic ties: the Italians versus everyone else.

There are few eras of American history that are remembered so romantically as the 1920s, a prosperous, free-wheeling and sometimes deadly time of flappers and jazz and illicit booze, the Murderers' Row Yankees, Louis Armstrong, Charles Lindbergh, Jack Dempsey, Prohibition, speakeasies, machine guns, the "untouchables," and Scarface Al Capone. The passage of time enhances the romance of any era, like our own childhoods for example, but add booze and bullets and bigger-than-life mobsters, cops and robbers, and that romance itself becomes bigger than the passing decades of posterity. Where it actually led, though, was much more dangerous than romantic: mob rule.

3

Family Secrets

An austere letter with a stunning message quietly found its way to the Chicago FBI office in August, 1998. It was old school—the hard copy kind with an envelope and a stamp, most fitting for a watershed moment that was about to cut the legs from under the Chicago Outfit. Someone wanted to *talk*, which meant the shroud of mob silence was about to be lifted. Since secrecy is the lifeblood of the Outfit, snitches are hard to come by, and they have a way of not lasting too long. Someone out there who wanted to spill his guts, and he had plenty to say. Better still, this was no run-of-the-mill stool pigeon; he was in a position to know. This guy was an Outfit member, a made man with connections straight to the top echelons, and he was ready.

Chicago summers are traditionally unpredictable, literally and figuratively. They bring humidity, heat, and extraordinary storms driven by towering thunderheads that often flash stunning shows of lightning over Lake Michigan. The heat can be oppressive, but when the winds suddenly shift cool lake breezes often bring a noticeable chill to downtown—nothing like the bone chilling lake effect of winter, but still dramatic. No matter—Chicago just shrugs, for we've seen it all before. Until now.

Addressed to FBI supervisor Tom Bourgeois, now retired, this letter would lead to a firestorm of controversy in and outside the mob. At the time, Tom was the organized crime section chief, and he immediately realized the explosive impact of the missive that lay before him. A fateful domino in the career of Bourgeois had just tipped over, and now there was no turning back. That one letter would spawn a seven year government investigation into the bowels of the Chicago crime hierarchy, followed by a penetrating indictment and the three-month federal criminal trial of five mob figures that was to follow. The most important part of the letter came at the very end. It was signed Frank Calabrese, Jr. Yes, the son of THAT Calabrese.

This was a genuine "holy shit" moment in the fight against organized crime that packed a once-in-career kind of wallop. Fathers and sons lead complicated, sometimes close, often impossible lives defined by relationships worthy of Freud and Shakespeare, but this episode was about to fly off the charts. I know about fathers and sons, and not just from many street smart years on the Chicago force. My own father had kidnapped me and my older brother when I was 9 years old, then took us to California—not exactly a good relationship builder. In the case of the Calabrese family, "Junior" had been dragged into the Outfit by his father Frank, and was forced to share and participate in the cut-throat family legacy for his whole life. At the time he wrote his letter to the FBI, Junior was already a convicted felon doing time in prison across the lake, not far from Chicago, in Milan, Michigan. Not surprisingly, the Federal Correctional Institution (the "FCI") at Milan is a stark place with a colorless name, sort of a black hole in life as most of us know it. Officially it is a low security facility housing male inmates located in southeast Michigan between Detroit and Toledo, Ohio, but in truth it is a one-way trip to nowhere. Ironically, the Milan prison sits only about 15 miles south of the University of Michigan at Ann Arbor, a sharp contrast of fate and misfortune—so near, and yet so far, as they say.

Decidedly user-*un*friendly, FCI Milan offers 13 pages of bleak regulations just for visitation alone. Exactly the place I don't even like to visit, let alone call home. Inmates are required to wear FCI-issued clothing, including collared shirts that are to be tucked in at all times; institutional shoes including "brown sued steel toe shoes" that can be purchased in the commissary; an approved belt, T-shirt, underwear, socks, and religious headwear. The only items that an inmate may also take while seeing a visitor include: "one pair of prescription eyeglasses, one comb, one wedding band, one handkerchief, and one approved religious medal (or more if specially approved by the warden)." If approved by the medical staff, prisoners can also keep their medication like nitroglycerine tablets, which are mentioned specifically—there must be something poignant about that. Importantly, inmates are expressly permitted to exchange and sign legal papers couriered by visitors from the outside: lawyers, clerks, wives, girlfriends, heart broken mothers.

Milan visitors have their own rules, too. If they are age 16 or older, they may arrive with up to $20.00 in cash but cannot give it to the prisoner which, of course, makes no sense at all. Why let them in with *any* money if keeping it from the inmates is an important rule? I wonder how many times the inmate gets the cash anyway—and who really cares? Visitors may also bring a small clear change purse, wallet, keys, coat, "life sustaining equipment" (presumably their own), and forms of identification. If they have infants with them, they may also carry a small see through diaper bag, one change of baby clothes, four extra diapers, and an approved collection of baby wipes, a "seasonal" blanket, two clear bottles of formula, and food—but no glass jars. No baby carriers or car seats are allowed, and everything must be inspected first.

The Calabrese family business was, of course, their branch of the Chicago mob. In some ways it was a smallish, lucrative, cash business like many others, but so very different where it counts the most. The Outfit has always maintained what looks like a decentralized organizational structure with an amalgam of titles strewn through the hierarchy in an awkward blend of military language and mob-speak, but looks can be deceiving. There is centralized control in one or more bosses, with the top boss having absolute power. The chain of command includes "crews" who operate something like territorial franchises, a little like McDonalds' restaurants but with less paperwork and big stakes that run much higher than too much cholesterol.

Frank Calabrese, Sr., was in charge of the south side crew. It is much the same as, and highly reminiscent of, the old territories in the days surrounding the Colosimo-Torrio-Capone era when crime became organized in the way most Americans understand it today. Captains, made guys, soldiers, crew chiefs, bosses, and even "advisors" permeate the mob structure. The advisors are usually retired or semi-retired bosses—old chiefs with the Outfit version of golden parachutes and the lingering respect of mob participation without the incumbent responsibilities. "Made" members are something like knights with tenure—anointed wise guys with lifetime employment handshakes, the price for which is a lifetime of mob loyalty.

Junior had the goods. He was ready to implicate his father and his uncle Nick Calabrese in the unsolved murder of Outfit hit man John Fecarotta. Agents were dispatched to Milan to verify Junior's story and his willingness to cooperate. The FBI dubbed their new-found investigation "Operation Family Secrets" because they intended to use Calabrese, Jr., to set up his father, implicate other mob figures, and penetrate the mob where it is most vulnerable: family ties. By most accounts, including his own, Junior was not a willing mob participant. He had been abducted by his own father into the family business, something like other recalcitrant sons who are forced into family empires with no real alternatives—but with a few profound and deadly differences. Don't get me wrong, once involved, Junior was a full-fledged mobster with ties to the typical mob activity from loan sharking to extortion, gambling, prostitution, drugs, and of course murder. But he wanted to escape, and his father unwittingly became a way out.

This is where Junior's letter comes in. It was a one-page, one-paragraph missive dated July 27, 1998. The letter was typed in pica font, addressed to Thomas Bourgeois. Junior knew the significance of this missile from the blue, and he admonished Bourgeois accordingly, evidenced by the following excerpt:

> The less people that know I am contacting you the more I can and will help and be able to help you ... I need for you and only you to come out to Milan FCI and we can talk face to face ... Please no recording of any kind just bring pen and lots of paper. This is no game. I feel I have to help you keep this sick man locked up forever.

Frank, Sr. liked to talk—not a good trait for mobsters, but hard to resist when you have the track record, power, standing, and ego of Frank. He didn't talk to everyone, though, indeed probably very few, but he certainly opened up to his son. Fortunately, Frank was willing to conduct business from prison, too, and since he was incarcerated at the same FCI-Milan as Junior, the Feds were overjoyed with the possibilities. Junior agreed to wear a wire in prison and, as it happens, most of the taped conversations between Junior and his father would take place in the prison visiting room. Among other things, Frank spilled the beans on three murders he was involved in, and Operation Family Secrets was under way.

Wearing a wire in prison has to be a tough assignment, and recording any mob kingpin is a risky chore, let alone one who is your father—and one with a history of beating you, at that. But Junior wanted a shot at a real life one day, or at least a meager chance at what might be left, and he knew it could never happen so long as his father was in power.

The FBI, meanwhile, was overjoyed and promptly proceeded to parlay its luck still further: court permission to tape record more conversations among Frank, Sr., and other visitors. Soon a strong case was built against Uncle Nick for the Fecarotta murder. True to form, Uncle Nick felt the weight of the government's foot on his chest, and he caved. Nick, too, decided to cooperate, but he soon did a lot more than spill a few extra beans to the FBI. Nick Calabrese spilled his guts with a jackpot bonus comprised of detail after detail on 18 previously unsolved murders. Agents soon found themselves pouring over thousands of documents, everything from old police reports to financial records and gambling receipts. The trail led all the way back to the 1970s, and all of it was eventually handed over to a federal grand jury that examined this treasure trove of guilt and ultimately returned a 43 page indictment in April of 2005. Think of it: 43 glaring pages shining on the darkest of mob secrets over the last three decades.

Altogether, fourteen mob figures were indicted, but only five of them would go to trial. Two of them—Frank Saladino and Michael Ricci—would die before trial. Six more bailed themselves out of the coming storm by pleading guilty to various charges, and still one more, Frank "the German" Schweihs, was hospitalized for cancer and too ill to stand trial. That left five hard-nosed mob defendants who rolled the dice and headed for trial: Frank Calabrese, Sr., James Marcello, Joey "the Clown" Lombardo, Paul "the Indian" Schiro, and Anthony "Twan" Doyle, the latter a discredited Chicago cop. The trial would become a front page extravaganza that began in June of 2007. Before its conclusion in September, the government would call over 100 witnesses and present more than 200 pieces of evidence.

The government would aptly describe this as an exceptional case, noting publically that "we haven't had an individual like Nick Calabrese cooperate like this and give this kind of detailed information before." The investigation would help the feds take out three crew bosses and the acting head of the Chicago Outfit. The official indictment was filed with the court and dated stamped March 8, 2007. It reads as a deliberate, cold, and solemn indictment not only of 12 specific individuals, but of the overall mob enterprise:

1. At times material to this indictment there existed a criminal organization which is referred to hereafter as "the Chicago Outfit." The Chicago Outfit was known to its members and associates as "the Outfit" and was also known to the public as "organized crime," the "Chicago Syndicate" and the "Chicago Mob." The Chicago Outfit was an "enterprise" as that term is used in Title 18, United States Code, Section 1961 (4), that is, it constituted a group of individuals associated in fact, which enterprise was engaged in and the activities of which affected interstate commerce. The enterprise constituted an ongoing organization whose member functioned as a continuing unit for a common purpose of achieving the objectives of the enterprise.
2. The Chicago Outfit existed to generate income for its members and associates through illegal activities. The illegal activities of the Chicago Outfit included, but were not limited to: (1) collecting "street tax," that is, extortion payments required as the cost of operating various businesses; (2) the operation of illegal gambling businesses, which included sports bookmaking and the use of video gambling machines; (3) making loans to individuals at usurious rates of interest (hereafter referred to as "juice loans"), which loans constituted "extortionate extensions of credit," as that term is defined in Title 18, Unites States Code, Section 891 (6); (4) "collecting" through "extortionate means" juice loans constituting "extensions of credit" . . . ; (5) collecting debts bettors incurred with the Chicago Outfit's illegal gambling businesses; (6) collecting debts incurred in the Chicago Outfit's juice loan business, which debts carried rates of interest at least twice the rate enforceable under Illinois

law; (7) using threats, violence and intimidation to collect street tax and juice loan debts; (8) using threats, violence, and intimidation to discipline Chicago Outfit members and associates; (9) using murder of Chicago Outfit members, associates and others to advance the interests of the Chicago Outfit's illegal activities; (10) obstructing justice and criminal investigations by intimidating, bribing, retaliating against, and murdering witnesses and potential witnesses who could provide information adverse to the enterprise's interests; and (11) traveling in interstate commerce to further the goals of the criminal enterprise.

The indictment continued on with a great deal of specificity as it described the criminal activities of each named defendant. It recounts in detail the organization of the Outfit structure and chain of command, including the "crews" and "sub-crews" assigned and "licensed" to operate in the various geographical territories in and around Chicago and known by the territories they operate like, for example, the North Side/Rush Street crew, the Chinatown crew, and so on. Each crew would be run by a crew leader known as a street boss or "capo," and these crew bosses reported to an underboss who was second in command in the Outfit organizational chart, often referred to, simply, as "Number Two," suggesting the role of the overall leader as "Boss" or, not surprisingly, as "Number One."

When a member of the mob proved especially trustworthy and valuable, he would be given special status as a "made" man. "Made" status normally required that the member be of Italian descent, and that he shall have committed at least one murder for the Outfit. He had to be sponsored by his capo, then participate in the "made ceremony" during which he swears allegiance to the mob. Members present would include the sponsoring capo and a number of other ranking Outfit members. Once "made," the individual was accorded great status and respect, but he also was obligated to the mob enterprise for life.

As on television and in the movies, disputes would arise over territories, activities and other aspect of the running the crews. The relevant capos would normally solve such issues, but if they could, then they all deferred to the Boss who would thus arbitrate and then decide the final resolution. During the time frame covered from the early days of the targeted Family Secrets activities, there were four key bosses: Tony "Big Tuna" Accardo, Joey "the Doves" Aiuppa, Sam "Wings" Carlisi, and John "Johnny Apes" Monteleone. Aiuppa and Jackie Cerone acted as underbosses and of course there were many acting crew chiefs and made members. One of the made members was Joseph Ferriola, who reported directly to the Boss.

On Monday June 18, 2007, at the Dirksen Federal Building[4] in Chicago, Nicholas Ferriola, one of the fourteen indicted in the Family Secrets investigation and the son of made man Joseph Ferriola, pleaded guilty to racketeering, extortion, and illegal gambling, and admitted to collecting "street tax" from at least one local restaurant.

Ferriola, age 32 at the time, was accused of being a member of the Chinatown 26th Street crew—a south side cartel linked to illegal gambling, extortion, and even political corruption. Apparently he made sweet plea agreement, because his deal did not require him to testify in the Family Secrets trial—perhaps saving his life, but from what, I'm not sure. He pled guilty in open court in front of federal Judge James Zagel, who was assigned the case and would preside over the trial. Judge Zagel happens to be a friend of mine from way back, and so his assignment gave me a leg up in attending and viewing the case. Not the kind of advantage that was improper, but I was treated with respect in open court everyday and given a special seat up front near the jury box and lawyer tables—close enough to exchange "pleasantries" with all the defendants, except Frank, Sr.

Assistant U.S. attorney Mitchell Mars read the charges aloud to Ferriola in open court, detailing how Ferriola had agreed to participate in the Outfit, including his role with the Chinatown crew. That crew was headed by none other than Frank Calabrese, Sr., and Ferriola admitted to taking orders from Frank while Frank was incarcerated. That same day another indicted defendant, Joe Venezia, age 64, of Hillside, Illinois, also appeared and pled guilty to gambling and cheating on his taxes. Among other things, Joe

---

4   The Dirksen Building is named for the long standing and esteemed senator from Illinois, Everett Dirksen, known for his eccentric wit, particularly his often quoted observation about government spending: "a billion here, a billion there, soon we're talking about real money."

happened to be employed by the brother of co-defendant Michael Marcello's brother—consistent with the numerous family ties one might expect. Joe's own attorney made a statement in court to the effect that it was "upsetting that Joe is older, the idea of going to jail was not particularly pleasant for him, and he wanted to take responsibility for his actions and put this part of his life behind him.

Michael Marcello himself pled guilty to hiding profits from federal tax collectors and obstructing justice. I was just a few feet from Mike as he stood before the judge wearing his bright orange prison jumpsuit and leg irons. The system was not done with him, however, although he already looked like a beaten man, a once proud mob honcho draped in a bright orange scarlet letter for all to see. Prosecutor Mars described James Marcello as head of the suburban Melrose Park crew. James Marcello would still stand trial for more serious offenses, and Mike Marcello faced up to 35 potential years in prison (although the actual term would be much less).

Thomas Johnson, age 52, of Willow Springs, pled guilty that Monday, too, as did his nephew Dennis Johnson, age 36, from the far west suburb of Plainfield. Both worked for Michael Marcello at M & M Entertainment of Cicero—the same Cicero that was originally entwined with the Capone empire in the 1920s and 1930s. Some bad habits are hard to break. The Johnson brothers admitted to altering video games so they could be used as gambling devices placed around there area taverns, restaurants, and social clubs—and of course they were also in charge of collecting the proceeds. Bogus records had been created to hide the profits. They were facing potential 10 and 5 years sentences.

The last official act of that first day was for Judge Zagel to rule that Frank "the German" Schweihs was too sick to stand trial and would be allowed to sit out the Family Secrets proceedings for health reasons. The trial would finally start the next day.

Between court dates I visited Judge Zagel in his chambers. The jury had not yet been selected, and I wanted to learn the system, especially for highly charged cases like this one. The judge and I go back many decades. He was appointed by Ronald Reagan, and is acquainted with my friend, former Illinois Governor Jim Thompson who grew up in the old neighborhoods of Chicago like I did. Over the years Governor Thompson appointed me to two separate commissions: The Illinois Crime Justice Information Council (1977-82), and the Juvenile Advisory Board (1984-86). About six months after the close of the trial, I asked Judge Zagel if mob cases in general pose any particular concerns about threats to prosecutors and jury tampering. Remarkably, he feels there is little outside influence from the mob, notwithstanding Frank Sr.'s muttered threat during closing at the Family Secrets festivities. Maybe this is a sign of respect for the system, or more likely, perhaps it is just an unwritten rule designed to keep the government from escalating any case to a vendetta—the last thing the Outfit would need.

This jury was selected not by name, though, but by assigned numbers—not so much to protect them from the mob but, as Judge Zagel explained to me, from the press. The judge was hoping to insulate the jurors from legions of reporters, gossip columnists, and photographers who are frequently unleashed upon unsuspecting and often unsophisticated jurors assigned to front page trials. The jury selection was a normal process in this case, with no extraordinary surprises along the way. And although Judge Zagel was present for every word of the trial, he told me later that the verdicts in any jury trial, including this one, are hard to predict. Most judges will admit the same thing, which is why the final verdicts can be so compelling, if not surprising.

For all its drama, high profile defendants, and strained tensions between the witnesses and the accused, Judge Zagel told me that Family Secrets was a pretty straightforward, orderly trial. He credited the defense lawyers for much of that, saying that as a group they had a "26th and Cal" background that made the process work. The judge was referring to the Cook County criminal courts building and jail compound located a little over 4 miles southwest of the Chicago's downtown Loop district. He meant these were highly experienced criminal lawyers who had tried many cases and were familiar with the system and its rules, but also the streets and their many unwritten rules, too. In other words, these guys were seasoned pros—and not naïve by any standards.

Judge Zagel is highly regarded as one of the brightest and most astute trial judges, a veteran of more than two decades on the federal bench in Chicago. He is something of a renaissance man of the trial bar who not only grew up trying criminal cases like the defense lawyers before him, but he also wrote "Money to Burn," a fictional thriller regarding a plot to rob the Federal Reserve Bank, and he played a judge in the 1989 motion picture "Music Box."

Rick Halprin, one of the defense lawyers, is colorful to say the least. He was long time counselor to Joey "the Clown" Lombardo, a mob kingpin who Halprin planned to portray as a "lifelong working man." That may technically be true, but in no way was Lombardo's life typical of the lunch bucket working men in America. "He doesn't have a home in River Forest" [a posh near west suburb known for its mob chieftains], Halprin noted. "He doesn't drive fancy cars." Sure, Rick—just a Buick-caliber working stiff that all the jurors could identify with.

Anthony "Twan" Doyle is a former Chicago police officer. He was charged in the conspiracy for passing messages from the imprisoned Frank, Sr., to other members of the Outfit. Frank was snooping to learn whether his brother was cooperating with the authorities, and Doyle was allegedly keeping him up to date on an investigation into the murder of mob hit man John Fecarotta. The nickname "Twan," by the way, came from Doyle's mother, who had a thick accent and found "Twan" easier to say than Tony.

Paul "the Indian" Schiro was called "Indian" because the rest of the mobster thought he looked like one. He was a 69 year old enforcer charged with one of the many gangland slayings leading to the Family Secrets trial. At the time of the Family Secrets indictment, Schiro was already doing time for his role in a jewelry theft ring headed by William Hanhardt, a former Chicago chief of detectives.

The biggest fish—and biggest name—was Joey "the Clown" Lombardo. Joey was always a character; and his charisma was almost charming. A reputed Capo in the Grand Avenue crew, Lombardo has been called a mob leader, a killer who controlled pornography and other Outfit business in the city of Chicago. Known for his alleged penchant for violence and his own unique brand of humor, the "clown" once took out a newspaper ad to publicly announce that he was officially "retired" from the mob. He was once convicted of attempting to bribe a U.S. Senator and conspiracy to skim $2 million from the Stardust Casino in Las Vegas along with mob bosses Joe "the doves" Aiuppa, John "Jackie" Cerone, and Angelo LaPietra.

James Marcello, age 65, was described by the FBI as the top boss of the Chicago Outfit at the time of the Family Secrets indictment. A resident of Lombard, Illinois, had previously been convicted in

1993 on various federal charges of racketeering, gambling, loan sharking, and extortion. Authorities alleged he passed money along to the family of Nick Calabrese in an attempt to buy silence. Federal agents recorded conversations he had with his brother Michael while James Marcello was in prison. The men allegedly discussed gambling operations and Calabrese's possible cooperation with law enforcement.

And then there was Frank Calabrese, Sr., the one time street boss of the mob's 26th Street crew, who was alleged to be Chicago's top loan shark. He was charged in connection with the 1980 murder of hit man William Petrocelli in Cicero, among a dozen other slayings. Frank pled guilty in 1997 to using threats, violence, and other intimidation to collect more than $2.6 million in juice loans. He was in prison, of course, when the Family Secrets indictments came down—which is where he was when Junior taped him, starting the whole investigation in the first place.

June 19, 2007, 9:00AM

On day 1 of the trial I arrived at the Dirksen Federal Building, 219 S. Dearborn Street, early enough to see Hon. Judge James B. Zagel just before the proceedings were to get underway. We reflected on the old days when he was executive director of the Illinois Enforcement Commission, appointed by Gov. James R. Thompson, when I was a member of the Commission, too. This is when I met Anne Wolf, Judge Zagel's dependable, energetic, helpful, and indeed charming secretary. Anne would be most gracious and helpful to me throughout the trial. I also met Ted Wiszowaty, court security officer whose duty was to govern and tend to the jury.

A judge's chambers are an extension of the judge's life and personality. Judge Zagel's chambers are unique to him, of course, which is obvious from the get-go. They looked and felt like home to me. He pointed out a Bobbie [London police] uniform hanging in the corner. There was a large mahogany conference table in the middle of his chambers surrounded by wall to wall bookshelves jammed with books of all sorts, not just works of law. The room was adorned by antiques and various figures, and an American flag stood upright behind his desk.

Then it was show time. Anne, who would be my best friend during the trial, escorted me to the courtroom and the seat I would occupy for over three months.

Jury selection had begun long before with a computer list of 150 prospective names in a special pool. These people would be sent in-depth questionnaires asking about personal information including opinions and perceptions of the justice system, the FBI, and organized crime in general. They were asked whether they were in law enforcement themselves or had ever been arrested for a crime—and of course whether they believed they could be fair in rendering a verdict. The prospects were also asked what they normally read and they listened to, including television shows that might touch upon the mob or mob topics, and whether they had ever written to an editor of a newspaper or magazine and, if so, on what topic.

Judge Zagel had already explained the selection process to me. On the first morning, 25 juror prospects would be led into the courtroom for questioning. They would appear in full view of the defense and prosecution, but identified by assigned numbers only. In the afternoon, another group of about 25 would come in, and the process of questioning would repeat itself until a full jury could be empanelled. Judge Zagel said he preferred 20 jurors, but he only had 19 chairs available. The difference would prove inconsequential. Twelve of those selected would be permanent jurors and the rest would be alternates—enough to survive any number of miscues, personal issues, health problems or other disruptive events that might arise during the course of a long trial.

When each group arrived, Judge Zagel read to them an outline of the case and asked whether they would be influenced either by the fact that most defendants were of Italian descent or by the graphic profanity that would be played from a number of tape recordings. Everything looks so slick on television, but I was struck by the obvious fact that these are real life, genuine people who do not often confront the system in any direct way. The whole process can easily be intimidating or at the very least confusing. One prospect, a retired tool and dye maker, said he once had to testify in a civil case once, and it was so strange that when he left the stand even he was confused about whether he had told the truth or not.

A web designer said he had discussed the case with a cousin, who happened to be an FBI agent, but still said he could be impartial. A retired maintenance man who had worked for the Chicago Board of Education admitted he had read a bit about the case but had not followed the developments closely.

By mid-afternoon, partway through the second group, Judge Zagel had dismissed five potential jurors from the pool, including one Latino man who had difficulty understanding English, and a medical technician who administers radiation and cancer treatments, who felt it would be difficult to replace him at work. I would occasionally note the defendants, who were present throughout the questions and answers. They sat at tables in front of the judge, along with their attorneys, and they did not seem outwardly alarmed—in fact, they appeared quite relaxed. I was situated where I could face the jurors, and Lombardo was in my line of sight. His counsel Rick Halprin and Susan Schatz kept handing him notes, which Lombardo read. He mostly kept to himself and did not seem to follow the proceedings closely.

By the following day, all 19 jurors and alternates (10 men and 9 women) had finally been chosen. This is when the judge announced for the first time that all the juror identities would be not be revealed during or after the trial. Attorney Halprin objected, arguing that such a ruling unfairly gives the impression that the defendants are dangerous people. They are, of course, but I understood his point. So did the judge, but the objection was overruled. I found this whole angle fascinating—sort of a "Catch-22" dilemma entwined with possible concerns of safety, privacy, fairness, and prejudice—all of which I later expressed to the judge's law clerk Steve Neuman. Steve gave me a short lesson on relevant case law concerning other mob figures. Remarkably, during this process, Judge Zagel was notified about the fake bomb that had been left at the back porch of Kurt Calabrese's home in posh suburban Kenilworth. Was that a coincidence? Was the mob trying to create a diversionary headline to drive home a point, or to intimidate? The bomb was a stupid fake, but authorities still evacuated the surrounding homes as a precaution, creating a stir.

Police walked a bomb sniffing dog though the Calabrese residence and car, but came up with nothing. Area residents were allowed to return after about three hours. Kurt Calabrese was not a defendant, but he was a reputed mob enforcer who would occasionally receive threats over the years, everything from dead rats to menacing letters. Attorney Lopez commented in open court, expressly stating that his client Frank Calabrese, Sr., had nothing to do with the bomb episode—indeed that he had the great alibi of being incarcerated by the federal authorities.

June 21, 2007, 10:00AM

Day 1 of the real trial, after jury selection, began promptly in the ceremonial courtroom 2525. It is a large, well adorned room with very high ceilings, carpeting, and an imposing federal seal perched on the wall behind the judge. This is the largest courtroom in the whole building, and an hour before trial the hallway was jammed with press, onlookers, and others. FBI agents were everywhere. When the doors officially opened at 9:30AM, the crowds rushed in, filling this room to capacity and requiring an overflow room with an audio feed for the public. The doors were guarded by U.S. Marshalls, and once an observer leaves the court room, he gives up his seat to the next in line.

The room buzzed with tension and anticipation. Artists were present and poised for sketching, pads and ballpoints in hand. The press was on pins and needles. I have been in hundreds of trials, but I had never witnessed a spectacle such as this. I was delighted to run into Curtis Blanc and John Glover, both retired Chicago detectives, and Jake Knight from the northern district and Mark Gunnoe of the eastern district, both of whom were now deputy U.S. Marshals. Before the courtroom was opened, Ed Gabes would run his bomb sniffing yellow lab named Comet through the room and surrounding area. Comet and I became good buddies, for he would lie each day near me with his paws crossed and head lying on top, taking it all in like everybody else. Knowing that I would spend hundreds of hours in that room, I had a keen personal appreciation for the job both Ed and Comet were doing.

As I sat that first day waiting for the jury, I counted 61 black and white portraits on the walls depicting past and present federal judges. I knew quite a few of them personally. At 10:15AM, Judge Zagel strode into the courtroom with Ted Wiszowaty, the chaperone who would govern the jurors for the following three months. There were five counsel tables, one for each defendant. The aging Joey Lombardo showed up in a wheelchair, giving the place a geriatric feel. All 19 jurors were methodically led in, all were asked to stand, and all were promptly sworn in.

Opening statements were about to begin. The prosecution team was led by two of the most seasoned U.S. attorneys: Mitchell A. Mars, the organized crime chief who headed the 1990s prosecution of mobster Rocco Infilice, and John Scully, who prosecuted William Hanhardt (the former Chicago Police Department detectives' chief who ran the stolen jewelry ring). They were assisted by assistant U.S. attorney and rising star Marcus Funk, who at closing would be treated to the Calabrese death threat.

With Chicago boss James "Little Jimmy" Marcello, top mobster Joey Lombardo, and reputed hit man Frank Calabrese, Sr. present along with their remaining two co-defendants, prosecutors would walk the jury through 18 previously unsolved mob hits that were carried out from 1970 to 1986. Two of those hits were made famous on the Hollywood silver screen by acclaimed director Martin Scorsese in the classic motion picture "Casino," which recounted the double murder of Tony "the Ant" Spilotro and his brother Michael, Chicago mobsters assigned to Las Vegas. According to the testimony that would emerge, the film guessed wrong on what had actually happened to the Spilotro brothers. The film depicted the Spilotro brothers being beaten with baseball bats at a remote Indiana cornfield where they were then buried alive. The jurors, though, would get a much different version, a compelling new account courtesy of the sworn testimony given by Nick Calabrese.

According to Calabrese, Jimmy Marcello instructed the brothers to drive from home in west suburban Oak Park to meet Marcello in the parking lot of a Howard Johnson Inn near Schiller Park, a stone's throw from Chicago's O'Hare Airport. Tony and Michael Spilotro did as they were told, arriving early for the meeting. The brothers were nervous, so instead of waiting in the car they entered the motel bar and had a drink to calm their nerves. When they returned to the parking lot at about 3:30pm, Marcello was waiting for them in a van. The Spilotro's climbed aboard the van, leaving the 1986 Lincoln Mark IV at the lot.

The pretext of the impending proceedings was that Michael was about to become a "made" man in the mob, while Tony was to be promoted as a top mob figure. There likely was an air of excitement in the van with the bothers looking forward to the ritual and related festivities. Within minutes they were pulling into the driveway of what would soon be the death house. Instead of being celebrated and promoted, the Spilotro brothers were taken promptly to the basement where they were kicked, beaten, and strangled to death by multiple waiting mobsters—and *then* their bodies were hauled and buried at the Indiana cornfield.

Finally, John Scully rose to break the silence with his opening statement. Scully struck like a great white shark scenting a full meal. "The government has made a deal with the devil," he said. Scully strode to the defense tables and pointed to each defendant, one by one, as he addressed the jurors in his low pitched voice. He methodically laid out his case on each of the 18 murders while a photo of each of the murdered victims was flashed on a large screen. Mug shots of all the accused were also shown for all to see as Scully recounted the killings and related crimes.

Frank, Sr., was charged with 13 of those slayings, many by strangulation—something of a trademark of his. Scully detailed how Marcello had lured Anthony Spilotro, the mob's top banana in Vegas, and his brother Michael, to their violent deaths at the hand of Nick Calabrese and others. Joey Lombardo was accused of the slaying of a businessman who was shot to death in front of his wife and young child before he was to testify in a union pension case against Lombardo. The tales of death and destruction went on and on. Schiro, an associate of the Spilotros, would be fingered for assisting in the 1986 murder of his own friend Emil Vaci. Hit man William Dauber and his wife were shot in their car in nearby Will County. A bomb went off in the car of Nicholas Sarillo when he failed to pay his "street tax."

Scully told the jury that much of the government's case would rely on secretly made tapes plus the testimony of witnesses Frank Calabrese, Jr., and his uncle Nick Calabrese. Nick would soon testify about his own involvement in 14 mob murders, while Junior had recorded his father Frank talking about the Outfit. Scully cautioned jurors that this case was no movie while Lombardo stared past Scully from behind his black rim glasses.

The mob is corrupt and violent and without honor, Scully emphasized. This is not the Sopranos or the Godfather, he stressed. It's about real people.

Three months later, when Frank would mutter "you're a fuckin dead man," I wonder if he wasn't referring to himself?

4

The Night Chicago Died

On January 26, 1947, the *New York Times* ran a matter-of-fact Associated Press piece that began as follows:

> MIAMA BEACH, FLA., Jan. 25—Al Capone, ex-Chicago gangster and prohibition era crime leader, died in his home here tonight.
>
> "Death came very suddenly," said Dr. Kenneth S. Phillips, who has been attending Capone since he was stricken with apoplexy Tuesday.
>
> "All the family was present. His wife, Mae, collapsed and is in very serious condition."
>
> Dr. Phillips said death was caused by heart failure.

In every way but one, this was an ordinary obituary that began much like any other story of a middle-aged man whose heart had finally given out. The rest of the story, of course, could not have been more extraordinary. Al Capone not only spent a meaningful portion of his life as the official "public enemy #1," he ruled Chicago with a grip of steel and bullets, ran a billion dollar liquor empire, changed American history, and left a legacy that reached all the way to the Family Secrets trial of 2007.

I did not cross paths with Al Capone personally, though I was a young boy in Chicago during the crime ridden heyday of Capone, Frank Nitti, Machine Gun Jack McGurn, and all the rest. But I did know Al's brother Ralph "Bottles" Capone, a booze hound who lived in Chicago, mostly off the scraps of his brother's reputation, until he died of a heart attack in 1974 at the age of 80.

The Family Secrets trial did not destroy the Chicago Outfit, but it did mark the end of the Outfit as it once was, the last bastion of a unique and powerful organized crime family with direct roots to Al Capone himself. Even Capone, though, was not the first boss. That honor goes to "Big Jim" Colosimo from 1910 to 1920, followed by Capone's mentor Johnny Torrio. Paul "the Waiter" DeLucia took over when Capone was sent to Alcatraz, but Tony "Big Tuna" Accardo, who officially was the boss from 1945 until 1957, was more famous nationally—and just as powerful, if not more so. Sam Giancana took over and ruled until 1966, a span that included the tinseled years of Frank Sinatra, the McGwire sisters, and all the innuendo surrounding John F. Kennedy and Marilyn Monroe. But even through those successions, Tony Accardo himself remained a top Outfit consigliore who retained the ultimate say in all major business issues and all decisions on internal mob hits from 1945 until he died in 1992, after almost a half-century of mob power.

The late 1960s saw the rise of the current crop of post-Giancana bosses like Jackie Cerone, Joey "the Doves" Aiuppa, John "No Nose" DiFronzo, Joey "the Clown" Lombardo, and Jimmy Marcello—the latter two both convicted by the Family Secrets jury. I came across many of them in my own career, especially Cerone and Lombardo. Two of them, Jackie Cerone (born in 1914) and Auippa (born 1907), had actually grown up during the Capone era. Auippa did not die until 1997, unofficially extending the Capone legacy for a full half-century after Capone's death. Joey Lombardo and I are almost the same age, he was born in 1929 and I just one year before in 1928. We both attended the Family Secrets trial, of course, although obviously from much different perspectives. Joey was indicted for murder, while I was there to witness the last chapter in a long Chicago history that included much of my own life and career. Joey maintained the dignity of a powerful chieftain during the trial, and he was unafraid to be warm and civil as the proceedings dragged on. He was more than willing to acknowledge me and pass pleasantries that revealed an unselfish respect for our long years together on the same streets of Chicago. He even asked if I would help him write his memoirs. Maybe I'll take him up on it, though his lawyer Rick Halprin might counsel him otherwise.

When Capone was sent to prison, Frank "the Enforcer" Nitti took over nominally because he was Capone's hand-picked successor, but Paul "the Waiter" DeLucia wrested the real power and moved the Outfit into new realms of racketeering, gambling, and loan sharking. Much of the Frank Calabrese street crew activity, as we shall see, focused on the racketeering and juice loan business, the latter a big money maker as well as a source of extraordinary havoc on the streets of Chicago.

The Outfit was caught extorting the Hollywood film industry in the early 1940s, causing Nitti to commit suicide and leaving DeLucia officially in control. DeLucia's individual rule did not last long, though, because he soon went down in the same Hollywood extortion trial along with several others. Accardo took over, but DeLucia remained in silent control with Accardo, including after DeLucia was released from prison because his parole required him not to associate with mob figures. When DeLucia died in 1972, the whole empire was left to Tony Accardo's control.

The Chicago Outfit is unique for many reasons, not the least of which is its colorful, famous history ignited by the Capone booze wars and the machine gun riddled 1920s and 1930s. But the Outfit is also a singular crime empire because of its ubiquitous central rule. New York City, of course, has no shortage of mafia figures, but there are five crime families in New York that share power. Chicago has had one dominant ruler for over a century, and its methods for shifting power smoothly have been surprisingly effective throughout several generations of bosses, sub-bosses, dual bosses, and even a recent triumvirate in the New Millennium that included DiFronzo, Marcello, and Lombardo.

As noted before, Johnny Torrio was severely injured during a 1925 assassination attempt, but once he recovered Torrio had the good sense to leave power and return to Italy where we remained unscathed. Capone was left to rule Chicago during the mob's most visible and most lucrative period, the Prohibition era. Although gambling and prostitution were dependable money makers, illicit booze was a windfall of staggering proportions. Some estimates suggest Capone raked in $10 million per year in 1930 dollars, and may have had a personal net worth over $100 million—perhaps translating to $1 Billion or more today.

The liquor distribution empire ran from Chicago to Detroit to the East Coast and even beyond, and the free flow of money allowed him to buy much more than hookers, cigars and fancy clothes, for Capone's reach also extended to politicians and law enforcement, solidifying his hold on Chicago. Capone was charismatic and loved the media attention, and he even held a certain charm for the common man with such straightforward quips as "All I do is satisfy a public demand."

Money begets greed of course, which leads to jealousy and power struggles, and so even Capone was not without his own problems. Rival gangsters Dion O'Banion, Bugs Moran and Hymie Weiss often tried to move in, and attempts on Capone's life were made more than once, evidenced by the occasional bullet holes in his Cadillac. He fortified the car with armor plates and bullet proof glass, and even installed a police siren, but he never became fully comfortable and often looked over his shoulder, in particular at Bugs Moran. When Capone's headquarters were shot up in one assassination attempt, a 10-minute barrage of gunfire according to some sources, which Capone escaped because an astute bodyguard had thrown him to the floor in time, Capone moved his headquarters to the posh, but more protectable Lexington Hotel on the near South Side. That move not only made him harder to reach, especially since it was heavily guarded round the clock, but it enhanced his celebrity status, making him sort of an underworld Donald Trump, a charmer and very high roller in his day. His luxurious hotel headquarters have been portrayed many times in television and film, including one of the more memorable scenes depicting Robert De Niro strolling down the plush lobby stairs as Capone in the 1984 film *The Untouchables*.

Unassailable as the mob figures may have been, the term "untouchables" nonetheless does not refer to them. It is a reference instead to the federal agents brought into Chicago to clean combat Capone and his war on Prohibition, the top corruption fighter being Eliot Ness, a name forever linked by history to Capone—and therefore almost as famous because of Scarface himself. Because they worked for the feds and not the local cops or politicians, they were deemed "untouchable" by Capone and his men.

Ness was actually a home grown boy who was the youngest of five children born in Chicago in 1903 to a pair of Norwegian bakers. Well educated, he graduated from the University of Chicago with degrees in law and business, then landed a job in Chicago with an Atlanta company that was in the private retail credit business. His brother-in-law, who worked in the federal government for the precursor to what would become the FBI, encouraged Ness to try law enforcement. So Ness was bought in, hooking up with the U.S. Treasury Department in 1927 where he was one of 300 staffers assigned to the Bureau of Prohibition in Chicago. Interestingly, although history and pop culture aggrandize the respective images of Capone and Ness as mature, seasoned adversaries, when Ness joined Treasury in 1927 he was actually only 24 years old, and Capone himself was just 28.

By that time, the educated and savvy Ness was squarely on the radar screen of the federal government, so Ness was given the task of tracking and destroying Capone's liquor business, an empire that had been fueled by the Volstead Act and Prohibition. Capone actually became a top priority of the Herbert Hoover administration, so the feds put Ness directly into Capone's line of fire, thus igniting the booze wars made so famous by literature, film, and history itself. Ness, it appears, may have created the label "Untouchables" himself when he publically used the term to expose and challenge efforts by the Capone organization to bribe Ness's own agents. Eventually Ness hand-picked 11 special agents for his Capone detail, who in turn had been whittled down from a group of 50 that Ness had already screened. The small, centralized, and fraternal nature of the group enhanced its accountability and helped assure the collective integrity of its elite members.

So just when Bugs Moran was taking shots at Capone from within, Ness found himself inflicting serious damage from the law enforcement side. Ness aggressively used wire tap procedures and proceeded to raid distilleries, breweries and distribution centers, destroying or confiscating contraband inventory, and seizing as much as $1 Million in Capone cash. The press ate it up, and so much of the Ness-Capone contention was played out in public, which enhanced the images of both.

Although the public was enraptured by the dangerous renegade Capone, it was also struck by the charismatic Ness who also had a knack for playing the media. Notwithstanding the romantic cops and robbers intrigue, the public also grew very fearful of Capone's bullets when the mob wars spilled onto the streets, which they sometimes did in spectacular fashion. Those street wars reached a deafening crescendo on February 14, 1929, when seven mob figures were bloodily gunned down in a garage at 2122 N. Clark Street near Chicago's Lincoln Park, just east of DePaul University's North Side campus. The St. Valentine's Day Massacre, as the press dubbed it, became the immediate stuff of legend and lore, and has therefore been depicted numerous times in literature and film, and was even parodied by a scene from Billy Wilder's *Some Like It Hot*. No one was officially arrested for the bullet riddled crime, but Capone's enforcer Machine Gun Jack McGurn is widely thought to have been behind the slaughter of those Bugs Moran loyalists, targeted as part of Capone's efforts to neutralize Moran's power.

The St. Valentine's Day operation was part of an elaborate scheme, not just a spur of the moment mob hit. Frank Nitti and other insiders had convinced Capone that he would either have to eliminate Moran or eventually be defeated *by* Moran's crew. They likely turned the planned attack over to Jack McGurn who orchestrated the stealth operation first by assembling a number of out-of-state hit men to help assure its secrecy, then planning an elaborate sting against the Moran gang. They methodically created a fake new gang that sold illicit liquor to both camps, Capone's and Moran's, giving them an air of credibility. One day a major shipment of Canadian whiskey was arranged for the garage on Clark Street, Moran's people fell for it, and the rest would soon become a very bloody chapter in Chicago's history. Capone and McGurn were hoping to nail Moran, too, but he was nowhere on the scene, but they certainly made a lasting point.

Part of the St. Valentine's intrigue has always been the apparent exertion style of the hit, with Moran's men all lined up and then methodically gunned down. It made quite a scene and created a lasting image. It probably was not planned that way, but it was a natural progression of the hit itself. The gunners were disguised as Chicago cops, giving them access to the illicit delivery whereupon they were to gain entry and open fire. Moran's gang apparently interpreted it as a typical police raid and promptly gave up, lining themselves up along the wall with faith that mob lawyers would spring them later. But instead of a drive to the police station, they were blasted with shotguns and machine gun fire.

In many ways the massacre represented "the night Chicago died," a dubious low point that later inspired a song of the same name, though the lyrics were not very accurate. Recorded by a British group named Paper Lace, the song was a fictionalized account of Roaring Twenties Chicago that likely was inspired by the dramatic February 14 shootings. It reached number 1 on the charts for one week in 1974, although it was not very true to history, misstating the facts, premise, and even injecting the wrong season of the year. In many ways, though, the massacre may have marked a turning point for Chicago by splattering the grotesque violence on the front pages and thereby boosting the visibility and political power of Ness and his agents, so although the mass murder itself have been a deadly milestone, ironically it inspired a renewed focus on law enforcement because of its patent brutality. Forensic evidence would show that all seven of the victims were nearly severed in two by the brutal machine gun fire, and several of them had their faces shot off to send a special message from McGurn and Capone.

Although the public and the press were appalled by the gruesome violence, the Chicago police were not especially interested in solving the crime. Maybe they were on the take from Capone, or maybe they just felt that justice was already done anytime seven key mob figures are eliminated. Interestingly, one of the men, Frank Gusenberg, actually survived for a few hours, long enough to be briefly questioned at a local Chicago hospital. When asked who had shot him, he denied Capone the glory in typical mob fashion. "Nobody shot me," he answered.

Ness was promoted to Chief Investigator for Chicago's Prohibition Bureau and launched his career at the expense of the Chicago mob. Following a period of great public acrimony and years of incumbent crime and violence, Prohibition was finally ended in 1933, after which Ness became a "moonshine" tax agent for Kentucky, Tennessee, and southern Ohio before being transferred to Cleveland in 1934. Ness became a powerful figure in Cleveland when the mayor installed him as the city's safety director directly responsible for both the police and fire departments. Ness proceeded to root out and rid the city of police corruption and declared war on labor racketeering, illegal gambling, and other criminal enterprises.

Ness threw himself into the job and focused on the key mob figures within Cleveland's organized crime families, an obsession which probably led to a divorce from his wife Edna, the first of three Ness wives. Ness moved on to Washington, D.C. in 1942 where he rejoined the federal government and was assigned the task of combating prostitution on military bases. That only lasted two years, then he entered private business to become chairman of the Diebold Corporation, an Ohio security company that specialized in safes. He actually ran for mayor of Cleveland in 1947, but was unsuccessful. He did have one last personal glimpse of fame, though, co-writing the book *The Untouchables* and thus revisiting those headline glory years in Chicago. Unfortunately, the still youthful Ness died of a sudden heart attack at age 54 just before the book was published in 1957, robbing him of the personal satisfaction and great distinction it would soon bring. The book lived on, however, and inspired the hit television series of the same name which starred Robert Stack, running on ABC from 1959 to 1963 and helping to assure a permanent place in history for Ness and his Chicago crime fighting legacy.

Capone's own legacy would likewise be bolstered by such enduring works, but Capone's place in history would have been secure without them. Fearing retribution from the St. Valentine's Day Massacre, Capone went into hiding. Moran was known to have said, "Only Capone kills like that," and he made a point of hunting down Capone. Scarface was a step ahead, and even arranged to have himself jailed in Philadelphia to keep out of harm's way. Back in Chicago, McGurn was eventually gunned down, but over time Moran ran out of time and money, so he fled Chicago. That allowed Capone to return, but his popularity and power had been severely damaged by the lingering headlines and graphic photos of the famed massacre on Clark Street. Although the cops had originally been passé about the crime, concerned civic leaders took matters into their own hands to force city reaction to the burgeoning mob violence. This public pressure, enhanced by federal fears that the Chicago wars had become a serious threat to society, soon caught the personal attention of President Hoover.

Since that time, the mob has been careful not to shine too bright a light on itself, preferring to operate in the dark safety of its own world rather than on the front page the headlines. Once Capone had caught the attention of Washington, his eventual demise was all but assured, an enduring lesson to the Outfit. Ness was soon assigned to disrupting the booze ring, while the rest of Treasury focused on the income tax implications of Capone's labyrinth of businesses from liquor to gambling and prostitution. Eventually the two approaches became merged into one, with Ness getting the headlines. Some sources wonder how much Ness had to do with Capone's actual capture and conviction, and others even wonder whether Ness ever actually met Capone. But thanks to the romantic attraction his own phrase "the untouchables," as well as his own book and the others books and movies that followed, the legend of Ness grew, harkening the closing line of a 1962 Hollywood film about justice in the Old West, *The Man Who Shot Liberty Valance*. When a small town newspaper editor learns the truth behind the legend of a revered home-town politician, and then is asked whether he would print the truth and destroy the legacy, his character replies, "When the legend becomes fact, print the legend."

Since the mob operates in the shadows, much of what it does becomes the stuff of legend, probably obscuring the truth since the days of Capone if not before. The Ness image is probably overblown, and the romance of Capone as been much too enhanced by history. But Capone was nonetheless a larger than life figure. He was a mainstay at local baseball games, perhaps with a hand in major league betting in the old days. He and his brothers were often seen at Cubs and White Sox games, often with team management and sometimes with Chicago's own Kenesaw Mountain Landis, a federal judge who became the major league commissioner in 1921 after, and mostly because of, the famous Black Sox scandal that marred the 1919 World Series.

Actually acting on the advice of a professional publicist, Capone was everywhere. He was one of the first people to push forward and shake Charles Lindbergh's hand after his world famous trans-Atlantic flight in 1927. He opened soup kitchens during the early days of the Great Depression, sent flowers to the funerals of key local figures, and once even paid the hospital bills of a woman accidentally shot during a gang war episode. But the St. Valentine's episode negated much of that goodwill, jolting the public back to reality and tipping the first of many dominoes that would reach all the way to the White House.

Federal agents and prosecutors eventually caught up to Capone, and he was brought to trial in a Chicago federal court in 1931. His lawyers actually tried to plea bargain and offered a guilty plea but the judge refused it and forced a trial. According to many sources, the judge actually replaced the original jury at the beginning of the trial to negate any possible efforts of Capone's gang to intimidate or bribe jurors. That bold move would bring a bevy of mistrial motions in today's judicial system, so one wonders whether the jury was replaced or just the panel of jurors from which to pick. Either way, the judge did intervene in some manner, the integrity of the jury was maintained, and Capone was convicted on five counts of tax evasion for 1925, 1926, and 1927, plus the willful failure to file tax returns for the two years following.

The celebrity of Capone was staggering. His fame reached far beyond Chicago and even America. Visiting dignitaries from foreign lands would often ask, "where is Capone" upon their arrival. It was a fame reminiscent of the Michael Jordan basketball years when children from Europe and Africa to China could be found wearing Bulls' jerseys or Nike shoes. Chicago has had its share of celebrity phenoms from Jordan to Oprah, and more recently a whiz kid named Obama, but Capone was the first, the biggest, and so for the one with the greatest legacy that still goes strong over eight decades later.

According to his *New York Times* obituary, Capone's gang wars killed at least 300 men "by knife, the shotgun, the tommy gun and the pineapple..." The tommy gun was the Thompson machine gun, and the pineapple was a hand grenade devised during World War I. The Times recounted Capone's exploits, including his conviction for tax evasion, then could not resist a little editorial license:

> For this [the tax convictions], he was sentenced to eleven years in Federal prison—serving first at Atlanta, then on the Rock, at Alcatraz—and was fined $50,000, with $20,000 additional for costs. With time out for good conduct, he finished this sentence in mid-January of 1939; but by then he was a slack-jawed paretic overcome by social disease, and paralytic to boot.

In Alcatraz, Capone met his match. One day, he allegedly cut in line against both written and unwritten rules, rankling Texas bank robber James C. Lucas. When Capone said "do you know who I am," Lucas is said to have grabbed Capone, shoved a pair of scissors to his throat, and offered this comeback: "Yeah, I know who you are, greaseball, and if you don't get back to the end of that fucking line, I'm gonna know who you *were*." After prison, Capone as released from prison and admitted to the Union Memorial Hospital in Baltimore, treated for paresis and who-knows-what venereal diseases, after which he lived out his live in Miami Beach. He died in 1947, just 48 years old at the time, after suffering from brain disease and dementia, pneumonia, a stroke, and then cardiac arrest, probably all brought on by complications from third-stage neurosyphilis which Capone had been reluctant to treat.

In 1930, Capone's brother Ralph, a sloppy bookkeeper, was convicted of tax evasion—a year before his more famous sibling. Al allegedly threw a party for his idiot brother where he publically humiliated Ralph. "You got caught because you weren't smart, you talked too much and put too many things in writing," he chastised. A year later, Al had the same problem, only much bigger.

After Al's conviction, Ralph's own image declined, but he lived off what was left of his brother's image for four more decades. Al ran a dance hall in Stickney, Illinois, had an interest in a bottling company that no doubt enhanced his images as "Bottles Capone," and owned a piece of a cigarette-vending firm. In 1950, Bottles had a glimpse of renewed fame when he was called to testify in Washington before the Kefauver Committee that was investigating organized crime. Ralph answered questions about his bootlegging days but refused to talk about any of the people he was associated with at the present time.

Brother Salvatore "Frank" Capone may have been the most likely to take over the Capone empire—had he lived. They say that of all the brothers, Frank fit the old Johnny Torrio mold the best, but he was gunned down in 1924. Brother John was two years younger than Al. When Al went to prison, John helped look after Al's wife Mae. John later changed his last name to Martin, then disappeared. He was glimpsed at a 1955 funeral, but the date and place of his eventual death is unclear.

Alphonse Capone also had a younger brother Albert, thus making two Al's in one family. The other Al lived longer, dying in 1980 at age 74. The youngest brother was named Amadoe, called Matt or

Mattie for short. Matt was a gangster in Chicago for years, and when he attended Al's funeral in 1947, he threatened a photographer for trying to take a picture of his mother. Matt died in 1967 at age 59.

The Chicago Outfit, though, through all its various iterations under its numerous bosses and sub-bosses, including many of my "friends" like Calabrese, Lombardo, Cerone, Tolomeo, and others, not only lived on, but it thrived. Although they would often avoid the limelight, they were not always successful, sometimes even being linked to John F. Kennedy, whose father Joe had many ties to Chicago business, including the famed Merchandize Mart which the Kennedy family owned for years.

And then came the Family Secrets trial, a three-month tell all that put the last 50 years of mob history back onto the front pages. That's where I come in.

5

Route 66

On a chilly Chicago day in November, 1961, James Bombenger, the secretary-treasurer of Lonergan Die Co., arrived for work at 8:15am. About an hour later, while he was working in the rear of the plant at 4615 W. Arthington, Bombenger heard four loud pops from near the front of the building. When he moved quickly to the other side to investigate, Bombenger saw a pink car outside and what looked to be someone lying next to it, probably some drunk who couldn't make it home. He left the building for a better look, and as he got closer Bombenger saw the victim bleeding from the head and gasping for breath, still alive, the car running, and blood rapidly pooling on the ground. Stunned, Bombenger raced back to call the police.

Albert Brown was a neighborhood guy graced with the athletic appearance of a tennis pro. With a square jaw, sculpted nose, and near-perfect hair parted on the right, he was a good looking man, one of those Hollywood types who always got the girls. Brown was no movie star, though. He was suspected in at least six safe-cracking burglaries and had already done time at the Joliet State Penitentiary, just south of Chicago, when he was arrested and convicted yet again for burglary on May 16, 1961 at the premises of the Candy Kit Co., 1809 N. Damen. The arresting officer had actually caught him in the act of cutting a safe. Free on $10,000 bond while appealing a new 5-10 year sentence, Albert Brown proceeded to evade his penalty the hard way, and quite involuntarily: he was the guy struggling for his life in the parking lot just east of the Lonergan Die Company, shot in the head and chest with an Italian Beretta pistol.

I was sent to the scene from Area 5 Homicide, where we promptly found Brown. He didn't make it. This guy Brown and I were almost the same age at the time, both in our early 30s, and we had the same Chicago roots, but we were certainly worlds apart. A couple of detectives were already on the scene from the 28th District when we arrived, and Brown's body was still lying next to his car, a 1955 Desoto, white over pink. We actually located the murder weapon, a 7.65 mm. Beretta blue steel automatic that had been dumped in a clump of weeds about 75 feet from the car. We left the gun undisturbed for the Crime Lab Technicians who dusted it for prints, but found nothing. The ammo clip was still in the gun, but empty, and a check of the serial number showed it was not registered. We inventoried the pistol, along with a number of recovered shell casings and pellets.

We interviewed a number witnesses and potential witnesses, including the victim's brother Stanley who had left Albert at home and still watching television around 11:00pm the night before. We spoke to the victim's ex-wife, too, who knew of his checkered life and had divorced him for it, but she knew nothing of the current incident.

Then we found Kathryn Hallam, a 64-year-old woman who lived near the parking lot. She had been seated in her living room watching out the window when she saw a pink and white car driving slowly down the street. She observed two men in the car before it turned to go down Arthington where she lost sight of it. Then she heard backfiring, or possibly gunshots.

We checked Brown's arrest record and saw that he had recently been nabbed along with a couple other burglars. One was Thomas Krause, alias Lawrence Krone, age 33, also a previously convicted burglar. He became a person of interest, and further investigation led my partner Frank Schira and me to the Blue Moon Tavern in suburban Melrose Park.

There was a minor jurisdiction and political issue since we were Chicago detective and not local Melrose cops. We called the Melrose Park Police several hours ahead as a courtesy, and we brought a lieutenant along from the Illinois State Police. Both problems were solved, so arrangements were then made to meet at the Blue Moon.

It was late at night when we all got there, about 1:30am, but we did not go in right away. My partner and I opted to sit about a block away in a squad car, facing the Blue Moon. With a burst of flashing light, another squad flew past us and we observed two fleeing men who ducked into the Blue Moon. We pursued, but when we got there the front door was locked. Our colleague from the state police ordered them to open up. They did. But when we entered, it looked like "Mandrake the Magician" had already been there and made everybody disappear. Except for the bartender, the joint looked completely empty.

The bartender grew very animated and even "ordered" the Melrose cops to throw us out—but there was no chance of that. We weren't leaving. He then picked up the phone and called somebody who apparently had some kind of authority. I don't know if it was a village official or a mob boss, but the barkeep slung F-bombs like a drunken sailor. "Fuck this, fuck them—motherfucker. I want them out!"

With the bartender still cursing, I walked to the rear of the lounge where I found a door leading to the basement. It was very dark, and I did not know what might be waiting for me in the shadows—one of the hazards of the job. I found some lights and flipped them on. To my surprise there were gambling sheets from every race track in the United States plastered everywhere, hanging on the walls from corner to corner. There were rows of chairs for customers, too, so apparently we had found some kind of illegal off-track betting operation—probably mob controlled. I looked behind the sheets and followed the walls, and soon I found a space between the inner and outer wall, about 3 feet high. I was stunned, because under this opening I could see the soles of a man's shoes. My pulse jumped a couple notches.

I drew my gun and was prepared to shoot as I ordered him to come out. I told him I would shoot, which I was not intending to do, but my goal was to scare him from out of that crawl space. I guess I made my point, because he soon emerged without further incident.

He was 6'1" tall with brown hair and eyes, and he had a tattoo on his right forearm and a 4.75" scar on his left cheek. It was Lawrence Krone, who promptly gave up and was placed under arrest. I escorted him up the stairs where I was blasted with another crock of shit from the bartender who was still pissed off and demanding help from the Melrose cops. No luck—I think they knew better.

My partner and I took Krone back to Area 5 for questioning. Our investigation produced a 6-page, singled spaced, written report, including how the victim had suffered multiple gunshot wound, one to the back of the head, another to the right cheek with a corresponding exit wound just under the nose, plus more gunshots to the chest, right hip, and back. Someone had clearly wanted this guy dead. My guess is that it was a mob hit—some of these guys were working burglaries in the area and not paying a share of the loot, a street tax, over to the Outfit. With a couple of these local guys off to prison, including the victim Brown who was facing 5-10 years, the Outfit must have decided to take no further chances. All at once they terminated a possible stool pigeon and sent a nice message in the process. That's what can happen to a couple of rogue stiffs out on bond.

As it happens, Krone was later released "for lack of evidence," all while spreading the same old shit, "I didn't do it." Right. He was soon picked up again by the burglary unit at Area 5 for another job. What a loser that guy was. And stupid, too. He wasn't in the mob, but did associate with them. He and Brown just did their burglaries and had decided to ignore the street tax, cutting the mob out of the action. In the Outfit or not, it just doesn't work that way.

By this time I had been on the job about 7 years and had drawn my gun hundreds of times. Maybe I should have become another stiff like this guy Krone or even the victim Albert Brown, lying shot to death next to his 6-year-old Desoto. It certainly *could* have been me—except maybe for luck or the grace of God. I was born on October 10, 1928, at St. Anthony's Hospital in Chicago, which made me about the same age as both Brown and Krone and a host of mob guys working their way up in the late 1950s and early 1960s, including eventual hit man Frankie Calabrese. And here I was—I had just canvassed a neighborhood not unlike a hundred others peppered across the Chicago sprawl. But somehow through fate, hard work, and luck, I was carrying a badge instead of a death warrant.

It was not easy. My father abandoned my mother when I was 8, forcing her to get a divorce in 1937, a lousy time for any woman to be a single mother. My father had come to the U.S. from Dunfermline, Scotland, and was able to find work as a janitor, not bad in those days during the teeth of the Great Depression. My father enjoyed his beer and booze more than work, though, and soon we were dealing with the horrors of domestic abuse. Then it got worse.

Not long after the divorce, when my brother Wally was 11 and I was 10, my father picked us up to go to the movies. We never made it there. Instead we were whisked away from Chicago altogether and headed straight for California on Route 66. Our son-of-a-bitch father had kidnapped us, stripping Wally and me from our mother, our home, our neighborhood. Wally and I were confused and angry, but mostly afraid. We could not understand what our father was thinking, and we had no idea when—or whether—we'd ever see our mother again. Making matters worse, our father brought another guy along for the trip, a random "nobody" named Charley to share expenses. He had to bring Charley, it turns out, because it was his car. My father had answered an ad in the paper from somebody looking for someone to share expenses to California. So far as I know, my father upheld his part of the deal.

Now a virtual icon of history, television, and pop culture, Route 66 in those days was almost brand new. It was commissioned on November 11, 1926 as one of the original routes in the new federal highway system. It ran from downtown Chicago beginning near Union Station, then on through Missouri, Oklahoma, Arizona, and eventually to California. Sometimes called "The Main Street of America" or "The Mother Road," as it was in John Steinbeck's *The Grapes of Wrath*, Route 66 stretched for an interminable 2,448 miles all the way to Los Angeles—and we saw every friggin inch. It was a state of the art four lane effort, but only sometimes was it a limited access highway. It was not even completely paved until 1938, just when we began our depressing journey with our father, a heartbreaking drive that lasted 7 full days and nights jammed into the backseat of his car along with our companion stranger. As best I can remember, it was a 1936 or 1937 four-door sedan with a trunk in the rear—I think it was a Desoto or maybe some other Chrysler make. Charley, its owner, was an older guy, maybe in his late fifties who I remember being a decent sort of person. But the car was really crowded for such a long trip.

When we finally arrived in sunny southern California, it was anything but bright for Wally and me. Our father found sporadic work and bounced around in various odd jobs. He made very little money, so we were relegated to sleeping on cots in dreary basements infested with all kinds of vermin. When he first found work, we had to sleep in the basement of the building where his job was, for about a week, because we had no money for a room—not even a flop house. Sometimes a rat would actually run across our feet—but later we found that the flop houses weren't much better. It sure seemed like there was a lot of rats in California. The vermin didn't seem to disturb our father, though, and that deeply hurt Wally and me because he paid us no mind and we had nowhere else to turn.

After that first week, when our father made a little extra money, he would sometimes upgrade us to a cheap flop house that had beds with disgusting mattresses, often featuring bedbugs that tormented Wally and me with their crawling and biting. We tried sleeping with the lights on, but that didn't help. In some ways this was even worse, because then we could see everything—like cockroaches that looked big enough to put a saddle on.

It was hard to get into the local schools during mid-year, but my father was nothing if not a hustler. He conned the nuns at one Catholic school into believing just about anything—amusing them with his flattery. Taken in by his charm, the nuns enrolled us the next day. That was a lucky break for Wally and me, and at least the daylight portion of our lives was looking up a bit. Except for one humiliation: our father would send us into bakery stores with a written note of hardship asking for any stale sweet rolls or other unsalable morsels. So there we were, tormented by bedbugs and cockroaches at night, and forced to beg for food during the day.

Wally and I lived this way for a year and a half. The whole country was mired in the Depression, and we were living like gypsies with no mother, no stability, little food, and few clothes. But there were plenty of bugs and rats. It was a living hell for both of us, but mostly it was fear that gripped Wally and me—we were scared we'd never settle down, never see our mother again, and never ever get out from under our father's grip. During this whole time, our mother never knew where we were or even whether we were alive. Then, one day in June, 1939, our father suddenly waved the white flag—even he had had enough, so at long last he would haul us back to Illinois. This, of course, meant that even our father didn't want us anymore, but that was an improvement. The good news was that Wally and I were finally headed back to Chicago—our real home. Our hustler father then found another stranger to share costs, and so we loaded up the car and headed back east once again on the all-too-familiar Route 66.

Back in Chicago, our father wasted no time finding a place to dump us. On just our second day in town, we found ourselves sitting in the vestibule of an office at the Holy Name Cathedral. Holy Name is one of the most revered cathedrals in the city, an upper class bastion located just west of the Michigan Avenue's "magnificent mile" and the church of choice for mayors and other civic and business leaders. But this was no shrine for Wally and me, for we shared the same singular thought: here we go again. After about two hours our father had conned some money out of a priest, which was hardly surprising. Then our father shoved us into a cab and gave an address to the driver: 739 E. 35th Street. The three of us were headed to the St. Joseph's Catholic Orphanage Home.

Orphanage? Damn him—we weren't orphans. So close to home and yet so far. Clearly, we still would not see our mother. Our hearts sank, and we asked our father why he was doing this to us. He seemed ashamed to answer—and certainly with good reason. Eventually we checked in, and then my father left. That was it. We did not see him again for about 8 years, until sometime in the late 1940s. He actually went back to California again where he wound up at a Veteran's Hospital in Long Beach. He underwent something like 10 operations there starting around 1952, including some on an amputated leg, and later died at that hospital.

As it happens, the orphanage was not all bad. It was clean, they cared for us there, provided medical treatment when we were sick, and educated us. But it wasn't family. And it was not much fun. Holidays and Sundays were visiting days. On Sunday we dressed for mass, then after lunch we were lead to a small assembly hall where all the orphans waited to hear their names called, which would signify there was a visitor. Many nights Wally and I cried in our beds hoping beyond hope that someone would come to see us. No one ever did, yet for all those Sundays we had to endure that same name calling ritual that cast such a painful pall over every Sunday and holiday.

Then one day, after two full years of such torture, Mother Superior informed us that we did have one surprise caller. Finally a new face, but were our prayers really answered? What if it was our father? Would he suddenly snatch us off to some faraway bug-ridden basement again?

We were led to the front and confronted by this mystery visitor. Wally and I had been right, but not about our father. Our prayers *had* been answered, for standing before us was an angel sent from Heaven: our mother. We cried with joy, embracing her at once, shoving the horrid past as far behind as we possibly could. Then the three of us shed our tears together, enough to fill Lake Michigan. I remember that moment as though it was yesterday—I will never forget it. Not in this life—or ever.

Our mother was a beautiful woman and very petite: about 5'2", maybe 115 pounds. She was kind, determined, and had a great deal of charm. After years of searching she had finally found us, but she had to do it the hard way. She earned about 95-cents an hour working full time in a bakery store during the Depression—not bad, but not enough to afford a private investigator. She pounded the streets, worked the phone, and networked the neighborhoods every day, though, getting the word out and never giving up until one day her efforts paid off. She finally heard about two boys that might be hers.

The next day the orphanage released us to her, and our lives began again. She took us straight to my grandparents' home on the west side at 503 S. Trumbull. We not only had family and a home, we were part of a neighborhood near Harrison and Homan. It was a mixed ethnic community where the people were clean and the rats and cockroaches were relegated to the allies and sewers. The Depression was in its final days and stubbornly holding on, but we had arrived in paradise. My brother and I were soon enrolled in the nearby Gregory Elementary School where Wally graduated in 1942, then I graduated one year later.

The life of a young teenage boy has never been simple or easy, and I was no exception. Looking for acceptance, I joined a neighborhood club awkwardly called the "Cen-Flo-S.A.C. Club." Named for the neighborhood streets Central Park and Flournoy, the "S.A.C." part meant "Social Athletic Club," but it was pure bullshit. We just made it up because it sounded good and made a nice acronym: SAC. The club was home to a number of thugs, which I suppose was the point. I proceeded to go to middle school and then high school with most of them: arrogant, vicious bullies—guys from some of the toughest neighborhoods in Chicago. After school we hung out in pool halls during an era when that was not flattering. The pool rooms in those days were smoky parlors full of bookies, cards, and neighborhood losers. Still in grammar school, we had become "pool hall junkies," mostly at a pool room at Harrison and Central Park. There was no supervision, no police control. Things were rough and anybody could do almost anything without being accountable. Many of the guys built their reputations this way, and several were eventually pinched for various petty crimes like shoplifting and purse snatching.

While some of us took the short-cut of crime, others had to work hard in the local meat markets and grocery stores, stocking shelves, making deliveries, cleaning up. That was me. I worked four hours a day after school for 25-cents an hour at the Garden City laundry in the 3300 block of West Harrison. It was tough work and I ached and sweated every day from lifting heavy wet bags of laundry. It was grueling, but that one dollar a day was really good to have.

I still have many warm memories of the old days, as many of us do. And I wince with nostalgia whenever I am reminded of local hangouts like Borik's Drug store at the corner of Homan and Harrison. There were friendly dice games conducted like clockwork after mass every Sunday either under the Garfield Park El tracks, on the docks at the Garden City Laundry, or sometimes at the Roscoe Laundry. No longer did I have to cry aloud for visitors—I had friends everywhere, though some of them were not too savory. But there I was, just 12 or 13, still in elementary school, hanging out with street thugs when I wasn't sweating in the laundry. Anytime I had 50-cents or a buck in my pocket, I looked for a little action at the pool hall or nearby laundry. It seems like poetic irony now, but like every person alive at the time I remember exactly what I was doing on December 7, 1941, when we first got word of the Japanese attack at Pearl Harbor: shooting dice. I had just turned 13.

At least I wasn't shooting other *people*. Vito Zaccagnini was one of the neighborhood guys who shot more than craps. He pleaded guilty to murder in 1949. After his release from prison Vito joined the mob—and eventually he landed in the witness protection program. Frank Santucci was convicted of armed robbery, burglary, and a federal charge of forged money orders. He drew a 5-year prison sentence. Joe Grieco was a juice banker who put money on the street for a mob boss named Fiore "Fifi" Buccieri. Joe is still affiliated with the north side crew. No surprise. Grieco would take the shoes off your feet, and I once caught him cheating me at cards for 10 cents a game. Junior Amadeo was convicted of armed robbery—I think his family still owns Milano's Restaurant on Rush Street. I hear it's a nice place, tucked among the restaurants and bars where tourists can find some of the city's best night life; I also hear you can find a number of Outfit regulars dining there.

I wasn't too popular, because the regulars knew they could never win more than $1.00 from me because that's the most I ever had. But I found a few games, sometimes playing 7-card-call rummy at 25-cents a game. Sometimes we'd bet an extra dime on the high spade. I wasn't a bad player, but whenever I played Joe Grieco, I just couldn't win. Then one day I caught Joey slipping high spades from the bottom of the deck. I called him on it, and he got insulted and arrogant, especially when I told him I was going to tell "Joe the Pelican" (who had one leg and definitely walked like a pelican) all about it. Joe the Pelican was an adult, and partly in charge at the pool hall. Grieco then flew into a rage and pulled a pocket knife, trying to bulldoze me, but I stood my ground.

I did in fact tell the Pelican, and he took one look at me and "so what." Case closed. I didn't win my appeal, so to speak, but at 14 I was still learning the ropes.

Everybody in the neighborhoods knew each other. Somebody was always dating somebody else's sister, and sometimes marrying into each other's family so over the years the families of all these guys would sometimes get all mixed together. Johnny "the Nose" Scaglione, arrested for narcotics, was the brother-in-law of Joe Grieco. Hell, I even dated Theresa Scaglione several times myself, and either she or her sister ended up married to Joey Grieco or Donald Grieco—it's hard to keep straight after 50 years, but I know at least one of the Scaglione sisters married one of the Grieco's.

The list of local wise guys seems endless. Richard Hinkel was arrested on bad check charges—you could paper your bathroom wall with all the bad checks Dick passed over the years. Tony Musto had his leg severed by an ice truck that rolled over him, Bobby Gaffney was hit by a train, killing him at Central and Lehigh, and Danny Petro died from a heroine overdose. There were more, but we all get the point. It was a rough crowd during rough times. It's a minor miracle that I never got dragged into the mob. Joining the service at a young age helped, aside from just not being cut out for that kind of work—or lifestyle.

But even the good times were dangerous. On August 14, 1945, there was jubilation across the world when Japan finally surrendered at the end of World War II. Lloyd Devitt fell off a car while we were all celebrating—he hit his head on the curb and died.

Good and bad came from those old neighborhoods. Most of the guys listed above were bad apples, but not all. And not all of those were bad all the time. And that same neighborhood produced its share—indeed more than its share—of community leaders. I went to school with the highly regarded Illinois Appellate Judge Warren Wolfson, and with Judge Charlie Barish, retired, who served on the Circuit Court of Cook County for many years, plus Judge Eugene Willens, also now retired.

At age 15 I dropped out of St. Mel's High School in Chicago, but I didn't choose a life of crime on the streets. Instead, at age 16, I joined the U.S. Merchant Marines in 1944 and then served in World War II. I had to lie to do it, though, since I was underage. No problem, I used my older brother Wally's name, social security number, and other info, and so I "became" Walter Thomas Jack. Identity theft is a big deal in today's computer world, but I did it over a half-century ago.

My father, who had the same name, had been drafted into the U.S. Air Force around that same time, where he then worked to keep the bombers flying. Things got confusing because my brother was in the service then, too, which meant there were *three* Walter Thomas Jack's in the service of their country, all from the same family. It's a wonder I didn't get my brother, who at the time had no idea I had stolen his identity, into trouble.

After several months I was shipped out of Newport News, Virginia on the S.S. Rosenthal, destination unknown—at least until we arrived at Oran, Algeria, in Africa. After the third night on the Rosenthal I went up onto the deck during the darkest of night, looked up at the stars and prayed to come home in one piece, all while wondering what-the-fuck a 16-year old was doing alone on a ship in the middle of nowhere during World War II. The very next morning I went on deck again where I could see we had joined a protective escort convoy. It was a moving sight, a line of ships so big and so long that the naked eye could not see the end of it stretching past the horizon in a shuddering display of Allied firepower. The war suddenly looked very real. I was nervous before, but now I was really shitting in my pants.

Meanwhile, the FBI began snooping around, wondering why all these people named Walter T. Jack were in the armed forces at the same time. They showed up at my mother's home and knocked on the door. She shrieked, of course, screaming "which one is dead," making a scene that must have been similar to the image from the film *Saving Private Ryan*, also about a group of brothers swept into the war. No one was dead, they explained, but they were looking for an explanation about all these Walter T. Jack's. My mother straightened it out with a thorough explanation about me, my brother, and our father.

The FBI told my mother to fill me in the next time she would hear from me, which she did. I was to call them, and they left a card with their number. Eventually I got word and I did speak to them. They were pleased I had joined up, saying "that's nice, but wait until you become of age." I was honorably discharged, and that was that. For awhile.

In 1950 I joined the armed forces again, this time as a U.S. Marine serving during the Korean War. I was of age this time and used my own name, so there were no more calls from the FBI. I went to training at Parris Island, South Carolina, then on to Camp LeJune, North Carolina, where I found myself in the 2nd Marine Division, 2nd Battalion, 6th Marines.

As time went on, most of us returned or stayed in the neighborhood. Several of us actually landed on the Chicago Police force. Ronnie Nadle passed away in the 1990s and Mike Marione lived next door to me, but Jackie Goggin, who is loving retirement, still sees me regularly at police breakfasts. Our most famous and most influential favorite son was James R. Thompson who became a long serving, highly popular and very influential governor of Illinois. Jim lived at Homan and Washington on the west side, and spent a lot of time with us in Garfield Park. Now the massive State of Illinois administration building in the heart of Chicago's loop is named for Jim.

I think it helped Governor Thompson to know the streets of Chicago the way he did: the wise guys, the card players, the losers, juice lenders, tough guys, and all the rest of us. Jim was elected to four consecutive terms (one of which was a shortened two year stint) and thus became the longest serving governor in the history of Illinois. Politically he was a Republican, something of an oddity for an inner city boy, but in his day much of suburban Cook County and most of downstate Illinois were staunchly Republican so he won his first term by a landslide in 1976 with 65% of the vote over Illinois' Democratic Secretary of State, Michael Howlett.

As a federal prosecutor Jim was tough and determined. That, along with his sheer size at a hefty 6'6", brought a popular moniker that stuck over the years: Big Jim Thompson. He nailed former governor Otto Kerner for abusing his influence in the racetrack industry, and he sent a number of Chicago political cronies of the original Mayor Richard J. Daley to the slammer, including the high profile Alderman Thomas Keane. Many thought that the youthful, charismatic, and steadfast governor was on a fast track for the presidency, but after serving as governor, Jim settled in as chairman and managing partner at Winston & Strawn, one of the country's most influential law firms. He took some heat recently when he pushed the firm to represent former Governor George Ryan *pro bono* for Ryan's own corruption trial, which Ryan then lost in April of 2006. George had been Jim's own Lieutenant Governor, and Jim was a big believer in loyalty—not only to individuals, but to the Republican Party. I think his loyalties have served him well.

In February of 1954 I graduated from police school and was sent to the 33rd District in Chicago at 5430 W. Gale Street, which is Jefferson Park. Like all the rookies, was placed on probation for my first 6 months so the department would have time to evaluate me. I was proud to be there, but I had already been in the service during two wars and had grown up with a big contingent of the mob, so I was no longer very naïve but I still had much to learn. I was assigned to the newly-founded three-wheel motorcycle unit at the district, and one of my first official acts got me two weeks off with broken ribs.

About a year later, in March of 1955, I was promoted to detective. At age 25, I was definitely one of the youngest detectives in the district. I was still learning the ropes—hell, I didn't even know where all the ropes *were* yet—when immediately on October 18, 1955, I found myself at the gruesome scene of a multiple murder of three young boys, a heinous crime that shocked the whole nation and terrified parents everywhere in the city. It would take 40 years to track down, locate, and convict their killer—a four decade odyssey that led to my first book in 2007, *Three Boys Missing*, a true crime epic that won three national book awards.[5]

---

[5] Third Place book of the Year for True Crime from Foreword Magazine; Silver Medal in the Ben Franklin Award for Mystery and Suspense from

My first partner was "Philly Beans" Tolomeo, a veteran but also a loose cannon who would end up entwined with the mob. Then came Frank Czech, a wonderful partner and friend who was with me for many of my early mob stories. After Frank passed away, I was paired with Frank J. Schira, Area #5 Homicide, was a great guy who became executive director of the National Police Officers Association of America. His son, Gary J. Schira, became chief of police in Bloomingdale, Illinois, where he also served as president of the Illinois Association of Chiefs of Police in 1997. One day I learned that my old partner Frank Schira from Homicide had been killed in an auto accident, but not in the line of duty. I don't know how it happened, but I immediately missed him.

To be fair to my father Walter T. Jack—or at least to give a balanced report—he was not all bad. He did serve his country in World War II, and he actually won a couple of worthy awards. He was presented a citation who wrote the prize-winning "Motorists Prayer" for a contest conducted by the Veteran's Administration nationwide. My father was discharged from the U.S. Army Air Force after his feet had been frozen while helping to keep bombers flying from their base in the Aleutian Islands. During World War II my father, a mechanic in the Air Force spent 10 years in the Veteran's Hospital facilities. He had undergone 10 major surgical operations, including a series of amputation of his right leg. My father later died at the Veteran's Hospital in Long Beach.

My friend and colleague in law enforcement, Big Jim Thompson, honored me with a dust jacket endorsement. Not bad for a couple of stiffs from the west side. It scares me, though, to think how it all could have been lost had my father not relented by giving Wally and me a round trip pass back home on Route 66. Between my tormented journey to California and my stint at the orphanage, not to mention all the neighborhood thugs, it's something of a miracle that I had managed to return, then survive, earn a badge, and later end up with a pen. Let alone have something worth saying.

PMA; and a Bronze Medal for Honorable mention in the Independent Book Publishers Association's 2007 Independent Publisher Book Awards.

6

Plymouth Fucking Rock

My partner Frank Czech and I squealed down Cicero Avenue at 85 mph in our unmarked squad, windows down, ready to blast our guns. This was a time when cops ruled and the public mostly just got out of the way, though today I suppose we might get sued, maybe even by the goons we were chasing.

We were in hot pursuit, and it wasn't pretty. On February 12, 1961, which happened to be Abraham Lincoln's birthday, a state holiday in Illinois, Frank and I were working midnights (midnight to 8:00am) in the 33rd Police District, not long before we were both assigned to Area #5 Homicide. We were informed by Det. Sgt. George Murphy that there was a sudden rash of thefts in the area, particularly of new tires and wheels from several automobile dealerships. Losses were mounting rapidly, already escalating into many thousands of dollars, and the local dealers were making some noise.

Frank and I staked out in an unmarked car and began the long waiting game. It was early Saturday morning, around 1:30am, when our efforts paid off. We spotted three men jacking up an auto while in the process of lifting tires and rims from a number of new automobiles at one of the Gateway Chevrolet car lots. This was an overflow lot at 4834 W. Lawrence, a little out of the way where surplus cars were stored by the dealer. It was a good target for hoodlums on the make.

There they were, right before us. Frank and I had caught these losers red-handed, but when they spotted us coming, all three jumped into a waiting car and raced away. We glanced at each other but did not hesitate. Frank floored it, and we peeled out after the fugitive suspects, screeching through Chicago's northwest side neighborhoods at breakneck speed. We reached 85 mph on the wide straight away lanes heading south on Cicero Avenue, a major thoroughfare that runs along the western edges of the city, named for Capone's old haunt of Cicero, Illinois,.

It was deep in the dark of night, but there were street lights, flickering signs, and other illumination along the way, not to mention our headlights. But at those rates of speed, it was still difficult to see. The fleeing auto was unable to make a turn at Cicero and Sunnyside when I called out to Frank, who was driving. "They won't make it," I said. Frank knew I was referring to an approaching area where a large boulder looms, big as Plymouth fucking Rock, right next to the retaining wall under a viaduct. I assume this random boulder was somehow left over from the ice age glaciers that once gouged their way through parts of the upper Midwest; but however it got there, it was certainly very real, decidedly immovable, and not far ahead of us.

Sure enough, the driver squealed his brakes and tried to veer away, but the momentum was too strong to fight. The fleeing car slid into the Rock, smashing it hard—so hard that it instantly bounced back into the street directly into our own path. Frank hit the brakes and steered hard. We missed the damned boulder, but our unmarked squad collided with the suspect car on the rebound, both mangled vehicles crashing noisily to a dead stop.

We were banged up pretty good, dazed, and hurting. I was able to pull myself from the squad, but Frank could not—he was pinned behind the steering wheel. Then I saw one of the thieves emerge from the other car and begin to run. Instinctively, I broke into a run, too, chasing as best I could given my cut and bruised body. I stayed right on his ass, though, both of us aching, both panting. He was looking ahead through the dark and at first did not see me approaching from behind. My whole body was throbbing, it seemed, but a boost of adrenaline kept me on his tail. As I closed the gap, I pulled my gun and began to yell. "Police! Stop or I'll shoot." He did—the prick stopped on a dime so fast he gave nine cents change.

We staggered back to the accident scene where all three subjects were arrested with the assistance of another squad that had raced to help. I was worried about Frank, though, since he had been trapped in the car, but meanwhile backup had arrived and an ambulance called. As it happened, two of the thieves were pinned in their car, too, which allowed the other officers and me to reel them all in. Frank and I were both whisked to the hospital where I was treated for a chipped jaw bone and bruises over my face and much of my body. I was soon released, but Frank, in much worse shape, was admitted for internal chest injuries.

There was no rest for the weary, though. Still hurting and decidedly pissed off, I returned directly to the District to continue my investigation. I was informed by the desk sergeant that the other three men had been taken to Resurrection Hospital, so I headed straight there to interrogate the suspects—hospital or no hospital, I was in no mood for formalities and intended to grill them on the spot. After all, this was back during the 1950s and 60s, an era that still belonged to the coppers during a time when our kids still played with toy guns while the adults watched *Gunsmoke*, *M-Squad*, and *The Untouchables* on television.

Two other detectives joined me, and as we arrived at the hospital I was still at the boiling point. We were told that all three were being held in the emergency room under police custody. As we approached, I finally lost it altogether. "You shit heads could have killed my partner and me!" With that introduction, I then determined who this trio of punks really were: Gary Garyn, 17 years old, of 7918 Strong and Larry Tully, 20, of 7525 Strong, both addresses in Norridge, plus Charles Pomeroy, 25, of 4343 N. Sacramento. Those three tough guys caved in immediately and implicated three other goofs involved from earlier thefts from that same Gateway Chevrolet: Richard Amundsen, 17; James Reichard, 18; and Robert Carole, 18, all from Chicago, all three fingered for buying stolen tires.

Then it hit me—I knew this asshole Robert Carole. He was one of four members of a gang I had arrested only a few months ago, in October of 1960, when a bunch of hooligan punks beat a 15-year-old boy at a pizza restaurant just across the street from a mob joint called the "Ivy/Bistro-a-Go-Go." The beaten boy had to be treated at nearby Resurrection Hospital for multiple cuts, bruises, and possible internal injuries.

Armed with these ID's, we went straight out and rounded up all three. Back at the station, I began to question Carole right away. "Well, well, well, if it isn't my favorite alter boy." He knew what I meant. Unfortunately, he had gotten off on the other charges when a jury acquitted him of the assault and battery against the boy. "You beat it in court last year, but it's not going to happen this time," I promised.

Each of Pomeroy, Tully, and Garyn was charged with attempted larceny; Tully and Garyn were also charged with grand larceny, as were Carole and Amundsen. Reichard faced a charge of receiving stolen goods. Since these guys were young, the case was to be scheduled for "boys court" but had to be continued because the three assholes involved in the auto accident were still hospitalized. My best memory is that all of them were eventually found guilty and did time in the joint, probably a year or less.

Most of those losers just disappeared into obscurity, but one of them kept turning up. Larry Tully, the 20-year-old who was one of the stiffs in the fleeing car we crashed into, became a low to middle tier mob goon.

He resurfaced a few years later when I was working part-time on my second job, something most policemen did in those days—with permission, which was standard procedure because our bosses didn't want us working certain types of joints like mob places, strip clubs and the like. My job was working the door at the Holiday Ballroom dance club along with my partner Frank, both of us taking tickets and checking the customers to be sure they were dressed properly according to management's dress code—and of course we also kept a general eye on the place.

One night late, out of the clear blue around 9:00pm, I found Larry Tully and his goons standing right in front of me wanting to come in. My greeting was to the point. "Not in a million years are you coming in here." Needless to say, that started an argument, but I held my ground. "You're not getting in, Tully, no way." He got in my face, and we exchanged a few Chicago pleasantries, but I made my point. "You're a fuckin' loser before you start." All this activity soon drew three other off-duty detectives working at the place, who asked if I needed help. "No thanks. I can take care of this lame-brain myself." That pissed Tully off, of course, so he tried to bait me to come outside. I actually did go out, but only after things had simmered down awhile, and only then because he was just hanging around and didn't seem to want to leave.

"What do you want, Tully?"

"A piece of your ass."

"Anytime, Tully." I wasn't kidding. Since I used to box in my younger days, I didn't give a shit. "Let's go now in the rear of the ballroom." Boxing was big during those days of Joe Louis and Jake LaMotta, so a lot of guys like me had spent some time in the ring at one time or another.

"No," replied Tully. "You'll arrest me after I kick your fucking ass, no way."

He was wrong on both counts, because I would not have lost to the sonovabitch. I actually did challenge him to box me at nearby Jefferson Park, though. I even gave him a day and time: Monday at 7:00pm. But tough guy Tully was nowhere to be seen on Monday. No surprise there. We even asked the Harwood Heights patrol cars to keep an eye out for him, but Tully made himself scarce.

The next time I heard Tully's name was about two years later. He was listed in the Police Daily Bulletin, arrested for the murder of an elderly woman at a rooming house in the Uptown area. I still wish I had kicked his ass—not only at the ballroom, but also when I had had the perfect chance years before at Plymouth Fuckin' Rock.

Later on, Area #6 Homicide picked up Tully, then age 21 and living in Harwood Heights, and Allan Phillips, also age 21 residing in Bensenville. In short order, both goons had graduated from tire theft and car chases to murder.

Both admitted to entering the fifth floor room of Mrs. Iva Baker, age 76, at the Leland Hotel. When they found her door ajar, the pair entered and grabbed her purse. They escaped with Mrs. Baker's purse, but then found it empty and apparently grew angry, returning to her room where they brutally beat the woman. Iva Baker died several days later at Weiss Memorial Hospital on the north side near Lake Shore Drive. The police received an anonymous tip fingering Phillips and Tully, both of whom were soon arrested.

Both men admitted to the Baker robbery in addition to two other heists in the hotel, but both steadfastly denied the fatal beating. Instead, after hours of police questioning, each one turned on the other with Tully and Phillips each blaming the other for the beating and the murder. As a result, both were charged with Mrs. Baker's murder in October of 1961.

Fewer than two years later, in May of 1963, a jury convicted Phillips for his part in the murder, and his sentence was fixed at 20 years. Inspired by that conviction, Tully then entered a guilty plea and received 14 years for his trouble. Over the years I have partly blamed myself for Mrs. Baker's demise, wishing I had done more to keep my piece of shit alter boy Larry Tully off the streets. I was not fast enough, although Tully took himself off the streets at the expense of poor Iva Baker.

When I first graduated from the Police Academy at Brighton Park in February of 1954, in the 3900 block of South California Avenue, I could envision car chases, hoodlums, and even bullets, although not boulders. My first assignment was to the 33rd District station at 5430 W. Gale Street. Now it's called Jefferson Park, the 16th District. Soon I was promoted to detective, one of the youngest detectives at the district level. I had a knack for being in the right places at the right time in those early days, and so I found myself on some of the most interesting, and sometimes most powerful, cases a gritty town like Chicago could offer. In the early days, Area #4 Homicide in 1962, I worked out of the stately precinct building that was featured two decades later on the popular television series "Hill Street Blues." [Photo available]

I was soon assigned to a three-wheeler motorcycle, the first time our particular station had them. The first thing I did, though, was get knocked down by a passing car while issuing a ticket to a driver at Elston and Milwaukee. It took me a week to recover, but I was soon back on the force and again fighting traffic. The hard way.

One evening, a local couple, the Grammels, were shopping at Siegel's Dept. Store at 5612 Milwaukee when their little girl suddenly ran into the busy street, both of them four lanes servicing an active commercial district on the Northwest side. When the mother lost sight of the child, she ran from the store to find her crossing in heavy traffic, three cars abreast at that point.

With the traffic bearing down on the girl, I jumped from my cycle and sprinted straight to her, dodging cars but not really focusing on the traffic itself. I reached the child, whose name I later learned was Hilde, grabbed her by the dress and snatched her to safety. Although one of the approaching cars brushed my uniform, I didn't really think about the gravity of my own situation, but clearly it had been a life-or-death incident for little Hilde. The mother later reported that 2 or 3 cars had already wheeled around Hilde, who was only 20 months old, by the time I had jumped into the fray. When my supervisors later asked what went through my head, I just told them I hadn't thought of anything—after all these decades, my wife might suggest that "not thinking" is one of my strong points. But I did vaguely remember an excited woman in my peripheral vision who was running and screaming, calling out "Hilde, Hilde!"

I was just glad to help, but Hilde's parents were understandably grateful, so they took the time to write a letter to the *Chicago Tribune* addressed for the benefit of Police Commissioner Tim O'Connor, all for the purpose of thanking Officer 2060, which turned out to be me, of course. I received the *Tribune* Traffic Award of the Month and a commendation from the Commissioner himself, proving once again that it is often better to be lucky than smart.

From car chases and loser thugs like Tully to commendations and little girls in distress, life on the force was an adventure. Some days were routine, though, and some downright boring, while others were filled with danger—and sometimes overwhelmed by uncontrollable grief. Those were the hardest. Little is more heart wrenching than the uncontrolled anguish of grieving parents. And I have seen more than my share.

Soon I was thrust into one of the most disturbing murder cases in Chicago history. Three boys went downtown on a Sunday afternoon, October 16, 1955, to see a Disney movie called *The African Lion*, but then never came home. I was the first detective assigned to the case. Two days later all three were found murdered near a forest preserve on the outskirts of the city, and with that the Peterson-Schuessler murders made national news and stunned Chicago. Concerned and frightened parents everywhere locked up their children, took their kids to school, and spent each day in fear as the speculation spread across the front pages and on television.

Two of the boys were brothers, Tony (age 11) and John (age 13) Schuessler, while the third was their friend and playmate Bobby Peterson, who was also 13. They had about $4.00 among them, but it was enough in those days for bus fare and the movie. The Loop Theater downtown was about 10 miles away, so they had not been expected home for awhile, specifically 8:00pm according to their parents. When they were not back by then, the two respective fathers began looking for them, then called the police when the boys still did not turn up. The police advised the fathers to first wait until midnight, then to let them know if the boys failed to appear. The parents did wait, but by 11:15pm Peterson's father was much too distraught and so he went directly to the Gale Street police station where he encountered Sgt. Petz at the desk.

My partner Frank and I were just finishing our regular shift, so we strolled into the station just then. Petz asked me to interview Peterson while other officers called to check with the local downtown theaters. The father filled me in, and during the interview was able to tell us what they had been wearing: Bobby was in a White Sox jacket, the brothers were each wearing Cubs jackets. It was mid-October, typically cool and rainy. Bobby's father was especially worried, he had a really bad feeling in his gut. We tried to reassure him that usually these cases end with missing children found the next day having been out all night with friends. Frank and I promised to check restaurants and bus stops the next day, but Malcom Peterson was unwavering in his fear.

Capt. Russell Corcoran, the 33rd District Commander, took charge of the investigation the following morning, first thing, at 7:00am. Police Commissioner O'Connor took a personal interest and assured all the necessary manpower would be made available. Meanwhile, Frank and I methodically combed the area conducting interviews at school and elsewhere. The boys turned out to be good kids. Bobby was a Boy Scout and an athlete, and the brothers were devoutly religious. None had a history of trouble and all had very good school attendance records. I was starting to feel nervous myself. Over the next couple days we interviewed bus drivers, bowling alley personnel, and others at places that might attract a trio of kids on the loose.

We found one high school student from Gordon Tech High School who saw the boys at The Monte-Cristo bowling alley after the movie, so we knew they had made it to the theater and had returned near home. On October 18, 1955, the second day after the boys had been missing, the dreaded call came into the stationhouse. Capt. Corcoran took the call, but soon turned ashen. "Oh, no!" he screamed, his voice trembling. "Men, we've got a triple homicide."

Frank and I, plus Det. Sgt. Murphy from the Chicago Police Dept. were the first detectives on the scene at Robinson's Woods. The badly beaten, nude bodies of all three boys, Bobby, Tony and John, had been discovered in a ditch at a picnic area in the woods. Victor Livingston, a liquor salesman, was hungry and decided to take a lunch break.

He normally brown-bagged his lunch, eating in the car parked at a customer's parking lot, but the weather had been especially good on this particular day so he took a short detour and found a place to eat outside in a forest preserve area known as Robinson's Woods. From that vantage point that he soon noticed something unusual back near the end of his car: the body of a young boy.

When we arrived, one body was face down and clutching a twig, and was stretched across the bodies of the other two boys. It was horrific, not like anything I had seen before. An autopsy the next day revealed that the boys had died from strangulation and that there was no evidence of sexual assault. Nonetheless, years of investigation would lead directly to a hidden world of pedophilia that still turns my stomach. Chief Pathologist Jerry Kearns examined the boys and determined they had been beaten, punched and mutilated based on the numerous abrasions and welts, plus a great deal of blood on the head of one of them. The time of death to have been between 9:00pm and midnight on the very Sunday night that they had seen the movie. Mr. Peterson's gut had been all too right. Tragically, the brothers were the only children of Anton Schuessler, Sr., and he was so grief-stricken that his heart suddenly gave out, killing him just a month after the bodies were found.

Clues were scant, but we did find that Bobby for some reason had signed into his dentist's building downtown not far from the theater at 6:00pm the night of the movie, and that a teenage boy reported seeing the boys hitchhiking along Milwaukee Avenue at Lawrence between 8:50 and 9:00pm that night. Interestingly, a woman reported hearing two loud screams from somewhere near the Idle Hour Stables around 9:00 or 10:00pm. We kept searching, and others after us continued the investigation, but the trail went totally cold six years later in 1961.

Nothing happened for almost 40 years after that horrific night in October, then, on August 11, 1994, one Kenneth Hansen, by this time a pathetic, bedraggled old man who had connections to the stable where the screams were heard four decades before, was arrested for the crimes. Hansen had been arrested for a separate stable fire in 1972, and the federal ATF stayed on his trail, eventually connecting him to the boys. The key witness turned out to be Roger Spry, who not only knew Hansen but who, at age 11 himself, had been something of a roommate and sex partner routinely molested by Hansen. Even more strangely, that same Spry later became Hanson's willing sex partner as an adult.

Spry said that Hansen had picked the boys up hitchhiking, and taken them to The Idle Hour Stables, then sent Bobby and John to see the horses in the stables while he tried to molest Tony. I'm not sure in what way, since the medical evidence did not reveal obvious penetration, but in any event John then returned sooner than expected. Hansen freaked out, killing all three. The stable owner was the notorious Silas Jayne, a friend of Hansen who, at least according to the accusation of Spry, had allegedly burned down the whole stable to destroy the evidence.

Jayne, by the way, had his own checkered history. One of two millionaire brothers who had a falling out over a horse doping scandal, Jayne often threatened to kill his brother George, age 47. Indeed, George was ultimately gunned down by hit men while playing cards in the basement of his home on Oct. 28, 1970. Despite being represented by the world famous defense lawyer F. Lee Bailey, Jayne was convicted of conspiracy to commit murder, then sentenced by Cook County Judge Richard Fitzgerald. Jayne ultimately served 9 years in prison.

Bailey hailed the conspiracy conviction as a great victory, since Jayne had escaped the more serious charge of murder. But one of the jurors had not seen it that way, later reporting that the verdict should have been first-degree murder. He believed that continued "icy stares" from Jayne, who was seated only 12 feet from the jurors, had intimidated the 9 women on the jury. It seemed as though he was "looking right through them," he said.

Over the years, Jayne had found himself traveling in dubious horse trading circles that were linked to the death of multi-millionaire candy heiress Helen Brach, who disappeared on Feb. 17, 1977 at age 65, possibly because she knew too much about a horse racketeering and insurance fraud scheme. Silas Jayne died on July 13, 1987, at age 80, from leukemia, leaving a trail of death and mystery.

Kenneth Hansen was tried for the Peterson-Schuessler murders and convicted in September of 1995, drawing a 300-year sentence. In 2000, though, an appellate court sprung him, citing prejudicial testimony from his trial, but he was retried in August 2002 and convicted again. This time the conviction held up on appeal, completing an odyssey of nearly 50 years.

Some people believe the boys may have fallen victim to someone else altogether, perhaps even John Wayne Gacy, one of the most infamous mass murderers in U.S. history. Gacy had not lived far from the boys, and he was ultimately executed in 1994 for the rape and murder of 33 young men between 1972 and 1978—most of whom were found buried under his house. Remarkably, Gacy was a frequent visitor to the Garland building where young Bobby Peterson had curiously signed in the night he was murdered. Hansen never saw freedom again, for he died on Sept. 12, 2007, of natural causes at age 74 while still in prison at the Pontiac [Illinois] Correctional Center.

Did Hansen murder those three boys? My belief is yes, partly because I don't buy the Gacy theory at all. In 1955, Gacy would have only been 13 years old himself and hardly could have handled all three boys at once. This whole episode was so compelling that it became the topic of my first book *Three Boys Missing* which won three awards at the New York Book Expo in 2007including third place in *Foreward Magazine's* True Crime Book of the Year, plus the silver medal in the Ben Franklin Awards for Mystery and Suspense.

The Peterson-Schuessler murders were not a mob hit, but they did make headlines and accelerated my own indoctrination as a detective, a career filled with murder and mob mayhem. While cruising through the neighborhoods as part of our assigned duty on March 31, 1959, we received a call from Lt. Paddy Diggins ordering us to respond to a shooting at the intersection of Raven and Nagle. I would soon be introduced for the first time to Joseph "Shorty" LaMantia.

When we arrived at the scene, we found Edmond Juzwik, age 48, shot in the left shoulder. He had taken a bullet while driving his 1959 Olds station wagon up to the intersection, and he was still in his car. Juzwik told us he had been on his way home to 6720 Edgebrook Terrace to gather documentation for a planned meeting with the IRS. When he stopped the car at a stop sign, a light blue Ford pulled up on his left and fired a volley of 10 shots, which later we would determine to be 10 rounds, one of which struck the victim in the left shoulder. They may not have been good shooters, but to me that many bullets meant they wanted him dead more than to just send a message. An ambulance soon appeared and whisked Juzwik off to Resurrection Hospital at 7400 W. Talcott.

We caught up to Juzwik at the hospital, where he was telling Captain William Szarat, Commander of the 33rd District, that he had not recognized the men in the other car and certainly could think of no reason why they would want to kill him, although he did recall a prior attack that might be connected. Juzwik was employed as general manager of the E/Zee Flow division of AFSCO Distribution Center on Harlem Avenue, and also had been the developer of a shopping center called the HIP (Harlem Irving Plaza) where three men had beaten him in the parking lot with pistols on the previous October 6th.

Both my partner Frank and I smelled a rat. The beating and subsequent shooting did not seem like random events. When we learned that Juzwik's office had also been looted and set on fire, we knew something was up. Juzwik then described his planned IRS meeting, during which he was to be questioned about financial transactions with three former partners in the development of the HIP shopping center. This confirmed our belief of hanky panky somewhere behind the scenes. The victim supplied us with those three names, so Capt. Szarat sent us to pick all three up for questioning.

Meanwhile, the crime lab found 10 bullets, all .38 caliber shells, in the vicinity of the shooting. One of the ballistic experts commented that it was a miracle that Juzwik had been hit only once. Frank and I also learned that Juzwik had been a witness in a trial where he identified one Joseph "Shorty" LaMantia, an ex-convict, who had beaten and robbed Juzwik of $460 in cash plus a $4000 diamond ring back in February of 1958, but was later acquitted of all charges. This was probably more than just a robbery, and we felt that three guys had apparently been chasing Juzwik for over a year.

LaMantia was acquitted in that trial because he had four alibi witnesses who placed him elsewhere, including a Chicago probationary police officer. I am convinced all four of them were phony, including the officer. The nerve of that guy, testifying for someone like LaMantia. Liars or not, all four testified under oath that LaMantia had been in a lot near 36th and Princeton precisely during the hour of the robbery, all helping the police officer repair an automobile. Now, if that ain't shit, I don't know what is.

Frank and I were ordered to haul LaMantia down to the station for questioning. We caught up with Shorty at 340 W. 30th Place, and told him why we had to bring him in. He resisted at first, and was offensive and obnoxious, but soon he calmed down and then came along willingly. At the station, we asked for his address and he gave 6435 S. Damen Avenue, different from where we had found him. I took Shorty's picture, then we questioned him for several hours before finally releasing him.

Then I took the photograph of LaMantia to the victim Juzwik who glanced at it but clearly wanted no part of LaMantia. Juzwik had already seen Shorty win in court, and he didn't want to aggravate the situation. Frank and I warned him that if LaMantia were back on the street, we could be dealing with murder the next time, "maybe even yours." He was not beaten again or shot, so I assume that charges were never filed.

Shorty had been running dice games for the mob ever since the 1960s. Eventually he became a supervisor within the mob's 26th Street Chinatown crew for many years, up to his eventual conviction on racketeering charges, along with conspiracy, gambling, and extortion. This, of course, was the same crew that Frank Calabrese, Sr., had been affiliated with for so long.

On September 26, 1996, Joseph Frank LaMantia entered into a federal plea agreement wherein he admitted to his role in the 26th Street crew from around 1978 until some time in 1989. In his plea, LaMantia described his street crew activities in detail, which included gambling, juice loans, and extortion.

Shorty found himself in the same federal prison as Frank Calabrese, Sr. and his son, Frank, Jr. That same prison housed some East Coast mob guys, too, and LaMantia made the mistake of introducing Frank, Sr., to them, violating one of the rules of Outfit protocol because LaMantia had not been a "made" member of the Chicago Outfit.

In part of the secretly recorded conversations that Junior would make of his father while in prison, the very tapes that would lay much foundation for the Family Secrets trial, Frank, Sr., blasted LaMantia's gaff.

"I said, what the fuck you [LaMantia] introducin' me to that guy like you were a made guy for? The man thinks you're made, doesn't he? Shorty, don't you fuckin' introduce me to nobody again."

Elsewhere on the same tapes, Frank can be heard dismissing LaMantia, telling how he was scared of being hit one time. Frank is heard describing how he and other mob figures were waiting at a "party," which is mob talk for a planned whack. LaMantia dropped by the party with sandwiches.

"One time he brought sandwiches to us. We were gonna have a party. Okay? And the Bull [Angelo LaPietra] brought him in and he's seen and he got fuckin' scared. He thought the party was for him.

"And, uh, Bull says, put the sandwiches over there and he said, do you see all these guys here? He says, they're all men. You go wait in the car.

"You shoulda seen him," Frank is heard talking to his son on the tapes. "He didn't even wanna look at us. We were sitting, we were all, we were ready. We were all dressed up, uh, ready to dance."

Ready to dance, Frank said. Of course. Little did he know that at that very moment he was helping to write the music to his own last dance, the eventual Family Secrets trial itself.

On Jan. 5, 1962, Gus V. Vivirito, age 43, was the victim of a gangland shooting. He was near death with six bullets pumped into his body when he was taken to St. Ann's Hospital. I was there. Gus told me he had been shot by a crime syndicate gambling chief who he fingered as Miles J. O'Donnell, age 35, the nephew of William Klondike O'Donnell, a beer runner in the Prohibition era and a labor racketeer. He was also running a crime syndicate gambling joint at 5941 Roosevelt Road in Cicero.

Vivirito had been shot in the cheek, neck, left and right ribs, and twice in the abdomen. He hung on for two weeks, but fifteen days later, on Jan. 20, 1962, Vivirito was pronounced dead—but not before we could obtain a dying declaration. An arrest warrant was immediately issued for Miles O'Donnell. His attorney, Robert McDonald, a lawyer for a number of syndicate members, called Area #5 Homicide and stated he was representing O'Donnell. On May 23, 1962, O'Donnell's bookie hall was raided and six persons were arrested. By November, four of the gamblers had been convicted, but charges against O'Donnell were dismissed. Vivirito also made several statements to the effect that he had given information to the State's Attorney's Office about syndicate gambling joints operating in Cicero. Vivirito then stated he started receiving pay from the prosecutors for information on Cicero horse betting joints.

Vivirito was one of the first to finger the mob, but he had little to lose at the time. "Miles O'Donnell is the man who shot me. I was in his Cicero gambling joint on Jan. 5. He must have followed me home from there. He shot me six times and left me for dead outside my home."

I still have my arrest report from January, 1962, describing Vivirito's wounds in detail: "Through and through gun shot wound entering about 2 inches right side of mouth, exit behind the right ear. Gun shot wound right upper abdomen, lodged. Through and through gun shot wound entering back, center belt line and exiting about 4 inches below left rib cage. Gun shot wound entering right neck, lodged behind left ear. Gun shot wound entering left neck and lodged in right shoulder area."

Mob hits were serious business. But even with six bullets, Vivirito hung on long enough to identify his own murderer. Years later, the Family Secrets investigation would drive a stake into the heart of the mob with more insiders spilling their guts. That's what it takes with these guys—insiders talking, a decidedly dangerous activity, of course.

Coming full circle almost, during the Family Secrets trial, in August of 2007, a man came over and grabbed my arm in the courtroom hallway. It was Rocco LaMantia, the 46-year-old son of Shorty himself. Rocco, too was a known convicted felon. He had been charged with the heinous murder of Martha DiCaro, only 19 years of age and Rocco's girlfriend at the time, by shooting her in the mouth on May 6, 1979, in Shorty's home. But in 1981 he was acquitted of that one—by Judge Thomas Maloney who, in my opinion and that of many others, was one of the most corrupt judges in Illinois history. But don't take just my word for it. Judge Maloney would soon be swept up by the Operation Greylord federal investigation and trial that uncovered extensive judicial corruption in the Cook County courts. Two lawyers who funneled bribes to Maloney over the years were two of the key witnesses against him at trial.

Maloney served as judge from 1977 until he retired in 1990, and some reports suggest he was the first and only Illinois judge ever to be convicted of fixing a murder case. Before going on the bench, Maloney was a practicing lawyer with mob connections. Eventually he was convicted in 1993 by a Federal District Court for conspiracy, racketeering, extortion, and obstruction of justice. In 1994 the former judge was sentenced to nearly 16 years for fixing three other murder cases. Prosecutors alleged that Shorty LaMantia had paid $20,000 to Maloney to fix Rocco's murder trial, although they never formally charged Shorty with fixing his son's case. Interestingly, though, before going on the bench Judge Maloney had once been Shorty LaMantia's own attorney.

According to various court records and published reports, Rocco had also allegedly helped set up a trucking business that would make over $400,000 from the City of Chicago in what became known as "the Hired Truck Program" scandal that developed when Rocco's wife was working for the mayor's budget office which ran the program for the City. Rocco had denied having any equity interest in the firm, though he did acknowledge helping to set it up. The company had been listed with headquarters at the LaMantia family home in the 2800 block of South Shields in Chicago, not many blocks north of Comiskey Park and now U.S. Cellular Field where the White Sox play. This was where Rocco's girlfriend had been shot in the mouth.

Apparently recalling the success of my first published book, Rocco asked if I'd write his own book with him. In turn, I asked if he knew that I had arrested his father, and he said he did, but that he didn't care. I have yet to take him up on it, though.

In August of 1965, Detective Sgt. Ed Flood, Homicide, sent Frank and me out to O'Hare Field. My assignment was to interview Alfonso Branch, age 49, a parking lot attendant. Branch had been sitting in a parking lot tow truck at 12:55pm when he saw a red 1964 Oldsmobile speeding down a parking lane before pulling to a stop in a no parking zone at aisle D-1. The driver emerged and started to lock the car when Branch tried to wave him off, signaling there was no parking at that space.

Making no progress, Branch approached the driver and said he'd have to tow the car if he left it there, then Branch returned to his own truck to write down the car's license plate number. The driver became agitated and followed Branch to his truck.

"What are you writing down?" the man challenged.

"I'm writing down your license number."

"And what are you going to do with it?"

Branch said that standard procedure required him to log the number in advance of towing any car.

"I should make you eat that number," said the stranger, who pointed his finger at Branch and then pulled a gun.

"I didn't know what make or model it was," Branch later explained to me, "all I knew is that it was a gun he pulled out from under his shoulder, and then pointed it at me."

"If this car is gone when I come back, I'll blow your goddamn fuckin' brains out." Then the man left for the terminal. Just like that.

We ran the plate DL-70486, and it checked out to HEJHALL, Elmhurst, Illinois, a near West suburb. The car had been rented to John Fecarotta of 201 Michaux, Riverside, Illinois, another Western suburb. Frank and I then learned that Fecarotta was a known syndicate member, an Outfit guy with a long arrest record. We returned to Area #5 Homicide, did a little more research, dug up some photos of Fecarotta, then went back to O'Hare with the pictures. Branch recognized the photos and was able to identify the man in the parking lot as John Fecarotta.

We decided to sit on the car, meaning to watch it round the clock until he returned. Frank and I couldn't be there 100% of the time, so we passed along Fecarotta's description: 6'2" tall, 230 pounds, black hair. He was a business agent and organizer for Laborers Local Union 8, and also a loan shark collector working for "Fifi" Buccieri, a ranking crime syndicate figure.

The red Olds remained under surveillance for two and a half days, then finally Frank and I observed a tall man who fit the description of Fecarotta approaching the car. We had to play it carefully, because we knew he had a gun when he left, so he probably still had one. Today we wouldn't be so sure, but there was virtually no airline security in 1965. We waited for him to put the key into the car lock, which would show possession of the key and the car. At that point, we would jump from our squad and catch him by surprise.

Sure enough, the suspect put the key in, so we launched ourselves forward, showing our badges and informing Fecarotta who we were. We had him place his hands on top of the car, but he was obstinate.

"What the fuck do you guys want?"

We immediately searched him and found nothing, then told him to open the door.

"It's not my car," he protested.

"Open the damned door," I ordered, showing no patience for games.

He still gave us a hard time, but finally started to understand our language. With the handwriting now on the wall, Fecarotta opened the door. We then placed him under arrest, I took his keys, and we proceeded to open the trunk.

We found no dead bodies, but we did uncover a pretty good smoking gun of sorts. In the trunk was a bag of burglar tools stuffed into an attaché case, plus 15 master keys for various automobiles. We hauled Fecarotta back to DDA#5, homicide, and questioned him. Like all these hoods do, John clammed up. He kept his mouth shut for the whole 2-3 hours that we grilled him, saying only "I want my lawyer, I want my lawyer." Finally we charged him with possession of burglar tools and aggravated assault, then Fecarotta was released on $6500 bond. I don't think he ever made it to trial, though, because I heard the FBI was interested and took over the case.

That was a lot of trouble for the privilege of parking in a no-park zone at the airport. Sometimes these guys are smart, then other times they seem so clueless. Apparently the mob bosses felt the same way about John, because over the ensuing years he would fall out of favor. He would botch a hit on Las Vegas boss Tony Spilotro after Spilotro became impossible for the Outfit to control. With that, time had run out on John Fecarotta, whose fate would be spelled out in great detail by Nick Calabrese, Frank's brother, during his sworn testimony at the Family Secrets trial decades later. The rise and fall of Tony Spilotro, and the downfall of John Fecarotta would provide some of the most riveting Family Secrets testimony.

7

Juice, Pizza & Vic Damone

At age 27 years, all Anthony Franchina wanted was a chance to live. The loan sharks would not give it to him.

Tony said he first fell into their clutches in November of 1963, right around the time JKF was assassinated. Tony's own death was set into motion, for it was then that he took his first juice loan from the mob. A little over two years later, Tony Franchina, working as a dock hand, squeezed the trigger of a small .22 caliber Derringer revolver that he had turned on himself. It was the best, last, and only way he knew to find peace.

Franchina borrowed $400 from Joseph and Donald Grieco, brothers who operated in the violent shadows of the juice loan racket. At first Tony was able to make the 10% weekly interest, but as the months passed he missed a payment or two so the mobsters doubled his interest as a penalty. At the time, Tony's take home pay was $78 a week.

Tony was beaten by hoodlums several times, once sending him home bleeding at 2:00am where he fell into the arms of his terror-stricken wife Dorothy. She would later testify before the Illinois Crime Commission.

Long before Dorothy would get to tell her story to the authorities, she and Tony endured many days and nights of hardship and terror. In addition to Tony's beatings, there were threatening phone calls in the night. When Dorothy pleaded with the juice collectors to give her husband a break, they suggested she become a prostitute to meet the payments.

By early 1964, it had become virtually impossible for Franchina to support his wife and their 7-year-old son. Franchina said that by then he had paid more than $1000 in interest, but the original amount of the $400 loan still stood. Tony was in a panic, unable to solve or even fully grasp the situation he had gotten himself and his family into. In March of 1964, Tony found himself telling his sorry story to Sgt. Michael O'Donnell of the Chicago Police Intelligence Unit.

But the mob was remained unintimidated and unrelenting. So although Tony forged ahead, telling his tale of juice, beatings and threats that followed his ill-advised loan from the Grieco's, he nonetheless refused to identify the thugs who had beaten him. There was no way out—if Tony remained silent, he could not escape the juice, and if he fingered his attackers he was a dead man. Ultimately, there was no difference, for Tony ended it himself by pulling the trigger in the bedroom of his family's apartment.

Two years later Mrs. Dorothy Franchina, age 33, while wearing a black lace veil over her face, steadfastly testified before the Illinois Crime Commission at the County Building. She would relate her sordid tale of despair and terror, including how hoodlums had once kidnapped their young son to send a clear message about keeping up the payments. She recounted years of horror that followed that first, relatively modest, loan of just $400. Yet paying off the balance was as elusive as when they started. When asked what the remaining balance was, Dorothy could only lament, "God only knows what that is." She recounted how the Grieco's urged her to turn to prostitution. One said she was "a good looking girl" and could earn good money in prostitution.

Dorothy told how, to her knowledge, payments fell behind only once, in 1964, and then her son, only 6 at the time, failed to return home from school. She became frantic, flagging a taxi and cruising the streets to look for him. She went to the Vic Damone Pizza factory on Larabee Street, which is where payments to the Grieco's were customarily made. She made a payment, then Donald Grieco assured her that her son would be home when she got there. Dorothy hurried home, where indeed she found their son Mike, who proceeded to report that two or three men identified themselves as friends of his father took him for an automobile ride—over his protests.

After Mrs. Franchina testified, Joey Grieco, accompanied by an attorney, proceeded to invoke the Fifth Amendment 51 times. He declined to answer questions dealing with his arrest record and connections with hoodlums.

Five other victims would testify at those same hearings. They told of paying 20% interest on loans and signing wage assignment forms. The juice racket has always been a crime that leads to other crime as victims become thieves, stealing money to make payments, or leads to the tragedy of broken or lost lives.

Tony Franchina was one of many such victims, as was his whole family. The police had told him they were powerless without Tony's testimony, but Tony could not risk turning on the mob. Tony's lips were sealed by terror. One day Tony went to visit his mother, and he told her he wanted to take his own life. Later that same night, Tony dined with his wife Dorothy in their small apartment on Chicago's north side. Dorothy later told the police that she and her husband quarreled over their predicament. She said her husband then went into the bedroom and changed into his pajamas, then took the .22 Derringer, pressed it to his chest, and fired one fatal shot.

His body fell across the bed, the pistol still in his hand. At the age of just 27 years, Tony Franchina was dead.

Little Joey Grieco did not pull the trigger that night only because he didn't have to. The young thug Joe Grieco, the one who pulled a knife when I caught him cheating at cards years before, became a top boss for the Outfit. He was ruthless, but Joey he wasn't entirely like Santucci or some of the other hoods of his day. Sometimes Joe managed to have some class, or at least he could look like he did. He was still wacko, mind you, but Joey Grieco cleaned up pretty good, as they say, when we were both kids. As teenagers in the 1940s, most of the guys I knew wore sneakers, T-shirts, and overalls—we call them jeans now, but at one time they were one-piece outfits with shoulder straps, much like painters wear today, and even the strapless regular blue jeans came to be called overalls. But they weren't for Joe Grieco—he operated on a different page. The rank and file, including me, dressed like slobs, jumped the El tracks, and wore the same clothes for a week, but Joe always looked like he might have walked straight out of *Esquire*.

When Joe Grieco strode into a poolroom—which he did often—everyone noticed. When we weren't playing pool, there was usually a dice or gin rummy game in the back room somewhere. That's where you could find Joe—and sometimes me. We would play rummy for a nickel or a dime—big money for some of us guys. But then Joe would pull from his pocket a greater sum, like a couple of dollars, and that would "one-up" everybody. He had charisma *and* money—making him something of a stud for his day, I suppose, even though the money was always a little shady, just like Joey himself. He probably had a few connections, too, even in those early days. The police never, ever came to check the poolroom where Joe hung out, and that impressed me more than Joey's fancy clothes did.

If the cops *had* shown up, they would have found a room full of 14-year-olds playing pool, parlay cards, and betting on the horses. We should have been geeky freshmen trying to kiss some elusive girl with braces—or even copping a feel if we got really lucky—but, no, there we were: pool, cards, gambling, and smoking.

To save my ass I couldn't beat Joe Grieco at "7 card call" rummy. We played at least once a week, sometimes twice, and I wasn't that bad of a player—but I just couldn't win. When I finally caught Joey cheating, I was really pissed and flew off the handle. I must have been a good show because my reaction brought the house down—and then brought a knife from Grieco's pocket.

I didn't get cut that day, but I knew I could be in trouble with the wrong people. Joe had more clout than a little piece of shit like me, which is why I decided to tell the on-site bookie Joe the Pelican, even though he never did anything. I also told Blackie Morelli, who helped run the joint. I didn't know what would happen next, if anything, but I wanted to let Grieco know that I wasn't a pushover. Eventually it all got smoothed over, but my early encounters with mobsters from Joey Grieco to Frankie Calabrese, who would bust my lip a decade later, suggested a definite pattern of confrontation during my earlier days. Maybe it was destiny at work—after all, I became a police detective, but most of the others just became more of what they were already. Until they found themselves on trial, in jail, or dead.

In 1958 a federal court fined Joey $5000, a huge sum in those days, and placed him on a year's probation for receiving stolen property. Over the years I followed Joe's career, partly because of our connection to the old neighborhood, but also because our paths crossed again after I was on the police force. Both Joey and brother Donald were arrested in February of 1964 by my dear friend and colleage Capt. Bill Duffy from the Police Intelligence Unit, where they operated the Independent Factoring Corporation, their small loan operation—presumably the one that led to the demise of Tony Franchina, among who knows how many others. They were then charged with aggravated battery for beating a juice loan victim who was behind in his payments. When I was a young detective, Joey was a mob lieutenant already experienced in the juice loan racket where he specialized in collections and terror along with his associate and mentor Fiore "Fifi" Buccieri. I didn't know who the shit Fifi was—no surprise because at first I did not know much at all about the mafia and rackets beyond our old neighborhood days. I began to learn fast, though, and the best way: on the job training. In 1965, Joey was busted for beating a juice loan victim and got 6 months in jail for his trouble. I was starting to catch on—wherever there was trouble in the Chicago neighborhoods, you could usually find the Outfit somewhere behind it.

A year later, in 1966, the Grieco brothers, Joey and Donald, were back at it, operating a loan shark racket from behind a new company selling frozen pizzas. The president of that pizza enterprise turned out to be Vic Damone—yeah, *that* Vic Damone, the singer, which should surprise no one since the name of the company was the Vic Damone Pizza Corporation. An ongoing investigation turned up Joey Grieco and Donald Grieco as company directors, and it also led to another company at the same address: Nicky's Frozen Pizza, a mob operation that fronted a juice loan racket. There was no Nicky, though, it was just a name for the business.

Word leaked out, and Damone was very upset when he was publicly linked to the Grieco's. He said it cost him a few TV show appearances. He was lucky it didn't cost more than that. The press asked Damone if he had made any inquiries of the Grieco or Buccieri brothers, and his answer was anything but inspired. "All I know about them is that they drove Cadillacs." With that, Mayor Daley's office revoked the license of Nicky's Frozen Pizza, which at the time was operating on the north side at 2015 Larabee Street, the same place Mrs. Franchina made the juice payment to free her son, and Damone was definitely embarrassed. A spokesman denied that Damone ever received any money from the pizza business. So how did he get involved? Damone said he had met Joey Grieco's wife while he was appearing at the Sahara Motel in Schiller Park, Illinois. The Sahara, by the way, was a mob establishment owned by

Mandel "Manny" Skar, a convicted three-time felon. He would later be murdered in front of his Lake Shore Drive apartment, a mob hit if I ever saw one.

According to Damone's explanation, he had been innocently "trapped" into becoming president of the Vic Damone Pizza Corp. while having friendly drinks with "Big Frank" Buccieri and the two Grieco brothers. Big Frank was a top crime syndicate loan shark and west side gambler. He was a director of the Damone Corporation, and his brother "Fifi" Buccieri was an established mob boss. After the Grieco's were arrested, the Intelligence Unit detectives inquired what the pizza firm's annual profits were and why the brothers had resorted to the juice loan racket. "The pizza business isn't as good as it looks," Joey explained.

Damone had worked his way up the hard way, and his reputation took a temporary hit with his ties to the "neighborhood" guys like the Buccieri's and Grieco's. Damone was actually born Vito Rocco Farinola—now there's a name. Although his father was an electrician by trade, he nonetheless played the guitar and liked to sing around the house. Damone's mother was proficient on the piano and actually gave lessons, so he clearly grew up in a musical environment. Soon he was taking voice lessons to emulate his favorite singer, none other than Frank Sinatra. Early in his career, Vito Farinola would take his mother's maiden name, Damone, and the rest is musical history.

In the 1950s Damone scored with dozens of records, appeared in several movies, and made a number of guest appearances on television's wildly popular Milton Berle Show and elsewhere. By 1966 when the press linked him to the Chicago mob, Damone was still recording but his career was on the wane. His last record to make the charts in the United States was released in 1969, and that was a cover tune from someone else.

Damone moved on with his career, but so did the Grieco brothers. They couldn't stop themselves from opening up small juice loan companies that operated in the backs of neighborhood joints like pizza stands and local lounges. Among others, they were involved in the Buccaneer Lounge in the heart of Old Town, not far from the Larabee address of the old Nicky's Frozen Pizza, and the School of Beauty Culture in far away Cicero. All were Outfit loan shark operations.

In 1958 Joey was found guilty of receiving stolen property, placed on probation, and fined $5000, after which they were charged with aggravated battery for beating a juice loan victim who was behind in his payments. In 1982, a grand jury indicted Joe for "conspiracy to collect a debt by extraordinary means," which obviously meant he was still active in the juice loan business. Two years later in 1984, Joe was tried for conspiracy and obstruction of justice and was found guilty by a federal jury. U.S. District Judge John Nordberg then sentenced Joe to prison for 5 years and slapped him with a $15,000 fine.

The fines were getting bigger, but Joe didn't always strike out. Also in 1984, in February I believe, he was tried and acquitted by a federal jury for obstruction of justice. After the not-guilty verdict came in, cocky Joey walked over and started shaking hands with the jurors. That was Joey, he never held anything back.

Judge Charlie Barish, my old grammar school buddy, went into law practice with a lawyer named Colonel Bill Kass, then he worked for the state's attorney's office as a prosecutor. Charlie went on the Cook County Circuit Court bench in 1980 where he stayed for 16 years before retiring in 1996.

Not long ago Charlie and I revisited the old days of our youth at Gregory Elementary, located at Lawndale and Arthington. We compared notes and even shared a few secrets. Sears Roebuck had a catalog plant only a half block from school. The B&O Railroad ran next to it and over nearly every major north-south thoroughfare in the city. Our class of 1943 included a number of eventual judges and cops, including Dean Wolfson, a prominent attorney, and his brother Warren Wolfson, a highly respected and accomplished judge, not to mention Judge Eugene Willens, Charlie himself, and me.

Charlie recounted how bad Vito Zaccagnini had been as a kid. Vito, for some reason, had hated Charlie, and on several occasions Vito would chase Charlie all the way home from school. Charlie said, "Guess what, Jim? He never caught me. If you remember, I was once on the track team." Charlie called Vito a bully and said he was cruel to other students at the school. Vito was always looking for a fight in those early days, though he never tangled with me. Charlie and his friends respected me over the years, maybe because in the early days I was there for them a lot—or at least at the right times.

One day years later Charlie was prosecuting cases in Racketeer Court when Vito Zaccagnini himself turned up on the docket. Charlie was amazed, so he walked straight over to him. "Do you remember me, Vito?"

"No."

Charlie filled Vito in and told him how he remembered Vito from years past. Vito got nervous and told his defense attorney Herb Barsey that he didn't want to go before this judge and this prosecutor—meaning, of course, Charlie. Barsey and Charlie chatted, and Charlie told the lawyer that he only wanted to scare Vito a little to get even.

Then Barsey told Charlie that Vito was about to enter the witness protections program and was wary that the prosecution—meaning Charlie again—wouldn't go along and might get in the way of Vito entering the program. Charlie told him not to worry about it, that everything would work out. In Chicago, like just about everywhere I'm sure, we like to say "what goes around comes around." Talk about getting the last laugh. Vito used to chase Charlie in the neighborhood just to scare him, and then Vito turns up frightened enough to hide in witness protection.

Vito had a brother everybody called "Cowboy." I never did know his real first name, but "Cowboy Zaccagnini" doesn't have much of a ring to it—unless you include sour notes. Cowboy was a little older than the rest of us, and he drove a cab. He would come to the poolroom and pick up the bets from the bookmaker Joe the Pelican, then run those bets over to the racetrack—all illegal, of course, but that was the point. Most of us see laws as boundaries, these guys always saw them as an opportunity. What a difference—Charlie was a prosecutor on his way to becoming a judge, and Vito was a murderer and mob operative headed for witness protection. It hardly seems like we came from the same place—it seems now more like different universes.

Vito terrorized many of the kids at school, not just Charlie. Most of the neighborhood guys would just stay away from Vito if they could. But that was not always possible. Vito would intimidate, fight, and slap the weak around, taking their money, not to mention dignity. If he pulled that crap when I was around, I normally jumped in, telling Vito to back off. I always felt I'd get my head ripped off for interceding, but I never did. Vito would just freeze, then walk away.

Vito always had money in those days, and most of us knew how he got it—stealing from the other kids, mugging a drunk, or purse snatching. Just about every day Vito would have dice games or penny pitching contests on the sidewalk across from Gregory Elementary. I was not a fan of Vito's, to say the least, and after we graduated I went my way he went his, and on to bigger things—like murder. In June of 1948 Vito, then just 22 years old, was involved with three other goons in the murder of John Onesto, the 72-year-old proprietor at the Onesto Shoe Repair shop on Taylor Street in an old Italian neighborhood. Onesto was the grandfather of a kid named Tino, one of the guys in our little neighborhood group, the Cen-Flo Club. His murder was really upsetting to many of us since Tino was one of our own, and we were furious that Vito would stoop so low.

As it happened, it was through a conversation with Tino himself that Vito had learned Tino's grandfather kept large sums of cash at the shop. Obviously that inside information gave Vito the idea of landing some easy money. On the night of the robbery, three hoods went into the shop first while Vito stayed behind. Since Vito knew Tino, he knew the grandfather might recognize him so he remained outside at first. By the time Vito entered, the old man Onesto was already bound and bindfolded with a towel forced over his mouth. Tino told me later they didn't get much money after all, given they ended up murdering Onesto. Tino thought the towel may have contributed to Onesto's death, since the old man had suffered from bronchial problems.

Needless to say, Tino was more than upset, telling me that if he ever got the chance he was determined to kill Vito. He didn't get the chance, for by June of 1949 Vito and three others—John Grath, age 21, Chris Lisallo, age 17, and Joseph Barbaro, age 22—were all indicted for murder. Only a few years removed from his tough guy grammar school days, Vito would spend the next 16 years in the Illinois State Penitentiary. When he finally got out, Vito picked up where he had left off, promptly becoming a muscleman for mobster Mad Sam Destefano.

Later, when Vito Zaccagnini spent 21 months in custody, mainly in the State's Attorney's witness quarters, had told a number of tales about how his own mob gang had worked. Often the gang would obtain information on valuable loads from cartage company employees who were hooked on juice loans. That was one of the biggest problems with the juice racket: the borrowers had to get the money repaid at all costs. So they would tip the Zaccagnini gang off, who would then hijack the trucks. Often the Zaccagnini boys would use portable red flashing lights atop their cars to stop truckers on the highways. After flashing phony police badges, the thieves would steal the trucks and their loads.

Zaccagnini was a government witness in a conspiracy case involving counterfeit travelers checks and United States Savings Bonds. Zaccagnini was one of the original 10 defendants, but he flipped and became a witness against the others. Zaccagnini himself admitted to being heavily in debt to the mob, including Sam Destefano, and at the time he was already under a state sentence of 5 to 14 years for forging checks. He flipped for the government, Zaccagnini explained, because he had no future in life. He was paying 11% juice every week on $10,000 he had borrowed from Destefano—that's $1100 per week forever, without ever reducing the principal. Over the years I would run into Vito at random places on the streets and in restaurants. Sometimes we would exchange small talk, appropriate since by then Vito was a small man with all the old junior high bravado long removed.

Richard "Dick" Hinkel was another classmate that Charlie and I both remember. Richie Hinkel was in my grade at grammar school, and Charlie was one year behind us. Much later, when Charlie was in private practice, he represented our old buddy Richie about 6 times for various deceptive practice charges usually involving bad checks. Richie was pretty proficient at passing "good paper," a term that referred to the really convincing bad, stolen, or forged checks. Charlie said that Richie called him one night from the Quad Cities, maybe it was Davenport, Iowa, along the Mississippi River about 180 miles west of Chicago. He had passed some really good stuff but got pinched for it and even hit the Chicago police daily bulletin—that was big time. Too bad Richie was just a big time loser.

As I watched the Family Secrets trial unfold in 2007, seven decades had passed since our father had abducted Wally and me. It was a sojourn that changed my life, and I'm certain our mother subsequently saved our lives, one way or another. The mob still exists, but those five Family Secret defendants have become relics of a distant day gone by. Maybe I'm a relic, too, but I have my dignity, as do Charlie Barish, Judge Wolfson, Big Jim Thompson, and the rest of us who managed not to cross over to the dark side. It's hard to imagine where our lives parted, precisely, since we were all in the same boat for so long. Maybe those five defendants thought they were taking the easy way, but after a lifetime of dodging bullets, other thugs, the feds, and even impromptu grave sites, it would be hard to describe life in the mob as "easy." Frankie "the Breeze" Calabrese, James "Little Jimmy" Marcello, Joey "the Clown" Lombardo were as powerful as one could be in the Outfit—yet there they were, still fighting for their lives, just as they had done for 70 years or more.

The movies sometimes get it right, but over the years the mob has been glorified with its money and women, gambling and booze, not to mention its brushes with fame. Television's Soprano family was basically accurate, mixing family, friends, and loyalty with murder, mayhem, booze, women and drugs. But money and power are hard not to glorify, especially since even the names of these guys have always been colorful, if not daunting, giving many a bigger than life visual image along the poetic lines of "bad, bad Leroy Brown" or "Mack the Knife." What could be more intimidating than the real life "Machine Gun" Jack McGurn or Frank "the Enforcer Nitti" from the 1930s? There was no doubt about what those guys did and what their claim to fame certainly was.

Sometimes the names are indeed self-evident. John "No Nose" DiFronzo, Frank "the German" Schweihs, Anthony "Little Tony" Zizzo, or "Big Tony" Chiaramonti, all bore obvious monikers. So did John "Apes" Monteleone, Bobby "the Beak" Siegel, and "Fat Herbie" Blitzstein, though a bit less flattering.

Tony "the Ant" Spilotro, the hood that virtually ran the streets of Las Vegas until his mob induced demise, was a good example, though there is some disagreement as to the meaning of his mob name. It may have just reference his smaller size, which he made up with a gigantic stature earned with violence and power—maybe the best example around of where the Napoleon complex can lead. Some sources attribute the label to the press, which picked up on it after FBI agent William f. Roemer, Jr. publicly referred to Spilotro as "that little pissant." I suppose both sources were probably right.

Some nicknames were not patently obvious. Ronnie Jarrett was "Menz" which meant "half and half," referring to his partial pedigree. Mike Ricci was "the Hotdog Man," Frank Saladino was "Gumba," Al Tarnabene became "the Pizza Man," and Micheal Albergo was called "Hambone." Anthony "Twan" Doyle, one of the Family Secrets defendants, derived his moniker from his mother's inability to say his own name due to her own thick ethnic accent, so instead of Anthony he became "Twan." Maybe Frank Santucci became "Frango" because he loved the famous Frango Mints sold by the renowned Marshall Fields store on Chicago's State Street, but I don't know. I do know how boss Joey "the Clown" Lombardo got his label: Joey was known for his quick wit and a talent for clever remarks.

When the cops stopped Lombardo once in the 1980s when he fled a gambling raid, Joey was carrying $12,000 in cash and a book filled with jokes. During a police booking photo in December, 1963, Lombardo would yawn widely to prevent the police from getting a good picture of him. In March of 1981, when leaving court, Lombardo used the *Chicago Sun-Times* newspaper to hide his face—with a hole cut out so he could see where he was going. So Joey was a cut-up, a bit of a performer, and "the clown" name stuck.

They spoke in colorful tongues, too—not just swearing or discussing women or murder, which they did frequently, but by talking in code half the time. This was driven home by testimony at the Family Secrets trial, too. With electronic surveillance and other ways of monitoring the mob—even just snitches listening in—it became prudent to develop a secret way of speaking to through the cops off and make overheard admissions harder to prove.

The "sisters" was code for two particular guys: Michael and James Marcello. The "hospital" was actually prison (in the old days the term for prison was "college"), "sickly sisters" meant any guys who might testify against the Outfit, and "not a nice girl" is a man cooperating with the authorities. Thus, one might be heard to say "the sisters went to the hospital because someone was not a nice girl."

Robberies were scores, "the purse" is evidence in the crime lab (like, say, bloody gloves), "the prostitute" is a cooperator, and criminal charges are "beefs." But of course, perhaps at the top of the list, the mob, the Outfit, is known as "The Family." And that brings us back to the investigation and trial that found five top kingpins sitting in front of me for three months with their lawyers all throughout the Family Secrets prosecution.

I don't know how much they taught me at Gregory Elementary, but somewhere along the way I learned the most important thing of my life: how to stay out of the wrong chair in a courtroom.

8

Philly Beans and Me

Phillip "Philly Beans" Tolomeo died on December 14, 1998. He was 71 years old. Phil was my first partner on the force when I made detective over a half century ago. But just who was this Philly Beans—cop or Outfit goon?

Working with Tolomeo was a nightmare. We had the midnight shift back in the spring of 1955, and one night we were driving and he suddenly stops at Harlem and Lawrence, a place called Meo's Norwood House, a restaurant. To this day, the restaurant still stands on that spot, now called the Warsaw Polish Restaurant, which occupies both a small corner of Norwood Park, just across the street from neighboring Chicago.

On our very first night of the midnight shift, while parked there in front of Meo's, Phil told me, "Wait here." Then he disappeared into the restaurant, a secluded joint with no windows or doors in the front. The only way inside was under a canopy over part of the driveway on the side of the building. It was an Outfit place, and they didn't like windows—sure, windows were nice for seeing out, but others could see in, too, and that wasn't good. I also was suspicious of the name, which seemed to echo the name Tolomeo. Phil left me in the parked car on Harlem in front of Meo's for way too long, and when he finally emerged I chewed his ass.

"I just wanted to see a few guys," he said.

"Do you know we're working?" I asked. "You can't be fucking around in some restaurant."

Philly Beans looked like a guy who just walked out of *Esquire Magazine*. I didn't care much for his Gucci shoes, plus I didn't like the last three letters of his name: MEO—same as the restaurant. It didn't feel right. I did a little of my own legwork about this place Meo's, then spoke with an anonymous source who reported that it was a favorite mob hangout. I was still green, a young guy on the force, and when I heard that Meo's was a favorite of the mob, I nearly shit. Not a day or night went by that you couldn't find a top Outfit chief at Meo's, and that included Tony "Big Tuna" Accardo, then the elder statesman of the Chicago mafia. You could find other top guys there, too, like Joey Aiuppa, Jackie Cerone, Sam Giancana, and Murray "the Camel" Humphreys. You couldn't miss these guys in there, and then I find my partner strolling inside in the middle of the night like nothing's happening. Meanwhile, I was adding two plus two, four came up real clear, and I was beginning to figure it out.

The last straw for me came when we were winding down our final few days on midnights. Phil drove me to Meo's, then left me waiting outside yet again. All of a sudden, I saw flashbulbs popping in the weeds, piercing through a dark vacant lot across the street on the east side. Somebody was clearly snapping pictures, which completely pissed me off. That was it. I had had it with all this Meo's nonsense and Phil's disappearing act, so I stayed over after our shift, which ended at 8:00am, so I could speak with Det. Sgt. George Murphy, my supervisor. I walked into Murphy's office and said I didn't like all this extracurricular stuff with Tolomeo, especially while we were working together. "I'm gonna get fired," I complained.

But Murphy assured me that all was okay, and he clued me in on the mystery of Philly Tolomeo. First, he said it was probably the FBI taking photos from the weeds. I said, "Oh, great, now I *am* gonna get fired." Then I found out that Phil was playing gin rummy with Outfit people. Playing cards with the mob! This guy would bet on raindrops if he could, which put me in a bad spot, but Murphy said *somebody* had to be this guy's partner. "You're new, Jim," Murphy explained, "and I didn't think you could get in trouble with him on the new shift." But that was that. Murphy took me off, and that's when I got my new partner Frank Czech, a great guy, really fantastic man and a true mentor. Frank and I would have a great career together, cracking cases and jokes for years to come.

Once I dumped Phil, things really changed, and my career took off. At first I didn't know what happened to Phil, but eventually I learned through the grapevine that he wasn't on the force anymore. Over time, I found out that in 1967 Phil had become a vending machine racketeer as a partner of, and good pal to, Joseph "Joe Gags" Gagliano. I also learned that Phil had been playing those gin rummy games big time, for big dollars. My source should have known, for he said that he, himself, was into Phil for about $8000—and he wanted to know if Phil was good for it. "Don't ask me," I said—the last thing I needed was to be vouching for Philly Beans to some connected guy.

Sooner or later all things good or bad come to an end. In April of 1969, my old partner Philly Beans was sentence to six months in Cook County Jail on charges of violating a court order to testify about his dubious vending machine operation. Circuit Court Judge Edward F. Healy had ordered Tolomeo to answer questions posed by the Illinois Crime Investigation Commission. As part of the order, Philly Beans had been granted immunity, essentially forcing him to testify.

Phil was reluctant. The Commission believed that the crime syndicate controlled the Preferred Cigarette Vending Company, located at 1920 W. Grand. By this time, Phil was the new associate of north side mob chieftains Joseph (Joe Gags) Gagliano and Joseph (Little Caesar) DiVarco. Preferred Vending was placing dozens of cigarette machines and juke boxes into locations around Chicago without benefit of a city license. Chicago Police soon began seizing 575 illegal vending machines in a mass raid personally endorsed by Chicago's original and powerful Mayor Richard J. Daley. Daley then ordered and authorized Police Supt. James B. Conlisk, Jr. to take any action necessary to stop the illegal operations.

Daley's order wasn't really about licensing, it was an assault on the mob that dispatched 160 police officers to round up the machines.

Phil became owner of the Preferred Cigarette Vending Co., Inc. (owner "on paper" only, I think he was the Outfit front man), and over the years I began to run into him in the neighborhoods. He was a steady at Dapper Dan's Restaurant located in the city, on the far northwest side at Belmont and Cumberland. Across the street, by the way, is a special place for me, St. Joseph's Cemetery. Two young boys are buried there, John and Anton Schuessler, two of the three murder victims in the mysterious triple murder in 1955—one of my first cases and a big enough deal that it became my first published book. I went there not long ago, to the St. Joseph's Cemetery, on the 50th anniversary of the deaths of those boys, and I put a rose on each gravesite.

Later I learned that Phil had gone to work for the Chinatown crew in 1978, where he made money in the juice loan business. His client list swelled to over 75 juice loan borrowers, and some reports put it as high as 100. That was pretty good—and lucrative. In 1983, though, it was apparently too lucrative because Frank Calabrese learned that Phil had been skimming money he collected off the top and had taken about $150,000 of Outfit money for himself. If anyone could have known better, it should have been Phil, a former cop who knew the score. But sooner or later these guys think they can rip off the mob itself, and a suicidal idea if ever there was one. Sometimes it arises out of sheer need, like from drugs or big gambling debts, but often it is just ego—they throw so much cash around that they start reading and believing their own press clippings. When Frank found out about Phil, it wasn't pretty. He had Phil beaten, and once when I ran into Phil at a restaurant he told me that Frank had personally broken his nose and took the deed to his mother's house as collateral until he paid back the cash.[6] By then, when I saw him, Phil had been taken down a few pegs and was working for a measly $100 a week—plus he had been told by Frank to turn his better accounts to other crew members like Jerry Scalise, John Rainone, and Phil Fiore. Fiore would rise rapidly through the ranks, and for awhile he and Tolomeo reversed roles with Philly Beans reporting to Fiore.

Later that same year, in 1983, Tolomeo's stupidity nearly cost him his life after he mishandled still more money. What a piece of work—if Phil had a brain, he would have been lonesome. Frank, Sr. and his brother Nick Calabrese went to Phil's house, confronted his mother, and put the fear of life into her when they said they were

---

[6] Years later, court records and published reports confirmed Phil's story. In 1983 Frank had indeed forced Phil to turn over his mother's house in Elmwood Park for collateral. The property found its way into a land trust with Salvatore Tenet as the listed beneficiary. Tenet was the father-in-law of Nick Calabrese.

personally going to beat Phil to death. I met that woman several times. She went through a lot over the years, not to mention transferring her house to the Calabrese family.

Phil had gotten in touch with one of his mafia buddies, I think it was Mario Rainone who was an enforcer for Lenny Patrick's street crew. Phil's idea was to set up his own money laundering business by making juice loans to borrowers that were real deadheads who had already been turned away by Frank's crew. How stupid does that sound?

I guess Rainone was just as brainless because he actually liked the idea and forked over $230,000 in cash with the understanding that he would collect on high-interest loans to a minimum of at least 35 juice customers, a book big enough to return $1,750,000 on the initial capital investment. Like I said, Phil was always on the edge, the kind of loser who would even bet on raindrops, so he then made a really big gamble: Phil took the money but decided not to loan it out like he said he would. Instead, Phil took most of Rainone's cash and used it to pay off the Calabrese street crew. Phil had his own Ponzie scheme going, robbing one to pay the other. That didn't work too well, though, because it turns out the $230,000 wasn't Rainone's money in the first place. The plan backfired, blowing up in Tolomeo's face because the money had really belonged to Black Sam Carlisi and Jimmy Marcello, two ranking Outfit guys.

And then things got *worse*. The Outfit suddenly wanted all their money called in after learning how incompetent the Lenny Patrick street crew was. Rainone was sure his time was up, surely there must be a contract out on his life, so he caved in. Rainone called the FBI shitting in his pants, then told them who he was and what he wanted. He sang like a bird in heat, spilling his guts about guys like Carlisi, Jimmy Marcello, and Frank Calabrese, Sr. Then, in 1990, Phil himself put the last nails in the coffin by filling the FBI in on the whole extortion racket—then he disappeared into the witness protection program.

With Rainone and Phil providing background and sworn testimony, Frank, Kurt, and Jerry Scalise entered into a plea agreement with the government. Frank, Sr. was actually sentenced to 10 years in the pen, and Frank, Jr., got 4 years for himself. In response to requests from the prosecution, the judge also ordered that Junior be given drug and mental health treatment while in prison.

With both Franks on ice and the government armed with a plethora of testimony, sweeping indictments came down hard on the Outfit during the 1990s. The federal grand jury returned a sealed 11-count indictment charging Frank, Sr. and 8 others with operating an illegal loan sharking racket that had thrived over the past 14 years, wreaking havoc on loser stiffs and their families.

Phil Tolomeo was sentenced in August of 1997 and drew 46 months in prison for racketeering. Assistant U.S. Attorney Mitchell Mars said that Phil's cooperation had enabled authorities to finally crack the ruthless street crew headed by Frank Calabrese, Sr. Philly Beans had come full circle, beginning with that bad feeling in my gut when Phil kept disappearing into his namesake joint Meo's during our shift, and ending with him actually spilling his guts to save his own life.

I say if you live by the sword, you die by the sword—Phil was just more proof. But it's always been that way—especially for the Outfit, and especially in Chicago during the bullet-riddled hey-days of the mob. I literally grew up in the shadows of the Capone era, then I matured as a young detective on the Chicago force at a time when the mob could still flex its national muscle from Las Vegas—Spilotro and the boys—to Washington, DC.

Philly Beans was a small-time hood lucky to live long enough to make it to witness protection. But the big guns were out there, too. Take, for instance, Frank "Frango" Santucci—Mr. Lucky, if you want to call it that. Me? I call it "taking care of business—the Outfit way." That's what Santucci could do as a prolific burglar, and that's why he rose through the Outfit ranks.

It was a bitter cold day in January, 1960, when my wonderful partner Frank Czech and I were in the area of Melrose and Central Avenue, heading for George Bell's Lounge at 5600 W. Melrose. George's had a 4:00am liquor license, and one of our duties was to keep an eye on all the late-license joints. At the time this was a booming lounge with live entertainment, though George would eventually have it taken away from him. George, you see, was a big time gambler who lost vast sums on sports betting. One night I stopped into Hoagie's on North Avenue—and there was George Bell, working. He said he couldn't talk then, so I came back and George and I got together the next day, when he told me he was actually living over the lounge. He would not discuss what had happened to his own George Bell's Lounge, but that only confirmed my best hunch: the mob was probably into George for big bucks, and they almost certainly shoved George out and took the place over. On our many routine visits to the place, my partner and I would often find top guys hanging out, like LaMontia, Calabrese, Destefano, and even Tony "the Ant" Spilotro.

On our way to George's place for a routine visit around 2:00am that night, Czech and I were stunned by a gut-shaking BOOM that suddenly thundered from behind an old Kresge Department Store (the forerunner to K-Marts) at 5626 Belmont Avenue. Police squads streamed in, and we gunned our unmarked car to the back just in time to find three men fleeing down the store's rear fire escape. Two got away on foot, but we cornered the third culprit. I recognized him as Frank Santucci, a mob guy.

"What are *you* doing here?" I said, completely surprised by our encounter.

Santucci wouldn't answer, so we had his ass hauled down to the 33rd District. Meanwhile, Czech and I went up to search the second floor of the store where we found the outer doors of an office vault had been pried open, while the inner doors bore the burns of an acetylene torch. But the safe itself was a tough hunk of steel that had resisted all efforts to crack it open. Obviously, we had caught Santucci and the boys in the act of blowing the doors open to penetrate the Kresge safe.

We headed down to the 33rd District to find Santucci, who by then was locked up at the Jefferson Park Station. We recognized each other right away, and neither was surprised to find the other for Santucci had a long history of crime, especially burglary and armed robbery. Most recently, he had been arrested earlier that spring, on May 24, 1960, when he and burglar Anthony DiPaolo were caught fleeing from a pawn shop at 3171 W. Madison, right next to a place called Little Jack's Restaurant & Cheesecake. They had entered the pawn shop through a rear door, then successfully cracked the safe—a well-known Santucci specialty—and absconded with a load of jewelry and cash. Dumb luck struck, though, and they were spotted. After a two-block chase, Santucci and DiPaolo were nabbed. Despite matching up mortar fragments and dust that tied Santucci to the pawn shop caper, Santucci nonetheless fought the arrest and eventually beat the rap altogether.

We knew we had an experienced safecracker on our hands, so we questioned Frank for two hours at the Jefferson Park station. But he refused to make a statement about the attempted Kresge heist, and would not finger either of the other two guys who got away. All he would say was "I don't know anything about it," so Lt. Mangan ordered us to strip his clothes and take them down to the crime lab for a magnetic examination. "We hope we can collect filings from the clothes," Mangan explained, "to match with scrapings of metal found around the damaged safe at Kresge's."

"Crime" was Frank Santucci's middle name—he just never stopped, he couldn't help himself. On Oct. 5, 1962, Santucci, Anthony DiDonato and Robert Chessher pulled an armed robbery of a tavern at 718 N. Albany Avenue where they got away with $1100 in cash. The owner, one Mrs. Norma McCluskie, a tough, no-nonsense proprietor, suddenly pulled a gun out and blasted the stiff holding the cash. Altogether she fired six shots at these guys. One of them shot back and another threw a bar stool at her, but Norma held her ground. Santucci took one of her bullets, and although he got away, he was arrested a few days later and hospitalized. He was then identified by the tavern owner, after which the other two were determined to be DiDonato and Chessher. All three were soon indicted, and Santucci was soon released from Bridewell Hospital on $15,000 bond.

But the robbery case did not end there. It just got better because "Mad Sam" DeStefano, a crazed goon who had already served prison terms for rape, burglary, bank robbery and racketeering, was soon arrested for conspiracy to commit perjury, charged with trying to fix Santucci's tavern case. DeStefano intimidated the two main witnesses, the gun-toting McCluskie along with one Mrs. Henrietta Burns, both of whom suddenly lost their memories and could not testify. No surprise there—Mad Sam had a reputation for torturing his victims with ice picks, just for effect, which got famously good results, even among hardened mobsters. Norma, bless her heart, may have won the gun battle, but she had met her match with DeStefano.

So, after Norma had already identified the attackers, she refused to finger them at trial, so the prosecution had to start over. Eventually DeStefano was tried on the tampering charges and found guilty by a federal jury, but Judge George Leighton set the verdict aside citing prejudicial conduct on the part of the prosecution during the trial.

I'm sure Judge Leighton was not intimidated—he was a defense minded African-American, a highly respected no-nonsense guy who held prosecutors to high standards.

Later in the same year DeStefano was tried for the second time, but Judge Edward Finnegal had no choice but to declare a mistrial when the jury reported it was hopelessly deadlocked. Finally, though, on September 10, 1965, Mad Sam was found guilty on the third try, convicted by a jury of 6 men and 6 women. He was then sentenced to 3-5 years by presiding Judge Nathan Cohen.

Meanwhile, Santucci, Chessher and DiDonato, all acquitted in the 1963 trial due to Norma McCluskie's memory lapse, feared for their own lives because of the money they took from Destefano.

In December, 1965, with Chicago ablaze from Christmas lights and the lure of shining windows along the Magnificent Mile, my crime poster boy, Frank Santucci was once again arrested and indicted for the latest of his notorious long crime sprees. He went down with three other syndicate hoodlums, plus one attorney by the name of Robert McDonnell. A few years later McDonnell would have a glimpse of fame by marrying the noted "mafia princess" Antionette "Toni" Giancana. She was the daughter of Sam Giancana, sometimes known as "Mooney" or "Mo," one of the most powerful of all the syndicate bosses, in Chicago and otherwise.

Santucci was a tough thug with 40 arrests. The others nabbed with Santucci included Ernest "Rocky" Infelice, an Outfit boss who would be sentenced to prison in 1993 for the rest of his life; Americo De Pietto, a convicted crime syndicate narcotics king who would eventually serve 20 years in Leavenworth Penitentiary; and James "Cowboy" Mirro, a lower echelon hoodlum who was a West Side gambling overseer and loan shark racketeer. All five were brought to trial together in May, 1966, charged with conspiracy to pass forged money orders that had been stolen from a supermarket and transported across state lines. They had lifted 14,700 blank money orders from a Melrose Park supermarket over a Memorial Day weekend. All five were convicted and four of them were sentenced to five years in prison. The chief witness against them was Fred Ackerman, a disbarred ex-attorney.

The fifth convicted defendant, lawyer Robert McDonnell, had his sentence reduced to two years by federal Judge Abraham Lincoln

Marovitz, a long-standing icon of the federal judiciary.[7] McDonnell had a few other issues, too. At the time, word had it that McDonnell was allegedly deep into juice loans to Mad Sam DeStefano, and that he had paid $150,000 on an $80,000 loan. He was known to represent a number of crime figures during his career, and given his conviction in Santucci's money order scheme, not to mention the juice owed to DeStefano, he apparently got a little too close to them.

Getting too close is what all the stiffs do. They think they can just "do a little business," but then they find themselves *in* the business. As I noted before, once they get comfortable they sometimes even get the idea to rip off the mob—why not, the money is easy, right? Sure, *getting* it is easy, but what comes later is the hard part. Maybe that's what happened to my ex-partner Philly Beans Tolomeo.

Tolomeo started by rubbing shoulders with top mob figures while he was still on the force, sometimes with me waiting in the car half the night at Meo's. I couldn't get far enough away from Phil and those guys fast enough, but Phil just kept moving in, getting closer, and then becoming one of them as a loan collector for the Calabrese street crew from 1978 to 1988. Tolomeo then fled Chicago after embezzling from Frank's street crew. To quote a 1999 U.S. Court of Appeals ruling in *United States v. Philip Fiore*, following Fiore's loan-sharking indictment for racketeering, conspiracy, and extortion, that stunt was "an act of incredible courage of incredible stupidity." Having worked with Phil, I can vouch for the latter.

When Phil took off for parts unknown, he took not only money, but also many comprehensive records detailing his juice loan collections on behalf of the Calabrese crew. According to court records, these included the names of individuals from whom he collected, the interest rates of the juice loans, and the amounts turned over to his superiors in the crew. When Phil later lost his nerve and entered

---

[7] Named for Abraham Lincoln and noted for his Lincoln memorabilia and his longevity on the bench, Judge Marovitz had been a boxer in his early years, was appointed to the bench by John F. Kennedy in 1963, and befriended many of the famous names of his day including Bob Hope, Frank Sinatra, and Jimmy Durante. He even escorted famed fan dancer Sally Rand to the Worlds Fair in 1933.

the Witness Security Program, all these records were turned over to the FBI. What happened next is a matter of court record in the Fiore appeal.

At Fiore's trial, Tolomeo identified all the members of the Crew. Tolomeo also testified as to the hierarchy of the Crew, the jobs performed by each member, and his extensive role as juice loan collector. According to Tolomeo's testimony, in 1983, Frank Calabrese, the leader of the Crew at that time, introduced Tolomeo to Fiore and instructed him to train Fiore, a career burglar from suburban Berwyn, in the juice loan collection business. While working under Tolomeo, Fiore became skilled in methods of debt collection, interest rate calculation, and bookkeeping.

The government had been watching Calabrese for years, even though they wouldn't nab him for good until the Family Secrets trial in 2007. Frank had been active in the loan-shark business for decades, and his arrest record goes back to my early days, when Frank was busted in 1954 for possession of stolen cars in Interstate Commerce.

The Crew set up shop with a command post at M&R Auto and Truck Repair Service, located in the 2400 block of Thatcher Avenue in River Grove. Beginning in 1990, the owner, Matthew A. Russo, Jr., was coaxed into a scheme to bilk three area car dealerships by filing false invoices for repair work that was never performed. The racket expanded from there, including the lucrative juice loan business that could return as much a 10% a week on invested capital.

Russo himself had made the mistake of borrowing $20,000 from the crew to pay down an old bank loan, but that only made his problems worse. The juice flew out of control, and just one year later Russo was instructed to turn his house over to Calabrese in return for $195,000—but Russo had to rent the house back for $1000 a month, in addition to weekly juice payments of $750, after which he was to buy his own house back at market rates two years later.

Shortly after Tolomeo trained Fiore, Tolomeo fell out of favor with Frank Calabrese—and of course, I knew why, after Philly Beans had filled me in. As a result, Fiore was officially promoted and assumed Tolomeo's juice collection accounts. This promotion required Fiore to meet directly with Frank Calabrese to discuss juice loan activity. Meanwhile, Tolomeo, who now answered to Fiore, continued his collection activity but was closely scrutinized by Fiore and other members of the Crew. Soon thereafter, though, Tolomeo left the Crew and entered the Witness Security Program.

Fiore testified in his own defense at trial—and to no one's surprise, he sold out Tolomeo—claiming that Tolomeo forced him into becoming a juice loan collector for the Crew when he was unable to pay a juice loan that he had made with Tolomeo. In support of his coercion defense, Fiore claimed that Tolomeo showed him a gun once and he "sort of felt threatened." Fiore also claimed that on another occasion, Tolomeo stated that "things could happen" if Fiore did not repay him. Fiore further testified that Tolomeo left town, claiming that he would be gone for a couple weeks, and asked that Fiore hold on to a green address book, several slips of paper, and some blank promissory notes. According to Fiore, Tolomeo never returned so he held on to Tolomeo's property until it was acquired by the FBI during the search of his house.

Fiore's testimony, a whitewashed version of how Tolomeo was forced out and his book taken over, did not fly with the jury. On May 1, 1997, the jury in fact found Fiore guilty on all charges, then returned a whopping forfeiture verdict of $2,600,000 against him. On September 3, 1997, the district court sentenced Fiore to 120 months on each count to run concurrently.

The juice racket is probably as old as money itself. But the business as we know it today can be traced at least to the 15th Century when Shakespeare wrote The Merchant of Venice, in which the character Shylock famously admonished a borrower: "If you repay me not on such a day, in such a place, let the forfeit be nominated for an equal pound of flesh, to be cut off and taken in what part of your body pleased me." In New York, the juice lenders are still commonly referred to as "Shylocks," and the loans themselves are called the "Shy business."

Just over a year after Fiore's conviction, Phil Tolomeo was dead. The house of Philly Beans Tolomeo was, in the end, a house of very fragile cards. It is daunting to think what could have happened had I gone into Meo's with Phil all those nights, instead of just fuming in the car, doing nothing. But I would not have gone in, of course, because that wasn't me. I was happy to have a job, especially as a detective. Phil wasn't so lucky—or smart.

9

Big Tuna, Little Jimmy

The 1960s was a high profile decade for the Chicago mob. Tony Accardo and Sam Giancana were the top Outfit guys in those days, and Giancana had a particular weakness for celebrities and politics. The mob looks unfavorably upon headlines, though, especially the ones that turn up the heat, so Giancana's weakness may have ultimately brought his personal downfall.

Giancana's ties to the Kennedy administration are legendary, including his possible involvement in the Bay of Pigs debacle in Cuba and his penchant for high profile women—indeed at one point he seems to have shared a girlfriend with JFK himself. Chicago, as it happens, was a Kennedy stronghold for years. The patriarch Joseph Kennedy had been a bootlegger during the years of Prohibition and necessarily had many Chicago underworld ties. The Kennedy family invested heavily in Chicago, and until recently had continued to own the famed Chicago Merchandise Mart, a mammoth commercial building in the heart of downtown that features hundreds of furniture and design showrooms. It is still the world's largest commercial building with 4.2 million gross square feet, 25 stories tall and spanning two full city blocks.

The most famous Kennedy connection to Chicago was the 1960 presidential election itself, whereby Sam Giancana and the Outfit helped provided union—and other?—votes to boost the election of JFK. My own ties to the Kennedy clan were much more routine. As fate would have it, in July of 1964, during the post-Kennedy era of Lyndon Johnson, The Beatles, and the very early stages of Vietnam, the recently widowed Jackie Kennedy came to Chicago with her sister Caroline Lee Bouvier. She wanted no police detail, but there is no way Chicago would leave her without some kind of protection. Acting Lt. Frank Kracker, in charge of O'Hare police operations, assigned me to watch over her. Sun-Times columnist Maggie Daly picked up the story, and I had a few moments of fame. She was the perfect lady, as I recall, though I did have to sneak off with them so Jackie could have a cigarette in private. But I won't hold that against her—that was the least of Mrs. Kennedy's concerns after all she had been through just months before.

Although the New York area claims as many as five mafia families, Chicago has maintained one essential "blood line" from the days of Al Capone. This gives the Windy City an edgy but uniquely romantic legacy of murder and mayhem that is still traced to the machine gun days of Prohibition. Though long removed by time and circumstances, names like Spilotro, Calabrese, Lombardo, Cerone, Aiuppa, and others are still entwined with the old guard, and that makes Chicago crime unique.

Two of Chicago's most powerful and high profile mob bosses were Sam Giancana and Tony Accardo. These two mob chieftains were contemporaries, both born in Chicago just two years apart. Accardo, born in 1906, was two years older than Giancana. Both were protégés of the Capone gang, and both eventually achieved great national visibility—and power.

Giancana grew up on Chicago's west side, as did I. Giancana was the right pedigree: his parents were Sicilian immigrants. Still in his teens, Sam led a street gang of thugs who did dirty work for the Capone empire in the 1920s. Eventually he became a "wheelman," a driver, for the Capone gang. By 1928, during the height of Chicago's roaring twenties, Giancana was promoted to triggerman.

Giancana was married to Angeline DeTolve in 1933 and the couple raised three daughters, one of whom, Antoinette, would later pen a widely publicized memoir called *Mafia Princess*. When Capone was sent to prison in 1931, the Chicago mob was wide open, and Sam made the most of it, first in the illicit whiskey business and later controlling the Chicago numbers rackets in the poorest of the city's black neighborhoods. Giancana muscled his way to the top of the Chicago gambling world through murder and strong arm tactics, then gained great favor by generating millions of dollars in fresh mob income from the numbers and related gaming operations.

Years ago my Uncle Ted, who had a few connections that were not my type, introduced me to a bartender named Carmen Manno at a place called the Pink Clock. Manno went on to marry Antoinette in, as I recall, 1959. Manno had been divorced, so the marriage was against her father's wishes, which had to create some interesting friction given who her father was. Sam never really liked Manno anyway, and felt he was not very bright. Antoinette—also known as Toni—loved her booze and spent a good deal of time in local lounges, especially hangouts of her father like the Armory Lounge, Andre's, and Airliner Lounge.

Toni had her share of mental issues to go along with a drinking problem, so Sam was always nervous about her possibly disgracing herself or her family in public. Manno was no angel, either, though. He turned out to be a wife beater. He was known to belt her in the mouth or stomach at parties, just to keep her in line. Manno is lucky he lived through such miscreant behavior, but word was that Sam did not intervene, telling Toni that "she had made her bed and had to sleep in it." Eventually she divorced Manno and later married an attorney named Bob McDonnell who in 1966 found himself facing conspiracy charges for passing forged money orders along with mobster Frank Santucci.

Bob introduced me to Toni in the Chicago criminal courts building at 26th and California one day. I never saw either of them again until I was in a Costco store in 2006 or 2007. I looked up, and there was the Mafia Princess herself working in the food section handing out samplers of her own gourmet food line to taste along with "Giancana marinara pasta sauce." We spoke and got reacquainted. At first she wasn't sure about me, but after I recounted tales of her husband and how we had met before, she opened up. She encouraged me to call her husband who was not in good health and might enjoy hearing from me. No dice, though—I did not need to go down that path.

Meanwhile, during Sam's youth another tough guy was growing up in Little Sicily on Chicago's Northwest Side where I spent considerable time as a young detective. Tony Accardo began his career as a pick pocket and small time car thief during Chicago's Prohibition era. He discovered a place on North Avenue called the Circus Café and became a regular there. It was owned by a gangster named John Moore who was directly connected to Johnny Torrio's organization. Soon Accardo found himself working for the Torrio gang, working his way up to an enforcer role where he bludgeoned slow payers with a baseball bat, hence one of his many nicknames, Tony "Joe Batters" Accardo.

Accardo got the attention of none other than Al Capone himself, soon joining the Capone gang and eventually becoming a "made man" at a ceremony personally attended by Capone. Accardo had a good sponsor, Machine Gun Jack McGurn who recruited Accardo for the Capone organization. Accardo took the opportunity seriously and gained considerable favor when he personally shielded Capone from a rain of bullets fired by rival hoodlums, after which he was officially promoted as Capone's own wheelman and personal body guard. By the 1930s, with Capone in jail, Accardo had become an Outfit capo with power over the Capone gambling operations.

Years later the feds secretly recorded Accardo boasting about his role in the 1929 St. Valentine's Day Massacre, although experts today question his direct involvement. Mob historians do believe, however, that Accardo was involved in the high profile slaying of Capone rival Hymie Weiss on October 26, 1926, near the famed Holy Name Cathedral just west of Michigan Avenue.

Accardo was given his own street crew where he developed a lucrative business in loan sharking, bookmaking, and extortion, not to mention the highly profitable illicit booze business that made Capone and his inner operatives extremely wealthy. In Accardo's crew was a youngster by the name of Joey "the Doves" Aiuppa, who himself would be boss one day and had personal ties to the eventual Family Secrets defendants.

Fate propelled Accardo to the top. In 1943, mob honcho and former Capone henchman Frank Nitti committed suicide after being indicted for extortion along with Paul "the Waiter" Ricca. Nitti was a known claustrophobic, which likely influenced his decision to commit suicide rather than return to prison. Ricca became a top mob chieftain and a particular fan of Accardo, once saying that "... Accardo had more brains for breakfast than Capone had all day." The Outfit told Nitti to take the fall, but he could not face jail again with his claustrophobia and he knew he would be terminated anyway if he failed to go along, so he shot himself. Accardo had ascended quickly and was close to Ricca, the next in line for the top spot. Ricca, though, was found guilty and drew a 10-year sentence, so suddenly Accardo found himself at the helm.

Accardo was drawn by the financial lure of Las Vegas, and he engineered the mob expansion into the Vegas hotels and casinos in the 1950s, triggering a string of events that would lead to the Spilotro problem years later. Under Accardo's direction, the mob invested heavy dollars in several Vegas properties including the well known Tropicana, Stardust, and Riviera hotels. He successfully ousted all five New York crime families from the lucrative Las Vegas gaming empire, then moved the mob into high priced call girl services instead of the usual brothels and racketeering activities.

Ricca had been correct—Accardo proved to be a brilliant business tycoon in his own right. His "Joe Batters" handle was bestowed by Al Capone himself, who was impressed by how Accardo theatrically bludgeoned two gangsters to death at a Chicago dinner Capone had thrown for the sole purpose of executing the two. "This kid's a real Joe Batters," Capone said, or so the story goes. A similar scene in the Kevin Costner film "The Untouchables" may have been inspired by Accardo's bat, although in the movie it was Capone depicted as doing the damage. Accardo's more famous nickname, Tony "Big Tuna" Accardo, had less dramatic origins: it came from the Chicago press after Tony was observed deep sea fishing where he indeed caught a giant tuna.

As Accardo thrived, the rising Chicago mob underboss was none other than Momo Salvatore "Sam" Giancana. Sam worked closely with Accardo, who clearly was still the top boss but sometimes acted more behind the scenes than up front. Giancana may be best known for his ties to Hollywood and politics, for it was Giancana who supposedly orchestrated a backroom deal with Joseph Kennedy to help elect Joe's son, John F. Kennedy, as president in 1960. Kennedy's very narrow 1960 victory over Richard Nixon is legendary, with Chicago providing an overwhelming number of votes in favor of Kennedy, tipping the election. In return, the story goes, the Kennedy administration was to ease off the mob, especially its lucrative Las Vegas connections.

How could Giancana implement such a plan? Again, fate played a role. In 1954 Giancana's wife Angeline died, freeing Sam who soon became addicted to Hollywood stars, the Vegas night life, and loose women. He became close to Frank Sinatra, and utilized Sinatra to get to Bobby Kennedy after he was appointed attorney general by his brother. Whatever deal may have been struck with the elder Joe Kennedy apparently was not honored by Bobby who launched a federal assault against organized crime. Soon thereafter in 1965, subsequent to the death of President Kennedy but still three years before Bobby's own assassination, Giancana was sent to prison on a contempt charge.

Sam only spent a year in jail, but Accardo and Ricca had had enough. They removed Giancana and demanded that he leave the country. Sam did leave, but he retained lucrative interests in a number of casinos, refusing to cut Accardo in—a bad idea. On June 18, 1975, after returning to the States, Sam Giancana was executed in his basement. By the mid-1970s, Joseph "the Doves" Aiuppa had become the official mob boss, but Accardo was only semi-retired and still wielded significant, if not ultimate, control. It was Joey "The Doves" Aiuppa who allegedly ordered the hit on Tony Spilotro, who himself had succumbed to the glitz, glamour, and power of Vegas and had grown virtually uncontrollable by the Chicago home Outfit.

Enter James J. "Little Jimmy" Marcello who became a front boss for the Outfit, which by that time was really run by a triumvirate of John "No Nose" DeFranzo, Joseph Andriacchi, and none other than Joey "the Clown" Lombardo. Both Marcello and Lombardo would much later find themselves on trial for murder, among other things, in the Family Secrets trial. Lombardo would testify at length in the trial, but Little Jimmy would remain silent for the entire proceedings. The jury, though, would nonetheless find Jimmy guilty of the Spilotro executions.

Accardo stepped down officially in the mid-1950s, some sources peg it at 1957, but he was only semi-retired and still maintained substantial power for many years. In the 1950s Giancana was officially installed in Accardo's place, at least for day to day operations. By 1955 he controlled Chicago's gambling, prostitution, drug distribution, and racketeering. Giancana publically proclaimed his "ownership" of Chicago, as well as mob satellite operations in Miami and Los Angeles. Such boasting was not all good for the mob, though. By 1959 the FBI had planted microphones at Giancana's headquarters in suburban Forest Park. Meanwhile, Giancana drew more attention by his romantic involvement with Hollywood entertainer Phyllis McGuire of the very popular McGuire Sisters, not to mention Sam's ties to Frank Sinatra. Sam had hoped Sinatra could mediate peace between the mob and the Kennedy administration in the early 1960s, but, again, those hopes were dashed when JFK's younger brother Bobby became Attorney General and declared war on the mob, then encouraged FBI top boss J. Edgar Hoover to place the Giancana home under constant surveillance.

Sinatra and Hoover were not Sam's only ties to John Kennedy, however. Giancana's girlfriends included one Judith Campbell Exner, yet another actress and entertainer, who also had a romantic relationship with the president. Many still feel that Giancana had helped stuff ballots to get JFK elected, and that he maintained a personal sense of immunity for having done so. If that were not enough, it was Giancana who may also have intervened to help the Kennedy administration plot the attempted assassination of Fidel Castro. With his ties to the Russians, the Cuban dictator had become a political thorn to the Kennedys. But he was also despised by Giancana, who resented losing Cuba's lucrative gaming operations when Castro took over. The eventual Bay of Pigs invasion was a mess, which did little to help Castro's standing in either the Kennedy White House or the Chicago Outfit.

Soon the Outfit grew tired of Giancana's antics, not to mention the heat he brought from Bobby Kennedy, so Tony Accardo essentially "fired" Giancana from the Outfit, after which Sam left town to lay low. After living a self-imposed life of exile in Mexico from 1965 to 1974, Giancana was extradited back to the U.S. to testify to Congress about the CIA, mafia, and Bay of Pigs. On June 17, 1975, before he could testify, Sam Giancana was shot in the head while cooking at his home in west suburban Oak Park, Illinois, a stately tree-lined community with an interesting history of notables who called Oak Park home. That exclusive list is topped by Ernest Hemingway, Frank Lloyd Wright, and McDonald's founder Ray Kroc, but it also includes comedian Bob Newhart, "Tarzan" creator Edgar Rice Burroughs, "golden girl" Betty White, and of course the most high profile crime syndicate figure of the 1950s to 1960s era, Sam Giancana.

Accardo, on the other hand, continued to maintain a lower profile and was able to control the Outfit longer than any of its other top bosses. Not only had he begun his mob career in the days of Capone, his mob powers expanded throughout the 1940s and 1950s. Once in control, Accardo expanded the mob into Las Vegas and a lucrative line of casinos, call girls, and other businesses. Under Accardo's leadership the Chicago mob at one time controlled almost all organized crime west of the Mississippi River in addition to Chicago, Illinois, and much of Wisconsin. With all of that, Accardo was hardly invisible, but the difference is that he was not drawn to publicity and fame the way Giancana was. Accardo made big money for the Outfit, maintained a lower public persona, and ruled with an iron hand when necessary. One example, often told, is how a band of mob low-lifes once decided to burglarize Accardo's home to steal back some jewelry they had already stolen from a legit businessman who was Tony's friend. They were all killed, most of them tortured with their faces burned off, and their bodies were scattered in various places around the Chicago area. All of these traits allowed Accardo to retain a great deal of mob power until his death in 1992.

Interestingly, by all accounts Accardo also had a strong marriage which began soon after he met Clarice Pordzany in 1934. Unlike many of his contemporaries, Accardo did not have a reputation for womanizing, even though his nationally recognized mob power must have been attractive to legions of women. Eventually Tony and Clarice had four children. One of Accardo's grandsons was Eric Kumerow who was a star local football player who eventually played in the NFL for the Miami Dolphins. Clarice outlived Tony for ten years, then died of natural causes in 2002 at age 91.

Accardo was also a man of perspective and discretion, and he made good on his commitments. There was a time in the late 1950s when the FBI stepped up its mob investigation and surveillance efforts, and that riled some members of the Outfit who began to harass members of one Chicago agent's family. Word is that that agent, William Roemer, sought out Accardo and made a man to man truce whereby they would leave each other's family alone. The threats stopped, and both men kept their word.

With legitimate interests in 20 office buildings, shopping centers, hotels, factories, trucking companies, and even newspapers, Accardo's personal holdings were extensive. Many of his later years were spent in the Palm Springs area, although he would still visit Chicago to settle disputes and otherwise mediate mob business. When he died at age 86, Accardo was buried in Queen of Heaven Cemetery in west suburban Hillside where he has plenty of company. Also at Queen of Heaven are the graves of Joey "the Doves" Aiuppa, Sam Battaglia (a Depression era gangster who robbed Mayor William Hale Thompson's wife at gunpoint in 1930), Mad Sam DeStefano, one time boss Paul "the Waiter" Ricca, and Tony "the Ant" Spilotro. (For more of the mob old guard, Mount Carmel Catholic Cemetery is the final resting place for such Outfit luminaries as Al Capone himself, Deanie O'Bannion, Hymie Weiss, Machine Gun Jack McGurn, and Chicago's notorious Genna brothers—not to mention the graves of Chicago's bishops and archbishops in its noted Bishops' Mausoleum.)

Widely reported legend has it that Tony Accardo, with all his mob history from Capone to Giancana and beyond, never spent a night in jail. Impressive under the circumstances given that his arrest record goes back to 1922, but hardly a great legacy in the larger scheme of things.

There are no Tony Accardo's in today's Outfit, but the remarkable Joey Lombardo was a colorful, widely respected and universally feared honcho as the Twentieth Century came to a close. When was the mob at its peak? Was it during the Capone hey days, the ascension of Accardo and Giancana, the Vegas windfall? Organized crime in Chicago may never again experience the wide open days of Capone, Nitti, and Machine Gun Jack McGurn, although it did glimpse the limelight again when Giancana was king and the Kennedy's were in Washington.

The beginning of the end may have occurred on Monday, April 25, 2005, when the Department of Justice issued a press release under a banner headline with a punch:

14 DEFENDANTS INDICTED FOR ALLEGED ORGANIZED CRIME ACTIVITIES; "CHICAGO OUTFIT" NAMED AS RICO ENTERPRISE IN FOUR-DECADE CONSPIRACY ALLEGING 18 MOB MURDERS AND 1 ATTEMPTED MURDER

The indictment recounted 17 slayings in the Chicago area, plus one more in Arizona and revealed the long-time federal probe of the Outfit under the code name *Operation Family Secrets*. The press learned that on that very morning, federal authorities, including both IRS and FBI agents, began arresting mob figures in Illinois, Arizona, and Florida. Remarkably, one such defendant was found dead, apparently of natural causes.

Eleven of the defendants were charged with conspiracy in connection with the Chicago Outfit as a criminal enterprise, including murder, attempted murder, loan sharking, bookmaking, and protecting the enterprise from law enforcement authorities. Patrick J. Fitzgerald, the United States Attorney for the Northern District of Illinois, reference the incumbent irony of the situation: "This unprecedented indictment puts a 'hit' on the Mob," he announced. "It is remarkable for both the breadth of the murders charged and for naming the entire Chicago Outfit as a criminal enterprise under the anti-racketeering law. It is a textbook example of the effective use of the RICO statute to prosecute an assortment of crimes spanning decades. After so many years, it lifts the veil of secrecy and exposes the violent underworld of organized crime."

These defendants were all arrested by the feds at various locations in Illinois on the morning of April 25, 2005: James Marcello, 63, of Lombard; Michael Marcello, 55, of Schaumburg; Nicholas Ferriola, 29, of Westchester; Joseph Venezia, 62, of Hillside; Thomas Johnson, 49, of Willow Springs; and his nephew, Dennis Johnson, 34, of Lombard. Frank Saladino, 59, was found dead in a hotel room in suburban Kane County. Another, Michael Ricci, 75, of Streamwood, was expected to voluntarily surrender later that day. Frank Schweihs, 75, was eventually picked up in Florida, and Anthony Doyle, 60, was being arrested in Arizona. The remaining three defendants were already in federal custody, doing time: brothers Nicholas Calabrese, 62, of Chicago, and Frank Calabrese, Sr. 68, of Oak Brook, plus Paul Schiro, 67, of Phoenix. True to form, Joseph Lombardo, 75, of Chicago, was a little different. He was on the run at the time, only to be arrested about 8 months later by the FBI.

Five of these defendants would eventually be tried together in federal court, which would become known as the Family Secrets trial of 2007.

The indictment sought forfeiture of $10 million in alleged illicit proceeds from the 11 racketeering conspiracy defendants, plus the specific forfeiture of M&M Amusement from the Marcello brothers. The indictment also set forth the following specific murders:

Michael Albergo, a/k/a "Hambone," in or about August, 1970, in Chicago;
Daniel Seifert, on or about September 27, 1974, in Bensenville;
Paul Haggerty, on or about June 24, 1976, in Chicago;

Henry Cosentino, on or about March 15, 1977;

John Mendell, on or about January 16, 1978, in Chicago;

Donald Renno and Vincent Moretti, on or about January 31, 1978, in Cicero;

William and Charlotte Dauber, on or about July 2, 1980, in Will County;

William Petrocelli, on or about December 30, 1980, in Cicero;

Michael Cagnoni, on or about June 24, 1981, in DuPage County;

Nicholas D'Andrea, on or about September 13, 1981, in Chicago Heights;

Richard D. Ortize and Arthur Morawski, on or about July 23, 1983, in Cicero;

Emil Vaci, on or about June 6, 1986, in Phoenix;

Anthony and Michael Spilotro, on or about June 14, 1986, in DuPage County;

John Fecarotta, on or about September 14, 1986, in Chicago.

Many of the murder victims were Outfit members or affiliates, such as John Fecarotta and the Spilotro brothers; some were business people who got too close to the mob; and some were victimized citizens. The seven defendants accused of the various murders, plus one attempted murder, included Marcello, Lombardo, Schweihs, Saladino, Schiro, and Nick and Frank Calabrese, Sr.

The trial would also detail the inner workings of the mob hierarchy and business structure, like how it operates through street crews which worked almost like local franchises defined by their neighborhood territories. There was the Elmwood Park crew from west suburban Elmwood Park; the North Side/Rush Street crew; the South Side/Chinatown crew; and the Grand Avenue, Melrose Park, and Chicago Heights crews. The structure was highly organized with each crew run by a "capo." Especially trustworthy and/or valuable members of these crews would be knighted, so to speak, as "made" members of the Outfit. A "made man" had to be nominated by his Capo, had to be of Italian descent, and must have already committed at least one murder on behalf of the Outfit. Once "made," there was no escape from the mob; at that point, the Outfit was a lifetime commitment. But of course it also ran the other way, the Outfit taking care of loyal made members and their families, even as made members were jailed or killed.

By operating outside the law, mob members were denied the protection of the law—at least until they turned states evidence. In reality, the mob operated a sub-culture within civilized America. It had its own rules, boundaries, rights and responsibilities, mores, tribal court system with bosses resolving disputes, and certainly "law enforcement" with crew members reeking havoc upon each other. All of this requires a sophisticated labyrinth of schemes beginning with a given criminal activity designed, ultimately, to make money for the Outfit. Examples include extortion, which might take the form of a "street tax" imposed upon a local business to allow that business to operate within a specific mob territory; high interest "juice loans" with mandatory repayments under threat of violence or murder; gambling; prostitution; and so on. As noted specifically by the indictment, such operations necessitate a strong structure of finance, tax fraud, obstruction of justice, and a host of other conspiracies to make the system work.

The obstruction activities would include intimidation; threatening witnesses or potential witnesses; false testimony; law enforcement payoffs; political deals and payoffs, and the like. To keep ahead of the law, the mob had to operate a number of legitimate businesses which were "fronts" for the real operations, giving the members the appearance of having legitimate incomes or jobs. There was an elaborate system of code words and names; law enforcement monitoring; the use of guns, explosives, and other instruments of violence; and maintaining sophisticated records to keep track of street taxes, juice loans, and other underground business profits and expenses.

M&M Amusement, the Marcello enterprise that the indictment sought to disgorge, offers a good example. The indictment stated that between 1996 and 2004, Jimmy Marcello, Michael Marcello, and others, operated the company—with the ironic name "Amusement"—to engage in a tax fraud conspiracy to obstruct the IRS in collecting legitimate corporate and individual taxes. Aside from being an annoyance to much of legitimate society, the entire tax code becomes an interesting instrument of the law of unintended consequences: the IRS is the bane of organized crime, the whole ultimate purpose of which is to generate illicit income. But that creates a necessary dilemma, because one cannot very well file tax returns outlining the gains of one's illegal activity; hence, the income goes underground, and sooner or later the paper trails lead the IRS and FBI to not only the income, but to the illicit criminal enterprise that generated the gains. This inherent dilemma brought down many criminal conspirators, not the least of whom was Al Capone himself who was convicted of tax fraud under the then relatively new Internal Revenue Code enacted only a decade before the Capone empire had hit full stride.

On a weekly basis for about 8 years, Michael Marcello allegedly deposited cash into the M&M bank accounts while knowing that he was deliberately "shorting" the firm of all its income; in other words, he was showing some cash to justify operations while concealing most of it from the authorities. Of course all that required the Marcello's to either involve or deceive their own accountants and tax preparers. The indictment suggested that they deceived them with deliberately false receipts, journal entries, and so on. That, in turn, caused M&M to file false corporate tax returns by under-reporting the gross receipts collected from illegal gambling machine operations that M&M had placed into various west suburban taverns, restaurants, and clubs. All such activity also caused the individual principals to file false personal tax returns, involving them directly in a conspiracy against the IRS.

How did the feds know? Among other things, on a number of dates in 2002 and 2003, both Michael and Jimmy Marcello engaged in intercepted conversations while incarcerated at the Federal Correctional Center in Milan, Michigan. In the grand tradition of Richard Nixon and others, it is hard to keep illegal activity to oneself, and sooner or later that means it may end up on tape. A great deal would be revealed on tape during the Family Secrets trial, some if it coming from taped conversations between Joey Lombardo and Allen Dorfman, but much of it stemming from the secretly recorded conversations that Frank Calabrese, Jr. had with his mob hit man father Frank, Sr., while both were incarcerated. It would make for compelling testimony, showing that the tangled web of mob activity extended not only between the mob and the civilized world, or among mobsters themselves, but also coming between blood family members as the house of cards first faltered and then came crashing down during the final dance of the mob as it used to be: the Family Secrets Trial of 2007.

10

Tough Guys

A courtroom clock peered over the crowded Family Secrets courtroom. It seemed to stand watch over the stately proceedings below while it methodically logged the hours and minutes, anguish, and intrigue as history passed by. Precisely how long this noble clock had gazed over Chicago courtrooms I do not know, but I am told the classic round timepiece dates back to 1902. It has seen and heard much over the years, ticking off each fleeting second of freedom that remained for the legions of souls who sat or stood below while their legal advisors pleaded a last chance pitch for absolution. Try as they may, though, it is perdition, rather than absolution, that has loomed for most.

It was a warm June day in Chicago, indeed the first day of summer, and Judge Zagel's packed courtroom was bursting of anticipation. The government had nabbed some of the top mobsters in the country, and over the ensuing months the judge, jury, gallery, and defendants would hear wretched tales of murder and mayhem, like how Tony Spilotro once ruled Las Vegas, including how Tony and his brother really met their violent demise. Names like Lombardo, Cerone, Dorfman, LaPietra, and scores of others would be skewered by federal prosecutors over the ensuing weeks. Even Jimmy Hoffa's name would come up. Some of the best drama would come from a Shakespearean son-against-father tragedy when Frank Calabrese, Jr. would testify against his father, reputed mob hit man and hustler Frank Calabrese, Sr., accused of no fewer than 13 murders himself. Junior, of course, had flipped for the government and recorded admissions from his father while both were in prison. We could not wait.

I took what would become my usual front row seat near the defense tables where Joey Lombardo and Frank Calabrese sat and would await their fate for three months during the summer of 2007. I was close enough to hear them breath.

We were reminded by prosecutor John Scully, an assistant U.S. attorney, that the stories we would hear were about real people and real crimes with real victims. This was not the Soprano's, he told us, referencing the equally bloody but sometimes likeable and wholly fictional mob families of HBO fame. The jury, a large group of 19 jurors and alternates that included 10 women, was attentive, even stoic, as they listened to the opening statements.

Seated in open court were James Marcello, "Little Jimmy" he was called. There would be no shortage of nicknames in this trial. Joey "the Clown" Lombardo was there, Anthony "Twan" Doyle—so named because his immigrant mother called him Twan not Tony, and Paul "the Indian" Schiro. The Calabrese family was well represented. Frank "the Breeze" Calabrese was on trial, and two of the chief government witnesses would be his son Frank, Jr. and Nick Calabrese, younger brother. Both would have plenty to say, like how Frank, Sr. was known for strangling his victims—then would often cut their throats "just to make sure" they were dead.

After a weekend recess, the government set the stage with former FBI agent James Wagner, who discussed the mob structure in Chicago. But soon the prosecution would get to the star material. On June 28, 2007, Emma Seifert rose from her seat and settled into the witness chair. Her son Joseph, age 37, was in the courtroom, too. He had been with his mother on one tragic day 33 years ago and was about to hear her relive that morning of September 27, 1974. Young Joseph, only 4 years old at the time, was actually named after Joey Lombardo. You could hear a pin drop on the carpet as Emma described that eventful day that changed the lives of so many.

Young Joseph, who had not been feeling well, was at the office of his father, Daniel Seifert. His mother Emma, still very young herself at the time, was with him, making coffee and otherwise tending to the day's routine. Suddenly two masked intruders burst through a back door brandishing guns. They shoved Emma and Joseph to the floor. Every juror leaned forward with their notepads. "I believe they said this is a robbery," she told them, all of whom were poised on the edges of their seats. According to Emma, these men also said something to the effect of "Where is—I don't know if they called him my husband or the SOB." But clearly they were looking for her husband Dan. Emma's voice was mellow. She was now in her 60s, a woman of dignity who had experience too many hard times. I was torn between taking my own notes and studying the faces of the jurors. They were engrossed by the testimony, their eyes fixed on a photo of Daniel Seifert that had been projected onto a large screen. It showed his shriveled body lying on the grass outside his plastics company. The jurors put down their pens and stared.

Emma fought to hold her tears as she described the morning her husband Daniel was shot gunned to death while she and their 4-year-old Joseph stood by, at one point with guns to their own heads. By this time, the gallery and several jurors were reaching for Kleenexes. It was a compelling moment. I looked directly at Lombardo, who was seated directly in front of me with his lawyers Susan Schatz and the high profile Rick Halprin. Joey was listening very intently, and seemed to be taking copious notes, which struck me as odd.

Emma, nicely dressed in a beautiful dark pantsuit, calmly used a laser pointer on another image overhead to show jurors where she was standing in the office when the gunmen surprised her. Again my eyes drifted toward Lombardo. His head was turned almost horizontally as he viewed the overhead screen, then looked back at Emma, defiantly scratching his head as if to be saying "bullshit."

Emma continued. "I screamed, but obviously not loud enough, because I heard nothing for a few seconds." The masked men bolted after her husband. She told her son to stay put, but Emma went back to her desk. At that moment she saw her husband running for his life, streaking across the factory parking lot. It was the last time she would see him alive. She locked the office door and called the police. Daniel Seifert ran to another building, but he did not make it before one of the gunmen shot him down. As he lay there, one of them came directly up to Daniel and blasted him in the head with a shotgun.

Daniel Seifert had been scheduled to testify as a key witness in a trial against top mobster Joey Lombardo who was charged with ripping off the Teamster's Central States Pension Fund. Seifert knew all the relevant facts, so without Daniel there was no trial. After he was gunned down, that particular case against Lombardo had been dropped. But Emma still had more to say. Even though the gunmen wore masks, she believed one of them was Lombardo himself, the namesake for her own son. She said that she recognized Lombardo "by his build and height, the way he moved." She testified that Joey was a boxer and light on his feet, and she felt that was him chasing down her husband.

Daniel had become entwined with the Chicago Outfit, Emma explained, when he did some carpentry work for "a mobbed up businessman" named Irwin Weiner who eventually put some money into a fiberglass company that Daniel managed. I was taken by Emma's courage and dignity as she spoke, so I met with her and Joseph as much as I could, interviewing them during lunch and routine court breaks. She didn't say much before her testimony, but afterward she opened up. At one point Joseph gave me his business card and invited me to stay in touch. At one point he even brought me three beautiful photos of him and his father, and encouraged me to use them for this book.

Emma told the jury Daniel had first been jumped in the entryway of the factory, then pistol whipped in the head. At that point she tried to get to her own office where there was a gun, but the drawer was locked. Then the shotgun went off outside, piercing the quiet day and changing the lives of Emma and her children.

She explained how Weiner had been friends with Lombardo, and how Lombardo had been hired by her husband's company. But she never saw him actually work there. By 1972 there was a falling out between Lombardo and Daniel. She said Daniel became fearful of Lombardo and others around that time. Emma said that she had seen Lombardo drive slowly by their house while she stood in the window waiting for her older son Nick to come home from school. She told Daniel, who advised her to keep the children inside, keep the door locked, and call the police. Daniel's brother Ronald also testified, informing the jury how Daniel had told him about testifying in the forthcoming Lombardo trial. At one point Lombardo actually called Ronald directly, warning Ronald to "straighten Danny out," or "you know what's going to happen to him." Ronald told his brother, who replied "to hell with them, I'm going to testify." But he never got the chance.

The gunmen had fled the scene in two cars. They left one at a dealership but outran police in the other, a white Dodge Challenger. The car they left behind was a real piece of work. It was a brown Ford

LTD outfitted with a quick-change license plate holder, a switch to kill the brake lights, heavy shocks, a police scanner and even a siren. This was considered a good "work car." It is if your work is murder.

Ronald later ignored a court gag order and spoke to reporters outside the Federal Building about his memories of Daniel. "I wish he was here. He was a good kid. He never hurt nobody."

Attorney Matt Lydon, now with the powerful national law firm Winston & Strawn, took the stand to corroborate Emma's testimony. He had been with the FBI during the 1960s and 1970s, and he explained that Daniel Seifert was the only witness who could link Lombardo to two checks that were key evidence in the old case against Lombardo.

Soon after Daniel was murdered, Emma said she got a call from Lombardo himself. "He says, you have something that belongs to me," Emma recounted. "I said anything I would have would be in the possession of the FBI because they had already gone through Daniel's things."

Attorney Rick Halprin attacked Emma's credibility on cross examination, and questioned why she had not told the FBI everything earlier than she did. Clearly Joey was denying the accusation that he was involved in the Seifert hit. But Emmy stuck to her story, and said that she and her family had been hesitant because they were all afraid.

Joseph's only memory of his father is the day the mobsters killed him. "We've never gotten over this," said Nick, the oldest of Daniel's three children. "Father's Day, we think about it. Mother's Day, we think about it. His birthday comes around, we think about it." It was one of many ironies in the life of Daniel Seifert, and in this trial, to be sure, but of course Daniel's own friend Lombardo had been fingered as the one responsible for his death. Not only had young Joseph been named after Joey Lombardo, but Lombardo had been his godfather. Nick explained that although Daniel had become peripherally involved with the mob, once he set his business up in suburban Bensenville he had been trying to extricate himself. "He was not afraid, Lombardo didn't scare him. That was the reason for his death. They threatened him, tried to intimidate him, and they only had one option left—that was to get rid of him."

The next day at trial found the huge image of a fingerprint on a large screen in front of the courtroom. Roy McDaniel, a former fingerprint expert for the FBI, explained. Another image was projected, another fingerprint on the face of an automobile title application for a 1973 Ford LTD. It was an application by "Acme Security Service," a bogus sounding name, but here's the kicker: the print, said the witness McDaniel, was from the left middle finger of Joey Lombardo himself. And the car in question was one of the two vehicles allegedly driven from the murder scene of federal witness Daniel Seifert. It was over three decades ago that McDaniel had found that incriminating print, but he remembered it well.

McDaniel described how he had retrieved more than a dozen documents from the Illinois Secretary of State's office that were tied to that Ford LTD getaway car. He explained how the documents were sent from Springfield, Illinois to the FBI in Washington, DC, where the title application was sprayed with a special solution which dried but then was steamed in a way to make latent prints visible. And there they were. The marks left on the document matched a finger on FBI fingerprint card 673515E, which carried the prints of Lombardo. "Only that one finger in the world could've made that particular print," McDaniel told the fascinated jurors.

The government paraded a number of corroborating witnesses through the courtroom, tying Lombardo one way or another to the various police scanners and even the Dodge Challenger which had been the other escape car.

As the trial moved into July, the heat was turning up both outside and inside the courtroom. One of the most interesting—and effective—early witnesses was Joel Glickman, who said nothing at all. That's right—nothing. Except for repeated saying that he would not testify. He was a fascinating witness, though, and his steadfast silence actually spoke volumes.

Glickman, now age 71, was a convicted bookie who had been sent to prison in 1976. He refused to testify against these mob defendants, Calabrese in particular, which made for some very compelling silence since he had already been granted immunity by the government—which meant both that he *had* to testify or be held in contempt, *and* that he could not be prosecuted for anything he would say in court under oath. Not a bad deal, yet this 71-year-old refused to talk.

Glickman's father Bernie had been a most interesting guy. He was a front for the Chicago mob in the mid-1960s, a time when he was also a boxing manager who promoted several world boxing championships involving top heavyweight names like Sonny Liston and Ernie Terrell. Ernie was born in Mississippi but he fought out of Chicago in the 1960's. He is the older brother of Jean Terrell who was a lead singer for The Supremes in the early 1970's. Ernie was a big fighter who stood six feet six inches. In 1967 he incurred the wrath of Muhammed Ali by calling him Cassius Clay instead of his chosen Muslim name. Terrell retired from boxing in 1973, staying in Chicago to become a music producer. He even ran unsuccessfully for the city council in 1987.

Liston was a heavy puncher bad boy who lost the heavyweight title in 1964 to a wild young kid named Cassius Clay who just before the fight announced to the world his new Muslim faith and new name, Muhammad Ali. When the heavy punching but slower Liston found himself being pummeled by the lightning fast Ali, suddenly in the fourth round a foreign substance found its way into Ali's eyes. Ali was not only in great pain, he was mostly blind, able to see only scant images of Liston or anything else. Ali was terrified and wanted his gloves cut off between rounds. Manager Angelo Dundee frantically sponged Ali's eyes, but all the challenger could do for the whole fifth round was run and hide. Ali endured the ordeal and his eyes cleared up. Liston had had enough, so he quit the fight—the brash new Muslim Muhammad Ali was champion.

Many fight historians, including numerous handlers close to Ali, believe that Liston's people had put a stinging salve on Liston's gloves knowing it would find its way to Ali's eyes. Liston had been accused of that very thing before, as many as three different times altogether. Fight historians also tied Liston to the mob, and it is widely believed that he was mob property. Perhaps the link had been Bernie Glickman, father of the recalcitrant witness Joel?

At one point Bernie owned the Hickory House Restaurant in the glitzy Rush Street area of Chicago. Son Joel became one of Chicago's leading bookmakers while father Bernie wielded mob influence over boxing not just locally, but nationwide. So there we were, on this July day during the Family Secrets trial, with Joel Glickman refusing to testify against the mob even though he could go back to jail for several months as a result. We all would have wondered why, except that the implied answer was growing more and more obvious.

Glickman simply refused to testify, instead saying "I respectfully refuse to testify." Each time he said it, he made a case against mob intimidation. Judge Zagel repeatedly warned Glickman that he could do jail time for refusing to testify, and finally the judge made good on his promises. Glickman was sent to jail at the Metropolitan Correction Center in downtown Chicago where he spent seven nights in solitary confinement, including the Fourth of July holiday, then relented. Jail is no good at any age, but at 71 years like Glickman, it is an especially trying, humbling experience. Glickman finally said he would talk.

On Monday July 9, Glickman was a surprise witness, ignited a buzz in the courtroom. When he took the stand again, Glickman's testimony was tentative. Glickman said he got a juice loan from Calabrese in the amount of $20,000, which was on behalf of Glickman's boss, an insurance executive. The loan was repaid without incident, although Glickman admitted that he could have been hurt had it not been paid back. Assistant U.S. Attorney Markus Funk took Glickman back to his bookie days and asked about street taxes paid to Frank Calabrese, Sr. Overall, he said he had paid over $350,000 to the Outfit as "tax" for the right to run his gambling operations. He admitted on the stand that he had to keep paying both for mob protection and the right to keep the gambling business going.

Connie's Pizza is one of the more successful pizza restaurant operations in Chicago, a town known for its world famous "Chicago Style" deep dish pizza ever since it was invented by Pizzeria Uno in 1943. One of the founders of Connie's Pizza testified in court, also on the topic of street tax. James Stolfe told the jury how he had given Frank, Sr. about $270,000 in street tax money over a twenty year period. Stolfe admitted, though, that he never complained and that Calabrese never threatened him. He even said that he had lied to a grand jury for Frank. Stolfe explained that he was intimidated by Frank, even though he had played handball with Frank, they had vacationed together, and had dinner together.

Stolfe told how he had sold his 1962 Oldsmobile Starfire to buy his first Connie's location on West 26th Street, near the Chinatown area—Frank's territory. At first Stolfe did not give up his day job for the Cook County Highway Department, and he said he operated for nearly two decades before the mob paid him a visit. When two Outfit thugs showed up one day, Stolfe thought they were salesmen. I guess they were, in a manner of speaking—selling "protection." Stolfe said he did not have time to talk, but the two said "find time."

After hearing them out, Stolfe went to Calabrese, his long time friend from the old neighborhoods where they had grown up together. He hoped that Frank would intercede on his behalf, and indeed Frank said he "would see what he could do." As it happens, according to Stolfe Frank had been in on the squeeze play from the beginning.

When Stolfe received two threatening phone calls at his restaurant, he knew the danger was real. At first they mentioned a payoff number exceeding $200,000, but Frank did intercede and "lowered" it to "$100,000. Fearing he could be beaten or see his restaurant burned down, Stolfe agreed to pay. He gave the first $50,000 to Frank in cash. When asked by the prosecution to identify the recipient in the courtroom, the white-haired Stolfe, then 67 years old, pointed to Frank. Stolfe said he never told his family about the payoffs, not even his wife or son, but he had told one person, his close associate Donald "Captain D" DiFazio.

To facilitate the payoffs, Stolfe then put Frank on the official payroll as a "spotter," someone who supposedly keeps track of the delivery trucks. [What kind of shit was this, I though, as I listened to Stolfe.] In reality, of course, the payments of $1000 per month were for protection money to Frank.

Federal authorities say that they first made the Connie's Pizza connection during a meeting of the Italian-American Club in Bridgeport during the original Operation Family Secrets investigation. They secretly recorded a conversation between Frank Calabrese, Jr., and club president "Captain D" DiFazio, learning of the street tax payments to the mob. Interestingly, when Frank, Sr., was sent to prison, where later his son had recording him extensively, the Connie's Pizza payments were cut in half from $1000 to $500 per month. I guess protection from guys in prison goes at half-price.

Prosecutors then called DiFazio himself to the stand, and he verified the delivery of payments to the mob, which he had done for years. He routinely gave cash-filled envelopes to Frank, Jr., who by then was already wearing a wire for the government. The feds then squeezed Stolfe, who was exposed to perjury charges, who then agreed to testify as a government witness.

On cross examination, Frank's attorney Joseph Lopez tried to portray the two—Frank and Stolfe—as friends, as pals. "Did anyone put a gun to your head and say you had to go play handball with him?" Lopez challenged.

Lopez continued. "They were friends. My client was employed there for a number of years. They were friends and they remain friends."

Lopez then tried to show that DiFazio had been a bookie in another mob street crew. Lopez then asked DiFazio what it means to be "special events director" for Connie's, his official title there.

"That means today I'm supposed to be at the Taste of Chicago," he said, referencing the summertime Chicago extravaganza in and around Grant Park. He referred to the various mob figures he confronted as "another tough guy." DiFazio said he was once confronted by Anthony "Tony the Hatch" Chiaramonti when Connie's wanted to open a location in Lyons Township. "Those plans were scrapped," DiFazio explained. "The name [Tony the Hatch] speaks for itself," he said of Chiaramonti—who later was gunned down at a chicken restaurant in the summer of 2001.

Lopez continued his cross-examination.

"You were a tough guy, too, weren't you?" Lopez asked.

"The whole neighborhood was filled with tough guys."

11

Too Many Suspects

Few cried at the death of Ronald William Jarrett, burglar, bookie, and mob loser.

Ronnie Jarrett was gunned down outside his Bridgeport home in 1999 just two days before Christmas, then held on for a month before finally passing. It was an Outfit hit.

Almost eight years later, on July 24, 2007, Jarrett's son Ron took the stand under oath. He, too, was a burglar, making thievery something of a family trade. He testified that his father had "brought him along" in the bookmaking business, so to speak.

Ron told the courtroom how his father ran the bookmaking operation, and how he ran afoul of the much feared Frank Calabrese, Sr., mob crew chief, enforcer, and prolific hit man. Ron, as it happens, was one of Frank's closest friends, explaining how he was a right hand man to Frank and had become an "MVP" for the Chinatown crew headed, at that time, by Angelo "the Hook" LaPietra.

In an audio clip played in open court, Frank seemed to express shock and dismay upon hearing from Ron that his father, the elder Jarrett, had been shot. "You're kidding," Frank said. "Oh my God. You're talking about Ronnie Jarrett. Oh my God. It was professional."

Nick Ferriola, son of the late Outfit boss Joe "Mr. Clean" Ferriola, had told the younger Ron that his father had been killed because he had fallen out with Johnny "Apes" Monteleone. Ron testified how it was his understanding that Monteleone had ordered the hit. He also explained that his father was reluctant to pay the usual mob street taxes, which partly led to his ultimate demise. But the street tax issues had not been his only problem. Jarrett had made a number of enemies in the Outfit—not a good idea by any means. Jarrett, as it happens, was known as one of the syndicate's more vicious thugs. One FBI agent, named O'Rourke, expressed how Jarrett had a taste for assaulting police officers and a confrontational penchant for luring women away from other men at bars. Around the time he was shot, Jarrett had been fighting with other Outfit members, including top leaders of the 26th Street crew which, of course, had strong ties to both Calabrese and LaPietra. "Everyone hated him," O'Rourke said of Jarrett. "When he was killed, we had more suspects than we could count."

While on the stand, Ron watched a large video screen in the courtroom where he saw a mustached face staring back. "That was my father," Ron said, who by this time was 35 years old. Ron told how his father had been a member of the 26th Street crew running a gambling operation. When he was sentenced to prison in 1980, both the Calabrese brothers, Frank and Nick, had dropped by his house to visit.

When Ron's father was released, the two of them became a father-son combination in a sports gambling ring that took bets on football, basketball, baseball, hockey, horse racing, and other sports. Some of the proceeds were directed to the family of Frank Calabrese, Sr., he explained. The operation was bankrolled by the elder Jarrett, who kept cash in a bedroom drawer or in a coat pocket in the closet. Their bookie operation had two offices, "one in Burbank and another on the South Side." Ron described how he, his father, and several others collected bets, sometimes adding up to $5,000 to $10,000 for one game. The corresponding gambling slips were hidden in the ceiling of the front porch of the South Side office.

Jarrett captivated the jury with details of the inner mob financial workings. When the bettors lost, the Jarrett's made money of course, which meant they would have to pay a "juice" to the mob in the amount of 10% of the bet. This was called a "Vig," which was short for "vigarish," a type of interest charge on a transaction. The Jarretts also had to gather $400 per week in "spiff," which Ron said was "like a tax," to Chicago mobster Nicholas Ferriola. Ron's father told him that some of this "spiff" was in turn directed to the Calabrese family.

"Times were good," Ron said, at least until his father's death. After the shooting, and with the permission of Ferriola and Calabrese, Ron re-opened the gambling operation along with his uncle Sam Bills. Ron remained only a short while, though, leaving the group in 2001.

Calabrese, Sr., told his son that he had learned the elder Jarrett was dealing cocaine and getting too much attention from the Feds, and a federal spotlight is almost always a precursor to disaster in mob circles. Calabrese believed that the FBI and the U.S. Attorney's office were about to bring a racketeering indictment against Jarrett which, as such indictments are wont to do, likely would have dragged more mob names into the picture. Frank told Jarrett to shut down his operation and pay a visit to Johnny "Apes" Monteleone. Perhaps sensing impending doom, or maybe just being stupid, Jarrett ignored the order and, as one might expect, paid the ultimate price when Monteleone called him.

Ronald Jarrett was a small time hit man and mob wannabe. Sure, he had his share of success, but in the end he was just another loser with an Outfit resume. He did have one other claim to fame, though. He was the model for the James Caan crime movie "Thief."

The younger Jarrett told the jury how he recalled other mob notables coming to the family home. He remembered Family Secrets defendant Twan Doyle coming over a lot beginning about a year and a half before his father's murder. Ron said that Doyle and his father would disappear into the basement or kitchen to talk, though he was not privy to the topics.

Darrell Goldberg, an attorney for Doyle, attacked the younger Jarrett on the stand, calling Doyle a childhood friend of Jarrett and suggesting there was nothing unusual about visiting with long time friends. Calabrese attorney Joe Lopez took his shots, too, then added his own editorial comments. "Unfortunately," said Lopez, attempting to deflect heat from his own client, "people get killed for various reasons all the time. The truth," he continued, loosely quoting an old Italian proverb, "is somewhere between the clouds."

Jarrett told the jury how he, himself had worked with mob operator Nick Ferriola, son of top honcho Joseph Ferriola, to run a bookmaking operation. Nick had explained to Ron that Frank Calabrese, Sr., had said there were certain people you could trust in the Bridgeport and Chinatown neighborhoods—and one of those was Frank "Tootsie Babe" Caruso. Tootsie Babe was the son of "Skids" Caruso who took over the Chinatown Crew from the late 1950's through the 1970's.

Terri Nevis took the stand and testified about the murder of Nicholas D'Andrea, who in turn had been suspected of an attempt on the life of reputed mob capo Al Pilotto on a golf course in Crete, Illinois. She said she began living with D'Andrea when he was in his late 40's and she was just 15 years old. I'm sure they made a wonderful couple. On the day D'Andrea died it was Sam Guzzino who called D'Andrea to set up a meeting. Nevis, now a mortgage banker living on the west coast, took the call when Guzzino said "get Nick on the phone." A follow-up witness, Karen Brill, testified that Sam Guzzino would come by his brother's cab company in Chicago Heights where she worked. The cab company, she added, had a garage that shared space with a bar and brothel called The Vagabond Lounge. Imagine that—a regular full service operation: drinks, hookers, and taxicabs. Brill was shown a photo of an old brown garage, and she identified it as the one. And it fit the description of where D'Andrea was killed.

Calabrese had already described the D'Andrea killing in detail. D'Andrea had been lured to a garage in Chicago Heights, and Calabrese was told to look for a tall man and a short man who would enter together. Frank was to club the short man to death with a bat. Sure enough, the two entered and the tall man immediately took off running—perhaps avoiding any chance of being mistaken as the intended victim. Of course his fast exit tipped off the short man, who was D'Andrea. It then took several members of the hit squad, including defendant James "Little Jimmy" Marcello, to overpower D'Andrea.

Then came the surprise of the day. Prosecutor's showed a photo of D'Andrea to his former wife Terri Nevis, and she said the man in the photo was not, in fact, her husband. When I heard this, I nearly shit right there in the courtroom. I suspect a few jurors felt the same way.

Calabrese had already said that the bosses showed him a news story about the hit, and he thought it was the taller man who was killed, not the shorter D'Andrea. Indeed the taller man, Sam Guzzino, was killed soon after the D'Andrea hit. The government believes that Guzzino was the taller man who lured D'Andrea to his death. "Absolutely not," Terri Nevis responded in a whispering voice when showed a photo by Thomas Breen, Marcello's lawyer.

During break, I found myself in a conversation with both Doyle and Joey Lombardo.

Another witness, Fred Pavlich, was once head of security for a trucking operation run by one Michael Cagnoni. He said that the head of a cooperative association that specialized in shipping fruits and vegetables would also deliver a briefcase stuffed with cash to various mob figures—just before his death. Prosecutors showed Pavlich a photo, and he identified the figure as one time top Outfit boss Tony "Big Tuna" Accardo, one of the most powerful mob bosses in the country. He said Accardo was on hand for at least one such meeting. Pavlich had resigned just weeks before Cagnoni and his Mercedes were blown to bits on June 24, 1981. The night before he resigned, Pavlich had gotten a threatening phone call that made it clear he should resign in a hurry. Pavlich did not argue the point, and indeed got out of the way.

Pavlich said Cagnoni was a brilliant trucking executive who had devised an intricate process for hauling produce to Chicago and New York from the California growers. Trucks were moving in all directions, efficiently delivering the goods. Unfortunately, Cagnoni also had to carry a briefcase stuffed with thousands of dollars in cash to another trucking operation, Flash Trucking, for deliveries into Chicago itself. Flash was a Cicero firm owned by the Spano brothers, Michael and Paul. Michael is serving a 12 year prison sentence for his 2002 conviction for helping former Cicero town president Betty Laren-Maltese swindle the suburb out of millions of dollars.

Cagnoni's widow, now known as Margaret Wenger, took the stand. She turned away from a computer screen as she identified a photo of her deceased husband Michael. She said that Michael had been acting strangely before the bombing, but he had not told her any details. She described how she had used the same car to take her son to school that day, corroborating an account offered by Nick Calabrese, Frank's brother. She was devastated to learn that had she driven toward the expressway instead of back home, the car would have blown up. Instead Michael took it, and met his demise.

"He hugged me and kissed me goodbye and said 'Remember, I love you very much,'" said Wenger, her voice dropping with emotion as her tears streamed down her face. She explained it was the day after her birthday, and she had not yet learned she was pregnant. "That was the last time I saw him alive," Wenger said.

The widow's testimony was heart felt, but it was the government informants that got a rise from the defense table. "It ain't fair." That's what I heard from the five defendants when FBI agents escorted Bobby "the Beak" Siegel into the courtroom. "What, another government protection witness? It ain't fair."

Siegel was by this time 71 years old. He was tall, about 6'2" and 220 pounds, with gray hair and a prominent nose, hence his descriptive nickname. Siegel was wearing a light colored T-shirt with a pair of eyeglasses stuffed into his front pocket. He would be the third government protection witness to testify in the trial. The other two were Wemette and Nick Calabrese. Frank, Jr., who is Nick's nephew and son of Frank, Sr., would provide great compelling details of mob mayhem and hits, but he was not a protected witness. At this writing, he lives in Arizona with his family and is not in the protection program, which has to be uncomfortable for Frank, Jr.

The five defendants were wary of Siegel, sensing he would hang them out to dry. All would easily have remembered that my old partner on the force, Philip "Philly Beans" Tolomeo had also entered the witness protection program over a decade ago, after which Frank Calabrese, Sr., was indicted in 1995. It was Tolomeo who testified against him at that time, helping to convict Frank who drew a 10 year prison sentence. The defendants' current take on all this? "Isn't there any honor anymore?"

Siegel took the stand and walked the jury through a number of Chicago crimes that he had committed, taking some of the sting out of the story before the defense lawyers could get hold of him on cross. I was interested in what Bobby had to say, for he hails from the same neighborhood areas that I come from. Bobby described how his career in crime had begun on the West side of Chicago sometime after he had dropped out of the 5th or 6th grade. He was 13 or 14 years old tagging along with other punk friends on the streets of Chicago, stealing "anything we could make a buck with." By the time he was 16, Bobby had graduated to armed robbery.

Bobby said most of the old neighbor hood guys were tough, and that "most made money and didn't go to jail." One reason, he explained, is that "most of the police were on the Outfit payroll" at the time. I don't know about "most," but clearly police corruption was an issue. Siegel's record was impressive. Bobby estimated that he had burglarized as many as 100 stores, robbed three or four banks and took part in three murders as an Outfit enforcer who collected juice loans for the mob.

Siegel's first connection to the mob came courtesy of Frank "the Calico Kid" Teutonico, who earned his wild west nickname by firing a gun into the ceiling before a card game just to warn would-be cheaters that things "would be on the square." The witness drove the point home by forming his hand into the shape of a gun and raising it above his head. Bobby proved to be a very demonstrative witness, often gesturing with his hands to emphasize various points for the jurors. Siegel said he was a collector for Teutonico, making $400 per week. "If a guy didn't pay the money, I would go out and get hold of him," Siegel explained, understating the real point.

By the late 1960s, Siegel was working for another mobster, Angelo Volpe, who ran a numbers racket on the South Side. Bobby testified how he once watched Volpe bribe a cop who was a boss in the vice unit. "He gave him a bag of money," Siegel said. Then the cop revealed a gambling site that the police were about to raid, but Volpe told him "that's okay, it wasn't one of ours." Siegel also alleged that William Hanhardt, a Chicago police officer in the intelligence unit at the time, was also on the take. According to Siegel, Hanhardt and his partner received $1000 each month from the mob, plus a new car every two years, in return for "seeing to it" that mobsters were not caught. Siegel reiterated that "most of the police were on the payroll" in the old days.

Hanhardt, a police deputy superintendent, was investigated and then ultimately sentenced to 15 years and 8 months by U.S. District Judge Charles Norgle. Hanhardt had been accused of heading a sophisticated jewelry theft ring that scored $40 million in jewelry from more than 100 salespeople scattered around Chicago area stores, and pleaded guilty in 2001. Hanhardt, ironically, had once played a retired mob hit man in an episode of the television series "Crime Story." Even more ironically, Hanhardt was at one time a very good friend of mine. Siegel also pleaded guilty to a series of jewelry store heists, then began cooperating with the FBI. Siegel's guilty plea and subsequent 19 year prison sentence came in 1994, and two years later he was working with the FBI from within the witness protection program. Convicted along with Siegel at that time was an impressive list of mob operatives, all accused of being in Hanhardt's gang: Joseph Basinske, Guy Altabello, William "Cherry Nose" Brown, Sam DeStefano (nephew of Outfit psycho Mad Sam DeStefano), and Family Secrets defendant "Paul Schiro.

Siegel testified about how he feared for his own life after a 1978 burglary of mob chief Tony Accardo's home in River Forest, Illinois, even though Siegel had not been involved in that burglary. But he in fact had been approached twice to get involved "to score some gold coins," but he wanted no part of the scheme. "I didn't have to be too bright to figure out what that was," he explained. Even so, Siegel felt he was too close to the situation and might be marked for death because of it, so after the burglary he went so far as to take a lie detector test to prove he wasn't involved. Siegel passed the test, then forwarded the results to the mob through various contacts.

The whole Accardo heist was an odd and needlessly reckless affair. Siegel testified that he later went to mob boss Gerald Scarpelli to ask why so many of his friends had been eliminated, and why he himself had been put on the same list. Scarpelli told him that it was a warning from the Outfit. They didn't necessarily think Siegel had been in on it, but "they just picked burglars of every ethnicity" to cover the bases. "You just happened to be the Jew," Scarpelli explained.

Siegel then told how he met a burglar named Mendell in 1973 while in federal prison at Sandstone, Minnesota. After both of them had been released, they teamed up on a few crimes together in Chicago. Siegel received a phone call from Mendell in 1978. "He called me on the phone and told me he got a call from 'the little guy,'" meaning reputed hit man Ronnie Jarrett. Jarrett had told Mendell that he had something good for him, and Mendell had promised to bring Siegel in. But Siegel never saw him again. Mendell's body turned up a month later in the trunk of his car—a fate so common that it has become a virtual cliché. It corroborated the same story from Nick Calabrese. Siegel then told jurors that another burglar, Buddy Ryan, contacted him just after Mendell disappeared and told Bobby that Johnny "Bananas" DiFranzo had called him about a job involving gold coins. Ryan called Siegel about joining in. "I never heard from him no more, neither."

It did not take much intelligence to connect the killing of six different burglars for invading Accardo's home. It was all about revenge and sending a deadly message. According to a government filing, a witness told authorities that Mendell admitted taking part in the Accardo break-in. Why? To reclaim gems that Mendell himself had stolen from a jewelry store. Later it would all seem similar to the

O.J. Simpson attempted heist of his own alleged memorabilia in Las Vegas. But Simpson was luckier—he just drew a prison sentence. Mendell got death.

Siegel's testimony was compelling, because here he was, a real life Outfit operative, now under government protection, spilling his guts about the mob. He even told how he had murdered three men himself: Sylvester Moore, Mel Young, and a third man whose name he could not recall. All the killings were in Chicago. Young, 41, from suburban Elk Grove Village, was found in the trunk of his car at O'Hare Airport in 1978, and Moore, as it happens, was himself a government informant.

Bobby the Beak was part of a crew of mobbed-up robbers who hit jewelry stores across the country, but mainly in California and Florida, raking in millions of dollars over the years. They usually wore Halloween masks and body armor, used automatic weapons, and performed their robberies with military style precision. Former U.S. Attorney Edmund Searby had a succinct take on the Siegel gang. "We prosecuted them in the fullest. We recognized they were the New York Yankees of robbers."

Siegel said that mob operations changed significantly after the RICO racketeering laws went into effect in the 1970s. The Racketeer Influenced Corrupt Organization Act put a dent into the Mafia ranks when legions of mobsters were prosecuted under the racketeering statutes and hauled off to jail. He said even "made" guys were nervous and became more and more secretive.

Interesting as Siegel was, jurors were mesmerized by the tales of Ernest Severino, age 60, a former Outfit footman and the co-owner of a Franklin Park gun store, who gave a chilling account of how he learned of his own boss' execution. As owner of both a gun shop and a cemetery—I think this is like a parlay in horse racing—this made Severino doubly valuable to the Chicago Outfit in the late 1970s. Mob figures called Ernie "The Oven" and would ask his staff for keys to the furnace. Just that name alone is daunting.

Severino told how mob hit man William "Butch" Petrocelli regularly wanted .38 caliber pistols, hunting rifles, and MAC-10 submachine guns from his store—but never managed to pay for any of them. Moreover, Petrocelli often wanted Severino to be his "go-fer," regularly asking Severino to hold envelopes, drive him around, and to do a number of errands and other little things—"this or that," as he put it. Petrocelli wasn't the kind of guy you said no to, so Severino obliged. "I didn't want to put myself in harm's way, let's say," explained Severino. It was a quarter century after Petrocelli's murder, and Severino still seemed nervous, almost looking over his shoulder at the prospect of Petrocelli's revenge.

Severino said he supplied Petrocelli with almost 100 guns over the years, including sawed-off shotguns and assault rifles. Severino said that he and Petrocelli remained friends—if you could call it that—until Petrocelli disappeared in the late 1980s. He never found out what happened—not until Gerald Scarpelli, Petrocelli's one-time partner in the Outfit, asked for Petrocelli's cash and bank documents that Severino had kept for Petrocelli. Severino was nervous about turning these things over, but Severino explained, "No, he's not coming back." The bosses had put Scarpelli in charge of Petrocelli's gang. The bosses had told Scarpelli and another mobster, Peter Basile "you can go in the next room and take care of the garbage if you want to." That meant Butch Petrocelli. No one ever saw Butch alive again.

From William Jarrett to Butch Petrocelli and hundreds of others, the mob has a way of taking care of its own problems. Some end up on shallow graves, many in the trunks of cars, and others just never turn up again. One of the most violent, prolific, and feared of all the hit men in recent times was my old nemesis, Frank "what the fuck you lookin at" Calabrese, Sr., and his three-decade legacy of extortion, mob hits, and buried bodies. Frank was up next, and he knew plenty. But how much would he actually say?

Anna Sage, the notorious "lady in red," may have famously betrayed Chicago crime legend John Dillinger who was shot and killed by the FBI on July 22, 1934 outside the Biograph Theater, but Connie Marcello, long time girlfriend to James Marcello, did her part, too, hanging Marcello out to dry during the Family Secrets trial. Marcello did not get shot, but he did get humiliated by Connie and virtually hung by the prosecutors as a result.

When the government called witness Connie Swanson, there was little that Marcello's lawyer could do to keep her quiet. Although Connie and Jimmy Marcello were close, with Connie even taking his name as the years went by, they were not really married—Connie was essentially Marcello's long-standing mistress. In some circles that may not be significant, but in a mob criminal trial it means that she was free to testify against Jimmy. Although there is a widely recognized spousal privilege that prevents wives from testifying against their husbands, there certainly is no corresponding "mistress privilege," as Jimmy Marcello learned the hard way.

Connie Swanson Marcello was 53 years old when she took the stand. With shoulder-length brown hair, Connie was attractive, poised, and soon-to-be very direct. Connie described how she met Jimmy in the mid-1980s while she was bartending at the Hollywood Lounge strip club in Cicero, Illinois. She testified that for more than 20 years she had been Jimmy's mistress, all while he had given her thousands of dollars each month. He even made sure she received monthly cash while he was in prison. Jimmy had "put her up" in a lovely suburban home where she continued to raise her two children—even while Jimmy was married to someone else.

When asked to provide details from Jimmy's past, Connie humiliated him by telling jurors how she conned Jimmy into believe she had said nothing to the federal grand jury in February of 2005. Even though she secretly had spilled her guts to the feds, for another two years she continued to receive up to $5,000 per month from Marcello, all in cash of course. The nature of the cash payments was important to the trial because prosecutors had alleged Jimmy Marcello ran an illegal cash-based gambling empire comprised of video poker machines placed in bars around the Chicago area.

Marcello had instructed Connie how to respond if anyone ever inquired about where all her cash came from. Connie was supposed to say that her mother gave it to her, but instead she told the truth to the grand jury when she was threatened with jail time and then promised immunity from prosecution if she told the whole truth. Connie then testified that she lied to Marcello in 2005 after the grand jury appearance, telling him the focus had been on "things about the 80s." When the prosecution asked Connie how long she received these payments from Marcello, Connie surprised more than a few. "I still was getting money from him as late as June," she admitted. "His brother or a friend would meet me at Baker's Square restaurant and hand her an envelope or a coffee cup stuffed with $100 bills." Marcello paid her lawyers, too, she said, and also took care of a $15,000 gambling debt she had run up in one month.

Describing how she had adopted the Marcello last name, Connie said that she and her children all acted as a "normal" family whenever Jimmy had visited them. On cross-examination, Connie was asked if Marcello was kind to her and the children, one of whom was adopted with the other having special needs. "That," she said before leaving the courtroom, "was true, too."

I listened intently all through Connie's testimony, but I also kept my eyes glued to Jimmy to study his reaction and body language. He put his head in the palm of his hands from time to time; he seemed emotionally disturbed over virtually every word, often shifting from side to side in his chair. At the conclusion of her testimony, Jimmy requested to leave the courtroom for a trip to the washroom, escorted by the U.S. marshals. My opinion: Jimmy was just too sickened by being hung out to dry by his otherwise loyal, long standing mistress of 20 years.

Sal Romano, silver haired and distinguished at age 72, took the stand on Monday, August 6, 2007. After introducing himself to the jury, Sal got the jurors' attention with a spicy answer to an otherwise routine question. When asked his past occupation during the 1960s and 1970s, Sal replied, "I was a thief."

Romano had been an accomplished burglar for many decades before becoming a government informant who turned on the old "Hole-in-the-Wall" gang that had been an important part of Tony "the ant" Spilotro's cabal. Although he entered the courtroom in a wheelchair, Romano appeared otherwise in control with his blue sports coat and yellow tie. Sal went on to explain that he had had a "rather good" childhood, but then ran into the right people—or maybe we should say wrong people—who helped him enter the burglary business. Romano worked a life of crime in Chicago and Las Vegas at a time when Tony Spilotro was effectively a commander for the Chicago Outfit.

"Locks and alarms fascinated me," he explained, telling jurors he would buy locks and take them apart to see how they worked. "I developed skills in those things," Romano said matter-of-factly. By the time he was 26 or 27 years old, Romano had become "an expert in lock and alarm systems."

At first Romano began burglarizing different types of coin-operated machines around the Chicago area. Other guys like him might have become installers or vending operators, but Sal's "skills" allowed him to go for the easier, bigger money right away. If and when he got caught, which happened occasionally, Sal Romano testified that he would simply pay off the police. How did that work? Sal explained that it was an indirect transaction. He would deliver money to "the lawyer they requested you get." That answer about lawyers got an immediate rise out of Lombardo's attorney Rick Halprin, who requested a side bar. Outside the presence of the jury, Romano was asked who those lawyers were and he fingered Sam Banks and Dean Wolfson. Sam Banks is the brother to Chicago 36th Ward Ald. William Banks, and Wolfson had been a notable Chicago lawyer who in 1985 pleaded guilty in connection to the front page Greylord sting operation, a sweeping federal investigation of corruption within the Cook County Court System. Moreover, I had gone to grammar school at Gregory with both Dean Wolfson and his distinguished brother Warren Wolfson, a highly regarding trial lawyer and law professor with no ties to the mob.

When asked to elaborate, Romano explained that on one occasion in particular he believed some of the payoff money had found its way to dirty cops from funds he had delivered to Banks—after which charges against him were thrown out. Romano testified that he moved to Las Vegas in 1979 at the request of another thief, Peter Basile, who was also a member of Spilotro's Hole-in-the-Wall gang. The gang had been having difficulty stealing some Las Vegas artwork and various other valuable because of troubling alarm systems—which was right up Romano's alley.

Romano described his Las Vegas days working with reputed mob criminals, including his friend Paul "the Indian" Schiro, one the Family Secrets defendants. According to his own testimony, Spilotro once warned Romano that if he did anything with Schiro, he should do what Schiro says. That was not the only time he had been cautioned about Schiro, who had been described to him as a "dangerous man." Romano conceded on cross-examination, however, that Schiro had never personally threatened him.

Sal did tell some entertaining stories about Schiro, though. One time they planned to rob a home safe belonging to a friend of Schiro. Since Schiro would need an alibi, Romano was chosen to make the actual heist. The friend planned to be at a family wedding in Phoenix, which Schiro would also attend, providing a convenient alibi. Schiro believed his friend had $50,000 in a closet safe—although he didn't elaborate on why he didn't mind ripping off his friend.

Romano testified that he and his men entered the house and took care of the alarm, but then the unexpected happened. A small yapping dog darted in from another room, barking its head off. While the burglars debated how to handle the dog, which normally would have been no problem, the dog escaped through a small doggie door, and then ran around the yard yapping, barking, and causing a commotion. The Romano band of thieves grew nervous about the dog calling attention to the house, so Romano called off the caper before emptying the safe. Romano said that later he got a lot of grief from Schiro for not solving the pooch problem. "Why didn't you take care of the dog?" Romano quoted Schiro, explaining that "take care of" really meant silencing the dog "for good."

Romano's explanation was concise and classic: "I don't do dogs." When he said that, the entire courtroom was thoroughly amused—but personally, I almost wet my pants. It was a stellar moment.

I felt it was strange that the Las Vegas crew did not know that Romano had been a federally protected witness from 1981 to 1987, had been cooperating with federal authorities, and had even spent two years undercover wearing a wire to gather evidence on Spilotro and his hole-in-the-wall gang. Romano left the federal program on his own accord in 1987, but he still is living under a secret identity in an unknown location.

In 1980-81, Tony Spilotro was indicted in Nevada for heading a burglary ring within the Las Vegas city limits. Romano said that he had been associated with Spilotro during their early years on the west side of Chicago when they did several "scores" together. Although associated with the mob for some time and had been involved in numerous robberies and home invasions, Romano said he had never actually become a "made man."

After Romano, the next government witness to take the stand was 85-year-old Dominic Calarco, who testified that he was a cook at his social club. Calarco proceeded to tell jurors that one day in January 2006, he heard a knock on his door. The man standing in front of him had a long somewhat unruly beard, so at first Calarco failed to recognize him. But once the mystery man spoke, Calarco knew immediately that he was none other than mob boss Joey "the clown" Lombardo. He was especially surprised to see Lombardo, because Joey had been "on the lam" hiding from the FBI after being indicted in April of 2005.

Lombardo, of course, was sitting at trial just a few feet away from me, and not too far from the witness. I watched him closely as Calarco spoke, but Lombardo showed no emotional reaction to the testimony. He only shifted in his chair occasionally, peering though his large black eyeglasses.

Calarco went on, describing how he then invited his friend Lombardo into his home, explaining to the court how the two had at one time been neighbors and now had known each other for virtually 70 years. Calarco allowed Lombardo to stay at his home for about a week, explaining that Lombardo said he "had a few more things to do." Among those was a trip to his dentist, who happened to be Patrick Spilotro, brother to Tony and Michael Spilotro, although Patrick was never alleged to be a part of the Outfit itself.

Dominic testified that he felt the case against Lombardo had been "none of my business," he nonetheless found himself urging Joey to turn himself in. According to Dominic, Lombardo had said he would do so, but only if he could be freed on bond and not "sit in jail" until trial. Calarco recounted how Lombardo actually cried some nights because he missed his family, and told the jury how he seemed to be in poor health—or at least that's how he appeared. Carlarco noted how Joey would not have to go far to turn himself in. "I said all we've got to do is walk across the street and down the block to the Elmwood Park police department."

As it happens, Joey's trip to the dentist Pat Spilotro proved most fateful, for Pat turned him in to authorities. Lombardo was soon arrested in January 2006, in the alley behind 2329 N. 74th Avenue, Elmwood Park, a Chicago suburb. It had been nine months since Joey Lombardo and the other defendants had been indicted in the Family Secrets case.

ATTN: Thomas Bourghois

I am sending you this letter in total confidentiality. IT is very important that you show or talk to nobody about this letter except who you have to. The less people that know I am contacting you the more I can and will help And be able to help you. What I am getting at is I want to help you and the GOVT. I need for you and only you to come out to MILAN FCI and we can talk face to face. NOBODY not even my lawyers know I am sending you this letter, it is better that way for my safety. Hopefully we can come to an agreement when and if you choose to COME HERE. Please if you decide to come make sure very few staff at MILAN know your reason for coming because if they do they might tell my father and that would be a danger to me. The best days to come would be TUES. OR WEDS. Please no recordings of any kind just bring pen and lots of paper. This is no game. I feel I have to help you keep this sick man locked up forever.

FRANK CALABRESE JR.

06738-424 inmate #

UNIT G-Right

FCI MILAN MICHIGAN

First letter sent by Frank Calabrese, Jr to F.B.I Supervisor Tom Bourgeois, letting him know that he wanted to flip and cooperate against his father.

The infamous "Last Supper" was the government #1 Exhibit taken at the Sicily Restaurant 2743 N. Harlem Ave in 1976, longtime outfit mob members seated in the front row from left to right, are, Tony "Big Tuna" Accardo, Joe Amato, Joseph "Little Caesar" Di Varco, and James "Turk" Torello. Pictured seated left to right in back row are Joey "Doves" Aiuppa, Dominick Di Bella, Vincent Solano, and Al Pilotto, standing in the back are Jackie Cerone (left) and Joey "The Clown" Lombardo (right).

The body of William "Action" Jackson was discovered in the trunk of his Cadillac on lower Wacker Dr. in Chicago.

Photo by James A. Jack

Remains left of Michael Cagnoni's Mercedes-Benz—car on a tollway ramp. transmitter activated a bomb and killed Cagnoni instantly. Courtesy of the U.S. Department of Justice

Ex-con Albert Brown well known burglar. He was suspected in a least six safe crackings Burglaries—shot in the head and chest, was a mob hit for not paying a share of the loot, a street tax to the outfit

Photo by James A. Jack

Mike Cagnoni
Murdered by car
Bomb Blast June 1981

Artist's rendition of all five defendants facing Judge James Zagel. (Left to Right) Frank Calabrese, Sr. James Marcello, Joey Lombardo, Paul Schiro, and Anthony Doyle. Courtesy of Verna Sadack

Assistant U.S. Attorney Mitchell Mars questions Joey Lombardo who trys to make a few points before the Jury.
Courtersy of Verna Sadack should come right after Jury.

Teamsters President Jimmy Hoffa (L) and Teamsters Union consultant Allen Dorfman.

Crime figure's Anthony Spilotro, second from left, and his brother, Michael Right, the two are shown entering a Las Vegas courtroom 1986, with attorneys Gerry Werksman (L) and Oscar Goodman Second from Right now Mayor of Las Vagas.

Curtesy of the Chicago Crime Commission

Det. Jack sluged in face by mob boss Frank Calabrese Sr, while making a routine check at the "nest" night club owned by outfit.
Photo By James A. Jack

Detective James Jack inspects stolen tiers and wheels, also tools used by gang.
Photo by James A. Jack

Lead Federal prosecutor Mitchell A. Mars, left, First assistant U.S. Attorney for the Northern District of Illinois Gary Shapiro, Center, and U.S. Attorney Patrick Fitzgerald meet with reporters Sept. 27, 2007 after the family secrets trial.

Philip T. "Philly Beans" Tolomeo was my first partner C.P.D. as a detective—then went to work for the Calabrese crew 1978. Tolomeo voluntarily entered the witness protection government program.
Courtesy of the Chicago Crime Commission

No. 5 Lawrence Stubitsch- Frank Calabrese, Sr.'s best friend and crew member. Shot and killed in front of Bistro A-Go-Go, 7055 W. Higgins Rd. Sept. 1966
Photo Courtesy of James A. Jack

Bullet riddled auto with Phillip and Ronald Scavo and Lydia Abshire were killed by the M/M Boys
Photos Courtesy of James A. Jack

Phillip Scavo
36 yrs

Ald. Benjamin F. Lewis was found in his office handcuffed and shot to death in his 24th Ward Democratic headquarters. No doubt this was a mob hit.
Photo Courtesy of James A. Jack

Sheriff's Chief investigator Richard Cain brought mob boss Ross Prio in for questioning. Cain (L) Prio (R)
Photo Courtesy of James A. Jack

Body of Richard Cain, once a lawman and then a syndicate gangster is carried from Rose's sandwich shop 1117 W. Grand where he was assassinated by two men wearing ski masked
Photo Courtesy James A. Jack

FBI surveillance photo of outfit bosses take their business outside in a mall parking lot—(left to right) Joe Ferriola, Jimmy Marcello, Rocky Infelice and Sam Carlisi July 1986
Courtesy of the U.S. Department of Justice

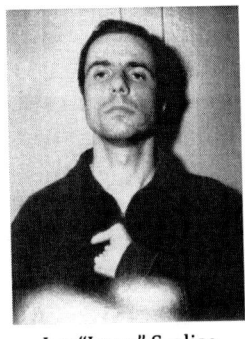

Joe "Jerry" Scalise

Joseph Grieco

Jimmy "Poker" Diforti

Frank "Gumba" Saladino

John "Johnny Apes" Monteleone

Joseph "Sharty" La Mantia

Frank "The German" Schweihs
Died July 24, 2008

Tony "Big Tuna" Accardo

Joey "The Clown" Lombardo

Jackie "The Lackey" Cerone

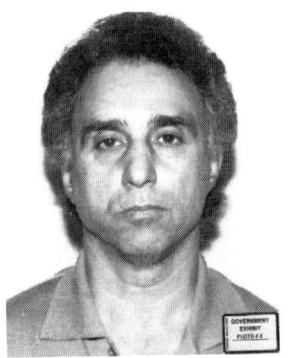
Harry Aleman

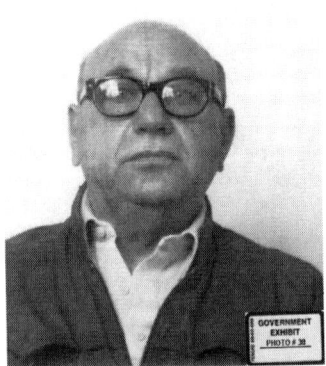
Angelo "The Hook" La Pietra

Emil Vaci

Sam "Wings" Carlisi

Joey "The Dove" Aiuppa

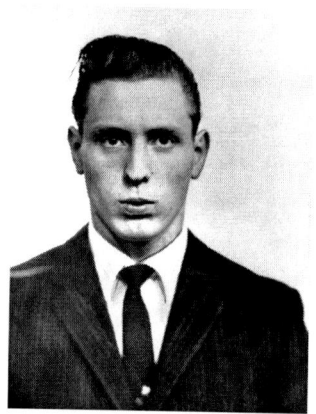

Billy McCarthy age 24
murdered May 1962
aka as the M & M Boys

James Miraglia age 25, aka as the M & M Boys—finding bodies stuffed in an auto trunk in the Southwest Side

Paul "The Indian" Schiro

Frank Calabrese Jr.

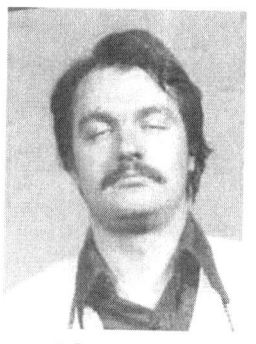

John Mendell

JOHN FECAROTTA - E31538
36, 6-1, 213, black hair, brown eyes

John "Big Stoop" Fecarotta

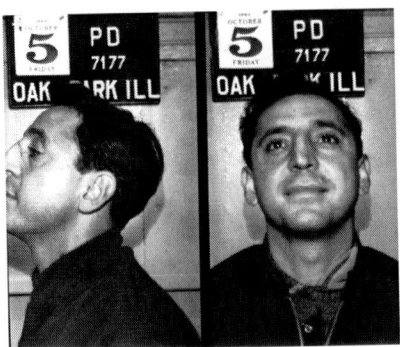

Frank "Frango" Santucci
Tavern Holdups

Gerald "Jerry" Scarpelli

James "Turk" Torello

Ronnie Jarrett

Dauber, William
Gunned down in rural Will County
with his wife—July 1980

Charlotte Dauber
wife of William

Joey Hanson
Tony Spilotro, Buddy in Vagas

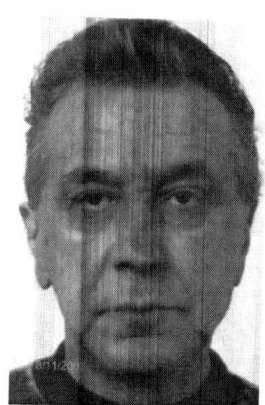
John "No Nose" Di Fronzo

Joseph "Joe Nagall" Ferriola

Anthony "The Ant" Spilotro

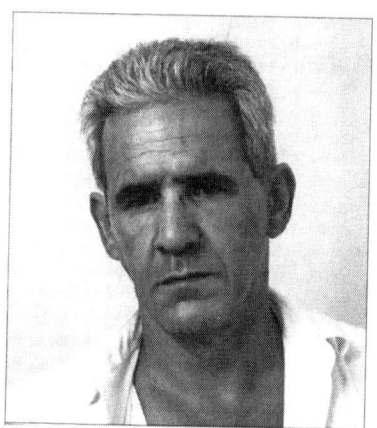
Nick Calabrese

Lawyers for the Defence

Rick Halprin
for Joseph Lombardo

Darrell Goldberg
for Anthony Doyle

Joseph R. Lopez for Frank Calabrese

Ralph E. Meczyk
for Anthony Doyle

(L) Marc W. Martin (R) Tom Breen
for James Marcello

12

The Killer Breeze

After two days of testimony, wise cracks, and cross examination courtesy of the 78-year-old Joey "the Clown" Lombardo, reputedly the one-time top boss of the entire Outfit, Lombardo left the stand still insisting he was nothing more than a dice game hustler. Such remarkable incredulity soured the jury's mood, which I felt would not help the next witness, defendant Frank Calabrese, Sr.

These were two old men, a pair of mob honchos—both of whom the government would implicate as liars and killers. Not exactly a legacy to be proud of, at least in most circles. When Frank "the Breeze" Calabrese took the stand on August 16, 2007, he was already well past his prime at 70 years of age. So was I.

Frank was sworn in, and as he took the stand he turned back toward Judge Zagel and said "Good afternoon." The judge responded, "Good afternoon ladies and gentlemen of the jury," then gave a slight nod to the expectant jurors.

Such pleasantries were in sharp contrast to the trial's overall theme of mayhem and murder, and such superficial civility may have provided a sense of irony but the most intriguing part is that Frank was testifying in the first place. We don't see high profile murder defendants testify very often, as was the case in the nationally followed O.J. Simpson trial, for example, when O.J. never took the stand. O.J. did attempt to try on the infamous glove, however, inspiring attorney Johnny Cochran's refrain, "If it doesn't fit, you must acquit." And that is why murder defendants don't testify on their own behalf too often—it is just too unpredictable, and too risky. Had O.J.'s glove indeed fit, it would have looked bad, even if he wasn't testifying for his own defense.

Lombardo's own testimony had been remarkable, too, of course, but Frank had a lot on the line and was really on the hot seat. He was the one implicated by his own son Frank, Jr., not to mention the damning testimony of his own brother Nick. Although Frank was motivated to spill as much reasonable doubt as he could all over his part of the case, I could not help but feel Frank would enjoy the show as its star attraction. Frank's attorney Joseph "the Shark" Lopez was allowing his client to testify on his own behalf for a reason.

The balding and visibly aging Frank Calabrese willingly strode to the stand nicely dressed with a sport coat and tie, wearing a short white beard that accentuated his years. At this point in our lives we were both a little long in the tooth, of course, and as Frank began I could not help but think of how we both got there. Frankie and I were in the same room, at the same trial, seated only 30 feet from each other, yet we were worlds apart. I watched Frank as he looked directly at the jury. It was hard to tell whether the jurors were glancing back or staring at his defense counsel's eccentric hot pink shirt and matching pink socks contrasted by his black suit and yellow lemon tie.

Joe Lopez is a personable, witty, and sharp attorney. A well known defense lawyer, he is unafraid to represent mob figures. Joe looked like a neon lamp in that get-up, but he purposely commanded the attention. It's part of his persona—and the act. Sure, he liked being a star of the show when working the courtroom, but he also wanted to keep some of the jury's focus—and the incumbent heat—away from Frank. He actually helped make Frank look conservative and reasonably normal by contrast, hardly an easy task. I've spent time with Joe, and although he may look unconventional in action, he is the consummate professional. To know Joe Lopez is to like him, a charm that is seldom lost on a jury.

Frank has one bad ear, which he complained about, so as we got underway he kept turning his head, and therefore the good ear, toward his lawyer Lopez, repositioning himself to hear better. It made him look old, naturally, but also somewhat normal if not sympathetic. For awhile.

I could not imagine what Frank might say after days of vivid, stunning, and incriminating testimony from his own son and brother, a shocking but understandable betrayal to most observers.

But there he was, complete with his own disarming necktie, plus his neon lawyer, so to speak. Frank looked eager, so I knew he must have quite a story lined up.

Lopez introduced Frank to the jury by touching on his family and distant youth. Frank had many brothers and sisters, and that made growing up a little rough. Frequently they all had to eat oatmeal for dinner to make ends meet. It was touching, but certainly a long way from making millions of dollars from illegal street loans, which Frank addressed head-on.

"My earning spoke for itself. I made millions so how would I have time to do this?" In Frank's language, "this" meant all these murders he was accused of, which he would soon deny one by one. He actually got himself worked up over the indignity and implied injustice of it all, and Lopez had to calm Frank down by refocusing on the planned testimony. So Frank returned to his personal story, gave his full name and told jurors that he was born in Chicago on March 17, 1937. The jury was all ears as Frank told how he was raised in the neighborhoods and grew up in the Taylor Street, Grand Avenue and Ogden area on the near northwest side, a region that many years ago was a strong Italian community.

Frank had no fewer than 7 brothers and sisters, and his highest education had been the fourth grade but he left school to work with his father on a coal truck, one of two concurrent jobs he held down in the early days. The other was working at night for the Jefferson Ice Company where they started around 7:00pm and drove a tractor and trailer, handling 400 pound cases of ice until 2:00 in the morning. Frank explained more of his early days: After I quit Jefferson Ice, I went to work for Hawthorn Melody Milk, a friend got me the job. I was the youngest man in transportation, driving a tractor-trailer. I delivered the trailer to an area that delivered, then filled up the milk trucks that delivered. The prosecutor John Scully objected to all this personal sympathy nonsense as irrelevant, but got nowhere. It is customary to give the jury a sense of who the defendant is.

"Did you get another job as you got older?"

"Yes, I worked on State and Grand selling newspapers. I would say I was about 13 and a half at that time. I attended a few grammar schools because I wasn't learning and I felt everybody was picking on me. It's just normal for a kid not learning nothing to understand that people are picking on him and they're not. They're not really picking on him, it took me many years to find this out. I had a learning disability, I found this out since I've been incarcerated, that I have dyslexia."

Frank was picked on as a kid, so here we go. I sensed the "victim defense" gearing up, not to mention the sympathy vote. Frank continued.

"I had it [dyslexia] real bad and I still have it. Sometimes I convert words, sometimes I convert numbers, and they found this out over at Milan when I was incarcerated."

"What year was your brother Nicky born?"

"I don't know. I believe Nicky is 64, I'm 70."

"How was your relationship with your brother as you were growing up, with Nicky?"

"When we were growing up we were very close, we were a close family. I was incarcerated at 16 years old and locked up. First I went to the service... my father stuck me in the service. I got incarcerated in the service and started going AWOL."

The prosecutor again objected on the grounds of relevance. This time the judge agreed, sustaining the objection, although Frank managed to continue anyway. He recounted how he had finished boot camp at Ft. Lenwood, Missouri, which was a 16 week program. Then everyone got shipped out. This was right after the Korean War, around 1953. Almost immediately Frank went AWOL for about 35-40 days. He was never apprehended, but his mother and father turned Frank back in, driving him straight to Ft. Lenwood. Frank didn't stay too long, for within 24 hours he was AWOL again.

All this went on for some time, then Scully again objected as to relevance.

"This is really, I think, not getting us anywhere," agreed the court.

After a little verbal jousting, Frank was back on track. All in all, he had gone AWOL from the service three times and had escaped custody twice. The final time on the run, he stole a car from the airport in St. Louis and eventually stopped at a gas station in Springfield, Illinois, located in the central part of the state about a couple hundred miles southwest of Chicago. But while the attendant was filling the tank—there were attendants who did that in those days—Frank floored it and pulled away, stealing the gas (which, around then, was probably under 25 cents a gallon). But it cost him a lot more, because Frank was soon caught, convicted, and sent to a federal penitentiary, a juvenile facility in Ashland, Kentucky.

Amidst all this, Frank and I already seemed much different, but it was clear that he and I really had much in common. Not only were we contemporaries from the streets of Chicago, but we both had endured tough times when we were young. I had been abducted to California by my father, and Frank had a series of mishaps with both the law and his own family. We were both in the service, too, and neither of us particularly liked it. But I didn't bolt. Frank did.

"Objection," Skully interrupted.

This time the judge responded directly to the witness. "Mr. Calabrese, your lawyer is trying to get you to a certain point in your life and he's trying to give a little background, but not everything, so that's why I'm sustaining the objections."

The objections were now being upheld, but Frank just kept right on with it. The judge was growing impatient, but he was not powerless—just flexible. Giving much latitude to the defense testimony is one way to help a guilty verdict to survive an appeal. Cutting the witness off, on the contrary, could give the appellate court something to hang its hat on.

Still, the prosecution objected repeatedly and the sympathy game played itself out again and again. Judge Zagel warned Joe Lopez, but then Frank himself protested and looked straight at the jury. "How are these people supposed to know what I'm doing?" The judge explained that he just wanted Frank to answer the questions that were asked.

Frank was released from the Ashland facility in 1956, when he was still just 19 years old. Frank recounted how he liked to get into fights, explaining that he hated bullies then, and that he still hates them now. He said he is "good with his hands," meaning that Frank was a proficient fighter.

"I had no . . . no shame of that," Frank said, "because there was many guys that picked on other people and even picked on me that I had to defend myself."

Court: "You know, I don't think this has anything to do with the case."

Lopez: "Okay."

Court: "Not in the level of detail that's been brought out. So why don't you ask a question and instruct Mr. Calabrese that if he ever answers a question yes or no, he should stop right there?"

Lopez: "Okay."

Lopez then asked Frank if he had heard what the judge said. He admitted to hearing part of it, and said that he would answer "yes" or "no" if he could.

"You mentioned that you didn't like bullies and you used to fight a lot," Lopez continued.

They should have asked *me*. Even I could have answered that one, since my first encounter with Frank was when he had suddenly split my lip at The Nest lounge in Chicago when we were much younger.

"When I was released from Ashland, Kentucky, I came back to Chicago. I met a young lady was my first wife, her name was Delores Hanley." Frank explained how he had met Delores at a place called Club Reunion in Chicago, located within the Austin Police District.

"I moved out of the family home after I got married which was 1961. I was 21 years old. At that time her father, my ex-wife's father, who was my father-in-law, got me a job with the 150 local. That's a union that handles heavy equipment, cranes, bulldozers, stuff like that. Before you became a heavy equipment operator, you had to become an oiler first before I did that, and learned about the equipment and to learn how to run the big equipment."

"After your marriage to Delores Hanley, did you have children?" asked Lopez.

"The first, Frankie, Kurt, and Nicky. Kurt is 15 months younger than Frankie. We were living in Elmwood Park, in an attic apartment."

The image of Frank, Sr., in the early days with those three young boys was a much different picture than we had already seen in court. Frank, Jr., went to jail, wore a wire, and even testified against his father.

Scully: Objection, Your Honor, to any of this detail. We're going on now for 20, 25 minutes.

Court: [To Lopez] Would you try to get to the point more quickly?

Lopez: Yes, Judge, I just want to lay a little more history for us.

Court: Yeah, but what's at issue here is a specific charge over a specific period of time, and his life, as a whole, is not what this jury is going to be asked to rule on . . . . and if you need a few moments for us to stop so that you can instruct your client in what is relevant, I'd be happy to give it to you, but you may want to just try a little—and you can lead.

The judge was giving Lopez the license to ask leading questions if that would keep Frank to the point. Normally leading questions are not allowed on direct examination, although they are often used on cross examination, to keep the witnesses own lawyer from virtually testifying. But sometimes it is helpful to allow leading questions for routine matters like the ones we had been plowing through for half hour already.

Lopez had been given much latitude, but the game with the jury and judge was coming to an end—sooner or later the jury would tire of Frank's vanilla stories, and that would begin to work against him.

"I just want to get—the indictment, it starts in the '60s, and I'm leading to the '60s. Let me just go right to the '60s and then we can be done with it," Lopez explained. So Frank continued.

"I met Larry Stubitsch around '63, '64, and I met Angelo La Pietra at Meo's Norwood House when I rented the house behind, they used to have fashion shows there on Saturday and Sunday."

That answer brought another legal skirmish and brought the judge closer to the real brink.

"Mr. Lopez," the judge interrupted.

"Yes, sir."

"If you ask 'what,' I expect an answer to what. If you ask 'when,' I expect an answer to when. If you ask 'how,' I expect an answer to how. If you ask 'where,' I expect an answer to where. I don't want a "why" question answered as well. I don't want to know because I simply want basic fundamental facts. There may come a point in time in which you may ask a 'why' question, but you haven't reached it. And what I find distressing, since it's your client and subject to you preparation, is that he's answering questions that you're not asking. He's answering 'why' questions and 'because' questions that you're not asking, and it's, frankly, irrelevant. His life's history is not at issue here. You can give a certain chronology, but I'm not getting a chronology, I'm getting a life story and that's not, in any respect, helping."

Lopez was being scolded. And it was all a war of credibility with the jury, which at this point the judge was effectively giving the jurors permission to be annoyed at Lopez and his client. The court had been careful not to overreact all along, but now Judge Zagel was impliedly threatening Frank's credibility with the jury without directly attacking Frank or punishing him with contempt—an overreaction that would perhaps sway the jury. And Lopez knew he was on a short leash not only with the judge, but more importantly with the jurors as well.

"And in the end," continued the judge, suddenly getting to the real point, "if it persists, it does not help your client. It's very much like somebody accused of a terrible crime who gets on the witness stand and for fifteen minutes tells you how nice he was to his mother. It's an interesting aspect of his life, but it is not relevant to the charge here."

Judge Zagel then gave Lopez a moment to explain all that to Frank, off the record but without adjourning court. Lopez then had a private conversation with Frank, and announced that he had complied with the judge's request.

"Judge, I did comply with your instructions," Lopez reported, "but like many people of Mr. Calabrese's ethnicity, they love to talk. And I understand that and I think that he understands it now and I think we're getting into a relevant time period of the 1'60s with Angelo La Pietra and everybody, I think, it'll be a little bit different now."

"Let us hope so," the judge sternly replied.

Then Lopez pushed the envelope. "But I do have to ask him some 'why' questions in regard to some of these people that have been named in this indictment."

The judge said he would allow some of those, if they were relevant, but he did not want to hear much about Frank's "incipient" military career. Lopez had managed to win a tactical victory. He gave up on the benign personal background in exchange for the right to ask the 'why' questions, even though the judge had not wanted those. It's all a part of the legal wrangling that goes on and on in a major case.

Lopez then directed his attention back to the witness.

"Now, Frankie, keep in mind what I explained to you a few minutes ago okay?"

"I'll try to do the best I can," Frank conceded.

"You met Angelo La Pietra at Meo's Norwood House, a restaurant and lounge on Harlem & Lawrence, through a guy named Rocky Potenza?"

"He used to hang out in Meo's all the time. I was working with the water department [for the city] running a high-lift at that time. I remembered Rocky called me over to the table and he said, 'Com on, I want you to sit here and have something to eat.' Then Angelo came in and sat with us, that's when he introduced me to him."

Finally, Frank got to the nitty gritty of how he waltzed his way into a career with the Outfit.

"I started doing other things besides working for the city. I was lending money out. I was lending money out and had about $14,000 on the street. I had people who would ask me to lend them the money. I started lending money around 1963. I was stealing also, like doing burglaries, whatever I could get my hands on, most of the people that were at Norwood Restaurant were involved in all types of criminal activities, that included Angelo and others. I began loaning money about the age of 23, when I used to hang around a place called Montana's on North Avenue east of Austin. A lot of the guys that hung around there I knew. They used to go to the track, they were gamblers, I wasn't."

As Frank spoke, I recalled knowing Montana's Restaurant myself. My cousin Ronnie used to hang around there, too.

Frank continued. "The $14,000 I had on the street was my nest egg, was from stealing and some of it was [from] working. I would see Angelo occasionally at the Norwood and started talking one day. When I say 'we started talking,' Angelo and me, we started talking and he asked me—I told him what I was doing. He says I shouldn't be doing that, he says, because 'it's not right.' Because I wasn't paying him, he wanted to tax me, but he didn't. I knew what he meant . . . that unless you belonged to the Club, which meant *his* Club, you weren't supposed to do this. I didn't know that. Angelo didn't have a Club, but he had a group of guys that worked with him, I met through the years.

"Angelo and me discussed the fact about loaning out money, we discussed future loans or doing business together in the future in any manner, he became a partner with me. He gave me $60,000.

"I told Angelo if I had more money, I know I can put it out on the street, and he says to me, 'what do you mean?' I said, well, I got guys who would want to borrow $10,000, pay $13,000 at the end of the year, pay $1,000 a month . . ."

Angelo said that Frank himself would have to guarantee the money. That's a risky proposition when dealing with a mob boss like La Pietra. It was dangerous, too, and gutsy for a kid like Frank. But Calabrese was on the rise, making friends in high places. More importantly, he was making money for friends in high places. So Frank said he'd guarantee the money.

"He not only gave me $60,000 once," Frank said, "he gave it to me a couple other times. He gave me $80,000 another time."

Frank described how he had met Larry Stubitsch in the Grand and Racine area on the near northwest side where there was a small restaurant, like a beef and sausage stand. Larry was already in the loan business, along with another guy named Steve Annerino who was with Angelo. When Frank got into the business with Angelo, he reported directly to Steve. Frank said that when Angelo gave him the first $60,000, it was paid in cash while Angelo's brother Jimmy was present. Consistent with mob practices, having a witness was a good idea in case there was a misunderstanding later.

Frank had first met up with Jimmy La Pietra at Montana's. Both Jimmy and his brother Angelo had come in one night to have dinner with Frank. That's when the advance of the first $60,000 had come up.

"I wanted to start working with Larry [Stubitsch]," continued Frank, "but Annerino wouldn't allow it. I then went to see Angelo one day and asked him 'how come this man would not allow us to work together?' He was hanging around in an Italian club in Cicero. I never socialized with Angelo, I just did business with him at this time. I was able to put the $60,000 out on the street, in only two weeks. There were six borrowers for the $60,000, so I needed more, they took $10,000 a piece, and it was very successful."

Frank explained that in the 1960s it was very difficult for people to get loans. He said times were difficult in the early '60s, around the time President Kennedy was shot, so he was able to find many borrowers for his juice loans on the street. Frank referenced the tapes he had already heard in court, then denied that he ever had to inflict physical injury to a borrower. "There was never a time that anybody that I ever had got a beating from me for money, 'cause I wouldn't do that." Sure, Frank said he put the loans on the street and gave his mob boss a cut from the proceeds, but firmly denied dishing out beatings to customers who didn't pay up.

As I sat in the courtroom listening to that nonsense, I had one thought: if anyone believes this shit, I'm Mary Poppins. That's how the juice business works, of course. The interest—the points—is very high, the repayment terms typically short. Frank had already guaranteed the money back to Angelo, so the best way to prioritize repayment is the threat of violence—and ultimately the violence itself. Without that, the mob would be just another creditor. But that's why the whole thing is illegal. Aside from being a scheme that often ended in violence, it created enough desperation on the part of the borrowers that they had no choice but to commit crimes to get the money to repay the Outfit. Juices loans are not just crimes on their own, they create other crime.

But Frank would have the jury believe that a friendly conversation did the trick. "I would sit and talk to them and ask 'em, 'what's the least you could pay' or 'what's the most you can pay' if they were having trouble and just take back the principal. I was successful this way, and go on to the next borrower."

Of course I believed he talked to his delinquent borrowers, and of course we all believe that they would come up with some money, even all of it—and probably without violence most of the time because they all knew the violent consequences were just a nod away.

Lopez asked if Frank had heard the tapes in court where his brother Nick said that Frank had accumulated millions of dollars over the years and that Nick had done his books over much of that time. "At one point," Frank answered, "the most amount of money I had on the street was about $350,000, that represented about 20, some people had 30, some of the people had less."

Frank told the jury how he started working with Larry Stubitsch, but also how he was required to go have "sit-downs with Angelo," a tough task for some because of Angelo's brutal reputation as a mob killer. His mob nickname—the Hook—was there for a reason. "Many people couldn't look him in the eye when they talked to him," Frank said calmly. "I never had that problem." If that was not to Frank's own twisted credit, at least it explained his fast rise in the mob. Frank had the guts.

The jury was then told about "sit-downs" and how they were mini-arbitrations of a sort where the boss resolved disputes.

"Steve was fighting with us, and he wanted all the big loans to come to him. I met with Steve Annerino one night with Angelo at a barber shop on 22nd Street, and Stevie was very shocked to see me there, and he got a little snotty, which wasn't very nice. And it was corrected, and that's when Angelo says to me, 'Larry goes with me,' and Larry [Stubitsch] and I became friends.

"I would then meet Jim Stolfe—I met Jimmy Stolfe before Larry had died. Larry was killed in 1966. I met Jimmy Stolfe at a small restaurant called Connie's Pizza, him and his dad used to work it. It was located at 26th and Lowe. Jimmy and me became friendly, very much friends.

"Larry and me worked together about two and a half years. Now as far as Angelo La Pietra was concerned, Angelo was Larry and me's partner with the money he gave me. I would repay him off the top of the book—whatever we got that was extra, I would give it to him."

According to Frank, the "top of the book" referred to money coming in that was extra money, funds that were not being circulated back onto the street. Instead of just holding it, Frank would give him a percentage of that back to take care of the loan. Frank said many, many months passed without making payments back to Angelo because we were building the book—reinvesting the interest in new loans to expand the whole book of loans they had on the street.

"I never had to pay street tax to Angelo, that was because he was my partner. I was Angelo's partner. I would say until he went away, that would be approximately in the early '80s—83, 84, in there.

"Larry got killed September, 1966. He was in front of the Bistro-A-Go-Go." Now there's a name—sort of reminds us of the absurd "Badda-Bing" from "The Sopranos" television series. Actually, the "Bistro" was formerly called the Ivy Lounge. One of my best friend owned it at one time: Joe Erskine, an ex-policeman.

The Ivy, located had quite a history. It was located at Montclare and Higgins Avenue on the Northwest side, just within the Chicago city limits. Chicago had a rule that the police and firemen had to live within the city, so there would be clusters of them on the fringes near some of the desirable suburbs like Park Ridge. The Ivy was a good after-hours place with a late liquor license, open until 5:00am on weekends and 4:00am on weeknights. They featured a good dancing combos there, too, like "Stardust Green" and "Tony Smith."

Mob bosses would come to the Ivy regularly, usually around 3:00am, including the likes of Angelo "the Hood" LaPietra, Frank Calabrese, Sr., Frank Santucci, Tony "the Ant" Spilotro, Phil "Philly Beans" Tolomeo, Billy McCarthy and Jimmy Miraglia (the M & M Boys), Joey Hansen, Bob "Crazy Bob" Sporadic, Felix "Milwaukee Phil" Alderisio. Sometimes the place was a living who's who of top mob figures. As a matter of fact, Milwaukee Phil and Tolomeo actually bought the place after it was closed down by the IRS for tax problems.

The Ivy Lounge was my beat. I was in the Ivy one night when several unidentified men came into the lounge, walked behind the bar and place bags with locks over all the cash registers to secure them. I became suspicious and managed to speak with owner Joe Erskine who told me the men were feds from the Treasury Department. Joe had big problems with the IRS and the Ivy never opened again—not until the mob took over and changed the name to Bistro-A-Go-Go.

I spent a lot of time in that area. A place called "Parse's Hot Dogs" is still located nearby at 7049 Higgins and was owned by Parse Tarpenian since 1953. In the early days, it was right next door to the Ivy Lounge. This is where Larry Stubitsch, 29, of 7101 Armitage, who was partner to Frank Calabrese, was shot in September of 1966. But Stubitsch did not die right away. He staggered next door to Parse's parking lot, was found there and then taken to Resurrection Hospital where he finally died. The Stubitsch shooting was well over 20 years ago, but I return to the scene often. Not only is Parse himself still there, I still see him twice a month when I stop in for my Parse's hotdog fix. In the old days Parse had a guy there making dogs, and now he's a top restaurateur at the famous Rosebud—but he served me hotdogs way back when.

The Stubitsch incident probably came with a hidden meaning, typical of some mob operations. Two other friends of Larry were also shot, and another was beaten: Richard Ferraro, 26, was shot in the left arm and chest; Charles Marzaho, 33, was badly bruised, and Richard De Angelo, 28, was shot. De Angelo was a former policeman who became the manager of the Bistro-A-Go-Go working for Alderisio and my old buddy Philly Beans Tolomeo. Cops and mobsters go together sometimes, I think for at least two reasons: the cops are enticed because they have already seen first hand how the fast money and women go with the job, plus they already know how the system works so they fit in quickly.

But I think there was much more to what was going on with Stubitsch and company. Four or five men showed up around 4:15am. The buzzer sounded at a side door, De Angelo opened it and encountered the men who announced, "This is a robbery." I don't think so. First, no money was missing and no one seemed to have stolen anything. Second, no weapon was found at the scene. Third, and perhaps most telling, Ferraro and De Angelo later refused to relate details of the shooting to the police. My personal opinion is that this was a mob hit on Larry Stubitsch, who was the friend and business partner of Frank Calabrese, Sr. Someone wanted to get even, either with Frank or Larry or both.

Look at it this way: Larry and his friends were at the lounge at 4:15am just after closing time. Then four (maybe five) guys come in and shoot and kill Larry. Later, as detailed below, Frank is implicated in the murder of someone who allegedly was involved in killing his friend Larry Stubitsch. Frank then has a mob "sit-down" where everything gets straightened out by Frank paying money. Why would that happen, unless Frank had to pay a penalty for taking someone out?

Obviously we are talking about a known mob hot spot for years, long before the Stubitsch episode itself. Way back in 1963 there was an incident involving my cousin Ronnie who once worked for Frank Calabrese at the La Luce joint. Ronnie and his father were actually arrested at the Ivy after another person picked up an envelope with money in it during a blackmail scheme that involved a suburban alderman from Des Plaines. Lots of action, if you know what I mean.

So back to Frank Calabrese, who continued his story from the stand, explaining the mob sit-down mentioned above, but of course denying that he killed the killer of partner Larry. "The lounge was on Higgins Avenue, two blocks east of Harlem at Higgins and Montclare. Phil Tolomeo was connected to 'Milwaukee Phil' Alderisio, and Phil Alderisio was the one that Philly had to account to. He was a police officer at one time; he was indicted [for charges] which he pled guilty to in the United States District Court here. It was the last case and the case before this, that's why I'm sitting in jail today. That's the same Philly Tolomeo from the Bistro-A-Go-Go that seen the man kill Larry and admitted it and he's never been pinched."[8]

Frank Calabrese continued his testimony. "I first met 'Philly Beans' Tolomeo sometime in 1965, I met him at Meo's Norwood house." And of course I was well acquainted with Philly Beans Tolomeo myself. He was an early partner of mine on the force. More on him later.

---

[8] As noted at length in Chapter 8, this is the same "Philly Beans" Tolomeo who was my first partner on the force.

"I didn't kill the person that killed Mr. Stubitsch, and I know who it was, definitely." Frank got the jury's attention with that one. See what I mean?

"I started to work with Philly in the late '70s, '76, '77. I'm not sure exactly of the dates, and also I met a person by the name of James Torello around 1966 when Larry got killed. I met him with Angelo La Pietra at the place that the killing took place [that] belonged to Milwaukee Phil—I never met Phil Alderisio.

"One day I had to go see "Turk" [Torello] because I was in trouble because the place belonged to Phil Alderisio and Philly Tolomeo, but Alderisio was the boss of it. He was his boss at the time and he [also] owned the Bistro-A-Go-Go.

"The first time I met John Monteleone was when I was having the problem with Steve Annerino. He used to hang in the same place that Stevie hung in, it was a lounge on 22nd Street. Johnny was called "Johnny Apes" and James Torello was called "Turk" and Jimmy La Pietra's nickname was Haime—I guess it means Jimmy in Jewish.[9] The reason for the meeting was a problem in regard to the shooting. Turk got it resolved. We had to pay $500 back a month to Milwaukee Phil for one year.

"The type of meeting that we had was commonly referred to as, like sort of an alternative resolution dispute meeting, which is known as a sit-down. [But] this was not a sit-down.

"A sit-down is when one group is having problems with another group of trying to steal their things—when they're trying to take and lie to the customers. If they got a card game, they would try to steal the card game from them by trying to divert these guys to come to them and telling them lies, and then you would have to have a sit-down for that. I heard some of those prison tapes, the ones where my son was talking about sit-downs with the 'wild bunch.' The sit-downs would be conducted by Joe Nagal who was Joe Ferriola, the wild bunch. The wild bunch consisted of Petrocelli, Tony Barcelino, Harry Aleman, some others I just can't think of now.

---

[9] Actually it is derived from the Hebrew name Jacob, meaning "holds the heel," referencing the story in Genesis whereby Jacob was born grasping Esau's heel and later bought Esau's birthright. It evolved into its English version courtesy of a French variation of "Gemmes."

Oh—Scarpelli, I never called him that. I called him Montejus. I have a nickname for everyone. Montejus means good hand, that was because he was supposed to be very tough with his hands.

"Now, I want to talk about these sit-downs. It wasn't conducted like these court proceedings, or a group sit-down at a table and shout at one another, and no conversation amongst each other to settle these disputes in a sit-down. No, no, it was all done diplomatically. There would be the head of that group sitting there, and then there would be somebody who was very important, and most of the time it was Joey Aiuppa. Aiuppa would make the decisions after listening to the conversation. Each side would tell its version of the events, and he would side with the truth. What I'm saying each side would present themselves with their argument. This was done in a diplomatic manner and no searing or cussing, that was a no, no, no. A decision would be made at this point or some point thereafter.

"I then met Ronald Jarrett at a hot dog stand called Larry's, at the corner of 26th—I was introduced to Jarrett by Pete 'Butch' Caruso. I wasn't part of that group. I was affiliated with Angelo, Angelo wasn't in charge down there then. Frank 'Skid' Caruso was. Angelo didn't take charge down there [in Chinatown] until Skid died, I think it was around . . . the mid '70s."

Frank pushed forward, dancing around the meat of his testimony. He told how he had pleaded guilty in the 1990s in connection with a mob loan sharking case. Calabrese was asked about whether Larry Stubitsch was working with a person named Michael Albergo. Michael hung out at Teet's Poolroom and Larry used to have him bring in customers for loans. That was where Frank met Albergo.

"I never killed Albergo, and I don't know who killed Albergo, even though the indictment says in August 1970 I committed the murder of Albergo. It's not true. Why would I want to kill him? Well, first of all, I have to tell you, and I would like the jury to hear this—he was dealing with everybody. He would get customers for Larry, then when Larry died he was bringing me customers, and how he was also bringing another fella customers. There was three of us. Michael "Hambone" Albergo was a freelancer, but he could've been considered an agent. But he used to bring me the loans that were a little larger than the other guys 'cause they couldn't handle them, and I would take those loans and I would give him a commission on those.

"I heard that there was a subpoena issued for me from some commission. This took place during the period, well, I can tell you because the man is dead today. My ex-father-in-law, Ed Hanley, found out and told me that 'you have a subpoena for you and you're going to be brought before a grand jury.'

"Hanley told me I should 'take a sneak' for awhile. My brother Nick and I took off to Arizona, we stayed a few weeks. My ex-father-in-law was involved in the Bartenders, Waiters and Waitresses Union—he was the president. He was president of the International which would be the whole United States, all of it. In fact Ed offered me a position in Las Vegas as president of the union in Las Vegas, which is one of the biggest locals in the country, but because of my education I was very embarrassed to that. I didn't think I could handle it. I was unable to read at that time, I still have difficulty reading and spelling, but I could write.

"I was having a rough time. I did most of my training and education at Milan, in prison, but taught myself to read and write on the street. But I learned more in prison about education.

"My brother Nick testified that I strangled Mr. Albergo [in the 1970s]. There's no truth to that at all. I knew Michael "Hambone" Albergo had been subpoenaed to testify before a crime commission, but I did not kill him. What did I do that he could testify to? There was no way that them loans meant that much. Larry and me put in 17 hours a day sometimes.

"My brother during the early period of time was hinting around that he wanted to work with me. Nick said 'how hard is it to do what you're doing?' I told him 'no, it was a lot of street driving, 7 days a week, there was no drop off.' It wasn't an easy job like you see in the movies."

Nick had already testified in court that Frank had expressly explained to him how Frank had to commit murders as part of his position in the Outfit. Frankie Calabrese was adamant on the stand.

"No way, no way did that ever take place, no way."

13

Heavy Work

Frank Calabrese sat stoically on the witness stand. His denials were persistent, if not entertaining. "It wasn't an easy job like you see in the movies." Frank was referring to the "job" of being a mob boss or, in his case, mob enforcer. Of course it wasn't easy—looking over your shoulder for 50 years, if you live that long, assassinating debtors and enemies, burying dead bodies, evading the police, then occasionally spending 5-10 years in the slammer only to get out and do it all over again. Isn't that precisely the point? It isn't *supposed* to be easy.

When brother Nick's testimony came up about murder being part of Nick's job description, Frank was defiant. "No way, no way did that ever take place, no way."

Frank explained that when he came back from Arizona he began to search for Michael "Hambone" Albergo because "there was money to be paid that I wasn't' getting. He was responsible for about $7000. He made collections, and he was supposed to give me the money he collected."

"I looked for him in the neighborhood around Grand Avenue, and he used to hang around a hotel on Lincoln Avenue at Ogden. I went there looking for him. I even spoke to his girlfriend, I even went to that location looking for her but I couldn't find her. I thought that he absconded with the money, the $7000. In fact, there came a time when Philly Tolomeo absconded with money. Nobody seen him. They told me they think he lambed, meaning he left town.

"I would have a write-off for the items in my book. We took the loss, Angelo and me, something like that, you just took it off of the top, meaning the top figure."

Then Frank explained how he began working with Ronnie Jarrett. Ronnie was a real nice fella, Frank told the jury, who got along really well with his brother Nicky. Ronnie, as it happens, liked to steal—I suppose that's no surprise—but he was particularly good at breaking into safes. Most of his burglaries were commercial jobs, like grocery stores with big safes stuffed with cash like at the old National Tea and the Jewel grocery stores. Ronnie stole a couple of trucks once, and another time he went away to the slammer for stealing a load of cameras. And another time he got five years for heisting another load, but Frank couldn't remember what it was.

Lopez, Frank's lawyer, jumped in. "Did you become involved in bookmaking?"

"No. Bookmaking is taking bets, when you take bets on horses and you take bets on sports. Bookmaking wasn't my thing, I didn't gamble. I was very happy handling the business of the loans, which I was very successful at."

At that point the court ordered a short recess, nothing more than routine and hardly worth mentioning except that during this particular break Joey Lombardo was wheeled in his chair right past me as he exited. Always personable, Joey looked me over and said, "Jack, I read your newspaper article in the *Sun-Times* Monday, very good. How about writing *my* book?" Joey was referring to an article about me and my first book, *Three Boys Missing*, about a 40-year police Odyssey triggered when three boys were murdered in Chicago when I was a young detective. It had been my case. Maybe I should write Joey's book—now that would be something—then again, we're both a little long in the tooth to tackle a story like that. Still, Joey seems persistent. He's written me from jail a few times after the trial, just to probe the idea.

When court resumed, I was still thinking about Lombardo's idea, but Frank jerked me back to reality. He picked up where he had left off about the bookmaking.

"Ronnie and Nicky both wanted to get into it [the bookmaking] because it was supposed to be very lucrative. I gave them $40,000 and then started doing business. I didn't know anything about bookmaking, and I don't know anything about odds and gambling."

Lopez then asked Frank if it was during this period that he became familiar with a guy named John Fecarotta. Frank said yes, but then came the big question.

Lopez: Did you kill John Fecarotta?

Frank: No. No way. I loved that guy.

Lopez: Did you help your brother kill that guy?

Frank: No way. I spent a lot of time with that man, he used to have a hotdog stand across from my house in Elmwood Park, during the 1970s. I met John Fecarotta through Johnny "Apes" Monteleone—Fecarotta and Johnny Apes were partners. They used to steal when they were younger together, then they got involved with the people—Angelo LaPietra and them. They were also friends with Turk Torello, I think Turk stole with them, when they were younger.

Talk about youth bonding—Frank made it sound almost like an "Old Yeller" moment. Young boys rafting, fishing, painting white fences—and ripping off the neighborhood.

"Johnny "Apes" stole cars. Johnny went away for a few of those. When I met Johnny Fecarotta they called him by his nickname "Big Stoop," and that was because he was big. Everybody had nicknames. I was called "Breeze."

"John and me spent time together. We'd go eat at restaurants, he used to like to gamble and we went to the trotters, the trotters in Maywood—the buggy races. Fecarotta and me hung out. I would spend time at the hotdog stand, we used to play gin together, he loved to play gin. We were good friends. We kind of respected one another. It doesn't mean that I held his hand and he held mine.

"Johnny liked girls. He had a wife and two girlfriends. There was no time that I worked with John Fecarotta—as I said before he worked with Johnny "Apes" Monteleone, and I believe with Turk and Angelo when they were younger.

"I met Jimmy DiForti for the first time at a car tire place off Cicero Avenue about two blocks south of 22nd Street which was his father's, I met him there with Johnny Fecarotta. Fecarotta use to play gin with him, Jimmy DiForti. As I know DiForti, he was a Fagan and a thief. In other words he would have kids go out and steal and bring him the stuff and he would buy it from them—it was all hot stuff.

"DiForti loaned some money out, I provided him with it, and it was a partnership with Angelo and Jimmy."

Lopez asked whether Angelo was Frank's boss.

"If he was my boss," Frank answered, "that meant he can control me, and he didn't never controlled me; never. He never told me what to do. He told me when something wasn't right or wrong, you can't do this or you can't do that and I would listen to him. He was a very well respected man and many people feared him. He was only about 5 feet, 7 inches in height, but built strong, that's why they called him "the Bull."

Lopez then brought Frank to the subject of extortion, namely the shakedown of a guy named Jimmy Stolfe. Frank said he used to go to Stolfe's restaurant in the 1970s, and told the jury he had great respect for the man. That was bullshit, by the way—Calabrese "had great respect" for every one of his customers. Right—that just sounds good for the jury, nothing more.

Frank told the story of how this guy Stolfe looked scared one day, so Frank asked about it. The story was that somebody had come into the restaurant looking to extort big money from him. So Frank intervened and went to boss Angelo LaPietra about it because he didn't want someone strong-arming his friend right under Frank's own nose.

Jimmy Stolfe told Frank that these guys wanted $300,000 or "he would have a problem." Frank said he got the money knocked down to $100,000, then loaned it to Stolfe who proceeded to pay Frank back. Stolfe put Frank on the restaurant payroll, giving him a net of $1000 a month.

Frank looked straight at the jury of five men, seven women, and did his best to seem sincere and convincing. Frank said that Stolfe was grateful for his help, and that he had then looked up to Frank as a great friend. Right, I thought—a $100,000 friend. One little problem: the prosecution believed that it was Frank all along who was extorting his "great friend" Jimmy Stolfe. But Frank stuck to his guns, so to speak, and insisted he had intervened on Stolfe's behalf, knocking down the extortion money and then loaning him cash to take care of it.

Then Frank expressly denied being in the Outfit.

"Joe—Mr. Lopez, I'm sorry. I call you Joe not to be disrespectful—when they say Outfit they're talking about guys like Angelo and Jimmy and Johnny Apes and Johnny Fecarotta, them are Outfit guys because they belonged to a group. I never belonged to any group, but I did hang around with a group and did business with them."

Lopez asked about Frank Santucci. Frank knew him, of course. He said Santucci worked for him. But he denied ever paying street tax up a chain to Angelo LaPietra—Frank said he'd never split profits like that.

But Frank did say there came a time when his brother Nick got involved with Angelo and Jimmy on a regular basis, around the end of the 1970s. Frank, though, said he didn't want to get involved personally.

Then Lopez threw a fat one down the middle, asking Frank if he killed Paul Haggerty on June 24, 1976—and then sliced his neck. "No way" came the familiar reply. But Frank did say he knew Haggerty, having met him at the house of Frank Lamonte, a friend of Calabrese from the old neighborhoods in the 1960s. Paul had a specialty—he would steal cartage and then sell it. He would sell pants, shirts—always something this guy was selling. Frank said everyone liked the guy because he was very respectful, did things for people, always went out of his way. If someone didn't have the money to pay, he'd tell them to just pay when they got it.

"So what about Henry Casentino?" Frank said he didn't even remember him, but Lopez reminded Frank that his brother had already testified how Frank had murdered Casentino.

"I murdered Casentino? For what? I didn't even remember knowing him."

Lopez went on to another victim named in the indictment against Frank—John Mendell. Frank said he knew him, that he was a friend of Ronnie Jarrett—he used to steal with him, and that Mendell and Jarrett were close friends.

Lopez: On June 16, 1978, did you commit the murder of John Mendell?

Frank: No way. I only met Mr. Mendell maybe once, maybe twice. And it was over by Ronnie's house, when I was driving by, because I used to hang in the neighborhood, and would wave to him and he would wave back. I went over there and he introduced me. He says if you ever need any jewelry, this fella sells jewelry. John Mendell has a business in Skokie, or up on the north side.

Lopez: Did you know an individual by the name of Donald Renno and Vincent Moretti?

Frank: Donald Renno I met in Elmwood Park, he used to hang around there. Vincent Moretti I never met. There was a restaurant that I used to go to once in awhile that he used to be in there. It was in River Grove, on Belmont and Central [sic].

That did not sound right to me. I think Calabrese was wrong about the location. According to him, it was a Greek restaurant on the corner in a shopping center at Belmont and Central—but that would be in Chicago city proper. Belmont at Cumberland would have been River Grove—this is where Phil Tolomeo used to hang out. I know that for a fact. The name of the place was Dappers.

"My brother worked for the Cook County Sheriff's Department and was stationed at Maybrook," Frank said. "And there was occasion he showed me police-type information, like a bulletin. They weren't for the public, these documents. I also learned about Vincent Moretti being killed through the newspaper. It was about the same time in 1978. I guess they found them both in a car. They talked about these type of things, it was all over the streets, different people would know about it, have different theories."

"Can you tell the jury," Lopez challenged, "did you strangle and slice their throats?"

"No."

Lopez continued. "What about July 2, 1980, the murder of William and Charlotte Dauber—do you know anything about that?"

"It was in the paper, on TV, too. John Drummond [a television crime reporter] did a nice story on it. There was big stories on there, all through the papers and in the TV—it was the headline. I wasn't in the area, Will County, to help anybody do that that day. No way."

Lopez asked Frank about the people he knew, how the process worked, how different assignments were made. He asked specifically about "earners" and people who do what is called "heavy work." Frank explained that "heavy work" means killing. Frank said he was an earner, but that he wasn't into the heavy work. He said that his earnings speak for themselves. "I made millions, so how would I have time to do this, I had too many responsibilities on the street, a lot."

"Did you know Butch Petrocelli?" quizzed Lopez.

"Yes, I did, he wasn't a friend of mine. I didn't like him."

"Did you murder him?"

"No way. He belonged to a particular group of individuals I just talked about. He was called the Wild Bunch from Talyor Street. He hung around a place called Momma Sue's, which was at Taylor and Loomis. He would constantly stick his nose up and try to take our things. We had a guy up on the South side that was running a card game. The card games—what happened is, you come to the game, they would buy the food, my friend would buy the food, and then we'd take so much out of the pot for each game. Sometimes the games would last a few days, and they weren't high-stakes. It was whatever they wanted to do at the table. This was before the gambling boats in Illinois, and before off-track betting—the games weren't really legal.

"If people wanted to play poker, organized poker, and they were gamblers and couldn't go to Vegas, there would be places here where they could participate in games. And also what they did in them games, in other words, sometimes they didn't have the money and they would play on credit. Nobody borrowed money, but they would owe the people they were playing on credit and pay them another time.

"These games made some good money. This is one of the reasons why I think Petrocelli and others would try to come in and take these games away—there's no doubt about it."

Lopez got to the point again. "Now, Frank, do you know who killed Butch Petrocelli?"

"No, I don't."

"Frank, let's talk about Michael Cagnoni—do you know who that is?"

"No, I don't."

"Does it look like anyone you know, after being shown Sketch #2?"

"No, I don't," Frank denied. "I did not kill businessman Michael Cagnoni with a bomb, as my brother testified to."

Frank, of course, was referring to the summer day in suburban Hinsdale when he allegedly blew Cagnoni's car on the expressway, as brother Nick had testified in detail.

He also denied his brother's account of how a blasting cap exploded in his hand during a trial run for the bombing. "I was served a search warrant, which required X-rays and it was a particle examination, and I was informed it was negative."

"Did you ever hold a detonator cap in your hand and have it blow up and blow a door off of a car? The man that was sitting right here would say it would blow your fingers off if you had one in your hand."

With that, Frank held his hands over his head and wiggled his fingers for the jury to see that he had no missing fingers. He also denied providing a remote starter unit for anyone to use in a bomb that blew up on June 24, 1981. "No way."

Frank explained further. "I never went to Michael Spilotro's and ask him for any of those devices, no way. I knew Michael Spilotro and I have been to his house in Williams Bay, Wisconsin. And I didn't participate in any arson in Fontana, in Lake Geneva, Wisconsin, and I don't know who did."

"The house in Williams Bay belonged to my father, which is not that far, just a few miles from Fontana. It's on the north shore, it's in Williams Bay. The house in question is in Fontana, that's Nick's house where he and his family would go. We bought it for a rental, to rent it out. I never instructed him to burn it."

"Did Michael Spilotro come to your house on more than one occasion?"

"No, just once."

"When they were there, did you discuss remote units with Michael?"

"No way."

"Did you yourself ever possess or order any type of remote starter units—computer starters?"

"I never ordered anything like that."

"Frank, did you ever travel from Cook County to Lake County on or about April 24th, and attempt to murder an individual?"

"No way. With a bomb—no way. That wasn't my M.O., my M.O. is loaning money."

"On July 23, 1983, I never pointed a carbine out the window at my brother as they unloaded shotguns into the car on Richard Ortiz. And prior to that I wasn't a part of any groups of individuals who traveled to a home in Cicero and attempted to shoot somebody on their backyard where Jimmy DiForti was—no way. And I never drove a car eastbound on Cermak road on July 23rd, 1983, away from a murder scene involving the victims Richard Ortiz and Arthur Marawski. No, I didn't."

"And finally, Mr. Calabrese—Big Stoop. On Sept. 24, 1986, did you formulate a plan with your brother and John "Apes" Monteleone to kill Johnny Fecarotta?"

"No way. Johnny was a good friend. I was under a doctor's care. I had a operation and got really sick in the '80s. Right before I was going through some tests, I was going real bad. I couldn't even keep my eyes open. In fact, I have records of all that stuff. The results of my illness affected my ability to earn money. It was slowing down, I didn't have the endurance, which I don't have anymore, that I had then. I had a pituitary tumor removed. It took many, many tests they ran on me before they can develop what was wrong, about three times a week, about a month or maybe even more. And there was a period of time I would be unable to do things. As a result of the operation, I turned it all over to my brother Nicky."

"Was there an agreement of any sort with him," Lopez asked.

"Well, I went to see Jimmy LaPietra, because Angelo was locked up at that time, he was incarcerated. Jimmy started taking over Angelo's business. He was the guy to see because he took over everything—all the business and all the interests that he had. I told Jimmy my condition, and he says to turn it over to Nicky, the whole thing. The condition which I was describing to the jury before, that condition affected my ability to be effective on the street. I then stepped back and Nicky took over.

"My brother Nicky took over the day-to-day operations of what was going on, but he screwed it all up. He was ruining the business I had. I think he ran it until around '89 when everything disappeared. All the money disappeared. He said he gave the money out and nobody was paying it no more.

"Nick described one of the incidents in regards to Philly Tolomeo when he was working for me. We were getting stiffed, no one was paying. Then before you know it, there was nothing, and the book died.

With that, the court adjourned for the weekend. Frank wished Judge Zagel a nice weekend.

"You have a nice weekend yourself, Mr. Calabrese."

I can't imagine Frank's weekend being especially nice, though in many ways I feel he relished the attention if not a stage to show off. After all, he was a top Outfit enforcer, and even though he was lying about it, the people who needed to know did. I also doubt whether Frank was intimidated by what was in store for the coming week, namely, his cross examination by Federal prosecutors. He would stick to his story, of course, but it would be less scripted, less predictable, and certainly more uncomfortable.

When Monday arrived, Frank was grilled about all the boasting to his son Frank, Jr. His response wasn't a bad effort. Frank said he lied to impress Frank, Jr., and gain his son's affections back from Nick Calabrese. Prosecutor John Scully pressed Frank for hours. Scully could not mask the look of sheer disgust on his face. I was very close, and I could see it, even feel it, as Scully leaned against the witness stand to crowd Frank and get into his head.

Scully played Frank, Jr.'s tapes over and over, pushing Frank hard on the stand. Frank kept his cool, but over the course of several hours began to lose his patience and then his composure. Finally, Frank showed his true colors, boiling over at the relentless pounding of questions from the government.

In one of the secretly recorded conversations, Senior appears to be referring to himself and another reputed killer as they took part in a mob hit together, repeatedly using the words "we" and "I" during the story. But Frank was ready with an explanation. According to him, those words simply didn't mean what they usually do.

Scully: Who is "we"?
Frank: It's not me.
Scully: So we is not you?
Frank: No, it's not.
Scully: So I is not I?
Frank: Correct.

Frank went on to deny his involvement in the car-bombing death of trucking executive Michael Cagnoni, even though Frank himself is on Junior's tape discussing in detail the blasting caps and transmitters. Frank even said he felt sorry for Cagnoni's widow when she herself had taken the stand earlier. "I was praying for the woman when she was up there," he said. I'm surprised he didn't tear up, too.

Referring to another tape, Frank said he had been lying to his son about stripping clothes off someone he killed and throwing lime on the body to decompose it.

"There was no lime. There was no body. There was no bones. There was nothing there."

As for Frank's own brother Nicholas, who also had testified at length describing hit after hit, Frank was both terse and condescending. "Lying like a pig," he explained.

When asked about a guilty plea Frank took in a 1997 loan sharking case, Frank said that the plea itself had not been fully explained to him. Frank should have just admitted the juice plea and conviction because he had been talking about that as his business all along anyway. But by discounting it, by blaming his former attorney for not explaining it to him, Frank was making a tactical error. The government pounced, threatening to call Frank's former attorney, Jeffrey Steinback, to come and testify. Normally attorney-client communications are privileged, but defendants can waive those privileges, sometimes by accident. Steinbeck would not be able to tell the jury whether Frank had ever admitted his own guilt to him, but Frank had put the extent of that attorney's explanation into issue, possibly creating a hole in the attorney-client shield. Still, Frank said that he didn't read the plea document and had not understood that he was pleading guilty to leading an Outfit crew that collected on juice loans by making threats.[10]

Scully moved forward, pushing Frank even further down a blind alley of deception, asking whether Frank had admitted to making "multiple extortionate extensions of credit." Calabrese said he didn't understand that plea, and that he never had looked at the allegation word for word. "I probably would've looked cross-eyed at myself," he said.

Scully: Did you know that Angelo and Jimmy LaPietra [who were brothers] were in the Outfit?

Frank: I knew they were affiliated in some way.

Scully: Did you know Angelo LaPietra was a capo?

Frank: I heard that.

Frank did admit to knowing Joey "the Doves" Aiuppa, but that was the extent of his knowledge or involvement.

Scully: Did you know that Joey Aiuppa was the head of the Chicago Outfit?

Frank: That I didn't know.

Perhaps even Frank realized how stupid that sounded, so he added a tag line: "I read about it."

Scully: Were you a burglar?

---

[10] The prosecution never did call Frank's former attorney Jeffrey Steinback to testify, however.

Frank: Yes. I was a thief when I was young. {But Frank also explained that he was not a home invader.}

Scully: Do you have any assets?

Frank: Yes. My son stole them.

Scully then asked if Frank's brother Nick was correct when he testified that Frank was part of the crew that did surveillance on bombing victim Michael Cagnoni.

"He's lying like a pig," Frank countered.

In a dramatic moment of derisive father-son contempt, Frank then pointed to Frank, Jr., who was in the courtroom, and then said, "That's my son. Ask him, he'd be *glad* to talk."

Frank continued, complaining that he had to pay off First Ward politicians in order to stay in business. The First Ward's connection to the mob is legendary, a legacy that has its roots in the old pre-Capone levy district days of downtown politics.

Frank had been fingered in at least 13 gangland slayings—and who knows how many others he may have been involved in over half a century, if not longer. But he steadfastly denied it all, every single one of them. Frank insisted he just had a money lending business that was independent of the Chicago mob. He did this, he said, by loaning money at high rates to gambling addicts who couldn't apply for traditional bank loans. I can't say he was lying about that one—that's pretty much how it works, although charging the exorbitant interest is a big part of it, not to mention the dark side of how to get repaid when the loan comes due—like when the Grieco boys kidnapped 6-year-old Mike Franchina for a day, suggesting his mother Dorothy take up prostitution to pay he husband's insurmountable debt. That, of course, had been the inspiration behind her husband Tony swallowing a bullet the hard way, the only way he knew to get out.

The practice of loan sharking, named for its predatory qualities, as we currently know it, has been around America for about 100 years. It first sprang up in big cities with factories that had workers with regular salaries, and originally took the form of paycheck lending where customers borrowed against their forthcoming payroll checks at inflated interest rates. In the old days it was not a crime; in fact there were few if any laws against it. Operators would operate from low profile store fronts, and at one time the practice was very common. Published sources suggest that during the early

Twentieth Century up to twenty percent of all American households had borrowed money in this manner.

With so much activity, though, the plight of the borrowers soon became a matter of national concern. Around the time of World War I, a new Uniform Small Loan Law attempted to regulate the practice. Many states adopted the law, and most had a version of it on the books by the middle part of the century. When the laws got tougher during the 1930s, much of the loan sharking activity was taken over by the underworld. At first the mob singled out small time borrowers and then intimidated them into paying at all costs, but soon the mob found itself preferring small business loans. These people had assets, business locations, and reputations, and it was easier to get repaid—plus the loans could be larger than the nickel-and-dime advances to pathetic small-time gamblers.

Some of the juice racket, ironically, has come full circle. Payday loans are now widely advertised by chains of lenders who specialize in the practice. They largely are able to navigate around the usury laws by charging a large check cashing fee, which makes it lucrative to "pre-cash" checks in advance of a customer's regular payroll. This practice actually cuts into potential mob business by taking away the small borrowers, but for those with bigger needs to fund drug or gambling habits, it can amount to a spiraling circle of destruction that perpetuates itself. To pay the first juice loan, the borrower has to get another loan from another lender, a process that repeats itself until something gives.

Frank Calabrese, the Grieco brothers, and scores of others have found the racket to be very lucrative over the years. As prosecutor John Scully forged ahead, and Frank eventually admitted to associating and doing business with members of the Chicago Outfit. But Frank continued to insist that he never took the oath of a so-called "made guy" and repeatedly maintained that he "never killed anybody."

Frank never fully denied his participation in the juice racket, though, and indeed testified about how he "had made millions," an argument he made under oath about having so little time to be a hit man on the side.

When Scully was through carving Frank up, leaving him an exposed broken old man and pathological liar, I wondered if Frank remembered the first thing he ever said to me, way back when he busted my lip at The Nest Lounge in 1958 when he didn't like my answer to his standard Chicago greeting, "What the fuck you lookin' at?"

Well, clearly I was "looking at Frank" once more, but this time I didn't see a cocky young hoodlum. Instead I saw what a life of crime on the streets of Chicago does to families, lives, and most of all, even to the most ruthless of the Outfit goons—the hit men enforcers who are feared but who also must live a life of fear, looking over their shoulders for the next hit—often their own. Frank outlasted all of it, to be sure, for he was still alive, a testament to his street savvy and obvious mob power. Yes, Frank Calabrese was alive, but he had no future.

And when you think about it, he didn't really have much of a past, either. Not one that counted, anyway. When all is said and done, it was all a big waste.

14

Strangers in the Night

When they wanted you dead, they got you dead.
                                        Nick Calabrese

Suburban Hinsdale businessman Michael Cagnoni, age 37, was a well-to-do trucking executive when he found himself in the middle of a dangerous mob dispute over truck routes and his cartage business, namely, who or what should control both. His mob ties went sour and Cagnoni knew he was in trouble, so he hired a bodyguard, carried a gun, and even began wearing a bulletproof vest—hardly the usual business attire for Chicago commerce. Except where the mob Outfit is concerned.

Cagnoni could feel the mob's presence among the quiet tree-lined streets of Hinsdale, an upscale suburb southwest of Chicago. He knew they were there—just not who or precisely where. So Cagnoni made himself unpredictable: he disguised his habits and made his daily routine difficult to track.

According to the sworn testimony of long time killer Nick Calabrese, the premier government witness during the Family Secrets trial, Cagnoni had already been deemed "uncooperative" and targeted for execution. An Outfit crew under the direction of Nick Calabrese began following Cagnoni, casing his routine and planning their hit.

According to Nick's testimony, Cagnoni and the mob had had a dispute about money, so reputed mobster Joe Ferriola was muscling in on Cagnoni's trucking business. But because Cagnoni had become more slippery than the usual target, the Calabrese crew members were forced to be more resourceful. Instead of deploying their usual tactics, which normally meant learning the victim's habits and routine well enough to engineer a precise execution, they decided to plant a "Godfather-style" bomb under the front seat of Cagnoni's green Mercedes.

The plan was simple enough: detonate the bomb by remote control as Cagnoni headed along Ogden Avenue to the expressway entrance of I-294 at Hinsdale. They rigged together a control device and tested it by using blasting caps to determine how close the remote trigger would have to be to detonate. They tried several times to orchestrate a viable trial run, without success, all while the crew tested various antennae to determine the optimum size to send the proper signal and even procuring an exact model of Cagnoni's car to practice unlocking the door. After several failed tests—nothing is easy, just try making a remote control bomb from scratch at home—the crew was finally ready. They set the murder scheme into motion and waited for the Mercedes to pass by, at which point it would be incinerated just as it reached the expressway.

On June 24, 1981, a typical summer day with Hinsdale's myriad old trees in bloom, birds chirping amidst the warm breezes, and the usual suburban hustle and bustle underway, Cagnoni's *wife* got into the car instead. She carefully placed their young son on the seat, buckled him in, and proceeded to drive to the local school unaware of the ridiculously crude instrument of death that lay just beneath. She pulled from the Cagnoni driveway with the boy, but by chance she headed away from the detonator instead of toward it. "This poor woman got in the car," Nick said from the stand, his voice beginning to shake of regret. "If she had come east, not west..." His words choked and he paused, his face showing a clear expression of concern. "I don't know what I felt." I was struck by his words. Remorse was not a common emotion among the mob faithful, especially executioners.

That same day, after Mrs. Cagnoni returned home safely in the Mercedes, Cagnoni himself took the car and left for his office located in an industrial area at 2608 S. Damen on Chicago's southwest side, exactly 26 city blocks south of the United Center where the Chicago Bulls and Blackhawks play. Cagnoni drove to Ogden Avenue, a main thoroughfare in Hinsdale, and then turned east toward the city and the expressway.

According to Nick, his brother Frank Calabrese trailed Cagnoni in a stolen 1974 black Buick. Frank drove ahead and positioned his car to observe Cagnoni and then detonate the bomb. As Cagnoni routinely drove onto northbound I-294 as he had done hundreds of times before, Frank coldly pulled the switch. Witnesses would later tell local police that they had seen a man, who apparently was "Frankie Breeze," as some called him, sitting in the same black Buick in the far side of the parking lot at a local upscale restaurant called The Cypress. When Frankie pulled the ignition switch, there was a quick flash of white smoke followed by a brilliant yellow explosion. What once was a Mercedes automobile was instantly blown in every direction, scattering twisted charred metal—and body parts—across a six-lane highway to the horror of passing motorists.

It was an incredible blast that rocked the normal hush of Hinsdale. It made an instant widow of Mrs. Cagnoni, of course, and it certainly conveyed a strong point about business with the mob—and that, after all, was the intended purpose. Cagnoni himself was strewn about the immediate area and far beyond. A day later, most of Cagnoni's right arm would be found in a wooded lot about 100 yards off the highway. Obviously, blowing a car in that manner, whether on a busy expressway or within the tranquil but bustling Hinsdale, was potentially very dangerous to legions of innocent people, whether Mrs. Cagnoni herself or other passersby. "Whoever prepared the explosive had to have some skill and some nerve," said a retired ATF supervisor who had investigated the case. "Once the bomb was in the car, a stray radio frequency could have set it off at any time." So Mrs. Cagnoni, after all, and for that matter half the village of Hinsdale, had been at risk that day in June—with dozens of lives just one slip away from becoming the unfortunate collateral damage of an Outfit dispute over money and power.

Nick Calabrese spoke clearly for the jury. He outlined how Cagnoni had first gotten into bed with gangsters because he felt they could help expand his business, which they in fact did. But everything has a price, and Cagnoni learned a simple mob truth the hard way, explained Nick, who definitely would know. "When they wanted you dead, they got you dead."

Ironically, Nick Calabrese found himself testifying on the witness stand years later, at the Family Secrets trial, for that very same reason. Notwithstanding his family ties to Frank, his longtime loyalty to the Outfit, and his record of successful hits and other mob business, Nick had been at risk for the botched execution of mobster John Fecarotta. According to sworn testimony of Frank Calabrese, Jr., Fecarotta himself had botched a hit on Las Vegas mob kingpin Tony "the ant" Spilotro and was slated for execution by Nick. But Nick almost blew that one, Fecarotta fighting Nick off in the attack before Nick tracked him down and finished him with a shot to the head. Later in prison, his brother Frank, Sr., actually told all this to his son in jail, who was already wired at the time by federal authorities. When the feds later played that tape for Nick Calabrese, Nick knew he was already dead, leaving him no real choice but to cut a deal, testify, and hope for the best.

Monday, July 16, 2007 (9:15AM)

Today Nick Calabrese would tell his chilling story of the Cagnoni car bomb in Hinsdale, and much more. The jury was largely unprepared for the breadth of mob malevolence they would soon hear. With the government about to unveil the testimony of its star witness in the Family Secrets trial, I arrived early to settle into my usual front row seat near the defense table of Calabrese and crime bosses Lombardo and Marcello. Although the testimony of Frank, Jr. had been dramatic for its insight and the obvious inner father-son conflicts, his uncle Nick Calabrese had been a much more active mob figure, a made man, and Outfit enforcer with a prolific intimate knowledge of mob inside activities over much of the last half-century. Nick's testimony, then, was highly anticipated and, like his account of the Cagnoni demise, would not disappoint.

I had punched the elevator button for the 25th floor as always, but when the doors opened I could barely exit. Something was clearly up—the lines were three deep outside courtroom 2525 with throngs of would-be onlookers pushing and squeezing closer, all competing for a chance at a courtroom seat. This was by far the largest hallway crowd since the start of the trial, for good reason, and this was just the overflow bunch. The courtroom itself was already jammed with spectators, family of the defendants, the press, and legions of security personnel. As I took my reserved seat in the front, I saw that every inch of the seating in that large courtroom was jam packed. FBI agents and federal marshals were lined up, too, filing most of the front two rows and providing a buffer between the defendants and the crowd, but specifically acting as a line of security for the witness Nick Calabrese to prevent other mobsters—maybe hit men—from getting anywhere near him.

Excitement spread through the air with a nervous buzz as the courtroom assumed the look and feel of a heavyweight fight from the old smoke-filled days of boxing, gambling, and mobsters. Notables were everywhere, and including prominent local trial lawyers, relatives of the victims, FBI brass, and even the top U.S. Attorney Patrick Fitzgerald. On the other side of the aisle were courtroom TV sketch artist Verna Sadock, the *Chicago Tribune's* Jeff Coen, Rob Olmstead from the *Daily Herald*, and many others, including my dear friend from 30 years in the trenches, John Drummond, a celebrated CBS Channel 2 crime reporter who's been around so long he actually played himself as a long-established newsman during press scenes in the acclaimed film *The Fugitive* many years before.

The artists waited nervously for the star of the show, witness Nick Calabrese, all eager to get their sketches going so they could finish in time for the evening news. A great deal of time passed before they got their wish, but eventually bailiff Ted Wiszowaty took center stage and commanded the courtroom with his customary "All rise, this Court resumes in session, so please be seated."

The atmosphere was thick with anticipation as the prosecutors announced their next witness. "The United States Government calls Nicholas William Calabrese." With that, Nick entered the courtroom with several hulking FBI agents at his side marching him to the witness stand where he was sworn in and seated.

Nick hardly appeared like a killer. At age 64, his white hair neatly parted, Nick wore rounded eye glasses and a grayish, almost white long sleeve shirt with white sweat pants. He looked much more like a typical senior citizen than a feared mob enforcer. With those sweat pants, he gave the appearance of one of those grandfathers in a group of mall walkers, speeding around the early morning hallways before slipping into McDonald's for their senior-discounted coffee.

I studied Nick closely. He seemed upbeat and anxious to begin his testimony. Perhaps this trial was a lifetime catharsis, or maybe it was just a big weight off his shoulders—though I think that selling out the most ruthless mob kingpins in Chicago would *add* considerable stress. Nick sat in the witness chair and stared straight ahead. His brother Frank glared back, looking Nick over while flashing a "knowing" smile. This was the second nightmare day in a week for Frank, who had just been carved up by his own son, but there he was, still smiling. Frank himself was accused of 13 Outfit murders, and defendant James Marcello, the current reputed to boss, allegedly had paid Nick $4000 per month to stay quiet while in prison.

I was anxious, too, thinking this testimony would be sweeping and fatal—to someone, possibly many—and perhaps slamming a last nail into the coffin of the mob as we know it. Nick focused at a darkened computer screen placed before him. He will soon be asked to identify people in a photo shown simultaneously on a screen behind him.

The moment he opened his mouth, Nick Calabrese commanded the entire courtroom. As Asst. U.S. Attorney Mitchell Mars began, there were no whispered conversations, no distant cell phones, no fidgeting or rustling of purses or papers. The gallery sat forward, motionless.

Nick expressed his understanding that he was testifying under a grant of government immunity. As part of his deal for cooperating, Nick will not be prosecuted for any of the 14 homicides that he will describe in detail. And if there are any resulting convictions, the government will recommend something less than life, which Nick surely would otherwise face.

Mars pressed forward. "Were you, in fact, what was known as a made member [of the Outfit]?"

"Yes," said Nick, began explaining the structure of the Outfit and its leadership. He told mesmerized jurors how the Outfit made money and how he had gotten his own start in the mob with his brother's help many decades ago.

Nick testified that he began cooperating with the government in January of 2002 after DNA evidence linked him to the 1986 murder of reputed mob hit man John Fecarotta.

"Did you in fact murder John Fecarotta?"

"Yes, I did. It was me, my brother Frank, and Johnny 'Apes' Monteleone [now deceased, natural causes]. We got the OK from Jimmy LaPietra, who was our capo [their captain]," Nick told the jurors.

This was stunning testimony about the inner workings of an admitted mob hit and, more remarkably, the nod from a top Outfit honcho that made it happen.

Mars continued his questioning and Nick admitted to various murders committed in conjunction with James "Jimmy" Marcello, one of the co-defendants, along with Paul "the Indian" Schiro, another co-defendant, as well as several others. Nick did not hesitate, offering a succinct "yes" each time another murder was described.

During a break, I studied Frank Calabrese at the defense table. He was leaning back in his chair, and seemed to be catching a quick snooze. Then he took off his glasses, cleaned and straightened them like a bored banker in a loan review session. It was as though he did not care at all, and something tells me he didn't. Frank was arrogant to a fault, not so much resigned to his likely fate of life in prison, but impervious to it.

When court resumed, Nick told how his brother Frank began working in the Outfit ahead of him. One day in May 1970, Nick got a call from brother Frank wherein Frank explained that he had gotten the OK from his mob supervisor for Nick to come and work for him within the mob organization. Nick told jurors how he learned the juice loan business from Frank, but that he had doubts about Frank's tactics since his brother was shorting the money he was supposed to be passing along to their supervisors.

"All that could lead to me and him, my brother Frank, getting killed," Nick said. Clearly Nick knew the ropes, that he was not entering what guys in my day called 'the life of Riley.' "If you got an order to go kill someone, you would have to do it," Nick explained.

Nick's unassuming appearance on the stand, the drama of his testimony, and the obvious danger he could now be in because of all this, gave him a sympathetic air. But I knew better, and occasionally reminded myself who Nick really was. Nick was a sick, sick killer who committed unspeakable acts, many of which would finally be recounted in open court. One time he even cut the head off a puppy and placed it in someone's car to send a message.

"When I'm on the stand, I can't lie," Calabrese emphasized to the jury, most of whom took notes throughout the first few hours of Nick's testimony. But I'm not sure the jury was ready for all the stark truth they were about to experience.

Tuesday, July 17, 2007 (10:00AM)

The next morning I again pushed through the crowded halls of the federal building and stopped to exchange pleasantries with Anne Wolf, Judge Zagel's secretary and my new best friend who made sure I was comfortable.

The prosecution had a big fish on the stand who would continue to mesmerize the court gallery. But Nick himself had been a vicious killer and mob insider, so the prosecutors were careful to maintain credibility by not sweeping such a brutal blemish under the rug. "It would be hard to come up with somebody more coldhearted than Nick Calabrese," they told the jury, reminding them of Nick's past but also inside knowledge and willingness to testify. The jury looked Nick over. Instead of the jogging outfit from yesterday, he was dressed in a pale collared shirt, untucked, with blue pants. Again, he should have seemed quite unassuming, but we all knew he was not.

"My brother told me we've got to put somebody in a hole," Nick began. The jam-packed gallery became hushed, and the jury turned to hear every word carefully. He explained that back in the summer of 1970, when Nick was still a young mob hopeful, Frank, Sr., announced they had to find a good location to dig a hole—for a body. Nick paused. At first the youthful Nick had thought his brother was kidding, like ribbing him with mob funny stuff, or at most that his brother was just testing him for a reaction. He soon learned it was no joke, and therefore if it was a test, it certainly wasn't hypothetical.

Nick's brother found a spot. It was inside a factory that was being built on the south side, a few blocks away from Comiskey Park, home of the Chicago White Sox baseball club. They located a convenient hole on the construction site, then left to get a shovel and two bags of lime. Nick told the story like it was just another day on the job which, I suppose, it was.

Nick shot a glance at his brother Frank who allowed a small smirk to emerge. Nick didn't even know the name of the man they were to murder, but he did know the victim was someone with too much knowledge who could potentially testify against Frank. The target turned out to be Michael "Hambone" Albergo, himself an Outfit enforcer who authorities had charged with mob loan sharking activity. With too much knowledge and already snared by the cops,

Albergo was more than expendable. Making matters worse, Albergo had once confided that if he ever were going to jail, he would not go alone—not exactly the kind of announcement that improves one's life expectancy where the Outfit is concerned. The situation was already out of control, for Albergo had been pinched for making illegal loans to undercover cops—a kiss of death for him.

Frank, Sr.'s close friend, the late Ronald (Ronnie) Jarrett, was also friends with Albergo. Ronnie lured Albergo into a four-door Chevy that Jarrett had stolen specifically for the hit. Jarrett proceeded to pick up the Calabrese brothers who sat in back with Albergo in the front passenger seat. Nick said it was a hot sunny day in August of 1970 when they all drove over to the targeted factory construction site. Once there, Jarrett, who was driving, suddenly grabbed Albergo's left arm. Nick reached from the back and immediately clutched the other arm. As they struggled, brother Frank wrapped a rope around the victim's neck, then strangled him as Albergo flailed and gasped for air. Nick was calm and kept his composure while telling the gruesome details for the jury, occasionally gesturing with his hands to make a point.

"Did he kill him?" asked prosecutor Mars.

"Yes," Nick said. He also explained how Frank then slashed the dead guy's throat, too.

"Do you know why your brother did that?"

"Just to make sure he was dead."

After removing the body's pants, they dumped him into the hole they had dug, then threw in the two bags of lime, refilling the hole with dirt. "At this point I wet my pants I was so scared," Nick told the stunned courtroom. But his brother Frank didn't catch on to that mishap because "I had a lot of dust and dirt on my pants so you really couldn't tell."

The prosecutor then asked Nick if he saw his brother Frank in the courtroom. Nick raised his left hand and pointed. Frank Calabrese, Sr., had been fingered by his own brother, by the secretive mob itself, in open court.

Nick said it would be years before he learned who they had murdered that day. He realized it had been "Bones" Albergo when, years later, he saw a photo in a pamphlet from the watchdog Chicago Crime Commission. In 2003 the FBI tore up the site, which now is a parking lot near Comiskey. It must have been a popular place, because dozens of bone sample turned up. Oddly, none were linked to Albergo, whose remains were never officially found.

Nick recounted how his brother was fond of talking in code and that he told Nick never to mention the murder by name. Frank told him to always refer to the slaying as "It." After all, he reasoned, "it" could be anything.

The prosecutors next focused on Paul Haggerty, age 27 in 1976, already a loser, who at the time was a former convict living in a Chicago halfway house. Haggerty had run afoul with the Outfit bosses who were eager to question him about his dealings with a suburban jewelry store. When Nick arrived at his brother Frank's house in suburban Elmwood Park, Frank's greeting was succinct. "Don't make any plans, we're gonna be busy." As Nick recounted the story, I noticed he refused to look in his brother's direction in the courtroom. I was about to learn why.

For weeks, Nick and Frank followed Haggerty with a hit team that included Frank "Gumba" Saladino and Ronnie Jarrett, nicknamed "Menz," the Italian word for half because Jarrett was half Italian and half Irish. The crew relentlessly watched Haggerty's movements as they tailed him to the bus and work. One day they struck, snatching Haggerty off the streets and into a stolen car. Haggerty struggled and frantically gripped the car roof while Frankie Breeze and Saladino punched and dragged him into the back seat. Once under control, they drove Haggerty to the garage of Ronnie Jarrett's mother-in-law.

Haggerty was cuffed and questioned in the garage, then they left him alone for a period of time with his mouth and eyes taped. Nick later gave Haggerty some water and helped him use the bathroom, after which the others returned to finish the job. "I held him and Ronnie held him," Nick said, "and my brother [Frankie] strangled him with a rope." Once again, just another day at the office.

The murder of John Mendell, though, proved anything but routine. As a matter of fact, the Mendell tale is one of the dumbest acts of mobster folly I had every encountered in all my years on the force. Mendell was the mob expert in electronics, but he was also a prolific jewelry thief. According to court records, especially one FBI witness whose name was blacked out of the file, Mendell headed a crew that burglarized many thousands of dollars in valuables from Levinson's Jewelry. Owned by Harry Levinson, the store was a major jewelry establishment with a big name in the Chicago area.

Most unfortunately for Mendell, Harry, who was not a mobster himself, counted Tony "Big Tuna" Accardo among his friends (perhaps Accardo was a significant customer of the store). As noted in prior chapters, at the time there was no bigger Chicago boss than Antonio Accardo, whose mob roots extended back to the Al Capone empire. At age 20 he had been recruited into the crew of mob enforcer "Machine Gun" Jack McGurn in 1926, after which Accardo continued to rise in the organization. Eventually he rose to a prominent position in the mob around 1943, running day to day operations. By 1972, Accardo had become the top boss of the entire Chicago crime syndicate, a post he held for twenty years until died of congestive heart failure in 1992.

When John Mendell knocked off Levinson's Jewelry in 1978, Accardo was at the peak of his power. Word has it that Harry Levinson personally asked if Tony would look into what had happened and, if possible, get the jewelry back. When Mendell learned that the top mob brass was angry and considering action, Mendell hid the loot in the rafters at his own place of business, then went into hiding.

Within weeks, mob operatives broke into Mendell's business, discovered the stolen jewelry, and re-stole it. This was more than Mendell could swallow—after all he had already stolen the stuff himself, fair and square—so Mendell led "his fucking crazy crew" on a mission to steal it back again. Unfortunately, by then the loot was stashed in Tony Accardo's sprawling mansion in River Forest, just west of Chicago. Later an undisclosed government witness confirmed the jewelry was stored in a walk-in vault within the Accardo residence. When the Mendell crew heard all the details of their mission, many of them wanted no part of it and backed out.

Mendell and some of the crew did eventually break into the Accardo mansion while he was away, a deadly act of stunning stupidity. Though Mendell insisted to the end he was only trying to get back what was his own "rightfully stolen" property, six members of that crew, including Mendell, would soon be tracked down and murdered.

According to Nick's testimony, the mob summoned Ronnie Jarrett, whom Mendell trusted, to lure Mendell to his death. Jarrett managed to take Mendell to the same garage where Paul Haggerty had been beaten and killed—the one belonging to Jarrett's mother-in-law.[11] This time, Nick said, he and his brother Frank, Sr., Jarrett, and mob hit man Frank Saladino carried out the brutal murder.

Nick supplied many details. John Mendell was beaten without mercy, his body punctured with an ice pick. Frankie strangled the hapless Mendell with a rope, but this time Frank added a sudden twist. "My brother handed me the knife and said 'you do it'," Nick explained. Prosecutor Mars asked if he performed as instructed. "Yeah, yes, I did." Frank was asking Nick to "do the honor" of slashing Mendell's throat after he had already been strangled—something of a trademark for Frank. Eventually, Mendell was found dead in the trunk of his car in Chicago, duly mutilated as a message from the Outfit.

The break-in at Accardo's house terrified the rank and file who knew about it. Mendell had clearly lost his mind, and before it was over Mendell and five others who were in on the caper would all be dead. One government witness who was NOT involved, a known career burglar with ties to Mendell, got wind of the mob retaliation plans. He was so concerned that Accardo would finger him among "the usual suspects" that he went to Accardo himself and offered to take a polygraph exam to show he had nothing to do with either offense—the burglary against Accardo or the original hit on Levinson's Jewelry. He passed the test and the Outfit heat on the relieved witness ended.

Others were not so lucky, including Vincent Moretti, a thief who was lured to a closed restaurant in Cicero in the wake of the Accardo burglary. He was strangled right there on the premises by brothers Nick and Frankie Calabrese while they played the Frank Sinatra hit "Strangers in the Night" on the jukebox. Frank wrapped the rope around Moretti's neck and pulled while Nick braced his foot against Moretti's head and yanked the other end until he was dead.

---

[11] Will his mother-in-law ever look at that garage the same way again? One can't help but wonder whether this woman had any clue how her garage was utilized. Assuming she did NOT know, which I think is more likely, she certainly must have been stunned when word got back regarding Nick's detailed testimony.

Another victim that night in the restaurant was Donald Renno who was not involved in the Accardo matter at all. Unfortunately, Renno was Moretti's companion that night and got swept into the hit just because he was there. Both men were beaten and strangled, then their throats were slashed Frankie-style before their bodies were dumped in the back seat of their Cadillac.

Frankie, who liked to speak in code, dubbed the killings as "strangers in the night," which is how he and Nick would forever refer to the double hit.

From the Cagnoni car bomb to Comiskey Park, mother's garage, Accardo's house, and "strangers in the night," Nick had already recounted years of mob mayhem. But he was just warming up.

Later, John Malooly, a former agent with the Federal Bureau of Alcohol, Tobacco, Firearms, and Explosives would revisit the Cagnoni murder as he testified against Frank, Sr. at trial. Malooly told how he had recovered parts of an explosive device used in the 1981 car bombing of trucking businessman Michael Cagnoni. Malooly caught the jury's attention when he said the device "... was still transmitting" when he found it.

Recalling that Nick Calabrese had testified that a blasting cap had gone off in brother Frank's hands in preparation for the Cagnoni hit, Frank's attorney Joe Lopez cross examined Malooly and asked about such a blast. Malooly said that an incident like that could cost someone his fingers, prompting Frank, Sr. to raise his hands for the courtroom to see—Frank's fingers were still there.

15

The Godfather of Las Vegas

Bill and Charlotte Dauber were a husband-wife couple executed by the Outfit in 1980. Nick Calabrese was not in on the hit, nor did he witness it, but he testified in detail about how his brother Frankie Calabrese had carried out the double murder.

Bill Dauber had been a suburban "chop shop" operator, dismantling stolen cars and selling the myriad parts onto the black market. He had been with the Chinatown crew since the old days of Jimmy "the Bomber" Catuara. When Catuara muscled in on the gambling and nightclub operations at the south end of Cook County, he had used Dauber as his lead soldier. In 1970 he tried to force a salvage operator to pay the Chinatown Crew street tax. Urged on by his attractive but loose-lipped and bitter wife Charlotte, Dauber began to badmouth the bosses and complain endlessly that he wasn't appreciated for his skills as an enforcer.

Dauber didn't know when to let up, so he continued bellyaching and soon fell into the bad graces of syndicate bosses Butch Petrocelli and Jerry Scalise who wanted Dauber dead anyway because they sensed he may have been cooperating with the government after an arrest on cocaine and gun charges. Nick said his brother Frank, Jerry Scalise, Butch Petrocelli, Gerry Scarpelli, and Ronnie Jarrett found the Daubers as the couple left the Will County Courthouse to drive home in Crete, Illinois. Frank caught up, then used his own car to cut off the Daubers. At that point, a van driven by Jerry Scalise pulled up along the Dauber vehicle allowing Butch Petrocelli to fire a 30-caliber semi-automatic at the Daubers, killing both of them within seconds. But to be sure they were dead, Scarpelli, with his own face concealed by a ski mask, walked up to the car and riddled the couple with a shotgun. Their bodies would eventually be found sprawled across the front seat of their Oldsmobile with three of its windows blown out and its front end crushed against a tree.

Fred Bruno Barbara is a wealthy businessman and a friend of Mayor Daley, but according to Nick Calabrese he was active in mob business. He was arrested a number of times, including a 1982 arrest for extortion in an FBI sting that included his cousin Frank "Tootsie Babe" Caruso. Barbara was acquitted in that case and has never actually been convicted of any crime. Nonetheless, Nick also testified about some of Barbara's alleged activities. Prosecutors have indicated that Barbara was "believed to be a major participant" in the illegal gambling operation run by LaPietra. Complicating matters, Barbara is a nephew of the late Chicago Alderman Fred Roti of the First Ward, a district with a notorious mob history. Roti himself had been tied to the mob and even identified as a made member himself.

According to Nick, Barbara supposedly teamed up with Angelo "the Hook" LaPietra and James DiForti to bomb Horwarth's Restaurant in Elmwood Park, a well known hangout for Outfit members. Nick fingered Barbara as one of six men who were split into teams to throw bombs on the roofs of two restaurants, including Horwarth's. Nick, though, had not personally witnessed the Horwarth bombing, but he did personally participate in a second restaurant hit and compared notes with those who had attacked Horwarth's.

Nick testified that on the same night as the Horwath bombing, he had joined up with his brother Frank, Sr., and reputed Outfit killer John "Big Stoop" Fecarotta to throw a bomb onto the roof of Tom's Steakhouse in Melrose Park. Nick said he was not officially informed why the mob brass had targeted Tom's, but he did confirm that he was place in charge of the bombing. "I lit the fuse in the bag," he testified. "I got out of the car and jumped up on a dumpster. I threw the device near an air conditioning unit on the roof and it exploded."

Nick was also part of a team that placed an explosive device against a wall of the Drury Lane Theatre in Oakbrook Terrace in the 1980s before it had opened. That crew included brother Frank, John Fecarotta, James DiForti, and of course himself. The prosecutor asked whether that device went off. "Yes, it did," Nick answered. "We talked about how loud it was."

But if Nick had not witnessed the bombing of Horwarth's Restaurant, how did he know who was involved? After both establishments were bombed that night, both demo teams met back at Fecarotta's hotdog stand in Melrose Park to compare notes. There the Horwarth crew made it clear that their bomb had indeed gone off.

Although he was not privy to the official motives for those hits, Nick speculated that they may have been related to the mob street taxes imposed as "protection" on legitimate neighborhood businesses. Nick himself would sometimes bring along "Gumba" Soladino, who was six feet tall and weighed around 300 pounds, to collect late payments on another mob activity: juice loans. "I told him [Soladino] you just stand behind me and don't say nothing, just look at the guy. Give him one of those looks." With "Gumba" in tow, Nick warned the hapless debtor that the "5% a week" loans weren't going away and that "next time I'm not gonna come, he's going to come," all while pointing at the imposing giant behind him.

Juice loans were good profit centers for the mob. Nick told jurors about a variety of activities he conducted with brother Frank, including the juice loans, but also the street tax angle and, of course, gambling operations. Frankie, in fact, had hundreds of thousands of dollars to lend "on the street" at exorbitant rates of interest. When Frank heard Nick say that in court, he rocked back in his chair, covered his mouth, and giggled. Nick said Frank had so much cash that his brother once lost almost $500,000, forgetting that he had it stashed in a safe deposit box. Frankie, Nick said, had about $1.6 million squirreled away in several safety deposit boxes in banks throughout Chicago but had completely forgotten about one of them.

The misplaced half-million bucks came to light one night when Frank became concerned and told Nick "there is a lot of money missing." Nick replied, "What's that got to do with me?" Nick then reminded his brother that at one of the banks he had reserved two boxes, not just one. Presto—the missing cash turned up.

Hoarding, loaning, and tracking such vast sums of cash presented many problems for the mob. Forgetting where it was hidden was just one of those issues. Nick had the courtroom in stitches when he told the hapless story of another stash buried in Wisconsin. Frankie had buried $250,000 in gambling and extortion cash in a steel box on a parcel of property that Frank had in Williams Bay,

Wisconsin, situated on Lake Geneva, a popular local hang-out north of Chicago—sort of a poor man's Lake Tahoe, sans the mountains but noticeably closer.

One day Frank went looking for the stash and dug up the box. It was a disaster. The case was wet, mildewed, and smelled bad enough to choke a mule. Frank brought the reeking cash back, and Nick said they tried everything to fix the stench. They even spread cologne on it, "but that made the smell worse." Nick said they eventually got rid of the disgusting loot by filtering it back into the system, loaning it to customers at 5 points per week. Nick said that the juice collections had to be split 50-50 with their mob boss Angelo LaPietra. Nick said that sometimes he drove the payments to LaPietra's Bridgeport[12] garage, stuffing the envelope into a large cooking mitt used for outdoor BBQ's. The mitt was hung on a nail, and Nick would flip it over, pointing the thumb in the opposite direction, to alert LaPietra of the hidden cash.

As the third day of Nick's testimony began, his voice remained quiet, resolute, but with little emotion as Nick continued to paint stunning word pictures of the Outfit crime family. Brother Frankie was responsible for killing mob hit man Butch Petrocelli for being "too flamboyant." In my own decades of mob experience, calling undue attention to the Outfit was always a sign of trouble—usually followed by death. Reckless egos may have brought down more mob figures than any other single cause, and Butch Petrocelli was no exception.

In 1980 Petrocelli through a sparking Christmas party at an exclusive Gold Coast hotel in Chicago. The over-the-top party was filled with hookers and mobsters, but that was not the biggest problem. It also featured a night long rant by Petrocelli, who boasted how he would one day be head of the Outfit. Current mob bosses were hardly impressed. To make matters worse, those same bosses began to suspect Petrocelli had skimmed collection money and shaken down a group of robbers without mob permission. Butch was called

---

12 Bridgeport is a Chicago city neighborhood, very white, very ethnic (especially Irish Catholic), and stocked with politicians and other bosses. It was the home of the original Mayor Daley, has been the home of the White Sox for over a century, and is now laced with row houses, tree lined streets, and ethnic taverns.

to a meeting in December 1980 where he was questioned, tortured, and murdered, his body eventually discovered in the back seat of his own car parked in the 4300 block of West 25th Street in Cicero almost three months later on March 15, 1981. The body was stuffed into a sleeping bag, and Petrocelli's face was charred, possibly from an acetylene torch.

Mob hit men are an enigma. The mob relies on them for muscle and executions, but those same people can easily get out of control—reading their own press clippings, so to speak. Petrocelli himself had been a feared killer, and the bosses were always on edge where he was concerned. Then he drew attention to himself with that party and all the boasting just when he was starting to dip into mob coffers without permission. He created a street tax in boss Joe Ferriola's name, which Ferriola knew nothing about, then withheld $100,000 in collected cash for himself. A bold move—but certainly not smart. The burglar crew that had to pay the tax complained to Outfit bigwig Jerry Scarpelli, to whom they were already paying a "legitimate" street tax. Scarpelli, a particularly unstable and violent mob figure, flew into a rage and drove to boss Ferriola's house at 3:00am for an immediate explanation. Ferriola, who had been sound asleep, answered the door in his boxer shorts. He was dumbfounded when he heard the story, and he immediately told Scarpelli that he never authorized such a tax and never worked with Petrocelli. Ferriola said he would look into it. Petrocelli then disappeared—for three whole months—until his charred body finally turned up.

According to brother Frankie, mobster Angelo "The Hook" LaPietra had burned Petrocelli's face with a torch. Surgical tape had been applied across Petrocelli's mouth, his throat was than slashed, after which he was fried. Angelo "The Hook" was the right man for the job. Standing about 5'5" with thick glasses and heavy lidded eyes, Angelo had earned a reputation for hanging enemies from meat hooks while torturing them to death.

Frank Calabrese, Sr., was a major mob operative and nearly always in the know. Once he tried to stop his friend Anthony Borcelino from being killed. Frank told the story of Borcelino to his son Frank, Jr., while they both were in jail, one of the many conversations secretly recorded by the feds. Butch Petrocelli had arranged for Borcelino, his rival, to be executed. "Butchie was a no good motherfucker," Frank said on tape—echoing the apparent feelings of Joe Ferriola who eventually ordered the hit on Butch. Frank, Sr., went to his own boss, Angelo "The Hook," to get the hit stopped. "I tried everything to save him," Frank told his son. Well, almost everything. "The Hook" came up with a solution, and offered to save Borcelino if Frankie would take his place. Borcelino was gunned down in 1979—but Petrocelli was already using up favors and mob goodwill, none of which helped when the mob finally had had enough after the infamous 1980 Christmas party.

As it happens, Frankie himself got the last laugh. LaPietra initially set Petrocelli up, sending him to a nearby office in Bridgeport. "Here he comes," said one of the waiting mobsters inside. Nick Calabrese was there. "It happened so fast, he was on the ground," Nick testified. "I remember holding him down, and my brother choking him." Helping out was Jimmy LaPietra and Frank Santucci. Outside waiting in cars were Frank Furio and Johnny "Apes" Montelione. Nick knew it was his brother who later cut Petrocelli's throat—after all, that was Frankie's trademark. Petrocelli's body was driven away, and Nick himself was in charge of burning the corpse.

Nick found a convenience store and bought two cans of Zippo lighter fluid, then emptied both cans into the car. "I threw a book of lit matches into the car and took off." Frank, Sr., who was supervising from a post nearby, scolded Nick. "You were supposed to leave a window open." With the car closed up, the windows were simply blackened, but the car itself failed to catch fire. The botched incineration did not sit well with boss Angelo LaPietra, who was concerned that Petrocelli may have somehow survived that attack and could still be alive. He needn't have worried, Nick told the jury. After the body was eventually found, Ferriola himself showed up at Petrocelli's funeral offering condolences and inspiring much insider snickering at the services.

Interesting as all these hits may have been, they are not nearly as compelling as a hit on a higher up figure—a mob boss. Nick witnessed the beating death of Nick D'Andrea who was tortured to generate information about the attempted shooting of mob boss Alfred Pilotto. D'Andrea, a 49-year-old Chicago Heights resident, known drug dealer, and an associate of reputed hoodlum Albert Tocco, was found dead in September 1981 in the trunk of his burned-out Mercedes near far south suburban Crete, Illinois. There was speculation that Tocco had been suspected of ordering the murder in connection with the attempted assassination of Pilotto, a south side boss.

On paper, Pilotto was president of Laborers Local #5. Unofficially, though, he was a noted Outfit boss of the Chicago south side suburbs. Pilotto extended the Melrose crew activities into vice and gambling, most of it centered in the Calumet area in the far south suburbs. In early 1981, Pilotto was indicted on a RICO charge for accepting kickbacks from an insurance company seeking to do business with the Laborers pension and benefit plans. Some in the Outfit assumed Pilotto would cut a deal with the government, putting the south side crew at risk. Pilotto's son-in-law, Salvatore Tricario, a Florida union official, had also been indicted, and wanted Pilotto dead. On July 28, 1981, Pilotto was playing golf at the 8th hole of the Lincolnshire Golf Club in Crete when a masked gunman suddenly stepped out from the nearby bushes and shot him five times. This was a remarkably bold act, because at the time Pilotto was playing a round with his brother Henry, the police chief of Chicago Heights.

The gunman, Danny Bounds, later reported that "I fired the first shot and it hit Pilotto in the shoulder. I came up out of the bushes and he turned and fell and looked at me and said 'please don't shoot.' I stood over him and shot three more times at close range. Five feet, six feet at most." Incredibly, Pilotto survived the attack. Bounds, the shooter, realized he was a dead man for not finishing the job, and scrambled to enter the witness protection program where he was free to tell his story.

Pilotto's own bodyguard, Sam Guzzino, who had masterminded the hit, was later found shot to death in a ditch. His throat had also been slashed. Pilotto was eventually convicted in the RICO case, then sentenced to serve 20 years in the federal prison at Sandstone, Minnesota, where he remained until his death in 1999. The Outfit, though, had made its point with the deaths of both D'Andrea and Guzzino—boss executions were high stakes and heavily disfavored.

Altogether, Nick Calabrese would take jurors through more than a dozen mob hits, mostly in gruesome detail, including two where he himself had been the trigger man. But no story proved more compelling than the high profile mob presence in Las Vegas that resulted in the brutal slayings of the virtual godfather of Vegas, one of the most colorful but out of control mob figures in Anthony "the Ant" Spilotro.

The original plan was to eliminate Tony Spilotro in Las Vegas, so a team of hit men was dispatched to Nevada. There was just one problem: they could not find Spilotro in Vegas. That was particularly bad news for Emil Vaci, age 73, a long time friend of Paul "the Indian" Schiro who the mob felt knew too much about the mob skimming operations at various Las Vegas casinos. Rather than return to Chicago empty-handed, the assassins took a detour to Phoenix to search for Vaci—all except for John "Big John" Fecarotta who skipped Phoenix and returned to Chicago. I never fully understood why Fecarotta did that, but as it happens his diversion back to Chicago did not sit well with Frank Calabrese, Sr., who had been seeking permission from the bosses to kill Fecarotta.

According to testimony of Nick Calabrese, four killers were left to hunt down Vaci, Nick Calabrese, James DiForti, Joey Hansen and Paul Schiro. They parked a van next to Vaci's Pontiac on June 6, 1986, then just waited for him to return, which they expected to occur sometime between 10:00pm and 11:00pm. Nick and Hansen hid the van while Schiro and DiForti were assigned lookout duty watching for the police. Nick left the van door open a crack so he could move fast when Vaci returned.

As expected, Vaci showed up. When Vaci was between his own car and the van, the hit was on. Nick explained what happened. "So I moved quickly, jumped out, and snatched Vaci, and had a difficult time with him." Vaci, even at age 73, put up such fuss that Joey Hansen had to help muscle Vaci into the van. According to Nick, Vaci actually thought he was being robbed, begging Nick to take his wallet. Then he started to get the real picture. Nick went on, "Then he says 'Oh no. I promise I'm not going to say anything.'" But Nick never gave an answer. Instead, he raised a .22 caliber revolver to Vaci's face, then pulled the trigger. But the gun jammed. While Vaci grew more nervous, Nick hit the gun and adjusted the clip trying to get it to work.

"What did you do then?" asked the prosecutor Mitch Mars. Nick paused slightly. "I shot him in the head," he answered. "I thought he was dead." But while Hansen drove the van away out of the lot there were more shots fired. Nick and Hansen ditched the gun, but they were terrified driving around Phoenix with a dead body. They wanted to rid themselves of Vaci as soon as they could. Although they had dug a grave in the desert outside of town, they did not want to chance getting caught along the way. Then they got confused driving around trying to improvise, taking a wrong turn and getting lost. The pair stopped the van, wrapped the body in a plastic bag and dumped it in a nearby dry water canal. Anxious to get out of town, they drove straight back to Phoenix that night.

Vaci had been a trusted associate of the Chicago Outfit whose primary responsibility was to skim millions of dollars from the Stardust Casino and Hotel in Las Vegas. Vaci was a big enough figure to earn a place in Scorcese's film "Casino," where he was portrayed by John Nance as the man with free reign of the casino counting room. Eventually Vaci was indicted for his role in the skim operation. Vaci was a dependable guy, and no one in the mob really believed he would break his silence even in the face of jail time, but still, the stakes were very high and Vaci knew so very, very much about who was in on the skim, how much was skimmed off, who delivered the cash, and where it was invested. He simply knew everything—and that made him dangerous.

In 1986 a federal grand jury subpoenaed Vaci, but true to form he refused to cooperate. Then the prosecution granted him immunity and upped the ante, compelling Vaci to testify or face contempt charges. The Outfit got nervous.

Vaci's ultimate death warrant came because he helped to hide a suspected Stardust slot skimmer named Jay Vandermark, who at one time had been the slot machine manager at the Freemont Casino. In 1976, both Vandermark and the estimated $7 million that he had embezzled, suddenly disappeared. Vandermark had successfully fled to Mexico, but he made the critical mistake of returning to the United States to hide out with Emil Vaci. Word of that reunion reached the mob bosses, and it was assumed that Vaci and Vandermark had been partners in the theft.

The Feds soon followed the Vandermark trail. By watching Vandermark's son Jeff, a Las Vegas casino employee, the FBI traced Vandermark to Mazatlan, Mexico, where he was living in a trail camp under the name of Steven Brown. But before official extradition could be made, the son was beaten to death with a hammer in his Las Vegas apartment. Dead or alive, his father, the elder Vandermark, has never been found.

Nick told jurors that he did not know officially why he was sent to Phoenix to kill Vaci, but he did know that Vaci was supposed to testify before a grand jury about someone who had skimmed money and run away. Nick also said that one of his mob superiors, James LaPietra, had told him that Vaci could hurt LaPietra with his testimony.

Nick testified that when he arrived at Phoenix, he met up with alleged mob killing machine Frank Schweihs, hit man John Fecarotta, and a third man nicknamed "Porky" whose real name is Fred Parclyla. Nick, though, said that he, himself, had been the gunman who shot Emil Vaci. He said that Fecarotta was supposed to be involved, too, but that he became skittish about the hit and headed back to Las Vegas.

Before recounting the dramatic Spilotro hit, Nick took a breather from his stories of mob executions to describe how he, himself, had become a "made man" in the Outfit. He had been driven to a restaurant on Roosevelt Road in Chicago where he sat before a table of Outfit kingpins, including boss Joey "the Doves" Aiuppa. Spread out before him were a gun, a knife, and a candle. Aiuppa threw a burning religious card onto the palm of Nick's hand and had Nick repeat the phrase, "If I give up my brothers, may I burn in hell like this old picture."

The ceremony was not particularly profound, but it certainly was ironic. There sat Nick Calabrese doing just that, testifying against anyone and everyone, giving up "his brothers" one after another, including he story of how Tony Spilotro met his demise—set up by a promised "made man" ceremony for his brother.

The Spilotro murder is one of the most infamous Outfit killings in Chicago mob history, a storied past that includes the St. Valentine's Day Massacre and countless Capone hits from the old days. Although Nick had admitted to participating in no fewer than 14 mob murders, many with his brother Frank, Sr., as it happens Frankie was not in on the Spilotro hit. But Nick was there, and he knew plenty.

In 1986, Joe Ferriola took over leadership of the Chicago mob. The FBI had gotten word that Ferriola was "cleaning house" to get rid of those in the Outfit who he felt could not be trusted, were a danger to him, or were no longer productive. At the top of that list was his own Las Vegas enforcer Anthony "the Ant" Spilotro.

Tony Spilotro was just 34 years old when he had arrived in Vegas in 1971 as the local Outfit representative and enforcer, a position that made him, in effect, one of the most powerful hoods in the country. But Spilotro was ill-suited for the job. He was a little man, hence the nickname "the ant," who was portrayed by the unnerving performance of Joe Pesci in the film "Casino."[13] Spilotro was both volatile and violent, a dangerous combination. In the past, the Vegas enforcers would kill only upon orders, but Spilotro seemed to solve every problem with murder, and that brought unnecessary heat on the mob activities. By 1986, the FBI suspected Spilotro of no fewer than 25 murders.

Spilotro was a native Chicagoan, the fourth of six children. His parents were immigrants who arrived in America from Italy in 1914. Spilotro's father ran Patsy's Restaurant, a notorious mob hangout often visited by the likes of Sam Giancana, Jackie Cerone, Gussie Alex, and Frank "the Enforcer" Nitto. Much later, upon direct examination at the Family Secrets trial, Joey Lombardo's counsel would ask Joey about his history with Patsy's. [see "The Last Supper"]

In 1962, Tony hooked up with Frank "Lefty" Rosenthal, a bookmaker. Eventually Tony was introduced to a number of key mob figures like Joey "the Doves" Aiuppa and Joey "the Clown" Lombardo, before joining a crew headed by Sam "Mad Sam" DeStefano. Tony rose quickly, becoming a "made man" in the mob by 1963.

By 1971, Tony was reunited in Las Vegas with old friend Lefty Rosenthal who ran several casinos for the Outfit, including the Stardust. A year later Spilotro found himself under indictment for the murder of Leo Foreman, a real estate agent and loan shark who pushed the envelop by throwing Mad Sam DeStefano out of his office back in 1963, the same year Tony became a "made man." Sam lured Foreman to Sam's home on Sayre Avenue on the pretext that Sam wanted to apologize to Leo so the two could "renew their good working relationship." Leo went for the bait, but clearly should have known better—but, once again, too often these guys would let their egos get the best of them. Leo thought it entirely possible that Mad Sam DeStefano would want to apologize to him.

The Foreman murder was a case that I personally worked on out of Area 4 Maxwell Homicide. It was an especially gruesome hit, and I am still amazed how Foreman had fallen for the trap.

What remained of Leo Foreman was eventually found in the trunk of his car at 5208 W. Gladys Avenue. He had been beaten with

---

[13] Some sources suggest "the Ant" originated with FBI agent William Roemer who referred to Spilotro as "that little pissant."

a baseball bat, stabbed several times with an ice pick, and then shot. We found out later that while he was dying and still bleeding, Foreman had pleaded with Mad Sam to spare him. Sam's reply was to the point. "I told you I'd get you."

When Leo arrived at Sam's house, they were met by Sam's brother Mario. Leo owed Sam $1000, but that was not the biggest problem. They drove the surprised Leo Foreman to Mario's house in Cicero—at gunpoint. There they all met up with Tony Spilotro and another hood, Charlie "Chuckie" Crimaldi. Foreman was forced into the basement where they beat him with a hammer, actually cut flesh out of his body, and then busted his knee caps. Crimaldi, a mob collections guy and hitman working for Mad Sam, later helped break the case when he was granted immunity by the government in exchange for testimony on the Foreman murder.

Investigators then leveraged the Crimaldi information to obtain a search warrant of Mario's house. When they entered the basement they found paint and wood chips to match those already found embedded in the fabric of Foreman's clothing by crime technicians who had thoroughly vacuumed his clothes, "CSI" style. Based upon the physical evidence and Crimaldi's testimony, prosecutors were able to obtain indictments against all three perpetrators: Mad Sam, brother Mario, and, most significantly, Tony Spilotro.

Another of the many suspected murders attributable to Spilotro was the fateful killing of DEA informant Sherwin Lisner, who along with 5 men from the Vegas crew had become a government witness to testify against the bosses back home. Spilotro himself was indicted in Nevada for heading a burglary ring called the Hole-in-the-Wall-Gang that operated within the Las Vegas city limits in 1980 and 1981. A prolific group, that crew was suspected in as many as 200 burglaries, 50 robberies, 25 extortions, and at least 4 murders for hire. Operating out of The Gold Rush, Ltd., a jewelry store just off the Vegas strip, the gang specialized in disabling alarm systems. The Gold Rush itself had been founded in 1976 by Tony, brother Michael, and a Chicago bookmaker named "Fat Herbie" Blitzstein. Officially it was a jewelry and electronics store, but mostly it was a very convenient and lucrative fencing operation.

Spilotro kept his role in the burglaries quiet, though, to avoid splitting his take with Chicago boss Ferriola. Spilotro quietly placed more than 5000 pieces of expensive stolen jewelry for sale on the black market in Vegas, then methodically assembled a massive portfolio of Las Vegas real estate, mostly vacant and undeveloped property near the Vegas strip. Although that was risky enough, Spilotro then made a critical error by mistakenly allowing an undercover FBI agent into the Outfit by vouching for his credibility. That agent eventually sat in on legal strategy discussions held to fend off a government investigation of boss Ferriola and others.

With power and money, Spilotro grew into a loose cannon well over a thousand miles from mob control in Chicago. He skimmed from the mob and committed murder without permission. He was also linked to the car bombing and attempted murder of his one-time great friend Frank "Lefty" Rosenthal (Robert De Niro in the "Casino" film) in 1982, and even slept with Rosenthal's wife (played by Sharon Stone). Eventually the order came down to kill Tony Spilotro, and to also knock off his kid brother Michael who was fast rising in the Vegas hierarchy. The task was assigned to the Chicago Chinatown crew, which meant the Calabrese brothers.

Frank transferred the order out to his brother Nick who immediately packed a bag full of explosives, and was provided a team of killers by underboss Jimmy Marcello, one of the Family Secrets defendants. That team included Frank "the German" Schweihs, James DeForti, and John Fecarotta. Nick drove to Las Vegas with all of them, intending to execute Spilotro with a car bomb.

Once in Vegas, the hit men tracked Spilotro, following Anthony to his lawyer's office located near the Federal Building, then to the cul-de-sac where Spilotro's home was located. The original plan was to either use explosives, or maybe a silencer-equipped Uzi submachine gun. Eventually, both brothers were lured to Chicago under the pretense of promoting Tony to "capo" and concurrently making brother Michael a "made" member, all under the direction of boss Ferriola.

Nick described how he had just returned from the Phoenix hit on Emil Vaci when he got the orders to round up Spilotro. Frankie was upset. "Why didn't they ask me? I wanted to be there."

Spilotro should have seen the end coming. Not only was he out of control, but three months before he and his brother would be killed, the Chicago bosses sent word for Tony to begin calling in loans and not to start any new projects. That should have been a fatal signal that the end was near, but the bosses covered any Spilotro suspicions by claiming that the Outfit needed the cash to pay for legal fees for several high-ranking members who were on trial.

Nick was sent to a large Venture store on 22nd Street west of Illinois Highway 83 in DuPage County (not all that far from the Cypress Restaurant where the Cagnoni car was detonated). Waiting there with Nick were John Fecarotta and mob boss Jimmy LaPietra, a leader of the 26th Street crew (the crew that included the Calabrese brothers).

The set-up was planned well. The day before, Jimmy Marcello kept in close contact with Tony while he was in Chicago, phoning him every half hour. Finally, the big call came, summoning Tony and brother Michael to attend a meeting. The brother's left Michael's house at 2:00pm on Saturday, June 14, 1986, taking the 1986 Lincoln Mark IV that belonged to Michael's wife Ann Spilotro. Tony told her they would be back by the late afternoon to watch Michael's son play in a little league baseball game.

Marcello then picked up Nick, Fecarotta and LaPietra in a "fancy blue van" in the early afternoon. Nick recounted how the men drove to a subdivision in west suburban Bensenville, near O'Hare Field. There were homes and brick walls, Nick recalled, one house with its garage door already raised. The group entered and was greeted by a number of top mob leaders including John "No Nose" DeFranzo, Sam "Wings" Carlisi, and Joe Ferriola. It must have been a daunting sight.

Carlisi made a comment about Nick's tan, which was still fresh from his Phoenix adventures. He also quipped about how much money Fecarotta lost out there, and Fecarotta wasn't sure he was joking—he dashed into a bathroom thinking the bosses had it in for him. "He came out, he was pale," Nick said. "I figured he thinks this is it for him." It wasn't. But Fecarotta would be dead three months later, anyway.

The group headed for the basement where still more mob figures were waiting, like Louis "the Mooch" Eboli and Louis Marino. Three more hoods were there, too, all wearing gloves, but Nick did not know them.

The jury leaned forward, transfixed. All eyes were trained on Nick as he wove the grimy Spilotro tale. Nick winced and shifted his weight in the witness chair, sometimes clearing his throat as he held a glass of water. The tension mounted as the jury listened, anxious to hear the first public account of the true fate of Tony Spilotro, the Godfather of Las Vegas, and his brother Michael.

The men waited in the house for about 30 minutes, then the Spilotros arrived upstairs. "I remember hearing talking and somebody coming in and saying 'hello' to everybody," Nick recounted. "I'm so wound up because I'm tense. I'm focusing on what I'm gonna do." I studied Nick's face, then I found myself searching the faces at the defense table as Nick spoke, especially Marcello's.

First down the stairs was Michael Spilotro. Nick spoke first. "I said, how you doing Mike, because I knew him." Then Michael took a few steps towards Marino and the others, and all hell broke loose. "I dove and grabbed his legs," Nick said, "I noticed right away that Louis "the Mooch" had a rope around his neck. Tony, who was right behind, was also nabbed. Nick heard Tony say "Can I say a prayer?" He knew he had walked into a fatal trap, but he still managed to go down with a threat. "You guys are going to get into trouble." I'm not sure with who, because much of the top brass was in the room right there.

"I handed DiFronzo a pocket sized .22 caliber revolver taken from Michael," Nick explained to the jury. Nick himself wrapped the rope around Michael's neck, then both brothers were savagely kicked and beaten to death. Nick helped wipe up a small spot of blood from where Tony had first fallen, but he had nothing to do with dumping the bodies later. Both Tony and Michael were murdered at the basement in Bensenville, then stuffed into a car. Their car was moved and eventually found at a Howard Johnson motel nearby, but the bodies were sent elsewhere.

What had gone wrong with the Spilotro brothers? Michael was just a punk in the wrong place at the wrong time, mostly just because he had the wrong brother. As for Tony himself, there were many rumors, of course. One had it that Tony was being told over and over that he was going to be murdered and so he had flipped to the government side. Knowing Spilotro, that was highly unlikely because he was addicted to the glamour and power that he had acquired as a top mob figure in Vegas. FBI agents stationed in Las Vegas later said that Spilotro had rejected every offer to enter the witness protection program. Maybe even that was too close a call for the bosses at home, but there were other rumors, too, some even more dangerous.

Some insiders thought Spilotro was trying to take over the Outfit altogether. He was ambitious enough—and crazy enough—to try it, but this would be the true kiss of death. Just as the flamboyant Butch Petrocelli met his demise for boasting of such thoughts, Spilotro could easily have met the same fate for the same reason. But what could he have been thinking—an attempted mob coup is the best way I know to see Jesus before your time. I don't believe he had his eye on the top. Spilotro already had his own mob haven in Vegas where he was king, the Godfather of it all in the glitziest town of them all. But he also had health problems. In 1981 he was in such poor condition that a doctor told him to get his will in order. Only 48 at the time, Tony was struggling with heart problems, which he had carefully kept secret until he underwent bypass surgery in 1984, followed by a second bypass in 1985. Under those circumstance, he probably had neither the energy nor the ambition to unseat the established boss Ferriola.

Nick testified that the murders of Tony and Michael were done quietly—no car bombs or shootouts, and the bodies were not intended to ever be found. This was completely different from most inside mob hits in Chicago, which often were over the top, even gruesome, and certainly high profile. These were intended to send a message to other to stay in line—which Tony certainly had not done. But why so low profile? It may have been to drive home the point of Tony Spilotro's high flying image, something of an intended irony, perhaps, to assure a simple disappearing act rather than another big Spilotro show that the mob had already lost patience for.

Nick was not involved in disposing of the bodies, but he knew who did. That job had been left to John Fecarotta who took the remains of Tony and Michael to a remote cornfield in Newton County, Indiana where they were buried five feet under the corn rows. The film "Casino" depicted the cornfield accurately, but the movie had the brothers beaten with baseball bats on-site, then shoved into their cornfield graves. But in truth, the brothers were long dead by the time they reached Indiana.

Just eight days later, on June 22, 1986, the Spilotro brothers were again making headlines. Their bodies had already been found, stripped to their underwear, by a local farmer, and that made the international news—exactly the kind of marquee attention the Outfit had sought to avoid. The cornfield had been leased from the wildlife preserve by farmer Michael King who was using weed killing chemicals one Sunday afternoon when he noticed freshly turned earth. He also said there were obvious marks in the soil indicating something had been dragged from the road.

King thought the suspicious evidence might have come from the work of deer poachers, so he called Dick Hudson, a biologist for the Indiana Division of Fish and Wildlife. When Hudson arrived, he and King began to dig at the site, thinking they would probably uncover a deer. About three feet down, his shovel hit a body in the midsection. Hudson said "I thought to myself, this is a person. I am not going to dig anymore." He turned to King and said, "We'd better call the sheriff."

The two bodies, partially decomposed, were found one on top of the other. They were dug up and removed, and soon were identified as the Spilotro brothers through dental charts supplied by their other brother Patrick, a working oral surgeon. The county coroner determined that the cause of death for both was "multiple head and neck injuries as a result of a blunt force trauma." Their lungs and airways were so full of blood that they couldn't breath—suggesting that they might have virtually drowned in their own blood. They also had sand in their lungs, suggesting the two had been buried alive. It appeared that they had not been tied up first, and both had what appeared to be defensive wounds on their hands and arms as though they had fought back or tried to shield themselves from the blows.

In a recording made in February 1999, Frankie Calabrese can be heard telling his son that the Spilotros were killed because Joey "Doves" Aiuppa, the reputed head of the Chicago Outfit at the time, had been angered that Tony Spilotro was growing so boastful. "It was on the street," Nick said. "Everyone knew about that." Later in 1986, federal investigators secretly wired the phones of Flash Trucking in Cicero, for years thought to be the alleged headquarters of the Cicero mob, in addition to being the home of Cicero boss Rocco Infelise. Investigators heard that Infelise, James Marcello, and top boss Joseph Ferriola exchanged phone calls to set up a meeting with the Outfit at a McDonald's restaurant in Oak Brook on June 13. The next day the Spilotros were slain.

John Fecarotta clearly had botched the burial, and that displeased the mob bosses enough to seal John's own fate. Fortunately for Nick, he wasn't in on the burial. After the executions, his job was done. At that point Nick Calabrese simply went out for a cup of coffee. But he would soon be assigned the job of executing Fecarotta himself for mishandling that same burial.

Ironically, that was the beginning of the end for Nick Calabrese, too. Eventually he was confronted by the feds with DNA evidence linking him to the Fecarotta hit. The squeeze was on, forcing Nick's hand and causing him to flip, all leading to his ultimate testimony in the Family Secrets trial.

The first Family Secrets government witness for the month of August, 2007, was sworn in and took immediate issue with Hollywood. Forensic Pathologist Dr. John Pless would proceed to testify that there was no evidence the Spilotro brothers had been buried alive in a cornfield—a fate popularized by the mob film "Casino." Dr. Pless also said the injuries both men received were more likely from fists than baseball bats as he told the jury in detail about the injuries both brothers had sustained.

The truth was no less gruesome than the Hollywood depiction, however. Michael and Tony each died from multiple blunt trauma injuries, and from having their lungs or airways so filled with blood from such trauma that they could not breathe—which essentially meant that they drowned in their own blood. Both had been found stripped to their underwear in a shallow Indiana grave just nine days after the murders. An immediate autopsy was performed at Indiana University Medical Center. There were abrasions around the neck of Michael Spilotro, which could have come from a rope. Multiple defense wounds were present on the backs of their hands, suggesting that Tony and Michael tried to shield themselves and fend off their attackers.

Some jurors visibly flinched as they viewed autopsy photos on the court monitors, pictures that clearly showed two swollen, discolored corpses with Tony Spilotro's face severely beaten and partially decomposed, barely recognizable as human. Tony Spilotro had been one of the most feared, high profile, and ruthless members of the Chicago Outfit, yet this was his fate—hardly an endorsement for the life of a syndicate mobster.

The trial would end on September 10, 2007, and by September 27 the door on the Spilotro killings was finally closed: on that date the Family Secrets federal jury would find defendant James Marcello guilty in the Spilotro executions.

16

The Fateful Gloves of Nicky C.

Nick Calabrese had watched for decades as bodies of his fellow mobsters piled up around him in a surreal world where anyone, himself included, was just one misstep from "ending up in a car trunk."

Yet with all that, many of those guys just never learned. Public boasting, threatening the organization higher-ups, too much partying, bringing heat on the mob brass—all sins in the eyes of the bosses, yet endless punks and even made guys simply could not control themselves. The egos, power, women, the loose cash—it was all intoxicating. But there was more, I think, something primal that was in control, driving many of these guys to self-destruct, an Achilles heel that brought down one wise guy after another. It had to be that way, really, because otherwise the mob, sooner or later, would take over the whole country. But it doesn't, mostly because it is self-programmed not to.

According to Nick, the Outfit hierarchy in the 1970s included top boss Joey "Doves" Aiuppa and underboss Jackie Cerone, known simply as "one" and "two." They ruled mob activities with a close watchful eye, the ultimate centralized management style enforced by swift retribution when necessary. Every murder, for example, had to be cleared by someone high in the chain of command. Disputes were settled in "sitdowns" with bosses, something of an arbitration where the arbitrator had unbridled power to invoke any remedy from dividing cash or territory to even the death penalty. Nick said he and his brother Frankie once had a dispute with mobster William

"Butch" Petrocelli that reached all the way to the top, involving Auippa himself. "If you guys can't straighten it out, then I'll straighten it out." The prosecutor Mars asked Nick what that meant. "They'd probably both get killed," Nick said, "if they didn't take care of the dispute themselves."

Mob life may have been dangerous, but it was potentially very lucrative—for awhile. In the 1970s Frankie's gambling operations pulled in $500,000 to $750,000 a year. Nick knew first hand, because he did all the paperwork for the crew. As was the custom, some of the profits passed up the chain, all the way to LaPietra.

The Spilotro problem itself was handled straight from the top down. Nick confirmed that boss Joey Aiuppa held a meeting—before many of the top figures would be sent to jail—and ruled that Spilotro was to be knocked down. "I don't care how you do it. Get him. I want him out."

Spilotro brought heat and trouble, and Auippa had had more than enough for too long. The mob had done much for Spilotro, and might have even fixed a murder case for Spilotro years before, but he had grown out of control, unappreciative. If they did fix that murder case, they had stuck their necks out, and that comes with a price: prosecutors eventually sniff it out, word gets around, the feds might get interested—it can cause a world of trouble. In 1983 Spilotro was indicted for the 1962 torture murders of a couple of Chicago burglars, James R. Miraglia, 24, and William J. McCarthy, also 24, known in mob circles as "the M&M boys." They had been found guilty of robbing Rudolph Churow, 68, president of the Almira Savings and Loan Association, 3434 W. North Avenue in Chicago. They were sentenced to two years but were out on bond awaiting appeal. When the last appeal was denied and jail was inevitable, Spilotro killed them both. But when Spilotro himself was charged with those murders, Cook County Judge Thomas J. Maloney suddenly discounted the testimony of the government chief witness Frank Cullotta and summarily acquitted Spilotro.

There was nothing subtle about Spilotro. Billy McCarthy had been held captive and tortured for three days. The coroner, Dr. Andrew Toman, said the autopsy later revealed that McCarthy's throat had been slit from ear to ear, but only after he had been severely beaten. James Miraglia had been strangled, beaten, and his voice box fractured possibly before the strangling. Dr. Toman said that both men had been hit so hard and often that their faces were not recognizable. True to form, their bodies turned up in the trunk of a car on the city's south side.

Had Spilotro simply dodged a bullet? Maybe. But ten years later Judge Maloney earned the dubious distinction of being the only Illinois judge ever convicted of fixing a murder case—not Spilotro's, but clearly Maloney was capable of it, and Spilotro was certainly motivated to keep himself out of prison. Maloney was one of many Cook County judges snared by the sweeping "Operation Greylord" investigation, a federal house cleaning of what had become a corrupt judiciary—not one of Chicago's finer moments. Maloney was convicted in Federal District Court for conspiracy, racketeering, extortion, and obstructing justice.

Maloney had served as a judge from 1977 until he retired in 1990. But his career before the bench is even more telling. Maloney had been a criminal defense lawyer with very close ties to the Outfit, and it appears he knew something about the art of bribing judges. When we ascended to the bench, Maloney brought his own bag men, one of whom became a bailiff. Did Judge Maloney give Tony Spilotro a pass? I think he did, but he certainly had the ability, the motive, and even the propensity to do such a thing.

When Spilotro and his brother finally met their demise under the blessing of Aiuppa, the Spilotro saga did not end, at least not yet. Not only were the bodies found soon after, causing a world of trouble for the mob, but even the Catholic Church got into the act. The next day after their bodies turned up, the Chicago Archdiocese ruled that the Spilotros could not be given a Catholic funeral at St. Bernadine in Forest Park due to their not-so-subtle links to organized crime. So, following a private service in a chapel at Queen of Heaven Cemetery in suburban Hillside, they were finally buried in the family plot. Tony's one time great friend Lefty Rosenthal, whom Tony had betrayed not only by plotting Lefty's death but also sleeping with his wife, must have hated Tony but was still diplomatic. "I'm glad I wasn't asked to be one of the pallbearers."

On the day before burial, three of Spilotro's alleged killers attended the wake a Salerno's Galewood Chapel on North Avenue: Ferriola, Infelise, and Marino. This was not the first time that Queen of Heaven Cemetery became the consolation prize for a top mob figure. Sam Giancanna, a top boss with national fame and well placed friends, is also buried there. Giancanna did not have a church funeral and his family did not request one.

In the case of the Spilotro brothers, St. Bernadine's was asked how the church can accept money from a parish family and then deny the same family a funeral. "I didn't ask whether they donated to the church," replied Father Paprocki. He went on to explain that most donations are given privately. "If there is a condition that gives rise to public scandal, then we must say 'no thank you.' If there is no notoriety, there is no scandal."

When Nick's testimony for the day was concluded, I focused on Nick and his brother Frankie at the defense table. Nicholas was careful to avoid Frank, choosing to stand facing the jury box as the jurors left the courtroom. Frank, though, continued to laugh, appearing unconcerned and notably unimpressed as he shook hands at day's end with his counsel Lopez. When the marshals led Frank past me once again, I hoped he might say something to me . . . but still no luck. But I remember thinking "we still have a long trial to go."

On July 19, 2007, Nick began his fifth and final day of testimony. It would not disappoint, for prosecutors led him straight to the John Fecarotta hit—perhaps the tipping point in the whole Family Secrets war that would soon unfold. John was targeted because he had screwed up a hit himself in Phoenix, and moreover because he was supposed to make sure the bodies of murdered Tony and Michael Spilotro would never be found. Nick was specially selected for the job because John was his friend and had wholly trusted Nick. That alone is tragic, worthy of an art-house stage play, one of those simple think-piece stories meant to stir the soul of the audience. But to Nick and John there was little irony and even less humanity—this was the ultimate cat and mouse game, complete with the biggest of stakes for them both.

When those Spilotro bodies were found, Nick said the reaction of the bosses was not pretty. "The shit hit the fan," displeasing the top guys enough to want John Fecarotta dead.

On paper, Fecarotta was a salaried business agent and organizer for the Laborers Local Union. But when Fecarotta's own union boss John Serpico was later questioned about John's role in the union, Serpico could not recall a single thing that John had done—plus he was at a loss to explain why a gangster like Fecarotta was given a leased luxury car paid for by the Locals. When Fecarotta himself was questioned, he admitted that he knew nothing about union organizing or about the Laborers at all, including its collective bargaining agreement, pension plan, or even the membership cards that Fecarotta was handing out. One thing that wasn't made up, though, was Fecarotta's Chicago PD arrest record dating back to 1940: 17 arrests and 2 felony convictions, one for armed robbery and the other for burglary. I arrested Fecarotta once myself. I nabbed him at O'Hare Airport on August 7, 1965. He had threatened a worker from the airport by putting a gun in his mouth and threatening "to shoot his fucking brains out." Nothing subtle about John—not in those days.

By the time the 1980s rolled around, Fecarotta had become just another sick asshole member of the mob. He was getting older and was substantially overweight, and suffered from heart, lung, and weight problems. He was suspected of carrying out a number of murders in the 1980s as a member of Chicago's Chinatown crew.

So what happened? Fecarotta had not just fallen from mob grace, he crash-landed. But it did not happen overnight.

Joe Ferriola and Sam Carlisi, topped ranked bosses at the time, had had enough and targeted John "Big Stoop" Fecarotta for a hit. The fatal contract was handed down to the 26th Street Chinatown crew—and that meant the Calabrese killing machine of brothers Frank, Sr., and Nick, both of whom were the most experienced of local enforcers.

Fecarotta had started to slack off with his performance and slowly got on the bad side of his immediate bosses who included Frank Calabrese, Sr. It seemed to the Outfit that John was not available for key jobs—he was M.I.A. way too many times. To make matters worse, he began to bad mouth the higher-ups, to even the bigger top bosses, all behind their backs. This is a sure kiss of death in mafia circles—especially since word always has a way of finding its way back to the right parties.

Aggravating the bosses even more, Fecarotta was carrying a sizable debt to the mob, particularly street loans from key figures like John "no nose" DiFronzo, John "apes" Monteleone, and the LaPietra brothers, Angelo and Jimmy. If that were not enough, he had also left Phoenix, AZ, too early without completing an important assigned hit on Emil Vaci. But there is still more, for the biggest of all was the botched hit and burial of the murdered Spilotro brothers, Tony and Michael, who had the misfortune of being planted in a distant cornfield only to again turn up—unexpectedly and quite literally. When their bodies were found in Indiana, a big spotlight was suddenly shining down on the mob—and nothing causes more mob reaction than front-page visibility. As a result, "the shit hit the fan."

Fecarotta was an experienced mob operator, a wise old owl in the ways of the underworld who wouldn't let any grass grow under his feet. The mob powers knew it would not be easy to take him out. Everything would have to be carefully planned and perfect; otherwise John would have a good chance of sniffing out the plan.

The Outfit, therefore, took its time. First, they waited for several months after the Spilotro murders and the botched grave debacle. Then, on Sunday, Sept. 18, 1986, the time was right with the plans in place. This would be the Calabrese brothers' hand-picked date to murder John Fecarotta.

Fecarotta was masterfully misled by the mob. They told him that he and his friend Nicky were assigned to perform a hit themselves on a dentist who had run afoul. Nicky would do the hit, and John would be the getaway driver. Nick knew all the right moves, but he had to be careful because Fecarotta, a seasoned hit man himself, also knew the lay of the land. But savvy as John was, he never suspected his friend Nicky Calabrese.

Nick stole a 1986 Buick Century from a suburban mall, then stole a set of license plates from another car and placed them on the Buick. The idea is to keep the stolen car trail confused until the end of the hit and the getaway. Such "work cars" are normally used in a hit only once, then abandoned—with or without a body in the trunk.

Nick's final preparation was to create a fake bomb that was to be used against their target. He took four emergency road flares and taped them snugly together with black duct tape, then placed the dud bomb into a brown paper bag. He then placed a .38 caliber revolver in the glove compartment, first disabling it by removing the firing pin. Then he put a second loaded .38 in the same paper bag holding the fake bomb. Not one to take many chances regarding his own life, Nick then tucked a third .38 revolver, fully loaded, into the waist band of his pants. This last gun was given to him by Frank, Sr., as a precaution.

With three guns, a dud bomb decoy, a fake hit contract, and a stolen work car, Nick was finally ready to rendezvous with John on the far northwest side of Chicago at Belmont and Austin in the shadow of St. Patrick's Catholic High School. Frank, Sr., was calling the shots, and his final instruction to Nick was to shoot John in the head as soon as he lets his guard down. Frank would be waiting close by in another car to pick up Nick for their own getaway. With that, Nick finally put on his usual black leather golf gloves, as he always did before going on hits, specifically to protect him from leaving any tell-tale fingerprints at or around the scene, or in the work car.

Nick was a shrewd operator. When he arrived in the neighborhood to pick up John he first scoped the area, driving around the block a few times. Eventually he parked the stolen Buick, then slid over to the passenger seat, holding the brown bag between his legs. Fecarotta, known as a good "wheel man," would be the driver.

The pair drove by the area where the dentist was to be found at his office, and drove down an alley past the local bingo hall as dusk was beginning to settle in. But they were not alone. A few neighbors were seen working in a garage nearby, so they continued on by, taking their time. Jobs like this were never all peaches and cream, there often was a hitch, and they knew they had to be careful. When Fecarotta took another pass at the designated area, it appeared to look safe. This time the garage door was closed and the neighbors were nowhere in sight. John found a good place to park. Nicky was prepared. The parking process gave Nick time to form a mental picture as events unfolded, and his gut told him "the time was right."

Nick reached into the brown paper bag at his feet, appearing to reach for the fake bomb. But something was in the air and John, a savvy hit man himself, had "caught the play," which meant that suddenly Big John understood what was really happening—the hit was going down, on himself. But it happened even faster than John expected, for Nick pulled the gun from the bag instead of the bomb. Fecarotta was stunned as Nick quickly held the gun to John's head, but then John reacted suddenly and violently, recoiling against Nick. The two hit men struggled in the front seat of the parked Buick, both knowing their mission was now a matter of life and death for themselves.

Hearing this story in open court, the jury was captivated. Nick went on, testifying that while he struggled with Fecarotta for control of the weapon, Nick was able to get one shot off. Unfortunately, he shot himself in the left shoulder, but the same bullet had also struck John in the chest. Survival of the fittest had never been more real. John either had to overcome and kill Nick or be killed himself. It was at once ironic and pathetic that these two old buddies, who had committed so many murders together, were now pitted against each other in a deadly battle for their own live. But so it is with life—and death—in the mob.

John was bleeding from the bullet to his chest, but he was impervious to the pain. His overriding purpose was to somehow latch onto that gun and kill his long time friend Nick Calabrese. In fact, John did manage to grab the gun, then tried to yank it from Nick. As they fought over the weapon, the cylinder opened, spilling the bullets over the front seat. This fleeting distraction gave John an opening to bolt from the car, and he took off, making one last reckless run for his life.

Nick was not about to botch this hit, however. His adrenaline was pumping like an oil gusher. He reached into his waist, pulling out the third gun. "My mind is going if I don't do this and he gets away, I'm dead," he told the jury. The hunter had already become the hunted, and Nick was worried the tables would turn yet again—and they would have, too. As Nick gathered himself, many things flashed across his mind, and he realized the consequences if John's escape was successful. He could hear what the bosses had said many times before if a target were to get away. "You'll take his place."

Nicky jumped from the passenger seat, and the chase was on. Down the alley they raced, both wounded, both desperate, leaving the hot Buick behind. With both bleeding from gunshots, they left a noticeable trail of blood down the alley. Big John was desperate, but he was still heavy and out of shape, so Nicky closed in. He caught up to his one-time friend at the bingo hall doorway. The game was finally over. Nick raised this last gun to John's head, aimed it point-blank execution style, and coldly squeezed the trigger. The bullet pierced the skull of John "Big Stoop" Fecarotta, and the deed was done.

Exhausted, Nick turned and walked away. Still exhilarated from the battle and the chase, Nick's simplistic hit man philosophy remained: "killing isn't murder, it's entertainment." But Nick still had to get away from the murder scene. He tried to avoid undue attention, a difficult task given all that had happened, not to mention the blood gushing from his shoulder wound. He tried to remain calm, but he knew that the shots may have alerted the neighborhood. There was a good chance that someone could have called the police—and still worse, that maybe someone could identify him.

By this time Nick was growing weak. He began to feel the throbbing pain, and was feeling the effects of so much blood loss. He worried about the evidence piling up around him, like the bloody clothes and the black gloves used in the job. He knew he had to get rid of these things as soon as he could—obviously the gloves could draw curious attention, since no one walks around with gloves on for no purpose, especially on a hot September day.

Nick continued walking and looked for his brother Frank, Sr., who should have been there with the second get-away car. But Frank was a no-show. While still walking, Nick pulled the gloves off and shoved them into his pocket, placing the gun in the other pocket. He felt the danger of the situation, especially if he were to be stopped and questioned, so he dropped the smoking gun down a city sewer grate. Later, Nick's nephew Frank, Jr., who worked a legitimate job on a Chicago city sewer crew, would be able to retrieve it.

A call for the police had indeed gone out, and within minutes the area was swarming with cops. Nick had barely stayed a step ahead of them and, while concerned that he might lose consciousness from the loss of blood, he nonetheless found a garden hose in a nearby yard and methodically washed himself off. Dizzy and confused while searching for his brother in the car, Nick had made a fatal mistake. He had accidentally dropped the pair of gloves near the scene—a miscue that would ultimately tie him to the murder of John Fecarotta.

Nick did manage to slip away from the area without detection or arrest, and he did finally hook up with Frank, Sr., who drove him to a suburban restaurant where they used a second floor apartment to clean Nick and get him treated by a "goon" doctor they knew, my guess is either a shady veterinarian or a real doctor who may have lost his license for one misdeed or another. Doctors like that were standard fare for the mob.

On September 14, 1986, the Chicago police picked up those wayward gloves and routinely placed the evidence into inventory. More than any other single piece of evidence, they would not only lead authorities directly to Nick Calabrese, they would set into motion the first in a long string of dominoes that would culminate in the Family Secrets "mob trial of the century."

Nick recounted the attempted assassination of Ken "Tokyo Joe" Eto, the mob's man in Chicago's Chinatown. Eto also headed the syndicate gambling operations within the Hispanic community, and he also controlled the action from illegal Fan Tan and Jai Jong games operating behind the neighborhood storefronts. Eventually he was pinched and found guilty on federal gambling charges, after which mob superiors felt Eto was a risk to spill the beans to the feds rather than do time. So they opted to have Eto hit.

Eto was shot in the head three times, but then lived to tell about it. On Feb. 10, 1983 Eto had picked up Jasper Campise, a Cook County sheriff's deputy, along with John Gattusa, all under the pretense of a dinner meeting with Vince Solano, one of Eto's bosses. Soon Eto smelled a rat, but they kept going, soon parking at a lot next to the Montclair Theatre where Solano was to meet up with them. Gattuso then shot Eto in the head at close range, making Eto one of the few people "taken for a ride" in Chicago who lived to tell about it. But this was clearly a botched hit, putting Campise and Gattuso themselves at risk.

The episode came to a close when both Campise and Gattuso were found stuffed in the trunk of a car. Both had been stabbed repeatedly. Eto himself had said the hit was ordered by Vince Solano after getting permission either from top figure Aiuppa or Jackie Cerone.

The Fecarotta murder case went unsolved for almost two decades. Then, in 2002, the FBI got a break from an informant who told them that Nick had been the killer. Agents pulled the bloodstained glove from CPD evidence and got a warrant to x-ray Nick's arm to look for the old gunshot wound, plus to obtain a DNA sample. The DNA was a match, placing Nick at the murder scene, and the wound was found definitely to be from a gunshot.

This was the very break the authorities needed, leading to Nick's own cooperation with the feds and launching the very Operation Family Secrets that eventually landed these top five figures on trial for their lives—but it would not come easy. Nick was confronted by the FBI, but even with the compelling evidence the government had, Nick initially refused to flip. Records show that the agents played on Nick's known dislike of his louder, more vicious brother Frankie, who often reneged on his promises over the years—even with his own family. The agent had already learned that Frank had often shortchanged and cheated Nick out of money from shared deals.

Agents knew by then that relations between Nick and Frank were very tense. Frank, true to form, was refusing to send money to Nick's family, which was his obligation as the crew boss, forcing Nick to take the issue to under boss Jimmy Marcello who solved the problem himself by sending Nick's wife weekly cash. Nick was grateful, and for that reason Nick tried hard to conceal Marcello's involvement in the Spilotro murders—even well after Nick's own arrest.

Nick was also upset over how Frank had treated his own sons Frank, Jr., and Kurt, in a loan sharking case, effectively hanging both of them out to dry. Then the agents pulled their trump card, playing for Nick the tapes that Frank's son had recorded of Frank in prison. One portion had Frank explaining to his son that Nick had fouled up the first plot to blow up Spilotro's car years earlier, then expressly named Nick and the others as Spilotro's killers. Then Nick was furious when he heard Frank also scoff on tape about Nick's botched murder of John Fecarotta—not that Fecarotta wasn't killed, of course, but how the hit had been screwed up in the process and then linked to Nick with that bloody glove. To top it off, those same tapes revealed Frank, Sr., telling his son that if his own brother Nick was helping investigators, he would have no objections to Nick himself being killed, explaining that those were the rules of the life they had both chosen.

With that, the handwriting was clearly on the wall, and Nick started cooperating. He was squired away to a federal prison in Ashland, Kentucky, and began giving investigators a detailed inside look into a host of mob murders that had gone unsolved for decades.

Thus the mob cycle of death: a never ending struggle where one thing triggers an avalanche of cause-and-affect mishaps, often escalating until something blows wide open. First, Tony Spilotro was out of control in Las Vegas, so the mob puts out a hit.

Then, when the FBI began snooping, Doyle became intrigued and felt that his superiors—the ones in the mob, not the Chicago police force—would be even more interested. The story was that Doyle told Frank Calabrese, Sr., about the crucial gloves left behind, a dangerous development for the mob since they could connect one, if not two, Calabrese family members to the Fecarotta hit. Prosecutor

John Scully called Doyle's actions an act of betrayal. "He betrayed his oath to the pubic," said Scully, "and decided to remain loyal to the Outfit interests."

Nick Calabrese summed his own testimony up with one pointed reaffirmation for the jurors: "When I'm on the stand, I can't lie."

Then attorney Joseph Lopez, counsel to defendant Frankie "The Breeze" Calabrese, finally got his turn at Frankie's brother Nick. Lopez began with "Good afternoon, Mr. Calabrese," then grilled Nick, who during the trial had already admitted to being "a coward," "a chicken," and "a rat" for testifying against his brother and other mob figures. But the defense was quick to add a more serious attribute: Nick was a mass murderer, racketeer, arsonist—and a liar committed to a live of mob mayhem that included shooting a man in the head as the victim begged for his life.

Nick Calabrese admitted to taking part in at least 14 mob murders, but balked when attorney Lopez called him a "serial killer."

"I am a killer," Nick explained, carefully leaving out the descriptive term "serial."

Lopez continued to provoke Nick during cross-examination, pointing out that Nick had alternatives to being a mob hit man—even suggesting he could have avoided it all by literally hanging himself.

Nick testified that he took responsibility for the 14 murders that he took part in, but also laid heavy blame on his brother Frank Calabrese and Nick's own belief that he, himself, would have been killed had he ever refused. Nick explained that ultimately it was his own fear of being executed for murder that led him to turn "stoolpigeon" for the federal government, hoping to avoid the death penalty and maybe even get something less than life in prison.

Nick told how his brother had brought him into the Outfit, and Lopez asked Nick if his brother thought him a coward. Nick acknowledged that over the years Frankie had called him both an idiot and a coward. "There's not many names he didn't call me," Nick emphasized. But he feared his brother would do a lot more than level insults if he had not gone through with his mob assignments, especially the ones that they had done together. He figured, quite simply, that sooner or later, his brother would kill him.

Lopez asked Nick if he really believed Frank would have killed him if he froze on a hit and let the victim escape. Nick confirmed that yes, he did feel that way.

"That's why you're sitting on the witness stand rather than sitting over at the table next to your brother," pressed Lopez.

"I didn't walk away from it," Nick answered. "To run away, you need money—I didn't have money. I didn't have money. Plus, I have a family." Nick recounted how he suffered over and over making his decisions to assist the government because he wanted to wait until his daughter finished high school, avoiding the embarrassment to his family as long as he could. It was not until 2002 that Nick contacted the FBI to free himself of a "load" that he had been carrying.

Nick found himself in prison finishing up a sentence he had received for helping his brother in the juice loan operations. Then he could hold himself back no longer, lashing out verbally about how his brother Frank had treated his own children, Frank, Jr., and Kurt. He blamed his brother for not doing more to save his sons from prison, especially Kurt, who had a limited role in the operation. (All four of the Calabreses, including Kurt, were charged in the 1995 racketeering case against their street crew.)

"Kurt was forced to do what he did by his father," Nick protested.

"His father didn't put a gun to his head, did he?" challenged Lopez.

"No, but he put a fist to his face," Nick shot back. Frankly, I think Nick could have scored a bigger punch himself by saying that, well, yes, in fact there was a gun to Kurt's heard, since at some point he knew he could be hit for disobeying orders.

"When did the beatings begin?"

"You name the time," Nick replied. "The kids went through hell with their father."

"And they gave *him* hell, didn't they?"

"No, they did not," Nick said.

Nick told the jury that he would have taken his nephew Kurt's prison time, but there was nothing he could do because his brother Frank was not interested in helping out early in the case "because it had to be both of us to do something."

Lopez then led Nick to when he had first learned in 2000 that the FBI had matched the DNA to him from the bloody glove at the Fecarotta murder scene.

"When you learned that," Lopez asked, "you really wet your pants, didn't you?" Lopez was humiliating Nick, partly referring to

Nick's earlier testimony when he admitted to wetting his pants from fear when he had buried his first murder victim.

"That's correct," said Nick, who was smooth under stress and remained cool as a cucumber.

"You didn't want to get fried, either, is that correct?"

"That's correct," Nick said, knowing they were both referring to the death penalty.

Lopez pressed on, challenging Nick's version of his Outfit work, asking over and over why he didn't just leave Chicago and move to California or anywhere else to avoid the mob and his evil brother.

"Once again," Nick replied, "that's why I'm a coward."

Watching Nick and Lopez do battle, I felt that the jury could identify with Nick's dilemma. He was anything but a sympathetic figure, but the jurors have been around long enough to know you can't just whisk your family to California and declare yourself safe from the ruthless arm of the mob. Nick wasn't just being a coward, he was being realistic. But Lopez had another take on it, asking Nick if he had not, in fact, reveled in the life of a mobster.

"No, I didn't like the fact that people would look at me and respect me for that," he said. "And [anyway] it was only a very few people that knew."

Nick explained that before joining the Outfit he had held a few legitimate jobs like working in radio communications for the Navy, as an ironworker who worked on Chicago's mammoth Hancock Center on Michigan Avenue, and even as a Cook County security officer at the courthouse in suburban Maywood. But then he drifted into crime, eventually becoming his brother Frank's "stooge."

Lopez questioned Nick about why he seemingly had no problem with killing. Nick had earlier testified that he simply, and coolly, had enjoyed a cup of coffee after taking part in the 1986 slaying of the Spilotro brothers.

"You didn't have a problem drinking that coffee, did you?" Lopez challenged.

"Yes, I did," Nick answered in a low-key voice, showing no emotion.

"You drank it anyway, didn't you?"

"I didn't drink it all."

Talk about mincing words. Did all this mean anything? It certainly was surreal—the two of them arguing about coffee and how much was sipped. It was symbolic of the mob in its entirety, I think—childish hooligans on the loose with guns in a concrete jungle called Chicago. They, personified by Nick, could drink coffee after one of the most notorious hits in Chicago mob history—but not all of it.

The cross examination of Nick spilled into a second day. Nick appeared much more confident than on the first day. He seemed to become more comfortable as a veteran witness, having endured the previous day's hostile examination.

Nick admitted that he had lied to the FBI even after he began his government cooperation. At first he had concealed the role of defendant James Marcello in the Spilotro killings out of loyalty—and money—since Marcello had been paying Nick's wife $4000 a month during Nick's prison stint. That was something Nick's brother had not done, even though it technically was Frankie's obligation to do so under mob custom.

Some of the other defense lawyers also took their shots at Nick. At one point, Judge Zagel was forced to halt the questioning by Doyle's lawyer Ralph Mecyzk who was relentlessly badgering Nick over inconsistencies in his statements to the FBI.

Rick Halprin, a top defense lawyer in Chicago and counsel to Joey Lombardo, leaned over the lectern and roared loudly about Nick's earlier accusation that John Fecarotta had once told him in a restaurant that Lombardo had been involved in the murder of a federal witness named Daniel Seifert in 1974. Halprin saw much sarcastic irony that Fecarotta himself could not appear in court to deny or explain, since Nick had already shot him in the head.

"Right?" asked Halprin.

"Right," said Nick.

Recounting Nick's coffee story, Halprin leveled further ridicule at Nick. "Did you order pie and coffee when he [Fecarotta] told you about the murder [allegedly by Lombardo]?"

Defense counsel made all the usual points. Lopez insinuated that it was impossible to know when Nick was truthful, under oath or otherwise. He specifically asked Nick if he lied to Fecarotta with a straight face before shooting him. "If I had a straight face, yes," Nick replied. Rick Halprin called Nick a rat whose testimony was flawed because it relies on hearsay—that is, based on things that he heard others say, not on his own personal observations as a direct witness.

But Nick, of course, had been personally involved in plenty, and his testimony was pervasive, complete, and consistent. In short, Nick's stories had mesmerized the jury and were eminently believable.

Nick recounted decades of complex, twisted tales of Outfit malevolence, keeping straight the names and dates and murders with the accuracy of a man spilling his guts—and emptying his conscience of a lifetime of murder. Those webs may have been tangled, but Nick unthreaded them, one by one, in painful but deliberate detail. He had betrayed the mob and family in a spectacular but mostly calm round of testimony that made the courtroom shudder and should have assured his own death sentence—not from the electric chair, but maybe, one day, much worse. But he is still alive. So far.

17

My Name is Joey

"Morris, the reason why I'm here, you don't know who I am."
"I'm..."
"My name is Joey."
"I'm, I'm assuming you're all right, if you're with Allen."
"That's right. That's right. Okay. Here's the reason why."

Those were the words of Joseph Lombardo, spoken to Morris Shenker in 1979. There is little doubt about their accuracy. The conversation was intercepted and taped by the federal authorities on May 22, 1979, then later used as a government exhibit. Dorfman's office, at Amalgamated Insurance, had been legally wire tapped by federal authorities.

This was an interesting if not daunting trio: Lombardo, Shenker, and Dorfman. Life Magazine once referred to St. Louis attorney Shenker as "lawyer to the mob." He included John F. Kennedy among his friends, he represented legendary union leader Jimmy Hoffa, and at one time he owned the Dunes Hotel in Las Vegas. Shenker was also heavily involved in Democratic politics and was acquainted with Harry Truman. He is credited with using pension money lifted from the Teamster Union's Central States Pension Fund as the seed capital for the mob's eventual penetration into the lucrative Las Vegas market.

Shenker's connections, legal work, business deals, and other activities were highly lucrative. When he died in 1989, he reportedly owed $55 million in back taxes. It takes a lot of earning power to run up a bill like that.

Lombardo and Shenker were referring to Allen Dorfman, who believed that Shenker was holding out on some very big dollars. Dorfman, too, is now dead, but he did not die of natural causes at age 82 like Shenker did. His death was a little more dramatic, as recounted in the *New York Times* on February 25, 2007:

> Longtime business associates Allen Dorfman and Irwin Weiner frequently lunched together. On a day in January 1983, they emerged from Dorfman's Cadillac onto the icy parking lot of a suburban Chicago restaurant, then minutes late for their one o'clock reservation. According to Weiner, they were walking between parked cars when two men ran up behind them and yelled, "This is a robbery." One of the men fired a .22 automatic at least half a dozen times. Only Dorfman was hit. He fell to the ground in a large pool of blood that quickly froze into red ice. When the paramedics arrived, he showed no signs of life.[14]

The restaurant was at an outpost Hilton Hotel in Lincolnwood, Illinois, a small community nestled among Skokie, Wilmette, and other near north Chicago suburbs. It was a peculiar hotel, known for its ugly 1970s use of color, purple for the most part. I knew the place well, and the gunning down of Dorfman, age 59, at the Hilton parking lot has long been the stuff of local Chicago lore.

Ironically, it was Shenker who once was on the mob bubble, but soon Dorfman was the one lying in his own pool of blood. Like Shenker, Dorfman had many ties to the teamsters and the Chicago mob. One of those connections was the speaker "Joey," who was Joseph Lombardo, one of the Family Secrets defendants and one-time mob boss also with ties to the Teamsters through its president Roy Williams. Just before the murder of Dorfman, which clearly was a mob hit, Lombardo, Williams, and Dorfman himself had all been convicted of attempting to bribe U.S. Senator Howard Cannon from Nevada. At the time of his death, Dorfman was free on

---

[14] Excerpted from "Bringing Down the Mob," by Thomas A Peppetto, February 25, 2007.

a $5 million bond while he awaited sentencing, which could have been five decades or more in prison.

With his pervasive connections to Hoffa, Williams, the Teamsters, Las Vegas, and the mob, clearly Dorfman knew way too much. His conviction, pending sentence, and life-long access to a multitude of mob secrets made Dorfman a dangerous threat to mob security. The Outfit was afraid Dorfman would cut a deal and testify, so Dorfman was eliminated. He had been around the mob a long time and should have known his days were numbered, but maybe his ego got in the way.

Lombardo himself has been widely implicated in the murder of Dorfman, notwithstanding that Dorfman was actually a close personal friend of Lombardo—so close that they went on Hawaiian golf vacations together. Shenker, Dorfman, and maybe even Joey Lombardo, had reason to know what may have happened to Jimmy Hoffa, whose disappearance has fascinated mob watchers for decades. I've got my own guess—at least to where the body is. Get the yellow pages from the phone book, then look under "cement."

Allen Dorfman had gotten his start in 1949 through his step-father "Red" Dorfman, a racketeer in his own right, then he was mentored by none other than Hoffa and rose through the ranks rapidly, becoming a highly visible millionaire and community leader at an early age. Lombardo's voice was recorded as he explained the meeting to Morris Shenker, referring initially to Allen Dorfman.

LOMBARDO: Allen belongs to Chicago. Now you know what I mean when he belongs to Chicago? I was sent here to find out what the story is. When they talk to Allen, he says he don't get this, he don't get this, he got this, he got this coming. It's 12 years—they're tired of listening to this bullshit, that he don't have this and Morris is this and Morris is that.

SHENKER: Okay, you . . .

LOMBARDO: You know where you belong, I mean, excuse me, you know where you belong, and he knows where he belongs and the other guy knows where he belongs—we all belong to certain people, to account to—it's a big world. And that's what I'm here for is to listen. And the word is that Morris says this and Morris says that, Morris says... and that's why I say, now what you say you got coming, you don't got coming... now you're here. According to what I see... hear you say.

\# \# \#

LOMBARDO: Now it's getting to the point now where you either gonna shit or get off the pot, ya know what I mean? We either get what we got coming or we don't get what we got coming.

SHENKER: Well, I, I can only tell you what he has coming.

LOMBARDO: Good, well, I, what he's got coming, the people in Chicago got coming.

SHENKER: Well, that's between you fellas.

LOMBARDO: I know that, dick.

That last remark embodies much of what one needs to know about Joey Lombardo, his power, and his rank in the Chicago mob: calling Shenker a dick to his face. The Outfit believed that Shenker owed them money, millions of dollars in fact. Lombardo was there to make the point—and he did so colorfully and most directly.

"Excuse me," continued Joey. "I'm just here to bring a message back. And what I think is what and what's, what and let me tell you something. If they make a decision and they tell me to come back and bring you a message to pay, you can fight the system if you wanna, but, I'll tell you one thing. You say you're 72, and you defy it, all you can do is send a guy like me to jail, one guy."

"I'm not going to send anybody to jail," Shenker protested.

"But, excuse me, but you ain't gonna send they system to jail."

"I'm not going to send anybody to jail.

"I'm just tellin' ya," Joey warned, raising his voice. "If they come back and tell me to give you a message and if you want to defy it, I assure you that you will never reach 73."

In one conversation, Lombardo had called Shenker a dick and then threatened his life. Why? What had happened to so infuriate the Chicago Outfit?

The government had the answer on tape, a prior conversation between Dorfman and Joseph Lombardo where the two discussed their planned confrontation with Shenker.

"... But, all you get from him [Shenker] are promises of bullshit," Dorfman complained. "You see, my statement to him today is going to be, listen, Morris, where is my twenty-five percent of the holdings that Hoffa and I are supposed to have? ... I says, all I know is all I'm going to say to him. Now where the fuck we goin'? Did you ever give me a fuckin' dime, Morris? Ever give Hoffa a fuckin' dime? If you did, I don't know about it. And if you did, I don't give a fuck because I didn't get nothin.'"

"Give me a ballpark figure," said Joey.

"I can find out exactly. The Fund has the records. The Fund would have..."

"It doesn't matter 'cause he'll be here at four o'clock, so, ah, think about a ball park figure."

The "figure" turned out to include $2.5 million, which was 25% of Shenker's cut of $10 million on a $20 million deal. But that was just the beginning; there was potentially more, much more, and as he spoke to Dorfman in preparation for the meeting, Lombardo became furious.

"He's gonna go run for help," said Lombardo. "You know where he'll run for help at? He's gonna run to St. Louis [meaning the St. Louis mob]. St. Louis says there's nothing we can do about it. It's out of our fuckin' hands. Now he's runnin' for help.... Now after you tell him everything, then I'll say excuse us Allen. Now you go out. Now, I'm gonna give him the fuckin' riot act. I'm going to tell him, listen, this is what you gotta come up with, if you don't [Lombardo bangs the table], this is what's going to happen to you, you understand? As long as we can't spend our money, you ain't gonna spend your fucking money. Do you understand? And you go wherever the fuck you wanna go. I'm just leavin' you a message. I'm just an errand boy. This is what they wanted me to tell you. Your bullshit's all through, it's all over with." Then Lombardo banged the table again, working himself up, maybe even psyched up, for the Shenker confrontation.

"You gotta be careful with him," suggested Dorfman.

"What's he gonna do?"

"He's a crabby, crabby motherfucker," explained Dorfman.

Lombardo and Dorfman focused on the big score, a Continental Connectors deal worth $174 million that should have netted Chicago, including Hoffa and Dorfman, something over $40 million. The number was so big that even Lombardo and Dorfman choked on it.

"How can he, how can he afford . . . fuckin' thing out, this cocksucker," Dorfman said. "It doesn't matter. You know, Uncle Joey, you know what really irritates me more than anything else about all this? All of this was made possible by Hoffa and myself."

That's because Hoffa and the Teamsters were funding Shenker and Vegas. Lombardo was so angry that he even practiced his planned death threat to Shenker. "You know what I'm gonna tell him? This is half of our fucking money that you got and know what we do, it ah, know what we do for less money than this? We do, we do a lot of bad things for less money than this. Imagine what we'd do for this kind of fuckin' money? You tell him, I'm gonna tell him, fuck you. I'm gonna tell him, you know. If we can't get our money, then you ain't gonna spend our money, then you ain't gonna spend a fuckin' penny of it either. Then when your heirs get it too, we're gonna give them a lot of fuckin' trouble, too. Whoever inherited. And they're gonna have a lotta fuckin' trouble. I'm gonna tell him, we don't want to fucking problem. All we want is our fuckin' money. Is that hard, hard to ask?"

Lombardo went on ranting to Dorfman. "And we ain't waiting another fucking month. One month is all we'll give ya, and after that the shits gonna hit the fan. You're not gotta spend a-fuckin'-nother penny after that. You're seventy-two years old? Well, you're not gonna reach seventy-three, I'll guarantee it, if you don't give us our fuckin' money."

Joey Lombardo was nothing if not colorful. He earned his nickname "the Clown" because he had a quick wit, always had something funny to say, and was known for his peculiar antics like yawning for mug shots or one time when he almost slipped out of police custody walking right out of the courthouse behind a newspaper with a peep hole. But there was nothing funny about his role as an Outfit enforcer. Joey was a feared mob figure who knew few boundaries. He had been with the Outfit since the 1950s, and by 1963 he stood trial for kidnapping but was acquitted. In 1965, Joey officially became a made member for allegedly killing Manny Skar, a hotel owner with mob affiliation. In 1974 Lombardo was to stand trial for embezzling over $1 million from the Teamsters Union pension fund, but the main government witness, Daniel Siefert, was murdered just two days before he was to testify. Later that same year a government informant implicated Lombardo in that death.

Lombardo escaped conviction on a series of felonies, including a number of murders, well into the 1980s. The bribery of Nevada Sen. Howard Cannon finally led to a 15 year sentence in 1985. A year later, Joey was also convicted of concealing mob ownership of the Stardust Casino in Vegas and skimming $2 million from casino coffers during a 5-year stretch in the 1970s. He drew another 10 years for that one.

Joey actually disappeared in the late 1970s when he became a fugitive and communicated through letters to his lawyer Rick Halprin. One of Lombardo's weaknesses, his family, finally caught up to him, for he was finally nabbed by the FBI at an 11th birthday party for his great great niece Shawanda Lombardo.

It would take 33 years, but Lombardo was eventually convicted of the 1974 Siefert murder by the Family Secrets jury, which also found him guilty of a number of other felonies including racketeering, extortion, loan sharking, and murder. The Siefert murder, though, was especially chilling, for he had been gunned down just outside his Bensenville fiberglass plant in front of his wife and 4-year-old son. Like Dorfman, Siefert himself had been a close friend of Lombardo, and Lombardo had actually baby-sat for Siefert's kids.

Befriending Joey was a dangerous proposition. Even Tony Spilotro, the mob's main enforcer in Las Vegas, felt close to Lombardo, for their respective families had actually come to America on the same boat. But Tony was too hard to control and was calling attention to himself and the mob in Vegas, so three years after Dorfman was eliminated, Spilotro was ceremoniously killed along with his brother Michael. One-time FBI agent Jack O'Rourke called Lombardo a vicious killer, one of the prime mob enforcers of his day.

Joey grew up in the Depression era streets of Chicago like I did. The son of a printer, Lombardo was from a huge family with 11 children. He graduated from Wells High School in Chicago and grew up the hard way, scraping money together from a series of odd jobs from shining shoes to delivering papers, loading boxcars, and even plucking chickens. He loved golf, too, and at one time caddied for Outfit boss Jackie Cerone, which no doubt influenced his early mob affinity.

When Joe Lombardo testified in court at his own Family Secrets trial, he said he never took an oat to any organization referring, of course, to the Outfit.

The prosecution pressed further. "Well, apart from that, your testimony is you are not a member of organized crime, whether an oath was required or not, right? . . . I'm asking, are you a member of organized crime, according to you?"

"I never took an oath, never put a Catholic card in my hand, I never took an oath of any secret organization in the world."

"And so you are telling me you are not a member of organized crime?"

"That is positively, sir." Joey stuck to his guns. And kept a straight face.

"Isn't it true, sir, that you were in fact the capo for the Grand Avenue crew, isn't that true?"

"That is positively no, sir."

Rarely does a "Perry Mason" moment occur in such high stakes proceedings, that is, where the witness breaks down and starts blurting admissions to the prosecution. Of course Joe was not going to admit he was a mob boss. But the prosecution kept pushing because it wanted the jury to see Joe's response, look at his eyes, hear his voice, and come to their own conclusions about his veracity. If they did not like what they saw and heard, Joey could hang himself with his own words.

"Mr. Lombardo, when you got out of jail in 1992, I think you said it was towards the end of the year, November?"

"1992. November, yes."

"You didn't quit the Outfit when you got out of jail, did you?"

This was a "when did you stop beating your wife question," and Joey refused to take the bait.

"I never belonged to the Outfit, sir."

"And isn't it true, though, that you were upset that the Outfit had taken away some of your power while you were in jail?"

"There is no such truth to that, sir."

"Well, you complained about that to Dr. Spilotro [the dentist, one of Tony Spilotro's brothers], didn't you?"

" . . . I have no reason to complain to Dr. Spilotro about a thing like that because it's not true."

"Well you told him sometime in 1993 that they were taking your guys away from you, right?"

"That is not true, sir."

"And isn't it true that the Outfit put you on the shelf for awhile, right?"

"The Outfit got no reason to put me on the shelf. I don't belong to an Outfit."

"Well, you told Dr. Spilotro a little later, in 2002, that you were concerned that New York mob guys were taking over Chicago Outfit business, did you not?"

"That is the most ridiculous thing I ever heard. No such thing was said to Dr. Spilotro."

"Well, you trust Dr. Spilotro, don't you?"

"No, I don't, sir."

"You did then."

"I trust him to a certain point."

"You trusted him with your freedom, didn't you?"

"No, I did not. I knew he was going to beef on me. I knew he was a beefer."

"You also told him that his brothers [Tony and Michael Spilotro] wouldn't have been killed if you had not been in jail, right?"

"That's not true, sir."

"Because you were their boss, right?"

"I was not their boss, sir."

"And you felt that you could speak up for them if you were out on the street and maybe save them from their murders, right?"

"That's not true, sir."

Joe Lombardo methodically denied everything, yet the government got what it wanted. Two things happened during that exchange. First, the prosecutor virtually did Joe's testifying for him. Even though Joey was saying no, no, no, the prosecution got the story before the jury. It is a perfectly legal and common tactic called leading the witness, which is allowed if the witness is adverse—meaning for the other side. The lawyers cannot testify for their own clients, just leading them through story after story with the witness just saying "yes" once in awhile, but they can lead hostile witnesses.

But a second thing happened, too. To strengthen his denial about trusting Dr. Spilotro, Joey added the comment " . . . I knew he was going to beef on me. He was a beefer." This, too, is a common tactic: keep the witness talking, for sooner or later he will slip up, get angry, or maybe fall victim to his own ego. It does not usually happen with such spectacular dramatic success as portrayed in the acclaimed film "A Few Good Men" when base commander Jack Nicholson blew up when his ego got the best of him, but little slip-ups are hard to avoid if one testifies long enough. The subtle point left for the jury was this: if Lombardo was not in the mob and had nothing to hide, why would he care if Dr. Spilotro had loose lips, a "beefer" who would beef, complain, or spill the beans?

One of the more bizarre events in recent Chicago mob history was Joey's infamous disappearance when he was indicted as part of the Family Secrets investigation. It made the television news every few nights, the press interviewed his lawyer Rick Halprin on camera, and local mob watchers were entertained for weeks by a game of "where's Joey." So Joey was asked on the stand about the indictment on April 21, 2005, and the events that transpired soon after.

"Well, you know arrest warrants had been issued for you, right?"

"I guess so, yes."

"Well, what do you mean you guess so? You read the papers, don't you?"

"Yes, I did."

"And you knew the U.S. marshals were looking for you, right?"

"That is correct, sir."

"And you hid from federal authorities, didn't you?"

"No, I was not hidden from federal authorities."

"Right. You hid yourself, didn't you?"

"Right."

"You hid yourself from this court, this very court, didn't you, Mr. Lombardo?"

"Yes, I did, sir."

"And you disguised yourself as well, didn't you?"

"No, I did not disguise myself."

"Well, you grew a beard, right?"

"No, I just let my beard grow, sir."

Here we have yet another prosecution tactic. A witness determined to deny everything can get so wrapped up in his denials that they begin to look contrived, even insulting. When the jury hears someone deny growing a beard, yet "just let the beard grow," they become skeptical, then insulted with such word twisting.

Mitch Mars, the prosecutor, then asked for permission to show a photo exhibit to the jury.

"I think it's safe to say, Mr. Lombardo, photo 33 does not depict the way you look now, does it?"

"No, there's a little difference." Joey was forced to concede that the freaky looking bearded man in the photo was clearly different from Joey the witness.

"A little difference in long hair and long beard, right?"

"Yeah, just a little bit."

"That's pretty funny, isn't it, Mr. Lombardo?"

"Well, a little joke once in a while ain't gonna hurt."

"And not only that, but you moved around from time to time so people couldn't find out where you were, right?"

"That's not true, sir."

"They arrested you after you came back from Dr. Spilotro's office, didn't they?"

"That is true. That's true, sir."

"And at the time you were staying with your friend, right?"

"That is true, sir."

"Mr. Calarco?"

"That is true, sir."

"You'd been there for a couple of weeks?"

"Maybe a few days more."

"And where did you stay before that?"

"I don't know where I was staying. I think I was staying somewhere in Oak Park, but the address I do not know."

"Who were you staying with?"

"I was staying with some guy that lived there, and would put me in the basement flat."

"Who is that?"

"His name is Joe."

"Do you know his last name?"

"No, I do not."

Joe and the prosecution continued to dance. Mitch Mars established that Joey had evaded the court jurisdiction for eight to nine months, that his friend George Kaluchi drove him to a place in Oak Park with Joey laying down in the back seat. There Joey remained for months, holed up in a basement apartment complete with its own kitchen, shower, bed, and a TV.

"And you went through a lot of lengths to avoid being arrested by the FBI, didn't you?"

"Yeah. Yes, I did."

"And your testimony here today is you didn't, you claim you didn't, know this was a federal crime to run from the FBI?"

"That is true."

"To run from this court?"

"That is true, sir."

"Well, you wrote a letter to the court, did you not?"

"Yes, I did, sir."

"And you made demands on the court in your letter, didn't you?"

"Yes, I did, sir, yeah."

"You demanded that you be given a bond, right?"

"No, I didn't say—"

"—you said you wouldn't surrender unless a bond was guaranteed for you, right?"

"That's true. That is true."

"And you also said that you wanted a separate trial, right?"

"That is true."

"That was another demand made by you on this court, right?"

"It wasn't a demand, sir. I was asking for it."

"Well, you said you wouldn't surrender unless those things were given to you, right?"

"I was discussing with the judge what my thinking was and what my feelings were, sir."

"And you wanted guarantees before you would submit to the jurisdiction of this court, isn't that true?"

"I wanted a guarantee?"

"Yeah, you wanted a guaranteed bond and a guaranteed separate trial, right?"

"No, I was stating—"

"—you were negotiating with the court, right?"

"No, I wasn't negotiating. I was telling him what my thinking is of why I didn't show up for court."

"You were telling the court what your conditions were before you would surrender. Isn't that true, Mr. Lombardo?"

"That is true, sir."

It took awhile to get there, but the government finally got Joey to admit to his demands and conditions to giving himself up. The government was scoring points with the jury, implying that Joey was toying with the court, the law, the FBI, and even the authority of this jury.

Mitch Mars pressed Joe still further. "And you spent a lot of time avoiding the whole process of this court, about 9 months, right?"

"Mr. Mars, I had 300,000,000 people against me."

"And isn't it true that you even went through the lengths of getting your teeth examined and fixed at night surreptitiously, correct?"

"That is not true, sir."

"You went there after business hours with Dr. Spilotro, didn't you?"

"That is true, sir."

"And you went there hoping that you weren't going to get caught, right?"

"That is true, sir."

"And you went there with your full beard and long hair and a band-aid over your nose? Right?"

"I went there with a beard."

"Well, the whole point was, you didn't want to get caught coming in or out of Dr. Spilotro's office, isn't that true?"

"That is true, sir."

"And during one of the visits, you gave Dr. Spilotro some documents involving this case, didn't you?"

"That is true, sir."

"Where did you get them from?"

"George Kaluchi gave them to me."

"Where did he get them from?"

"I have no idea."

"And you gave them to Dr. Spilotro, didn't you?"

"That is true, sir."

"You trusted him with your freedom, didn't you?"

Joe was suddenly caught in another trap. He had said he didn't really trust the doctor, but then he trusted the dentist with documents, not to mention his very after-hours presence at a time when Joey was clearly on the lamb.

"No, I was a little leery," Joey explained, "but I had nowhere else to go. I had an infected tooth and a big cavity. I was in pain and he pulled it out for me."

"And even at the very end, Mr. Lombardo, you told Dr. Spilotro his brothers were killed because people had to follow orders, isn't that true?"

"That's not true, sir."

"They had to follow orders of the Outfit, isn't that true, Mr. Lombardo?"

"That is not true. He didn't tell you the truth—Dr. Pat."

"Dr. Pat was lying, as well?"

"He was lying about whatever he said about me."

As I listened to all this unfold while the cross examination was coming to an end, I could not help but wonder whether the jury would believe Lombardo's story, his alibis, his denials, his "pay no attention to the man behind the curtain" logic, all in the face of the obvious, especially Joey's key role in the mob.

The paths of Joey Lombardo and the Spilotro family would cross many times during their respective mob careers and the ensuing Family Secrets trial. But no encounter was more poignant, perhaps, than when Dr. Patrick Spilotro, the respected dentist from suburban Park Ridge, Illinois, took the stand on August 7, 2007. Patrick, an acquaintance of mine, is the older brother of the murdered gangsters Michael and Tony. When Joey Lombardo was on the run after news of the Family Secrets investigation broke, Joey reached out to Dr. Spilotro. By the time he took the stand, Pat Spilotro was aging, but at 70 years still had a head of white hair and a professional dignity about him. He wore a blue suit, and as he took the stand his lineage was obvious—Pat's face was a carbon copy of his brother Tony "the Ant" Spilotro. Pat, a legit dentist and wholly straight, had fixed the teeth of mobsters for years.

While under oath, Pat Spilotro testified that Joey Lombardo made an unscheduled visit for pain from an abscessed tooth. Pat testified that he received a call on Jan. 6, 2006 and was informed that Joey was in trouble and had a serious dental problem. Pat arranged to meet Joey in the basement of Spilotro's office building. Joey showed up with a hooded jacket sporting a beard and a band-aid on his nose. Pat worked on Joey's teeth for about 45 minutes to an hour.

When Joey arrived, he asked Pat, "Are we on video camera?" Hardly the first question most of us have at the dentist, but Pat responded as one might expect. "No, I don't think so." Joey trusted

Pat, and at no time suspected the dentist as an FBI tipster—though for years Pat had worked with the Feds years before hoping to learn the true fate of his brothers. Pat then testified that Lombardo had repeatedly told him over the years that had Lombardo not been in prison at the time, those murders of his brothers never would have happened.

But that night, in the dentist's office, Joey offered something quite different. According to Pat's testimony, Joey, who at the time was on the run from the law, made a comment much different than his courtroom testimony. "I recall his words very vividly," Spilotro said. "He said 'Doc, you get an order, you follow the order. If you don't follow the order, you go, too.'" Spilotro called the FBI and gave them the exact time of Joey's appointment.

Pat went on, telling the juror's about a conversation he had with Lombardo in December, 2002. Spilotro said that Lombardo was upset because a New York mobster had come into the city to try to take over certain functions of the Chicago Outfit. But that story was contrary to Joey's testimony, the effect of which was that he had long been retired from mob activities and, in any event, that Joey had never been a mob leader. I watched Joey as Pat spoke. Lombardo listened intently while leaning on his cane, and periodically turned his head toward attorney Rick Halprin.

Pat also told the jury how he knew Nicholas Calabrese, that he did his dental work, and that he once visited Nick in prison and actually recorded him. But Nick offered nothing about the murders of the Spilotro brothers. He did send Pat a Christmas card from prison in 2001, telling Pat that he had made a decision he never believed he would ever make. We all know now what Nick Calabrese was referring to, a decision that would contribute to the success of the Family Secrets investigation.

The last time he saw his brother Tony, according to Pat's testimony, was June 12, 1986, just two days before Tony vanished and one day after he last saw brother Michael. Pat explained that while Tony was in his office, Tony had access to a phone and apparently called the home of mob boss James Marcello, at least according to phone records retrieved later. Pat testified that he had been in Wisconsin when he got a call from his brother Victor who told him that his brothers Michael and Tony had not come home. "Something is terribly wrong," Victor feared.

Spilotro said he never knew of Nick Calabrese's involvement in his brothers' murder. "They never told me they did it. But there's no honor amongst these men," he continued. "No respect. They are all a different breed. Money and power are their gods, nothing else."

Joey told the court and the jury that he was just a working man who held legitimate jobs and that his only connection to the mobsters came from friendships with powerful men like Dorfman. Along the way, Joey's personal health became an issue, too, a recurring theme that his counsel prayed upon. At one point when asked if he had seen a physician lately, Joey alluded to his widely reported disappearance by answering that he had been "what do they call it, unavailable." A true jokester all the way was Joey "the Clown" Lombardo.

Joey explained much of his predicament by blaming others. "There are a lot of liars and mistaken people out there." He continued to maintain that the legions of witnesses and others were wrong or making things up. While in custody a year earlier, Joey had undergone heart surgery, and his lawyer often brought up Joey's complaints of chest pains. While still on the lamb before trial, Joey had even written Judge Zagel to explain that he was not giving himself up because "medical care in prison was a farce."

He went on to say that his only relationship with Jackie "the Lackey" Cerone, a top mob boss, was as a friend, that he would meet him at the golf course at White Pines and at the Riverwoods Country Club. And of course, Joey would also meet up with Cerone at his house in Elmwood Park and even at Cerone's summer home in Fox Lake in the countryside northwest of Chicago.

Some days during the trial Joey seemed tired and showed his age. Other days, though, there were flashes of Lombardo the jokester. One day, while in a happy-go-lucky mood, he seemed to joke around with everyone—especially me. I recall that Joey was chewing candy at one point, and he suddenly turned to me with a playful expression and said, "Hey, Jack, it tastes like lobster." I replied in kind, "Don't you wish."

Throughout Joey's testimony portion of the trial, Frank Calabrese, Sr., and Jimmy Marcello would have frequent hand-over-mouth discussions, sometimes for several minutes. Maybe they spoke of the witnesses against them, or their respective families, contempt for the system of justice—where Jimmy Hoffa is, who knows?

I suspect at least some of these defendants know a lot of answers, including where plenty of bones are buried, maybe even Hoffa's. I do know that Jimmy Hoffa, the man who made the Teamsters the most powerful union in the country, has been missing for over 30 years, and no doubt has been long dead. On July 30, 1975, Hoffa waited for his luncheon appointment at a restaurant in Bloomfield Township in Michigan. According to published reports, Hoffa was wearing Gucci loafers with blue pants and a blue short sleeve shirt that day. According to his wife and acquaintances, Hoffa seemed jittery, perhaps with good reason. His lunch date was with two certifiable mobsters, one from New Jersey and one, I believe, from Detroit.

Hoffa had been stirring the pot with his intent to run again as president of the union. He had been removed from the union over a decade before after a 1964 conviction for jury tampering, conspiracy, and other crimes. Hoffa had spent five years in the slammer when none other than President Richard Nixon granted him clemency in 1971. Frank Fitzsimmons, a well like union man, was Hoffa's successor, and most of the mob bosses wanted Frank to stay. Hoffa was potentially a loose cannon, but even worse he was a lightning rod. And they liked the arrangement with Fitzsimmons.

Witnesses said that a maroon 1975 Mercury pulled out of the parking lot in a hurry, and the driver of a truck recognized Hoffa in the back seat. Both mobsters Hoffa was meeting that day had alibis, and the car itself belonged to the son of another mobster who said he had loaned it to a good friend of Hoffa's, a teamster colleague—indeed his son-in-law— named Chuckie O'Brien. Hoffa would have been savvy enough not to enter a car like that with mob guys, but he might have been comfortable with someone like Chuckie. But Chuckie later had his own alibis, yet they were weak and failed to fully check out.

Police dogs and DNA testing years later both confirmed Hoffa was in the back seat of that car, as well as the trunk. But no one has seen him since.

As far back as 1959, Hoffa was publically linked to organized crime in a spectacular way. Bobby Kennedy, was at the time chief counsel to the Senate labor Rackets Committee, appeared on the nationally televised Jack Paar Show, the precursor to the Tonight Show on NBC, looked at Paar and the television camera and pointed fingers at Hoffa, Johnny Dio, and Tony "Ducks" Corallo. Hoffa hated Kennedy, publically demeaned him, and even had a physical altercation with him. That kind of baiting was dangerous, and even though Bobby Kennedy was already dead when Hoffa disappeared, Hoffa was still a lightning rod for the government.

Prosecutor Mitch Mars brought the Family Secrets trial full circle to Hoffa and the Teamsters. As his cross of Joey Lombardo was coming to a close, Mars referred to a 1973 indictment of Lombardo, the one where he allegedly ended up with a pile of union money, when he asked whether Joey knew that a conviction would have barred him from the Teamsters Union. Lombardo said he was already barred, but that wasn't the prosecution's point. Mars used that as foundation to ask if he knew that Dorfman could have been likewise barred, and he confirmed that he did.

"And that's the golden goose, isn't it, the Teamsters money?" asked Mars, punctuating the day's testimony. That it was. Union money was a bottomless pit, a lucrative golden goose for those with fancy tastes—and an appetite for power.

I am personally convinced that Hoffa's disappearance was a mob hit. When he returned from prison in 1970, Hoffa wanted his lucrative and prestigious job back as Teamsters president. Hoffa had been convicted for jury tampering and diverting pension funds for his own use, then cooled his heels in federal prison at Lewisburg, Pennsylvania, a high security joint where its G-Block is unofficially called Mafia row. The prison has housed a number of crime figures including Hoffa and John Gotti, not to mention other luminaries like Alger Hess and even civil rights activist Bayard Rustin.

While Hoffa was away and Frank Fitzsimmons was president of the Teamster, things ran smoothly and the feds did not sniff around as much. When Hoffa was paroled, though, he started to make noise in Detroit and Chicago, but the Chicago mob nixed his return to head the Teamsters. James Riddle Hoffa was acting tough, and the mob was annoyed. Hoffa was taken out in July 1975. He was expected to meet Tony Giacalone, a top Detroit mob figure, at the Red Fox Restaurant outside Detroit. Giacalone never showed up, but Hoffa's stepson Chuckie O'Brien did. Trusting O'Brien, Hoffa got into the car—and was never seen again. The Hoffa disappearance is still an ongoing, open case. The FBI code name is "Hofex," short for "Hoffa Execution." I guess they feel it was a hit, too.

Was Joey Lombardo involved? He sure doesn't admit anything about it in open court, but he did stun the jury with an endless series of denials, continuing to stonewall his role with the Outfit. Certainly he was involved with Dorfman and the threats to Shenker, both of which put him close to the Hoffa situation. Shenker had wriggled out of his own jam, by the way, dying of natural causes in 1989 at age 82. Hoffa was not so lucky.

Joey's testimony would still provide plenty of drama. When he got to the Last Supper, a mob gathering of top bosses in Chicago depicted by a government photo showing Joey right there with Auippa, Cerone, and a handful of other top figures, his explanation would leave the jury shell shocked.

Jimmy: Chapter 18 is about Joey and contains some testimony excerpts for effect; Chapter 19 is about the trial and Joey on the stand, it is more chronological and linear.

18

The Last Supper

August 14, 2007

    When I arrived early for court on the 14th of August, I found the hallways clogged by a long line of spectators, hundreds of them, all eager to catch a glimpse of Joey "the Clown" Lombardo on the stand.
    Onlookers jammed the hallways two and three abreast. Except for those who had already been keeping an eye on the trial, most had never seen Joey Lombardo in person before. All were anxious for a first hand look at one of the most notorious of all the ranking Outfit crime figures. I was curious, too. What would Joey say? Would he spill the beans or stay mum? Fat chance he would talk now after all these years—still, there was a great deal of excitement in the air.
    Joey was dressed in a conservative gray sports coat with a silver tie. His hair, tidily cropped still sporting a hint of Roman style bangs, always reminded me of Julius Caesar, but today those strands were accented by a salt & pepper aging that looked good on his 78 years. Joey sat in his wheelchair at the defense table, cane in hand, and he still he retained an air of dignity and the great power that once defined him—and to a degree still does.
    By the time the doors opened to Judge Zagel's courtroom at 9:30am, room 2525 quickly filled to capacity with other federal judges, FBI supervisors, federal prosecutors, and a flock of reporters from television and other media. I took my usual seat under the stately old courtroom clock that dates back to 1902. It steadfastly hung from the wall as it had done for decades and seemed to keep

watch over these five fallen stars at the defense table, but really it was just keeping time—or should I say marking off time, for that is what was happening to them, to me, to history.

Before court officially began, I had one of my brief personal chats with Joey. He held his oversized Harry Caray 1980s style eyeglasses in his hands, shuffling back and forth from one hand to the other. All of us could feel the mounting tension in the courtroom, but I was close enough to sense how nervous Joey himself really was. Did I feel for him? How *could* I—yet, indeed, how could I not?

"Do you clean those off before you testify?" I said, glancing at his glasses, hoping to ease the tension.

Joey raised them into the air for a better look, searching for smudges. "Thanks, Jack." He consciously used my last name, a nod of respect I think, not necessarily for me personally, but perhaps for the many decades that we had shared from opposite sides of the street.

Joey would be on the stand in a matter of moments. What would he say? What would he feel? This is a man who for over half a century had eaten fear for breakfast and had built a career on the shoulders of terror inflicted by him and his cohorts. Yet he was still nervous, a fish out of water, nabbed by something bigger than us all—not just the feds, but by humanity itself. The reckoning had arrived.

As the crowd buzzed, James Marcello's attorney Marc W. Martin introduced me to his father William J. Martin, age 71. As a young states attorney himself, the senior Martin once headed the team who prosecuted Richard Speck, one of the most notorious, cold blooded mass murderers in U.S. history who went down in the 1960s for slashing no fewer than 8 student nurses in Chicago. He even wrote an acclaimed book about the ordeal called *Crime of the Century*. William found it interesting that I, too, was an author, having recently published my own *Three Boys Missing* about another stunning Chicago murder case. We sat together most of the day, trading war stories from the old days at 26th and California during numerous breaks in the trial.

When court finally began, the defense opened with a handful of preliminary witnesses. Joey's attorney Rick Halprin did the direct examination.

First up was Eli Jacobs, age 69, a purchasing agent for a company that did business with the slain Danny Seifert. Lombardo himself had been a supervisor, and the point was that Joey had held a real job in the 1970s. Next came a former FBI agent, Peter Wacks, who testified that Emma Seifert, Danny's widow, have never told him that she believed Lombardo had been one of the masked gunmen who had murdered her husband. A third witness, named Bonnie, now age 65, told how she had been a former mistress of Joey, told how he would take money from his pockets to pay vendors—again showing Lombardo in business, and with a sympathetic spin.

Finally, at 3:05pm, after one of several breaks, a waiting U.S. marshal broke the silence. "All rise."

Rick Halprin called Joseph P. Lombardo, age 78, to the stand. Joey was steered forward in his wheelchair by the marshals, who were forced to navigate a virtual obstacle course before wheeling him to the stand from a rear hallway. On the way he paused to flirt with Blanca Lara, the blond court reporter seated up front, getting her to smile. Lombardo could be very charming in his day, and some habits do die hard.

Joey swore to tell the truth with a terse "I do" delivered by a grating voice that showed its age.

This was the test of Joey's life. The marbles had all finally landed in one fateful basket that was about to play itself out with Joey trying to convince a jury that he was neither a killer nor a top mob boss. To do so, he had to also convince those jurors that he had worked a real job, including real work at Danny Seifert's business. This was Joey's last dance, and he had to get it right. Otherwise, justice and his own failing health would probably send him to a federal prison for the rest of his life, destined to die alone somewhere behind maximum security bars.

Joseph "the Clown" Lombardo leaned toward the microphone and directly faced the jury. It was a dramatic moment: alleged mob boss and accused murderer about to take the stand, under oath, in his own defense. He was ready.

HALPRIN: Good afternoon. Would you state your name, first and last.
LOMBARDO: Joseph P. Lombardo.
HALPRIN: I'm going to call you Joey, is that okay?
LOMBARDO: It's okay with me, sir.

Rick wanted Joey to seem more human, but then he got straight to the meat and potatoes.

HALPRIN: On September 27th, 1974, sir, did you kill Danny Seifert?
LOMBARDO: Positively no.
HALPRIN: Have you ever been a capo or a member of the Chicago Outfit?
LOMBARDO: Positively no.

Rick hit the jury with the big questions right up front, then drifted to the background material, asking Joey about his old neighborhood where he had grown up. Joey had lived at 510 N. Elizabeth Street and went to the local James Otis Grammar School. The "old neighborhood" was established as the Elizabeth, Grand Avenue, and Ogden area, where Joey had lived all his life. How long? "I would say about 78 years," Joey reported.

Rick then asked if Joey knew a local restaurant called Patsy's. Joey did, of course—we all knew the place, anybody on one side of law enforcement or the other knew Patsy's Restaurant, and that meant we knew Patsy, too. The place was located at Ogden and Grand on the near west side, a working class area along the way to the old Chicago Stadium where boxers, hockey players, and even Michael Jordan first made their marks on the city. Patsy had a famous name, as well—or at least it would soon be famous. He was Patsy Spilotro, Tony's father. "Patsy" was short for Pasquale.

Patsy's Restaurant was originally opened in 1920, on the eve of the Capone era, by Patsy himself, the immigrant father of six Spilotro brothers, including of course Tony, Michael, and the dentist Pat. The restaurant was at 470 N. Ogden, at the corner of Grand Avenue, in the Italian neighborhoods on the near west side a few miles from "the patch," a relatively safe neighborhood not far from Chicago's loop. The Grand-Ogden "patch" would produce "the circus café" gang whose leader would be none other than Tony Accardo, who also grew up in the area. Later, of course, Accardo would graduate to bigger things: the Outfit itself.

According to Pat, another well known regular was Chicago Mayor Martin H. Kennelly, a reformer from the Irish Bridgeport neighborhood who was elected in 1947 and re-elected in 1951. Sensing Kennelly was growing too independent, he was dumped by the Democratic machine, which opted for an Irish new comer by the name of Richard J. Daley, who was elected in 1955. With regulars like Accardo and Mayor Kennelly, and family staff like Tony and Michael Spilotro, Patsy's had become a fixture of Chicago lore.

Patsy ran the restaurant until his death in 1954. I knew the place, of course, and I became acquainted with his son Pat, a respected dentist with no ties to the darker side of the Spilotro legacy, as the Family Secrets trial wore on. Pat tells me that all six Spilotro brothers worked the restaurant when they were young. The mother lived for many years after the original Patsy died; she did not pass on until 1995

For the better part of two days during the Family Secrets trial, Rick Halprin lobbed softball questions to Joey, who was well prepared and hit them all on the sweet spot. When Lombardo was then grilled by prosecutor Mitch Mars, he stuck to his guns, pleading ignorance, blaming coincidences, or accusing witnesses of lying about his finances, the Seifert murder, and Joey's role in the Outfit. [Jimmy: This is condensed because two days of Joey denying everything is boring and unnecessary.]

Mars went after Lombardo, suggesting that Joey was much more than a lowly "gofer" for the mob, just running small errands for the bigger guys. The two combatants went head to head, with neither backing down. Mars then played the tape of Joey, Allen Dorfman, and St. Louis mob attorney Morris Shenker. This was the conversation picked up by the government, which had bugged Dorfman's office, catching both the practice session Joey had with Dorfman while working himself up for the confrontation with Shenker who the mob felt was holding back Chicago mob money, and later picking up the actual discussion between Joey and Shenker. The jury was on the edge of their seats. So was I.

It's hard to argue with a taped recording that memorializes a plan to threaten a top St. Louis attorney, then later showing how Lombardo actually delivered those threats. This was no small potatoes meeting. Shenker, of course, was Jimmy Hoffa's lawyer, Joey was a top Chicago mob figure, and Dorfman would soon be eliminated by a bullet to the head—for knowing too much—possibly ordered by Joey himself. Shenker kept denying everything, and then everyone in the courtroom heard Joey say to the 72-year-old Shenker, loud and clear: "I'm just telling you if they come back and give you a message and if you want to defy it, I'm sure you'll never reach 73."

Mars pressed Joey, but Lombardo insisted that all he was doing was play acting—playing tough guy mobster to get a point across, to get Shenker to repay funds to the local teamster boss Dorfman. "That was a role that was particularly suited to you, wasn't it?" Mars countered.

"A good role?" Joey answered.

"The role of a gangster, yeah."

"Yeah, like James Cagney, Edward G. Robinson . . ." said Joey, referencing these tough guy star actors from the 1940s to make the point about his own supposed play-acting.

Mars responded that it was an especially good role for Joey "as a member of the Outfit."

"No, that's not true, sir."

"Boss of the Grand Avenue crew?"

"That's not true, sir."

Mars was relentless, going for "the Clown's" jugular.

"You did threaten a man's life, didn't you?"

"I threatened my wife, too, when I was married." He meant he was big on idle threats, but I'm not sure that was a good way to present it to the jurors.

Mars hammered away, and as Joey insisted he was only play acting, he nervously moved his cane from hand to hand.

"Did you threaten the man with his life, Mr. Lombardo, yes or no?"

"I didn't threaten him, I just told him he won't reach 73."

"And how do you interpret that for a man that's 72?"

"He lived past 72," Joey answered, making a fairly good point.

"That's not what you told him, Mr. Lombardo. You threatened him with his life, yes or no?"

"No, no, no, he didn't pay, sir, and he lived to be 73, 74, 75. He still didn't pay."

Then Mars addressed the Danny Seifert murder. Daniel Seifert was allegedly gunned down when Lombardo and his crew, including Frank "the German" Schwiehs, were trying to handcuff the man. But Seifert, a Bensenville businessman, got free and ran off, so they shot him. Seifert was Lombardo's partner in a fiberglass molding company, then turned snitch against Joey and was due to testify in court against Lombardo for laundering money from Teamster pension fund.

The case fell apart after Seifert's murder, so the charges against Joey were dropped. The Outfit and the Teamsters had new life, all of which took immense pressure off the backs of Dorfman, Spilotro, Lombardo himself, and many others.

Mars drilled Lombardo still more about Siefert, riveting the courtroom with questions that showed how Seifert had been gunned down while running away, finally shot in front of his wife and child.

"I had no idea that Mr. Siefert was going to testify against us until he got killed," Joey insisted.

"You knew," continued Mars, "that if you got convicted in that case and if Dorfman got convicted in that case, the "golden goose" was gone for you?"

"That is not true, sir."

"Mr. Lombardo, the next day you were at a golf course—you were at a golf course after Danny Siefert was murdered?"

"That is not true, sir."

"You were there with Marshall Caifano?"

"No, that's not true."

"And with Johnny Rodgers?"

"No, that is not true, sir."

"You told Johnny Rodgers and Marshall Caifano the very next day, quote, 'that son of a bitch won't testify against anybody now, will he.' That's what you said to Rodgers and Caifano, isn't that true, Mr. Lombardo?"

"That is not true, sir. He's a liar. I can tell a liar when I hear it."

The court took a break. Joey needed it, he was taking a real beating on the stand.

Back in session, Joey was questioned by his own counsel who explored what can only be described as Joey's missing wallet defense.

Lombardo said someone had lifted his wallet and driver's license from his car glove compartment, so he slipped into a pancake house at California and Diversey where two uniformed policemen were having breakfast. One of them was Richard Orissy. Joey said he wanted to file a police report. The officers asked Joey to wait until they were finished, after which they had Joey follow them to the station where he made out the report.

"What time did you arrive at the police station?" Halprin asked.

"I would say about 8:15am."

"What time did you leave the police station?"

"I would say about 9:00, 9:30—10:00."

"Joey, did you do anything else about the missing wallet?"

Yes, I went to the Secretary of State's office to get a new license that same day. I was there around 2:00 or 3:00pm, then heard on the news about the Daniel Seifert murder as he was leaving."

So there we have it: when Mr. Siefert was being gunned down in front of his family, Joey had allegedly surrounded by cops and government officials. A perfect alibi?

On further cross examination, Mars delved into the wallet story. Had the car been broken into? No, the windows were open, it was a warm day. "The officer told you to go to the Shakespeare district police station, right?"

Lombardo snapped back. "You're not hearing right, sir. I said I went into the restaurant, there's two policemen there eating, I told them that someone took my wallet and stuff out of my compartment and I would like to make a police report. 'Wait until we get through eating, you have to follow us to the station.' That's the story I told before."

It seemed like Joey had scored a couple points, keeping Mars to the facts. But not for long. It was a trap. Either Mars had set it, or Joey stumbled there all on his own, but a trap is what presented itself.

Mars responded. "That's not the story you told when you were first interviewed by FBI agents, isn't that true? Mr. Lombardo, let me direct your attention to the day of the murder."

"Go right ahead," said Joey.

"September 27, 1974, the FBI came to see you."

"You know they did," Joey challenged. It seemed like Mars was getting to Lombardo because his answers were becoming obnoxious, even hostile.

"It was at 8:30 in the morning, roughly, that Danny Siefert was murdered, right?"

"That's what I understand."

"And FBI agents came to you at about 6:00 o'clock that day, at night?"

Mars established that two agents named Robert Whiting and Larry Damion came to Lombardo's residence at 2210 West Ohio, and that the Siefert murder was already in the papers by then.

"When they came to see you, you were reading the *Chicago Daily News* weren't you?"

"I don't recall, sir."

"And you were reading the article about the murder of Danny Siefert, weren't you?"

"I don't recall."

"And your name was in that article, was it not?"

"I don't recall, go ahead." Joey sounded well prepared. Lawyers will caution witnesses to say "I don't recall" instead of saying "I don't know." It may seem like a fine line, but "I don't know" technically means that one never knew and simply doesn't know. Like what is the diameter of the moon—I don't know means you don't, while I don't recall means that you knew but can't think of it. People who don't know at all suddenly cannot remember something, while those who cannot recall can later have their memory triggered without impeaching their own credibility.

"And the agents came and wanted to talk to you and you're reading the paper and you said this article is—quote—"full of crap," do you remember that?"

"Well, I might have said that. Go ahead."

"And you didn't say anything further to them, did you, Mr. Lombardo?"

At that point Rick Halprin jumped in, asking the judge for a sidebar. "No," the court answered.

"Isn't it true, sir, at that point you did not tell them about this alibi that you say you had for your whereabouts that morning?"

"I don't recall, sir."

"You didn't tell them you were in a restaurant, did you?"

"I don't recall."

"You didn't tell them your wallet was stolen, did you?"

"I don't recall, sir."

"You didn't say 'this newspaper article is full of crap and isn't it lucky I got an alibi for where I was today,' did you?"

"Let me give you the answer, sir."

"I'd like an answer yes or no, Mr. Lombardo."

"Just a yes or no?"

"Yeah."

"I don't speak to the FBI when I have a problem."

"So the answer is no, you didn't tell them about the alibi?"

"I don't think—I don't recall the conversation."

I don't think the jury was buying the story—or in some ways, the lack of a story. I was thinking, and I suspect the jurors were, too, that if the FBI ever comes after me for a crime that takes place while I happen to be surrounded by police officers, I think I'm going to say so right off the bat.

Upon re-direct, Halprin asked Joey about a photograph that had previously been introduced as an exhibit in the trial. It was a group shot of top mobsters, something of a "last supper" gathering of who's who in the Outfit.

"Joey, see that picture?"

"I couldn't begin to count the number of times that's been shown in this trial."

"I'm sure you're tired of looking at it, but—"

"Objection," Mars interrupted, weary of this set-up.

The Court's patience was running thin, too. "I believe," said Judge Zagel, "the prosecution would like you to ask a question which is what you're standing there for."

Halprin groped for, and found, a question. "Where are you located in that picture?"

"I'm standing up with a suit."

"And can you identify any of the other individuals in that picture?"

"Sure can."

"Go ahead."

Joey agreed the photo was from 1976, and he proceeded to ID a virtual "family" reunion. The man to Joey's right, with arms folded, was Jack Cerone, a big Outfit hitter and one time mob boss. Seated on the far right, in a white shirt, was a fat guy named Turk Torello, and next to him was Cesar D'Varco. Joe D'Amato was there, too, plus another character who used to play golf with Cerone. The two men in the front were Tony Accardo, one of the most powerful figures in mob history, along with top boss Joseph Aiuppa. Another man was present, Dominic DiBella, a north side capo, who was clearly emaciated—Joey said the man was dying of cancer at the time. This man was the reason for the "last supper" get-together and photograph. DiBella did his part—he died shortly after the photo was taken.

"That's the purpose of that meeting with them guys, because this guy is dying and they want to have a last meal with him. He has three months to live, three to six months to live."

I knew Jackie "the Lackey" Cerone. He was a ruthless, even frightening, top mob figure. A longtime mobster, Jackie had become chauffeur to Outfit boss Tony Accardo. Then Sam Giancana took Jackie under his wing, and eventually Cerone became boss himself after the semi-retirements of Accardo and Joey Auippa. At one time, Cerone was part of an enforcer team that had tortured and murdered loan shark William "Action" Jackson. Cerone was no stranger to the courtroom, for he had been arrested over 20 times for everything from armed robbery to embezzlement. As a matter of fact, in 1986 Cerone, Joey Auippa, and two others were convicted of skimming $2 million from a Las Vegas casino—the very caper that inspired the acclaimed film *Casino*. He died in 1996, not long after his release from prison.

I became acquainted with Cerone through my uncle who introduced us many, many years ago. Both Jackie and my uncle were from the old West Side neighborhoods, and eventually they went into business together—which lasted until my uncle died of a heart attack in 1980. Jackie was civil to me, but I was wary of his reputation as a mob executioner.

Another man in the Last Supper photo, who was next to the sick man, was identified as Vince Solano. Another mob figure, a union guy named Al Pilotto, was there, too. It was quite a group. But if Lombardo was not in the mob, what was he doing there?

"Well, I went to a wake. So I went to the wake. After I was there for awhile I met a friend of mine named Albert Milleri, and I said I was hungry, and he lives up west around there, around Elmwood Park somewhere. And I says, 'I can go for a nice beef sandwich. He says 'let's go.' So he brought me to this here place.

"Do you remember the name of the restaurant?"

"I have no idea what the name of the restaurant is. I know it's on Harlem Avenue."

Joey told the story. He had been in the washroom, then came out and suddenly he's invited over to see some people and have a drink. "I said hello to everybody, and then after a few minutes, five or ten minutes, fifteen minutes, I don't know, and then I left."

The Last Dance

I was acquainted with Pilotto, too, the union man in the photo. It was around 1967 when my partner and I had stopped a lone driver headed to O'Hare Airport at 3:00am. We checked his driver's license and recognized the name. It was Alfred Pilotto. We surveyed the car, inside and out, including the trunk. We found nothing unusual (like a dead body). Pilotto was very pleasant, and he gave me his business card. "If you or your family need a job, just bring this card to my office," he said. I still have that business card. It identifies Alfred Pilotto as president of the "International Hod Carriers, Building and Common Laborers Union." Being union president can be dangerous work. This is the same Alfred Pilotto who gunman Danny Bounds testified about, an attack which resulted in a retaliatory hit on Pilotto's own bodyguard who apparently had planned the Pilotto shooting in the first place. One day while Pilotto was playing golf when a waiting gunman jumped from the bushes and ambushed him, pumping four bullets into Pilotto's body. Remarkably, Pilotto survived and later stood trial in Miami.

Halprin continued. "Did you, Joey, ever commit any crimes with Mr. Accardo?"

"Positively no."

"Did you ever receive any money from Mr. Accardo?"

"Not a penny."

"And, Joey, what does the term "Chicago Outfit" mean to you?"

"A group of people that get together and conspire. They do illegal things or legitimate things, they go partners."

The Clown had some explaining to do. He just happened to be in this underworld version of "the last supper," an image that has since become a highlight at Congressional hearings on organized crime in the United States? What a coincidence. It could happen to anyone, right? Did the jurors believe that any of them could stumble into having a drink with Tony Accardo, then get their picture taken with him and a cadre of mob brass?

Mars identified the restaurant in question as the Sicily Restaurant at 2743 N. Harlem Avenue. I believe this "last supper" meeting was held around noon to assure added privacy—the restaurant did not open until 4:00pm for the dinner trade. The joint wasn't too far from where I once lived, actually, and I had eaten there myself a few times—but not on this occasion. Mars continued to question Joey about the gathering.

"Do I know the people?" Joey repeated. "Yes, I do."

"And it's true, isn't it, that they are all members of the Outfit?"

"Let me tell you," Lombardo answered, "there's not one member there that I know that was told to me that they took an oath of a secret organization."

Now there's an evasive answer if I ever heard one. Apparently Mars felt the same way.

"I'm not asking about the oath, Mr. Lombardo. I'm asking about organized crime. These men that you see in this photograph were members of organized crime, weren't they?"

"They never told me they were," Lombardo insisted.

"And more than that, they were bosses in organized crime, right?"

"They never told me that."

Lombardo was not winning the exchange, however. Even though Mars was getting nowhere on the surface, the jury heard Joey mince words like they had never been sliced and diced before. He was not giving an inch to the prosecution, but by digging in so hard he seemed disingenuous, even arrogant.

Mars continued. "Well, didn't you just testify earlier today that Joey Aiuppa, the guy on the far left, was the boss of Cicero?"

"That is correct, sir."

"And by that you meant boss of the mob, right, in Cicero?"

"The Cicero crew? That is true, the jury heard me."

"No, I don't think they heard you say the Cicero crew."

"Well, ask them." Joey was getting a little cocky—and the jury was sitting just a few feet to his right.

"I'm asking *you*, Mr. Lombardo," Mars pressed, emphasizing *you*.

"I say he was the boss of Cicero, and I didn't say he was a member of organized crime. I said he was the boss of Cicero."

"And the boss of Cicero is the boss of the Cicero crew of the Outfit, right?"

"He's the boss, if you want something done in Cicero, you want something done and you couldn't get it through a politician, you go see him and he get's it done."

"And you reported to him from time to time, didn't you?" Mars questioned.

"No, I never reported to him. I seen him from time to time but I didn't report to him."

"You know a man named Solano in that photograph?"

"Solano? Yean, Vince Solano, yeah, I know him. He's a union guy."

"He's a member of the Laborers Union at one time, right?"

"That's what he was."

"And he was also the boss of the Rush Street crew, wasn't he?"

"Not that I know about."

"How about Mr. Pilotto, the guy sitting next to him, you know him, right?"

"Yes, I did."

"You called him a union guy?"

"Absolutely."

"He was also the boss of the Chicago Heights crew, wasn't he?"

"I don't know if he was the boss of Chicago Heights."

"You know he had that accident where he got shot at a golf course?"

The word "accident" resonated through the courtroom. We all reflected on the number of times we've dodged bullets on the golf course: none.

"I read about it in the paper."

"And then the man standing behind him is Jack Cerone?"

"Yes, I knew him."

"He's the underboss of the Outfit, isn't he?"

"I don't know if he is the underboss, but I know him."

"Going around the table, the guy you have slated in the white shirt is Mr. Torello, isn't he?"

"That is correct."

"You know him as Turk?"

"That's him."

Mars soon got around to Cesar D'Varco, who once headed the Rush Street crew. Rush Street was at one time the center of Chicago night life, in the old days featuring the likes of Frank Sinatra, Lenny Bruce, George Carlin at such popular hangouts as the nationally known Mr. Kelly's. The area is known for its bars, hoards of young people, and virtual armies of tourists who poured in from nearby Michigan Avenue hotels.

D'Varco was a sore spot for Joey. Red Wemette, who was the third witness in the trial, testified that he had to pay a street tax to Joey. But Joey steadfastly denied any such arrangement, even though Wemette ran a porno store right there in the Rush Street district. But since the porno shop was near Rush, D'Varco felt he should be getting the street tax.

"You testified today, Mr. Lombardo, that you happened to be in this photograph by accident? Is that correct, Mr. Lombardo?"

"By chance, right, by chance to get something to eat."

"You were getting something to eat and you walk into a restaurant with a dozen Outfit bosses, by chance?"

"I walked in there, like I say, and there's two, four, six, eight, nine people in there."

"And they all happened to be Outfit bosses, Mr. Lombardo?"

"That's what you're saying, but I say I went in there and saw nine people in there that I knew."

"Mr. Lombardo, you say you were there with somebody else, right?"

"Yes."

"And who was that?"

"Albert Gilary."

"We don't see him in the picture, do we?"

"No, he's in the other room."

Mars made his point. Maybe this guy Gilary wasn't there at all.

Mars then asked Lombardo about Frank "the German" Schweihs, one of the most violent and ruthless of all mob figures—a really wacked out guy. But this "German" was helping Joey collect, working for Joey Lombardo—which put Joey in a pretty lofty position in the Chicago mob.

I noticed that Joey finally seemed very uncomfortable, shifting around, side to side, in his seat, restlessly moving his hands and fingers over his cane. Joey was wearing the exact same gray jacket and silver tie from the day before, but it provided little comfort as Mars relentlessly grilled him with questions about mob figures and all these alleged coincidences.

But Joey was not afraid of the mad man Frank "the German." Mars reminded Joey of a tape with "the German" discussing his collection activities for Lombardo, then asked if Schweihs had said those things on tape. Joey stunned the crowd.

"He sure did, and he's a liar."

Joey Lombardo had just called the inexorable Frank "the German" Schweihs a liar. Nobody does that—unless that nobody is an extraordinarily powerful "somebody."

This was a compelling moment, one of several times during Lombardo's testimony when the jurors were so engaged that they put down their note pads and focused completely on Joey. Even the reporters were perched on the edge of their seats taking in every word from this top reputed mob boss as he evaded charges of murder, racketeering, and conspiracy.

Lombardo went on, denying mob actions over and over. The feds had Lombardo on tape threatening an uncooperative massage parlor. "We'll flatten the joint." He was grilled further about street taxes, loser guys who worked for Joey like Louie "the Mooch" Eboli, one of Joey's collectors who put the arm on porn operator Red Wemette.

Lombardo denied it, over and over, then began to lose his cool.

"Where's the evidence?" Joey challenged, unable to resist getting into Mars' face a little. "Where's the picture? Where's the conversation?"

Mars countered sharply. "How about where's the *tape*? Let's play a tape, shall we?"

"You have a tape from 1979 in Allen Dorfman's office about them two massage joints," said Joey.

"Yeah, I'm going to play that now. Yeah. Your lawyer asked you about it earlier today, right??

"Right. Right."

"He read parts of it to you?"

"Yes, he did."

"He didn't read all of them to you, though, did he?"

"No, I know it was about, whatchacall—about a building that a guy wanted to buy."

"It's about a street tax, isn't it, Mr. Lombardo?"

"He's talking about you ought to put a street tax on that place. And you say 'tax that business,' don't you, in that conversation?"

"I sure said something about tax."

"Yeah, and you said you were going to flatten the joint if they don't pay, right?"

"I didn't say flatten. I said—"

"Well, let's see what you said. Play the tape, let's go over it. Play the tape."

Lombardo tried to interrupt. "Let me say something before you say anything—"

"No, I have a question for you."

"Okay."

"And my question is, didn't you tell us today 'there's no one there, we don't have nothing to do with it'? And you say 'we' doesn't mean 'we,' right?"

"That's true."

"Your testimony is 'we' means what?"

"Him."

"We means him?"

"He doesn't have nothing to do with it?"

"Louie don't have nothin to do with it."

Mars kept the heat up, pressing Lombardo. "But Louis Eboli doesn't say 'no, I don't,' does he? What's he say? He says 'we don't.' Right, Mr. Lombardo? So, Mr. Lombardo, you're saying both of you are wrong?"

"Right. Right. Absolutely."

Double talk is downright tiring. Lombardo and Mars were dancing around in circles, ultimately establishing that wrong is right, leaving the jury to wonder not only about Joey's truthfulness, but maybe his sanity.

"This is about a massage parlor, right?"

"That is correct."

"And this is about a massage parlor that your crew is going to charge a street tax to, right?"

Joey sat silent, not responding.

"Isn't that true?"

"This is not my crew to charge a street tax," Joey finally said.

"Whose crew is it?"

"It's Louie's gonna do it. Louis is by himself. Louie puts juke boxes at all places all over."

They debated the meaning of the word "we" almost interminably. Mars pressed Joey, reminding him that when he was recorded he had no reason to lie, no reason to choose words carefully because he had no idea at the time that he was on tape. Mars said Joey was lying, Joey said he just wasn't picking the right words.

Then Lombardo invoked President Clinton. "Just like the president, that he said he didn't choose his right word on certain things." Joey was referring to President Clinton's own double talk standard, which ended with something like "it depends on the meaning of *is*." If ever there was definitive proof that honesty should start at the top, this was it. An accused top mob boss was sitting here on the stand, under oath in front of God and jury, and using the Clinton bullshit argument to justify lying in court.

I couldn't understand what Joey was trying to do. It seemed that Joey was attempting to needle the prosecutor, but why? It just didn't seem to work, and we could all see it on the jurors' faces.

Mars continued. "And then you say 'you got to go out and tax them for $2000.' And they say 'okay.' Right?"

No response from Lombardo.

"And you say go tax them. You're giving directions to Louis Eboli, right?"

"No, I'm not giving him directions."

"It's a muscle tax, isn't it, Mr. Lombardo?"

"No, no, no. He saw me that day—a couple of days—before, and he told me he was making an investment there, sir. You don't have all that conversation."

"So your testimony is, this is just a return of Louie Eboli's investment?"

"That's what it is."

"And how is it that you have to say a penalty by flattening the joint if you don't have a return on the investment?"

Lombardo explained that the business had moved near Club 26 and some of Joe Ferriola's guys, bad guys, and that it was important to move away. Lombardo said that the Club 26, the "mansion," is Joe Nicki's, meaning Ferriola, and said that "we can't have a guy open up by a friend of ours."

Mars jumped. "And here's the 'we' again. 'We' meaning you and Louie Eboli?"

"Right. Right."

But Mars brought the subject back to street taxes. "Well, Mr. Lombardo, you say on page 5, lines 10 to 15, there's a reference there to Joe Nagal. Joe Nagal is the same as Joe Nick, right?"

"That's correct."

"And the same as Joseph Ferriola, right?"

"That is correct."

"And you again tell Mr. Eboli that he better take his—take out the juke box boxes that he has in there because the joint is going to be flattened if the tax isn't paid, correct?"

After many hours of testimony, Joey eventually became short-tempered with the prosecutor. During cross-examination they argued over the meaning of transcripts and words, then Joey, growing more frustrated, said to Mars, "No, no, can't you read?" And later he added, "Sir, sir, sir, let's read it together." Then came the finale to Mars. "Are you having trouble understanding me?" Joey challenged.

"At time, I am, Mr. Lombardo, I must admit." It was the perfect retort, for I could see the jury was thinking the same thing.

After a break in mid-afternoon, we heard about how years ago Allen Dorfman had brought an alleged real estate deal where Lombardo's family invested $43,000 that remarkably turned into $2 million. Lombardo had no credit at the time, but Tony Spilotro co-signed for him on a lucrative piece of Las Vegas property. And there was another deal where Dorfman himself co-signed, and another deal called the California Club, a $1.4 million golf course deal in the early 1980s at a time when Lombardo was under indictment for bribing a U.S. senator.

After going through these myriad multi-million dollar deals, Mars focused on a golf course venture and made the point that Joey didn't even have a job at the time. Joey admitted he did not, but offered that he did have a dice game.

"Dice game?"

"Yeah."

"Worth $1.1 million?"

"Now you're trying to make something that's not there."

"I'm not trying to do anything, Mr. Lombardo. I want to know your interest in this particular golf course for $1.1 million."

"$100,000 was invested by my family, my wife. She's divorced from me and I still call her my wife."

"Because you've lived with her for basically your entire life, right, Mr. Lombardo?"

"That's not true. I did not live with her my entire life. I'm divorced from her. The last 15—since 1992, I do not live with her. I live in a different apartment in the basement."

"You lived at the same address?" Mars could see the jury was curious, if not skeptical.

"That's not true."

"Well, let me ask you, with this golf course proposition you say you're willing to buy this deal for $1.1 million, right?"

"Not me, my family. My wife and two kids."

"Well, your wife wasn't at this meeting, right?"

"No, she was not."

"And your children weren't at this meeting, right?"

"No."

"You were at this meeting?"

"Absolutely."

"I said that you're interested in that deal—what about me, right?"

"Absolutely, absolutely."

"Okay. And why—we're about to see why, because it was a pretty good deal, wasn't it?"

"Absolutely."

"It was a sweetheart deal, wasn't it?"

"Absolutely."

"And so when you got this deal, Mr. Lombardo, you didn't have to put up $1.1 million, did you?"

"No, I did not, I put up $100,000."

"And it was $100,000 in a joint account with your wife, right?"

"That is correct."

"And so you put up $100,000, you didn't have to put up the additional million dollars, did you?"

"No, it was borrowed from the lessee."

"And you got a loan for $1 million, right?"

"My wife and kids got a loan for $1 million."

"Well, you were at the closing, weren't you?"

"Yes, I was."

"You, Joe Lombardo, without a job except for a dice game, right?"

It was a fascinating exchange. And it went on and on, one deal after another, Mars exposing each one for what it was—either a miracle or a sham: $800,000 here and $1.4 million there, lands trusts, no job, million dollar gains—and no corresponding taxes paid.

Then Mars circled back to the central question. "You are not a member of organized crime, your testimony is today?"

"That is positively true."

"Isn't it true, Mr. Lombardo?"

"I never took an oath, sir."

Joey meant an oath to the Outfit. I wonder if he remembered he was under oath on the witness stand.

The next day Lombardo's attorney Rick Halprin conducted the redirect examination of his client and attempted to counter the damage done by the prosecution.

He tried to establish that Joey had a real job at the time Danny Siefert was assassinated, that Joey was an athlete in high school, and that he also had worked as a boy shining shoes, even for some policemen who Joey said "were very cheap people."

"Let's not press our luck," Halprin said, sensing a lighter moment.

"You told me to tell the truth," defended Joey. "I'm telling the truth.

A prompt outburst of laughter shook the courtroom. The crowd saw the humor in Joey calling the cops cheap, but we also laughed at the irony of Joey insisting he was telling the truth. It was a stretch, to say the least. The Judge may have sensed the later, for he saw fit to intervene before it got out of hand.

THE COURT: I don't see anything funny about a sweeping conspiracy case that includes the murders of 18 individuals.

Mr. Halprin focused on Joey's card games, crap games. Joey said they never got caught because they knew how to get permission from Chicago's various aldermen.

Joey kept testifying, but it seemed more like a stream of consciousness, with Joey attempting to justify his actions over a lifetime of crime, all disguised as constant coincidences, lies by others, misunderstandings, or false accusations.

The jury was not buying it. I did not buy it. But Joey was Joey: clown, boss, kingpin, family man, for nearly six decades Joey Lombardo was a fixture in the streets of Chicago. And so was I. But I had a badge.

When he was finished with his testimony, Joey asked me for a copy of my first book *Three Boys Missing*. I sent an autographed copy to him at the Metropolitan Correction Center—the federal jail housing all the defendants during trial. I heard later through one of his attorneys, Susan Shatz, that he enjoyed the book. A jailed mob chieftain enjoying the book of an old retired detective like me. Just one of the many ironies of life—especially on the streets of Chicago.

19

The Last Dance

How many pallbearers do you need for an Outfit funeral? One—to slam the trunk.

Okay, it's a silly joke, but it's still a gem for those of us in homicide. Yet there was nothing funny about the tragedies that were retold daily during the Family Secrets trial, or those that took place on the streets for the decades before. But clichés exist for a reason, and we heard many a tale of life in the shadows: car trunks, cornfields, construction sites, house basements, wherever. As one witness put it, when the mob wanted you dead, they got you dead.

We expected the jury to continue deliberations in Monday September 10, 2007, and beyond. I arrived in court that morning as usual. After the normal greetings, including a short chat with Judge Zagel's clerk Steve Neuman and Anne Wolf, word came down—the jury had reached a verdict.

Those words energized the courtroom. But the excitement would not soon pass, for Judge Zagel postpone the reading of the verdict for three hours to allow family members of slain victims time to appear in open court. About 20 of them would choose to do so.

As I left the courtroom, I was besieged by the ravenous media. "What's up, Jim?" they demanded. There must have been something in the air, or maybe my expression, that tipped them off. I couldn't say anything directly, though, because the judge had asked me not to say anything yet to the waiting media outside. But word soon spread.

At 2:30pm, all eyes were on Judge Zagel as he deliberately approached the bench. The courtroom was quiet as a morgue when Judge Zagel asked the foreman, "Has the jury reached a verdict?"

"Yes, Sir."

The envelope containing the fateful verdict was handed to Deputy Donald Walker, who passed it along to the bench. The judge read the paper silently before returning it to the deputy, who read it aloud. "We the jury find all five [defendants] guilty as to all counts charged in the indictment." The judge then polled all the jurors to verify that what was about to be reported was their true verdict, and that they all were in agreement. Each one said "yes" or "yes it is."

This was a sweeping victory for the prosecutors Mitchell Mars, John Scully, and Marcus Funk. All five defendants were found guilty on all counts, which variously included racketeering, conspiracy, bribery, illegal gambling, and tax fraud.

But there was more. Jimmy Marcello, age 65, who two years before was considered the boss of the entire Chicago mob, was also found guilty of obstructing justice by paying hush money to witness Nickolas Calabrese, and for conspiracy to defraud the government by not reporting his gambling income.

Frank Calabrese, Sr., age 70, was also found guilty of extortion for demanding and collecting "street tax" from Connie's Pizza, as well as guilty of conducting an illegal bookmaking operation.

Joey Lombardo, age 78, was found guilty of obstructing justice for remaining on the lamb (on the run) for several moths after an arrest warrant had been issued for the Family Secrets indictments and trial.

The main mob man in Phoenix, Paul Schiro, age 70, was convicted of racketeering conspiracy and will face life in prison.

The defendants showed little reaction, as the courtroom breathed a collective sigh. Marcello embraced his counsel Marc Martin, kissing him on the cheek. Lombardo visibly found no humor in the proceedings, cocking his head to glance in my direction. He was soon throwing something of a tantrum, poking his cane at the courtroom floor and holding visible disdain for his lawyer Rick Halprin. Doyle sat like a frozen popsicle; Schiro appeared stunned, growing pale as he stared at the floor.

With all that, there would still be more, for there were many murder counts still pending. The next day, on September 11, 2007, the jurors were to begin deliberating on the 18 mob slayings that were the heart, soul, and high drama of the case.

September 27, 2007, there finally was a requiem of a different sort. I was in Judge Zagel's chambers. It was mid-afternoon around 3:45pm when word came that the jury had reached a verdict. Judge Zagel immediately arranged for the U.S. Marshall's Office to have the defendants sent over from the Metropolitan Corrections Center to the holding area in court.

When word of a verdict circulated, reporters and spectators rushed to the courtroom on the 25th floor of the Federal Building where they found one wrinkle. Judge Zagel's own courtroom was being used for a swearing in ceremony for new federal judge Susan Cox, so the judge arranged for a new, but smaller, courtroom, for the reading of the verdict.

I raced ahead of the impending hoards so I could nab a seat. After three months in the front row and a lifetime of jousting with the Chicago Outfit, this was no time to be left out. As it happens, I still got my front row position, seated right next to U.S. Attorney Patrick Fitzgerald and the first assistant for the Northern District of Illinois Gary Shapiro.

The defendants arrived and were seated at the defense table. Judge Zagel entered and took the bench at 5:27pm. There was a hushed but very tense courtroom as the defendants took their seats one by one. Lombardo was decked out in a blue suit with a blue shirt, open neck. Calabrese had a tan sport coat; Marcello a light green sport coat, light brown shirt, no tie. Schiro wore a light green coat.

Shortly before 5:30pm, the jurors filed into the courtroom, somber-faced. None looked toward the defendants.

Judge Zagel began. "Have you the jury reached a verdict?"

"Yes, sir," announced the foreman. Many secrets were exposed during the course of the trial, but at least 12 secrets remained, including the identities of all the jurors.

The envelope containing the verdict was handed to the court crier who ceremoniously gave it to court clerk Don Walker who then passed it to Judge Zagel. The judge read it silently and handed the paper back to Don who proceeded to read it aloud to a stilled audience.

"We the jury find Frank Calabrese, Sr., James Marcello, and Joey Lombardo guilty in 10 of 18 murders and Paul Schiro dead locked in one killing. The defense attorneys asked that the jurors be polled individually, and one by one they confirmed their verdict.

Some of the defendants exchanged whispers as the verdict came in. There was visible dejection at the defense table and obvious elation on the side of the prosecution. All attorneys would finally be freed from a trial-long gag order, and they promptly met with reporters in the lobby of the Federal Building. They took turns stepping to the live microphones and television cameras to discuss their roles in the Family Secrets trial, attack the verdict, threaten appeals, and all the rest.

Throughout the trial, the jurors were known only by numbers, their true identities closely guarded all these months. Judge Zagel made a point of thanking them personally for their time and service. When they were dismissed, the jurors returned to the jury room and then were escorted from the Dirksen Federal Building through a specially built underground tunnel. They would surface across the street inside the companion Kluczynski Building to escape the hoards of media. Both building are big black skyscraper boxes located in downtown Chicago only a couple blocks from the famed State Street shopping and theater area. The Dirksen Building is were the federal courts are, while the twin Kluczynski Building houses other federal agencies, notably the Midwest offices of the IRS.

Both buildings enjoy immense security, including underground egress, the tunnel mentioned above, metal detectors, video cameras, armed guards, and so on. For this reason, the Kluczynski Building became the interim headquarters of President elect Barrack Obama before the inauguration in early 2009. From the Kluczynski Building the jurors would exit on the south side at Jackson Boulevard, free to return to their normal lives—almost. The jurors had been asked if they preferred to speak to the media. They declined, but it wasn't that easy.

Reporters soon sniffed out the escape of the jury, spotting the jurors as they exited the sister building across Dearborn Street. The media approached the jurors and bombarded them with questions. One juror stopped and simply said "just get away" before disappearing into the crowd. I saw two female jurors walked briskly away toward the river, refusing to answer questions.

One reporter persisted, catching another juror, a woman, who relented. "We did the best we could," she said. "We thought we did a very fair job. And we were very reasonable with each other so we could do a good job." She would not, however, comment on the trial details or the specific atmosphere inside the jury room during deliberations. She was then asked the obvious question about whether she feared the men she had just convicted of racketeering and murder. The woman answered in a calm, easy voice. "I don't have any fear because I'm just a person that's picked to do this. I did my job. I think everybody though they were very fair."

Attorneys for the defense would make the point that although found guilty of racketeering, their clients were not guilty of murder. Few were listening. After an era than spanned four decades as the beginning of the end slowly evolved, the last dance of the Outfit as we know it was finally over. On Thursday, September 27, 2007, a jury of everyday people called these defendants killers. The jury obviously concurred with the strong closing statements of the prosecution, that the mob used fists, ropes, knives, guns, and bombs to conduct their business the way they wanted with little retribution. Until now.

The jury convicted various defendants of 10 homicides. They remained, however, deadlocked on the other 8 homicides, supporting the belief of the one woman juror that she and her colleagues had performed their duty and done a good and thorough job. One of those 8 deadlocked murders was the only killing that Paul Schiro was accused of. Even so, he would not walk. He still faced up to 20 years for the racketeering charge.

Remaining in the jammed courtroom just after the verdict, I had glanced over my shoulder and got an immediate reaction from Dr. Patrick Spilotro, brother of the Spilotro brothers who had been murdered at the hands of some of these defendants, who was seated directly behind me. He tightly grabbed his wife's hand.

Joey Lombardo, at age 78 the oldest defendant, leaned over on the defense table and rested his chin on his hand and remained motionless as the deputy read that the jury had found him guilty of the infamous 1974 murder of Daniel Seifert who, as it happens, was shot and killed exactly 33 years ago to the day, on September 27. Seifert's murder was the only killing that Lombardo had been specifically accused of. As the jury moved on to the other defendants, Lombardo's looked over to the jury and delivered a murderous glare as if to give one final warning. But by this time it was all over, and such glares were largely empty. The world, and the jury, were moving on.

After court I strolled down the hallway with my good friend John Drummond, the long time crime reporter for CBS-channel 2 news in Chicago. We compared notes and together observed the relief and other emotions pouring from families of the various victims.

There had been great relief throughout the courtroom as relatives of the victims found closure. Anthony Ortiz, the son of victim Richard Ortiz, and his mother Ellen Ortiz, wife of Richard, were overwhelmed. "Now he [her husband Richard] can rest in peace after 24 years," said Ellen. "The lord punishes in many, many ways."

Anthony Ortiz said he was glad that Frank Calabrese, Sr. was found guilty of his father's shotgun murder, as well as the collateral killing of his father's friend Arthur Morawski, who had been in the wrong place at the wrong time. "Finally, it's over," Anthony told me. "There's closure. He's not bragging about double-aught buckshot now," Anthony added, referring to Calabrese. "We've been waiting for this for a very long time. Now he wasn't sitting there smirking. I drove in frantically from Addison when I heard the news that the jury was coming back with its verdict. There's a lot of stop signs and stop lights I blew through," he said.

Just before the verdict, Charlene Maravecek, the widow of Paul Haggerty, who was slain in a mob hit during 1976, wept at the front desk of the Federal Building, telling security she needed to get upstairs to the courtroom. "I've waited 31-and-a-half years for this" she said, tears flowing. She raced to the courtroom, but was too late. Charlene missed the reading of the verdict, then collapsed in the arms of a government victims' assistance worker as she left. Her husband's murder was one that the jury had been deadlocked over. "I waited 31 years," she repeated. "That bastard ruined my life. They couldn't come to a decision. I could have made a decision in five minutes. I'm disappointed in the jury."

"Why? Why?" Charlene persisted, her face bright as a red rose from relentless crying. "Why did they find everyone else guilty except the man who killed my husband? She remembered the day she was told her husband was murdered, that it seemed like it were yesterday. "I was eight and a half months pregnant when they told me. My baby only lived six months."

Haggerty wasn't the only deadlock, of course. The jury was also deadlocked over the murder of Nicholas D'Andrea who was found bludgeoned in the back of a burning trunk of a car in September of 1981. John Drummond and I caught up to Bob D'Andrea, son of the deceased, as he leaned on the building outside. "I'm feeling pretty shitty," Bob said, his eyes slightly reddened as he spoke. "The whole world knows he did it," D'Andrea said. "I didn't wait 26 years to hear this. Deadlock might as well be innocent."

I spoke directly with Patrick Spilotro in the hallway, catching him just ahead of the news media. "We are very satisfied that it came down like it did," he told me. "It will let the families rest in peace. These people are going away."

Patrick was right. No one got off, not even the deadlocks saved any of the defendants. I took time to sigh and to reflect. Many decades had passed since Frank Calabrese, Sr. first punched me in the mouth when I was a young cop on the force. I knew a number of these young thugs during my youth on the West Side, arrested many, and danced with a few myself during a career of homicides, car chases, skirmishes, fights, arrests, and trials.

Poignantly, Joseph Seifert said that this was the anniversary of his father's death, referring to the murder of Daniel Seifert in front of Daniel's wife and son many years before. Joey Lombardo denied being involved, a most ironic twist given that young Joseph had been named after Joey in the first place.

After all was said and done, Frank Calabrese was moved to solitary confinement to protect him from threats on the inside. Joey Lombardo, to whom I had showed civility but not necessarily respect, later asked if I would help write his own book. Maybe I will do just that—depending on what Joey has to say. They are both aging, and neither will again see the light of freedom.

There will be more mobsters, more criminals, more homicides, of course. Where there is money to be made outside the law, there will be thugs ready to cash in. But when you live outside the law, you lose the protection of the law. It becomes a lonely and dangerous life out there, almost providing its own punishment for careers gone bad.

The Outfit in Chicago was like none other. Its legacy began before Capone, then thrived during the Capone empire in those notorious Chicago days of booze and machine guns, an era that our sprawling city is still known for across the globe. Then came the heydays of Giancana and Accardo, the Las Vegas windfall, and then the new guard bosses like Cerone, Auippa, and Lombardo himself.

The final songs have not yet been played, but the music has grown feint. We are all old now—Calabrese, Lombardo, and me—but I've got my freedom. And dignity. And no regrets.

20

Epilogue

Were the legions of mob operatives just play acting when they were caught on tape, one after the other, admitting to, sometimes bragging about, heinous crimes over the course of the Family Secrets investigation?

That question was posed by prosecutor Markus Funk, who began his closing argument by observing that for these defendants to really be innocent, they had to be remarkably unlucky for each one to just be fooling and "play acting" just as they were being recorded by the Feds.

Assistant U.S. Attorney Markus Funk attacked the alibis of Frank Calabrese, Sr., and made no secret of his contempt for these Family Secrets defendants. "The evidence tells you that these men are guilty," blasted Funk, who told the jury that these five defendants were responsible for 18 known murders consistent with the 43 page indictment that ignited the most important Chicago mob trial since the days of Capone himself.

Notwithstanding the thousands of pages of testimony over the course of three long months, Funk was quick to the point. "It's actually a fairly easy job," Funk announced, referring to the issue of guilt or innocence. "The evidence makes it very clear that these defendants are guilty many times over," he pressed. "It would be enough," Funk continued, "to convict the men on racketeering charge if they simply knew of mob activities and helped plan them. But each defendant personally committed crimes as well."

"These men are about making money," Funk said. "They are about accruing power for themselves and about accruing power for the Chicago Outfit. You can hear that man laughing about the murders," Funk charged, showing his contempt as he pointed toward Frank Calabrese, Sr., as he referred to one of the secret government recordings where Frank mocked these murders to his son. "There's nothing funny about that, is there?" he challenged, staring down toward Calabrese at the defense table.

"Are you asking us?" Frank's attorney Joseph Lopez shot back. Calabrese, Sr. would at times shake his head and smile during Funk's closing argument. In so doing, I sensed that he was helping to prove the case against himself. Did the jury feel that Frank was mocking life, justice, the court, even the jurors themselves?

Funk hammered away for three solid hours, often pointed to Frank, reminding the jury of evidence that Frank, Sr. was involved in the murder of 13 human beings. Frank just sat back in his chair and giggled.

Funk turned Frank's obvious contempt against him. "Frank Calabrese, Sr., the man with the smile," Funk continued, his voice loud and strong. "The man with the smile. There's nothing to smile about in this case."

Funk turned his attention to the others as well, uttering a few choice words about defendant James Marcello, another made member of the mob who profited from illegal gambling, paid hush money, and all the rest. I noticed that Jimmy Marcello's son Jimmy, Jr., was in court with Marcello's brother-in-law Joe Monaco. Marcello is married to Monaco's sister—and I know Joe Monaco from the West side. In my experience, he seems like a really nice guy.

"Joey the Clown Lombardo is a made member who extorted victims and businesses for the Outfit and participated in the killing of federal witness Daniel Seifert.

"Paul the Indian Schiro was the mob's man in Phoenix who helped kill his friend, witness Emil Vaci.

"And the final defendant Anthony Twan Doyle was a corrupt Chicago police officer who passed investigative data from the Family Secrets case to imprisoned mob leaders," Funk told the attentive jury.

Funk then turned his attention to the government's own witness, Nicholas Calabrese. "Nicholas Calabrese told the truth when he testified about being a part of Outfit hit squads that carried our many of the murders," Funk said, "and four of the five defendants were captured on audio and video tapes that pointed to their guilt."

Funk ridiculed the play acting defenses of Frank, "Twan" Doyle, and Joey. Funk argued that the jury should focus on the underlying threads that connected all these alleged activities. Why did so many individuals and businesses buckle under Outfit pressure? "Fear. The Outfit is an organization that thrives on its ability to instill fear, and the men on trial were a big part of it," continued Funk.

Funk walked through details of 18 murders that were at the center of the case. He suggested that some of the best witnesses were the defendants themselves, whose testimony simply was not credible.

"Lombardo, for example, testified that he wound up in what has become known as the 'Last Supper' photo of mob leaders at a restaurant because he haplessly wandered in for food. Frank Calabrese, Sr., said he ran a street loan business but never got rough as he tried to collect debts.

"This isn't Chase Bank here. Look at Frank Calabrese," Funk challenged as he again motioned toward the smiling defendant.

Funk also focused on the high profile murders of Tony and Michael Spilotro, killed in 1986 for attracting too much "heat" on mob activities in Las Vegas. Another murder revisited in closing was that of Daniel Seifert in Bensenville, who was gunned down in 1974 at his factory after signing up to testify against Joey Lombardo from stealing from Teamster funds. Lombardo himself testified that he did not know Seifert was going to give testimony against him, but Funk noted for the jury that as part of the case Lombardo would have had papers delivered to him giving actual notice of the pending Seifert testimony. "So [the murder] paid off in a perverse way for Mr. Lombardo," Funk added.

Funk revisited the incriminating evidence against Joey Lombardo, then took time to expose Lombardo for what Funk said he really is. Funk took apart Joey's alibi that he was busy filling out a police report on his stolen wallet at the time, exposing that story as contrived.

Funk encouraged jurors not to simply believe or disbelieve the testimony of government witness Nick Calabrese, who Funk conceded was also a "cold blooded killer," but also to consider the corroborating evidence in making up their minds. Then Funk went on the attack.

"Who give them the right to take the lives of other human beings?" he pressed. "How is it that they can just walk into a business and demand money? Because they know how to instill fear in other human beings," said Funk, answering his own question. "Kill another human being if he gets in your way."

Of course Funk was not the only one to offer his version of the trial and the conclusions the jury should reach. The defendants had their own shot through counsel. First up was Thomas Breen, James Marcello's attorney, who proceeded to attack the testimony of Nick Calabrese. "If you find he's lying about the Spilotro murders—and he is—then you can't believe a word he says," Breen argued.

Nick Calabrese testified that Marcello took part in three murders and one attempted murder, including his involvement in the fate of the Spilotro brothers, but Breen said that Calabrese lied to save himself from the death penalty. "Do you think he would lie?" Breen asked, referring to Nick. "Do you think he would lie to save his live?" The defense lawyers lined up against the credibility of Nick Calabrese, describing Nick as a mob serial killer who spent most of his adult life "lying, cheating, conniving, committing crimes and getting away with it."

Breen continued. "Why would the killers [of the Spilotros] risk driving more than 100 miles with two bloody bodies in a car to find a burial spot?" It would be reasonable, Breen argued, for the jurors to infer that Calabrese simply made all this up to sweeten his own deal by solving for prosecutors one of Chicago's greatest mob murder mysteries.

Then came perhaps Breen's most entertaining argument on behalf of his client Jimmy Marcello. "Is Marcello Irish? Well, look at his birth certificate. His mother is Irene Flynn. Her father was James Flynn. Her mother was Katherine Lavin, who had 14 children and was a Irish as Paddy's pig." Breen stressed that in addition to requiring at least one murder as a prerequisite, only those who are of 100 percent Italian descent can be "made" members of the mob; therefore, he argued, when Nick Calabrese testified that Jimmy himself was a made member, it could not have been true. "The only thing 'made' about Nicholas Calabrese's testimony about James Marcello is that he made it up."

Five defendants, legions of murders, and more victims than we can count. After three months of trial, it all added up to five guilty verdicts but very little closure. Sure, the families of the victims could breathe easier, but no guilty verdict can rewrite history.

Interestingly, if not ironically, one of the most ruthless mob figures never made it to trial.

Francis John "Frankie" Schweihs died of cancer in 2008 at that age of 76. He was slated for trial with the others, but his health declined and his trial was delayed pending his health. The cancer caught up to him before the prosecution did.

In the mid-summer of 2007 when I was waiting outside courtroom 2525, I saw an old acquaintance down the hall, a criminal trial lawyer. "Paul!" I shouted. "Paul Brayman, nice to see you. It's been years, what are you doing here—getting a glimpse of the trial?"

"No," replied Paul. "My client is Frankie Schweihs. "The German," I said. Indeed, Frankie "the German" Schweihs, a cold-blooded cutthroat if ever there was one. "I'm here to get a hearing date for Frankie later in the year," explained Paul.

Brayman told me that Schweihs had cancer, and until recently had been convalescing in a Westchester, New York, hospital under protective custody. Paul didn't think Frankie would make it to a new trial date, though.

Frank "the German" Schweihs had eluded law enforcement after the government's sweeping operation and related family secrets indictments against the top mob echelon because, quite simply, Frankie wasn't available. He had been M.I.A. before FBI agents finally swooped down on his hideaway nest deep in the Berea, Kentucky hills where they found him with his girlfriend and finally arrested him. His cancer soon bought him a reprieve of sorts, causing his own trial to be separated from the other family secrets defendants.

Frankie's health had improved enough that the prosecution was pressing for trial, and the date of June 10, 2008 was set for the initial hearing. By this time Frankie had been transferred from New York to the MCC, the Metropolitan Correction Center in Chicago, which was the federal jail. In fact, when June 10 arrived, I was in court to witness the proceedings before Judge Zagel. "The German" was wheeled into the courtroom by federal marshals, along with attorney Ellen Domph. He looked pale and gaunt, and wasted little time in front of the judge. The cancer overrunning his body had done little to soften Frankie's attitude, not to mention his big mouth.

Schweihs noticed federal prosecutor Amarjeet Bhachus, who is Sikh, and sarcastically, and audibly, asked his counsel if they were in a foreign country. Schweihs taunted another prosecutor, Markus Funk. "You're making eyes at me." When Funk did not respond, Frankie continued. "Yeah, you. You making eyes at me? Do I look like a fag to you?"

Funk had a way with bringing out the worst in these guys. It was last year that he had inspired the "you're a dead man" threat from Frank Calabrese, Sr.

Schweihs would not let up. After the hearing he called Funk "another asshole." But the prosecutors ignored him and continued to handle the routine business of setting a firm trial date in October. Judge Zagel did not specifically reprimand Schweihs, but he did end the hearing quickly. The fun, though, wasn't over. As the marshals wheeled Frankie out, I heard Funk bode Schweihs "farewell" in German. It sounded like the familiar "aufweidersehen," with the right accent, for Funk himself had grown up in Germany. I almost sh*t in my pants when I heard that remark.

Outside, attorney Domph said Frankie is usually very polite, but I wasn't buying it.

The government was serious, and ready. Prosecutors had told Judge Zagel that they expected to call as many as 110 witnesses for the trial. Judge Zagel wasn't sure if the fall date could hold up, but hoped to get the trial started by the end of the year. Of course by now, Frankie had acquired yet another count against him for evading law enforcement while on the lamb during 2005.

Schweihs may have been sarcastic, but he was a no-nonsense mobster. One time another mobster was taking street tax from one of Frankie's porn shops in Chicago's Old Town area, but that activity stopped on a dime once Frankie found out. "The German" took care of the matter. As mob operative William "Red" Wemette put it, the other mobster, then missing, had suddenly gone "to open up a hot dog stand in Alaska."

"I don't care who it is," Frankie was heard saying on an undercover tape. "If it's Al Capone's brother and he came back reincarnated, this is a declared fucking joint."

I was at home one day relaxing in front of the TV when a notice came across the tube. "Ruthless enforcer, age 78, dies awaiting trial." Few mobsters talked tougher than Frank "the German" Schweihs. He made the most hard-core mobsters tremble with fear at the sight of him, had died of cancer while in federal custody awaiting trial. I called my friend, Frankie's lawyer Paul Brayman. Paul told me that Frankie had signed a "do not resuscitate" order, but then rescinded it. Paul had visited Schweihs frequently while he was incarcerated at the MCC in Chicago, and later had been with Frankie only hours before he died. Paul had to open cans of coke for him, because he was too weak to do even that. Paul said that during that very day he had gotten Frankie transferred to Thorek Medical Center in the city because he was dehydrated, virtually comatose, and needed emergency treatment. Just four hours later Paul received a telephone call. Frank "the German" Schweihs had died.

Paul said that Frankie had been determined to fight the government's case to the end. When the funeral service was held, Frankie one again was a no-show. The prosecution had transferred his remains to the Cook County Medical Examiner, leaving the family distraught. The Examiner had not originally been notified, and by law anyone who dies in custody has to undergo an examination. So the feds stepped in. Brayman said the hospital told him no one had ever died there while in custody before, so they were unaware of the procedures. Frankie was still causing trouble, even after the end had come.

Schweihs' standing among mobsters was legendary. John Mallul, an FBI supervisory special agent, said that virtually every Outfit guy feared him. "They didn't necessarily even want to be around this guy. If they saw this guy coming, they would have to kill him or be killed." None wanted any part of that.

In secret recordings, the FBI once heard Frankie say to "Red" Wimette that he wouldn't be around later because he had to go kill someone. He said it casually like other people speak of taking out the garbage. According to testimony during the Family Secrets trial, even the mobster Michael Spilotro once warned his teenage daughter to lock the doors and call 911 immediately if she ever saw him sneaking around their house. Quite a guy.

Later I personally spoke with 38-year-old Joe Seifert by phone in the fall of 2008, maybe October. Joe is the son of the late Danny Seifert. Schweihs was one of the mobsters accused of killing Danny Seifert during an ambush hit in front of witnesses. Joe said that Frankie's death gave him no comfort, but he applauded the news. "No relief, no justice. No peace," Joe told me. Schweihs' death simply had not been "unpleasant enough." "I know he died from cancer," Joe explained, "but I think he got off easy."

On Monday July 14, 2008, the indictment was dismissed against Frank Schweihs. Good riddance. His death may have been the easy way out—but at least he saved the taxpayers a lot of money with his early exit.

Case closed.

On January 26, 2009, I walked into Judge Zagel's courtroom 2525 where it all started back in June of 2007. The sentencing phase for the surviving defendants who perhaps not as lucky at Schweihs with his early exit, was about to begin. At long last, the end had finally come—for these defendants, the end was a daunting finale to a life of crime, corruption, and mayhem, some dating back to those early Gregory Elementary School days of my youth, over six long decades.

The mob has had a strangle hold in Chicago since before the Capone days, and they said years ago that "Scarface" Capone could never be convicted. Wrong. They said John Gotti could never be convicted in New York, but that was proved wrong in 1992. Even though various Chicago crime figures had been convicted before, after five full decades of mob rule by these Family Secrets defendants, few observers believed the government could indict so many powerful crime syndicate figures all at once, let alone convict the likes of Marcello, Lombardo, Calabrese, Schiro, and Doyle. Wrong again.

I arrived early this fateful day, taking my seat along with Judge Zagel's secretary Anne Wolf, courtesy of court security officer Ted Wiszowaty. Judge Zagel entered and took the bench at 2:20pm, and soon three U.S. Marshalls brought Paul "the Indian" Schiro from the federal corrections center. Schiro, clad in the customary orange jump suit complete with the indignity of leg irons, took a seat at the defense table. Schiro calmly adjusted his glasses while his counsel requested the removal of the chains. Judge Zagal agreed, and the leg irons were removed.

In the summer of 1986, Paul Schiro had been sent to Las Vegas to help a crew of hired killers to silence Emil Vaci, age 73, before he could talk to a federal grand jury about the mysterious disappearance of a man who was tied to a sweeping mob skimming operation at a Vegas casino. Testimony from Nick Calabrese described in detail Schiro's role in the killing. On a hot summer night, June 6, 1986, as Vaci was leaving work, he was abruptly pulled into a van and shot in the head. His body was wrapped in plastic and promptly dumped in a local dry water gully.

Judge Zagel would learn from a letter sent by Vaci's daughter, Drena Garrison, as read aloud by victim witness coordinator Felice Weiler, which read, in part, "Till this day, I still cannot shake the image I have of my mother hunched over, clutching my father's new suit, now wrinkled and stained with tears from the news of my father's death." It was a new suit her father had recently bought to renew his wedding vows, but he never got to wear it for its original purpose—he was buried in it instead.

The jury convicted Schiro of racketeering and conspiracy in September, 2007, but was unable to unanimously agree on whether he was responsible for Vaci's murder in Arizona in 1986. Judge Zagel found Schiro was involved in the killing by a preponderance of the evidence, and held Schiro accountable for his murder and taking that into consideration during sentencing. He gave Schiro 20 years, the most Schiro could face on the racketeering count.

When the judge asked Schiro whether he had anything to say in open court, Schiro leaped at the chance, jumping up with arms flailing, denying any conspiracy, racketeering, or any accountability at all.

After his outburst, Schiro's leg irons were re-applied and the marshals hauled him off to prison and into obscurity.

Two days later I was back in court, this time to witness the sentencing of Frank Calabrese, Sr., then age 71, mob enforcer, killer, loan shark, and extortionist. The first time I saw Frank was a half-century ago when he was young, cocky, and arrogant enough to punch out a cop—me. Today he looked terrible, something like what the cat might drag in from the alley. Frank was wearing the standard issue orange government jump suit, an old pair of glasses attached to his head with a thick white felt strap. Frank's shoes looked like a gym shoe taken from a rummage sale.

The courtroom was packed yet strangely silent. The first of the family victims proceeded to be heard. "You broke my heart but you didn't take my dignity," announced Charlene Moravecek, the widow of murder victim Paul Haggerty, who was just 27 years old when he died at Frank's hand. She confronted Calabrese and yelled at him for cutting her husband's throat and stuffing him into a trunk years ago. "My husband had no connection to the mob," she told Calabrese with rivers of tears pouring down her cheeks. "You murdered the wrong person," she cried. "That shows how smart you all are."

Frank replied softly but audibly to Mrs. Moravecek from his chair at the defense table. "God will bless you for what you say."

"Don't you mock me, ever," she blasted back. "Your Honor, I don't want to hear from him."

Then Frank's son Kurt Calabrese strode to the lectern where he proceeded to unleash the proverbial riot act, telling the judge how his father beat him throughout his life, belittled him, and threatened to bite his nose off. "I could make you disappear anytime I want," Kurt said his father would tell him. "My father was never a father, but more or less an enforcer." Still, Kurt said that he managed to forgive his father. With that, Kurt turned, looked Frank straight in the eye, and said, "I want you to apologize for what you did to me and my brother."

With all this, the shit hit the fan. Frank was ready to blow, and he exploded on cue. "You better apologize for the lies you're telling," Frank demanded. "You were treated like a king for all the things I've done for you."

"You never hit me and never beat me?" Kurt challenged.

"I hit you with a strap and a paddle when you were younger,:" Frank answered. But he could not stop himself. In a deep but strong voice, Frank pressed on. "Tell them about the money you stole, the million dollars in cash, and the $110,000 that didn't belong to you," said Frank, referring to mob cash that had been stashed away before Frank went to prison in the 1990s. I could feel the tension, and emotions ran high as Kurt walked stiffly from the courtroom, tears flowing freely down his cheeks.

Next, Tony Ortiz, son of Richard Ortiz, reported that he was only 12 years old when his father was shot in a car outside his Cicero bar. A large screen would show a number of family photos, one showing Tony's father holding him at the age of 12. Tony said he had to give up Little League baseball because he was so keenly aware of his father's absence in the stands.

When the murder was carried out, Tony raced to the spot where his father had been shot. "I remember the grinding noise of the broken glass under my feet," he told the courtroom, also recounting how he could recall seeing his father's cigar still lying on the ground at the scene. "I picked it up and held onto it, knowing it was all I had left of him." Tony finished with contempt. "You are a cold hearted killer, Calabrese."

With that, it was Frank's turn. Calabrese walked over to the lectern squarely in front of the judge where he began yapping away, true to form. "I've been living in a hell hole, I'm a sick man. I got high blood pressure, prostrate problems, and a bad heart. Judge can you tell me why I'm in confinement? I don't know, please tell me."

Frank then turned to the prosecutors and apologized for the reckless comment "you're a fucking dead man." Then he told the judge that when he had laughed aloud during the trial, it was because of the ridiculous testimony he had to endure from his brother Nick and some of the other witnesses.

"I'm not no big shot," Frank announced. "I'm nothing but a human being, and when you cut my hand I bleed like everybody else." Among other things, Frank was a walking, talking cliché. He gave a 40 minute speech to the judge, rambling on about his own family and how they stole from him, portraying himself as a purported victim but never actually denying that he had killed anyone. Judge Zagel, who knew how Frank would strangle many victims before cutting their throats, was unimpressed with the performance. He held Calabrese responsible for six additional murders. The judge noted how the case against Frank, Sr., was unique. Not only had his brother Nick testified against him, his own son Frank, Jr., had stepped forward, too.

"I just want to say that your crimes are unspeakable," Judge Zagel announced. "I sentence you to life in prison." I kept my eye squarely on Frank as the judge spoke. There was little reaction from what was left of Frank Calabrese, Sr., as his counsel Joseph Lopez patting him on the back.

February 2, 2009, was to be a day of reckoning for one of the Outfit's most humorous, colorful, eccentric, and certainly ruthless mob characters in the last 40 years, Joseph "Joey the Clown"

Lombardo, 80. Lombardo, too, was decked out in government orange as he awaited his fate. He had already been convicted of racketeering and the 1974 murder of Daniel Seifert before Seifert himself could testify against Lombardo. Seifert had been the sole witness to tie Lombardo to two checks that were critical evidence in that case, so when Seifert was eliminated the whole case unraveled.

Joey arrived at 2:10pm in a wheelchair, escorted by four U.S. Marshalls who wheeled him to the table where his defense counsel, Rick Halprin, waited. After the usual preliminaries, the courtroom clerk Donald Walker announced "all rise" as the judge took the bench.

Emma Seifert, widow of the deceased Danny, and her two sons then stepped before Judge Zagel to read pain-filled letters about what they had to endure throughout the prior 34 years after a masked hit team ambushed Seifert who then ran for his life. The attackers caught up to him, though, then beat and shot him to death as Emma and their four-year-old son watched in horror. The widow Emma Seifert stood courageously in court, wearing a charming black dress as she addressed the judge.

She could not find the words to explain what had happened to her son Joseph, ironically named after Joseph Lombardo himself. It was a struggle to preserve her own Joseph's innocence when he later would hug her at the funeral and offer his own support. "Don't cry, Mommy," he had said. "I don't think those men meant to hurt my daddy." The murder destroyed their family, Emma explained, and asked, "How do you explain to your four-year-old why his daddy died?"

Joseph himself then addressed the judge. He told how he had been just 4 years old when he was playing with match box cars and a Fischer-Price toy garage when he suddenly saw the killers outside shooting his father. He said the last memory of his father was the sight of Daniel Seifert's body lying twisted on the lawn. "I wonder if I ever said good-bye," he added.

Then brother Nicholas Seifert spoke about the disturbing and difficult years he had spent, and how his marriage had dissolved amidst the stress of the Family Secrets trial. Nicholas told how he had left home for 15 years without notifying his family where he was all that time. He said that years after his father's death he would often walk from his home in Bensenville to the cemetery in Elmhurst to spend time at his father's grave. "Even to this day I would think about my father who never got a chance to guide me about money, business, girls, even how to tie a necktie."

The prosecution showed a number of Seifert family photos on the large courtroom screen, then added clips from home movies complete with Beatles music, especially "In My Life," playing in the background. I focused on Joey Lombardo as he sat in his wheelchair taking this all in. He never let on that any of it affected him, and it even seemed like he may have had a difficult time hearing the proceedings.

The judge asked Joey if he wanted to address the court. That was like asking someone if his heart was ticking. You didn't have to hold your breath for the answer. Lombardo could not wait for his chance. The one-time Outfit boss wheeled his chair into position in front of the judge, then strained to pull himself up where he stood, addressing the court.

"First, I want to say to Emma Seifert, Joe Seifert, and Nicky Seifert, I was sorry for their loss then, I'm sorry for their loss now," Joey began. "I want the court and the Seifert family to know I did not kill Danny Seifert and had nothing to do with it, before, during or after."

Joey told the judge that he had an alibi for when the killing of Danny Seifert took place, referring to the police report from when he allegedly had his wallet stolen. Lombardo actually read directly from the report. The alibi was a bit too perfect, though, and seemed very contrived—not to mention irrelevant. Even if Joey was in the police station at the time, it does not mean he didn't order the hit in the first place. Then, after making his report, Joey conveniently spent time at the Illinois Secretary of State's office getting his driver's license renewed. Corroborating his own story, Joey reported how he even ran into an old friend of his there, Anthony "Tee" Bongiarno. I knew "Tee" myself, I used to work with him at the Area #5 Detectives Division.

Lombardo's stacks of witness statements and reports as to his whereabouts were not allowed into evidence during the trial, prompting Joey to complain at his sentencing about how he had not received a fair trial. Indicting the court for its unfairness was not the wisest course of action for a sentencing hearing. Nonetheless, he rambled on, saying how the government didn't put "one ounce" of evidence in to prove he was involved in organized crime after he had served his time for the skimming and bribery conviction. "Now I suppose the court is going to sentence me to life in prison for something I didn't do," he complained, portraying himself as the victim.

Joey's counsel Rick Halprin jumped into the fray, raising questions about double jeopardy since his client had already done time for loan sharking, extortion, and other wrongdoing that was the subject of the Family Secrets prosecution.

Prosecutor Markus Funk would have none of this and urged Judge Zagel to impose the maximum allowable sentence. "Mr. Lombardo is . . . an Outfit boss with no remorse," Funk added. Lombardo has long been described by authorities as the long time capo of the Grand Avenue street crew.

Then Judge Zagel spoke. "In the end we are judged by our actions, not by our wit or our smiles. In cases like this," the judge continued, addressing Lombardo directly, "we are judged by the worst things we have done, and the worst things you have done are terrible. I see no regret in you."

Lombardo was then sentenced to life in prison. Even though Lombardo will never see green grass again—at least not as a free man—the sentence provided neither comfort nor the requisite closure for the Seifert family. "I'll never feel safe," Emma Seifert said. "Never." Emma confirmed her feelings directly to me both before and after the hearing, stressing how she can never feel safe again, no matter what.

It would be "Little Jimmy" Marcello's turn on Thursday February 5, 2009. Unlike Calabrese and Lombardo, though, who had entered court decked out in jumpsuit orange, Jimmy Marcello appeared to have just stepped out of a Giorgio Armani designer store. Jimmy was shackled, but otherwise fully outfitted to the nines in a dark olive silk sport coat, nicely pressed slacks, and an open neck sports shirt.

The first to address the court was Bob D'Andrea, son of Nicholas D'Andrea who was beaten to death in the back of a car in 1981 while mob bosses were questioning him about a botched hit of a mob boss. Marcello was implicated in the hit along with several high ranking mob bosses who were there, including Sam Carlisi, who had pulled Nicholas into a car and then beat him with the butt end of a shotgun while D'Andrea was tied up in the back seat. They roughed D'Andrea up so much, they decided they had to kill him, which they proceeded to do. Marcello had been the driver of the car.

Bob D'Andrea looked Marcello straight in the eye, telling him how he wished Marcello could imagine the pain his father went through. Marcello stared right back. Tom Breen, one of Marcello's attorneys, objected to how D'Andrea addressed Marcello rather than the court directly.

Michael Spilotro's widow also had a turn at Marcello, who had been implicated in the notorious Spilotro hit made infamous by the Hollywood film *Casino*. Smartly dressed in black with dark glasses, Ann walked right to the lectern with a painful letter she was about to read. She praised the Department of Justice, the prosecutors and others who had worked hard to bring the closure of a happy ending, as she put it. But Ann stressed how she never, ever would forgive Marcello for what he had done to her family so many years ago, recounting years of pain and suffering as she raised her children after the murder.

I watched Ann closely as she read from her letter and addressed the court. She refused to use Marcello's name, and avoided looking at him directly.

Patrick Spilotro, the dentist who ultimately helped prosecutors to nab Joey Lombardo, was next. He reeled off a list of dirty mob laundry, including the names of Outfit members who were responsible for his brother's death. As he went through the list, it occurred to me that most of those cited were already dead—not much of an endorsement for the life of a mobster. One top mob figure who was neither dead nor indicted was John "No Nose" DiFronzo who somehow was never charged. But I believe the Family Secrets prosecution was not the end of mob prosecutions, just the beginning of the end. At this writing DiFronzo is widely believe to be the top boss, and I personally feel he could be among those to be indicted next.

Spilotro expressed great contempt for how his brothers were killed. "Denied my brothers a prayer" is how he put it, stressing that their killers deserved no mercy. "I stand here not because I want to, it's because I have to."

Dr. Spilotro then jolted the courtroom, recounting how Little Jimmy Marcello had lost his own father, Sam Marcello, to mob violence in 1973. Sam had been collecting juice loans from a sandwich shop owner in the old Western and Taylor Street neighborhood. Sam was a small guy, like his son, but he worked in tandem with a gorilla named Joseph Grisafe. The restaurant had once been owned by Sam Rantis, 43, who served 11 months in prison after Secret Service agents confiscated nearly a half million dollars in counterfeit bills. His frozen body was found after he disappeared in December, 1973, when it turned up in the trunk of a car parked at O'Hare Airport.

Pat chided Marcello, saying he should have known better, since he had lost his own father to mob violence. Yet even Pat really didn't know the whole story of what had happened—but he didn't really have to know to make his point. But I *do* know the full story.

On July 6, 1974, the badly decomposed bodies of two men were found stuffed into a pair of 55-gallon oil drums in the storage area of a sandwich shop on the west side of Chicago. Those bodies were identified as Sam J. Marcello, 57, of Rosemont, Illinois—Little Jimmy's father, and mob goon Joseph Grisafe, 34, of Mount Prospect. The proprietor of the restaurant found both men. Marcello was jammed head down with a plastic bag covering the top half of his body. He had been shot once in the head. Grisafe, though, was 6 feet 4 inches and 240 pounds, so stuffing him into the drum had proved more difficult. To do so, his legs had been cut off, both of which were found nearby in a separate box. Both men were believed to be victims of a gangland execution in response to an extortion investigation that was raising way too much heat from the government.

As Pat spoke in court, I kept an eye on Jimmy Marcello. I strained to read his expression, searching for clues on his face. Throughout the sentencing process, he showed no emotion whatsoever and continued to appear relaxed, sitting cool as a cucumber at the defense table, one hand resting on his cheek most of the time.

Judge Zagel addressed Marcello. "You could have done better, you know now to do better, and I regret that you did not. You could have led a better life. But now you will have to pay for your crimes." Even as the judge sentenced him to life in prison, Marcello's stoic expression failed to change.

The remaining defendant, Anthony "Twan" Doyle was sentenced on March 12, 2009. Before the judge took the bench, I found myself chatting with Bruce Meczyk, my good personal friend and the attorney for Doyle. He said he was nervous, but was going to request probation for Doyle with no further incarceration. I thought he must be smoking some funny cigarettes, and I told him so.

Doyle was eventually escorted in, decked out in shackles and orange jump suit, and took a seat next to his attorneys Meczyk and co-counsel Darrell Goldberg. Doyle had changed a lot since the trial in 2007. He was wearing glasses, his hair was totally white and slicked back. The last time I saw him was in 2007, when we had spoken some, and his hair then had been completely black. I don't think they offered much in the way of hair coloring and other niceties in the pen.

Markus Funk began, introducing Doyle as a former police officer. Funk reminded the court that when Doyle had been assigned to the evidence room of the Chicago Police Department, he would log into a police computer and gather information on a pair of gloves that had been left behind at the John Fecarotta hit in 1986. Doyle was looking to tamper with evidence, even willing to destroy crucial DNA evidence, which could have jeopardized much of the Family Secrets trial. Prosecutors were seeking up to 20 years for Doyle, who had passed information about the evidence along to Frank Calabrese, Sr., then in prison. "He betrayed his oath as a law enforcement officer," Funk chided. "He betrayed the public trust. Mr. Doyle is a disgrace."

For 40 minutes my friend Ralph Meczyk would respond, arguing that his client was defendant only because of his loyalty to his friend Calabrese—but that he did not know the monster that Calabrese really was. Anthony Doyle was a good cop, Meczyk argued, one who earned an honest living as a police officer who at one time had been a street sweeper for the City of Chicago. He disputed Funk's description of Doyle as a "sleeper agent" for the mob.

Meczyk recounted how Doyle had saved several people from a burning building, and had saved a robbery victim after she had been thrown onto the "L" tracks. Doyle had jumped down after her, pulling the woman to safety as a train approached, a heroic deed that earned him police officer of the month honors.

Doyle, though, had allegedly become a "chumbolone," street slang for "chum," a fool. Doyle had used these words during his testimony at trial. The judge asked whether Doyle wanted to address the court. He did, approaching the bench with a yellow pad of notes, his lawyer standing at his side. Doyle then read his apologies to the court, expressing that he was deeply sorry and ashamed—to his friends and especially his family. Doyle's wife was in the courtroom, having arrived from Wickenberg, Arizona, for the proceedings. Doyle's apology was short, but very emotional for Mrs. Doyle who cried throughout.

Judge Zagel sentenced Doyle to 144 months in prison for leaking evidence information and helping mob killer Frank Calabrese, Sr. "He picked the wrong people to try to help," the judge added. But Doyle did catch a small break because of his otherwise splendid career. Judge Zagel could have given him 15 full years, but did consider his years of good service.

Afterward I asked Maczyk how he felt about the sentence. "Great, just great," he replied. "It could have been devastating." Not that 12 years is any picnic—but at least it wasn't 15.

Judge Zagel's work still was not done, though. There was the lingering matter of one-time mob operative Nick Calabrese, brother to Frank and a key government witness. This would be the last tune played for this, the last dance of the Chicago mob as we once knew it, for Nick had to be sentenced as well.

Nick Calabrese had been one of the mist "made members" of the Chicago Outfit to openly testify against the mob. Interestingly, Judge Zagel moved the proceedings for Nick, opting to use the smaller courtroom 2503 for symbolic reasons. Nick had not been a defendant in the case, the Judge explained, so he did not want to give the implied appearance that he was being treated the same as the real defendants. This was to be something different altogether.

One thing was not different: the courtroom was jammed packed, wall to wall, with government agents scattered throughout the gallery. Many family members of victims were present, as well as the head United States Attorney for the Northern District of Illinois, Patrick J. Fitzgerald and First Assistant Gary Shapiro.

On March 26, 2009, at 2:15pm, Nicholas Calabrese was escorted into court where he took a seat with his counsel John Theis. I was struck by Nick's demeanor as he walked gingerly through the room, an old man, a defeated man it seemed, with white hair and glasses but no orange jump suit. Nick wore blue jeans, a gray sweat shirt, and white gym shoes as he settled in.

The mood was different on this day. Nick had been a mob figure, to be sure, but he had also brought some closure for many of these families, risking his own life to do it. The judge openly announced that

Nick's sentence had to reflect his level of cooperation to incentivize other potential mob turn-coats to provide information as well.

"On this day there are many other hundreds of fathers and mothers and brothers and sisters," the judge announced, referring to families needing to know more about the fate of their loved ones. "Many of them still wait."

Felice Weiler, an assistant in the U.S. Attorneys Office assigned to victim witnesses, read letters sent by the Spilotro and Vaci families. They were heartbreaking letters that set the stage for a number of family members to step forward.

The daughter of Arthur Morawski approached to tell of her father, an innocent man gunned down in cold blood while simply sitting in his car in Cicero, Illinois—the wrong place at the wrong time. She said "no more hugging, kissing him, and his grand daughter will never know him and her children never got to know him, only for a few family pictures."

Janet Ortiz, daughter of Richard Ortiz who was shot to death along with Morawski, read from her notes and cried throughout. "I have waited half a life for a chance to come face to face with the person responsible for my father's death," she said. I glanced at Nick who seemed to have been weeping as well, all while family photos kept flashing overhead on the large screen set up in court.

Anthony Ortiz was next. Son of Richard, Anthony called the sentence pathetic. "To me, that's a serial killer," he said coldly, referring to Calabrese. "Mr. Calabrese will tell you he should get leniency and still have his life; it's more than I had with my father." Still referring to Nick's sentence, Anthony continued. "I've never heard of something so ridiculous. That's less than a year for every person that he killed."

The widow of Paul Haggerty, Charlene Moravicek was next. "You ruined my life," she began. "You killed my husband by cutting his throat and putting a plastic bag over his head and put him in the trunk of a car." Looking over her right shoulder, she stared directly at Nick Calabrese. "He is the devil," she announced, sobbing throughout her emotional address. Then, as she left, she stopped and looked directly at him again and vented a sudden loud cry. "You make me sick to my stomach." The intensity finally got to her, for as Charlene Moravicek left the courtroom, she finally collapsed and had to be wheeled from the Federal Building by paramedics.

Then Peggy Cagnoni approached the bench. She said she would always remember her husband Michael's last words to her before he was to be blown apart by a Calabrese car bomb in 1981. "I'll always love you."

Addressing Calabrese directly, she went on. "I feel you are truly heartless and deserve no mercy. You got in a trap and had nowhere to go. Do you have any idea how I felt [upon learning] that I had been driving a car with a live bomb and with my 8-year old son—and also pregnant at the time?"

I watched Calabrese, his head hanging, but his face showing no visible signs of remorse.

Bob D'Andrea, son of mobster Nicholas D'Andrea who had been beaten to death with a baseball bat in 1981, told the court that he knew his father was part of the mafia, "but I still love my father."

"You are here," Bob continued, "quite simply because you dropped your gloves." Cynical, perhaps, but true. Bob D'Andrea was always a huge man that you would not want to tangle with, but he had become a much different man than the last time I had seen and spoken with him. In court he was very mild-mannered, almost in deference to the fading last dance playing out before us all.

Then Nick himself took a turn. He apologized for his wrongdoing and his crimes, and said he thinks of those crimes all the time. "I can't go back and undo what I done. It's there every day. It doesn't go away, and rightly so. I ask my wife and children for their forgiveness. I let fear control my life, and beneath that fear was a coward who didn't walk away from that life," he admitted in front of his wife and children. "I stand before you a different man, a changed man. I throw myself on the mercy of the court. Thank you."

Judge Zagel then reminded Calabrese and the entire gallery, "Whenever he's a free man, Calabrese will never draw a secure breath. The organization will not forgive or relent in their pursuit of you," he said to Nick before sentencing him to 12 years and 4 months behind bars. Calabrese was age 66, and under federal guidelines he would serve 85% of his sentence. But he had already been incarcerated for 6 years, so he would be given credit for time served. Nick Calabrese might, indeed, once again see the light of freedom, though as Judge Zagel had observed, nothing in Nick's life could ever be truly free again.

Months later, on Thursday, February 21, 2008, I was stunned to learn that that prosecutor Mitch Mars was dead. "Humble mob prosecutor dies at 55," the Sun-Times reported.

I did not know Mitch well, although I had met him on day one of the Family Secrets trial and would chat with him occasionally throughout the trial. It would be the last case for Mitch Mars, a modest man who wore suits off the Robert Hall rack. Just two weeks after the trial, Mitch saw a doctor about a nagging cough, only to learn he had lung cancer. He kept the diagnosis quiet, and took a leave of absence.

I found myself at Mars' funeral on Saturday, February 23, 2008 at the St. Cletus Roman Catholic Church. Many wept as Father Charles spoke of his courageous life. "You are not forgotten, loved one, nor will you ever be, as long as life and memory last we will remember thee."

Later, at a celebration for Mitch at the Federal Building, the Federal deputy chief of organized crime, Mark Vogel, paid tribute. "Mitch gave his last measure of devotion to that case," he said, referring to the Family Secrets investigation and trial, "which was Mitch's finest accomplishment."

Mitch's closing arguments in the trial had indeed been stirring, one of the best closing arguments ever in courtroom 2525, according to colleagues. Personally, I feel I was privileged to be one of the lucky few to see Mars deliver that closing, live, in the courtroom. A quote from the closing is now featured on a memorial plaque honoring Mars that is hung in a third-floor conference room.

And so courtroom 2525 was dedicated to the late Mitch Mars. I never heard the great Clarence Darrow, who once spoke for 12 hours to save the lives of young murderers Nathan Leopold and Richard Loeb, but I did hear Mitch. His Family Secrets closing would be second to none, with the following words forever memorialized in his honor:

"Criminal cases are about accountability and justice, not only for the defendants, but also justice for our system, justice for our society, and justice for the victims.

"Our system works. It is the greatest system in the world. But it only works when those who should be held accountable are held accountable."

These were the last words he would utter in open court, the last breath of the last dance. And now they will live on, speaking every day to every defendant and victim who touches courtroom 2525.

Index

A

Accardo, Tony "Big Tuna," 14-15, 18, 54, 66-67, 122, 134-41, 160, 224-25, 283, 290-91, 309
Ackerman, Fred, 129
African Lion, The, 97
Aiuppa, Joey "The Doves," 54, 66, 136, 138, 140, 210, 236-37
Albergo, Michael "Hambone," 119, 142, 198-200, 221-22
Alderisio, Felix "Milwaukee Phil," 194
Aleman, Harry, 178, 197
Almira Savings and Loan Association, 246
Altabello, Guy, 162
Amadeo, Junior, 85
Amundsen, Richard, 93
Andriacchi, Joseph, 138
Annerino, Steve, 192-93, 197
Anselmi, Albert, 45

B

Bailey, F. Lee, 100
Baker, Iva, 95-96
Banks, Sam, 168
Barbara, Fred Bruno, 228
Barbaro, Joseph, 117
Barcelino, Tony, 197
Barish, Charlie, 87, 115, 118
Barnum, P.T., 39
Basile, Peter, 165, 168
Basinske, Joseph, 162
Battaglia, Sam, 140
Battle of 22nd Street, 43
Bay of Pigs, 133, 139
Bell, George, 126-27
Bhachus, Amarjeet, 315
Bills, Sam, 158
Bistro-a-Go-Go, 93, 194-97
Black Hand, 40, 45
Blair, Kevin, 28-29
Blanc, Curtis, 10, 61
Blitzstein, "Fat Herbie," 119, 238
Blue Moon Tavern, 78
Bombenger, James, 77
Bonnie (witness), 282
bookmaking, 52, 136, 142, 156, 158, 201, 303
Borcelino, Anthony, 231
Bounds, Danny, 233, 291
Bourgeois, Tom, 47
Brach, Helen, 100
Branch, Alfonso, 106

Brayman, Paul, 314, 316
Breen, Thomas, 159, 313
Brill, Karen, 159
Brown, Albert, 77, 80
Brown, William "Cherry Nose," 162
Buccaneer Lounge, 114
Buccieri, Fiore "Fifi," 85, 107, 113-14
Burns, Henrietta, 128

C

Cagnoni, Michael, 143, 160, 206, 209, 211, 214, 226
Cagnoni, Peggy, 10, 329
Caifano, Marshall, 286
Cain, Michael J., 10, 18
Cain, Richard, 18, 176
Calabrese, Frank Jr., 13, 27, 29, 48, 50-51, 58, 63, 85, 103, 125, 146, 154, 209, 217
Calabrese, Frank Sr. "The Breeze," 10, 13, 17, 23, 26, 49, 51, 54, 61-62, 103, 125-26, 183, 303-4, 307-8, 310-12, 326-27
  bookmaking, 156, 158, 303
  denial, 203-4
  dyslexia, 186
  forty-minute speech, 320
  Jefferson Ice Company, 185
  on John Feracotta's murder, 202
  marriage, 188
  murder of Dauber couple, 143
  murder of John Mendell, 204
  on Paul Haggerty's murder, 204
Calabrese, Kurt, 28, 60, 125, 188, 255, 257, 319
Calabrese, Nicholas William. *See* Calabrese, Nick

Calabrese, Nick, 23, 26, 50-52, 58, 62-63, 108, 124, 160-61, 214, 216-17, 232-34, 243-45, 256, 275-76, 313, 327-29
  Barbara's alleged activities, 228
  Cagnoni murder, 217-22
  murder of John Fecarotta, 219-20, 251-53
  serial killer, 256, 313
Calabrese, Wemette, 161
Campise, Jasper, 254
Candy Kit Co., 77
Cannon, Howard, 262, 267
Capone, Albert, 75
Capone, Alphonse, 15, 21-22, 26, 28, 30-32, 35, 41-43, 45-46, 65-68, 75, 92, 134, 137, 145, 224, 308
  in Alcatraz, 75
  brought to trial, 74
  convicted on five counts, 74
  death of, 75
  fame, 74
  "Scarface," 32, 46, 68, 72, 317
  treated for paresis, 75
Capone, Amadoe, 75
Capone, Bottles, 14, 31, 66, 75
Capone, Ralph, 14, 17, 31, 66, 75, 259, 326
Capone, Salvatore "Frank," 75
Carlisi, Black Sam, 125, 240, 249, 323
Carlisi, Sam "Wings," 54, 240
Carole, Robert, 93
Caruso, Carmen, 26
Caruso, Frank "Skid," 158, 198
Caruso, Frank "Tootsie Babe," 158, 228
Caruso, Pete "Butch," 198

Casentino, Henry, 204
Casino, 14, 62, 235, 237, 239, 242, 244, 290
Castro, Fidel, 139
Catuara, Jimmy "The Bomber," 227
Cerone, Jackie, 54, 57, 66, 122, 172, 237, 245, 254, 267
Chessher, Robert, 128
Chiaramonti, Anthony "Tony the Hatch," 119, 155
Chicago Board of Education, 60
Chicago Crime Commission, 174-75, 222
Chicago Daily News, 288
Chicago Merchandise Mart, 133
Chicago mob, 3, 13, 15, 22, 26, 31, 49, 52, 71, 114, 133-34, 139, 151, 211, 236, 262
Chicago Police Department, 13, 62, 326
Chicago River, 36-37
Chicago Sun-Times, 10-11, 28, 120
Chicago Syndicate, 13, 21, 26, 52
Chicago Tribune, 97, 218
Chinatown 26th Street, 54
Churow, Rudolph, 246
Cicero, 28-29, 42-44, 55, 58, 91-92, 104-5, 114, 143, 160, 166, 192, 202, 207, 225, 243, 292
Clay, Cassius. *See* Muhammad Ali
"clubs," 24
Coconate, Frank, 27
Cohen, Nathan, 129
Colosimo, James "Big Jim," 39, 66
Colvin, Harvey, 39
Comet (dog), 10, 61
Conlisk, James B. Jr., 123
Connie's Pizza, 153-54, 194, 303

Corcoran, Russell, 98
Cosentino, Henry, 143
Cox, Susan, 304
Crimaldi, Charlie "Chuckie," 238
Crime of the Century (Martin), 10, 281
Cullotta, Frank, 246
Czech, Frank, 9, 24, 90-91, 122, 126

D

Daily Herald, 218
Daley, Richard J., 22, 89, 123, 284
Daly, Maggie, 134
D'Amato, Joe, 289
Damion, Larry, 288
Damone, Vic, 5, 109-10, 113-14
D'Andrea, Bob, 308, 323-24, 329
D'Andrea, Nicholas, 143, 159, 308, 323, 329
Dauber, Charlotte, 143, 205, 227
Dauber, William, 63, 143, 205
De Angelo, Richard, 195
Dean O'Banion Gang, 44
DeLucia, Paul "The Waiter," 66-67
Dempsey, Jack, 46
De Pietto, Americo, 129
Destefano, Sam "Mad Sam," 117, 128, 130, 140, 162, 237
Dever, William, 41
Devitt, Lloyd, 87
DiCaro, Martha, 105
DiDonato, Anthony, 128-29, 289
DiFazio, Donald "Captain D," 154-55
DiForti, James, 28, 228, 234
DiFranzo, Johnny "Bananas," 163
DiFronzo, John "No Nose," 26, 66, 119, 324

Diggins, Paddy, 101
Dillinger, John, 35, 165
Dio, Johnny, 277
DiPaolo, Anthony, 127
Dirksen Federal Building, 54, 58, 305
DiVarco, Joseph (Little Caesar), 123
Domph, Ellen, 315
Dorfman, "Red," 263
Doyle, Anthony "Twan," 10, 17, 29, 51, 57, 120, 147, 312, 325
Druggan, Terry, 44
Drummond, John, 205, 218, 307-8
Drury Lane Theatre, 228
Ducks" Corallo, 277
Duffy, Bill, 112
Dundee, Angelo, 152
D'Varco, Cesar, 289, 293

E

Eboli, Louis "The Mooch," 240, 295
Ernie "The Oven," 164
Erskine, Joe, 194-95
Eto, Ken "Tokyo Joe," 254
Everleigh Club, 39-40
Exner, Judith Campbell, 139
extortion, 40, 50, 52, 54, 58, 67, 103, 106, 125, 130, 136, 144, 165, 203, 228-29, 238

F

Fan Tan, 254
Farinola, Vito Rocco. *See* Damone
Fecarotta, John, 50, 57, 107-8, 143, 202, 217, 219, 228, 236, 239-40, 242-43, 248, 250, 253, 255, 259
Federal Correctional Institution, 48
Federal Mann Act, 35

Federal Reserve Bank, 57
Ferraro, Richard, 195
Ferriola, Joseph "Mr. Clean," 54, 158, 243, 297
Ferriola, Nicholas, 54, 142, 157
Finn, Mickey, 38
Finnegal, Edward, 129
Fiore, Phil, 124
First Ward, 34, 39-40, 211, 228
Fitzgerald, Patrick J., 9, 142, 327
Fitzgerald, Richard, 100
Fitzsimmons, Frank, 277-78
Flash Trucking, 160, 243
Flood, Ed, 106
Flynn, Irene, 313
Flynn, James, 313
Foreman, Leo, 237-38
Four Deuces Café, 41
Franchina, Anthony, 109-11, 113
Frank, 26-29, 50-51, 90-93, 102-4, 109-11, 124-26, 153-54, 156-59, 183-94, 196-213, 219-23, 225-27, 229-32, 255, 311-12, 318-20
Freemont Casino, 235
Fugitive, The, 37, 218
Funk, Markus, 11, 21, 153, 310, 315, 323, 326

G

Gabes, Ed, 61
Gacy, John Wayne, 101
Gaffney, Bobby, 86
Gagliano, Joseph "Joe Gags," 123
Garyn, Gary, 93
Gattusa, John, 254
G-Block, 278
Giacalone, Tony, 278

Giancana, Antoinette "Toni," 129
Giancana, Sam, 14-15, 18, 26, 32, 66,
   122, 129, 137-41, 237, 290, 309
  Bay of Pigs, 133, 139
  extradited back to the U.S., 139
  growing up years, 134-35
  murder of, 139
Gilary, Albert, 294
Glickman, Bernie, 151-52
Glickman, Joel, 151-52
Glover, John, 10, 61
Goggin, Jackie, 88
Goldberg, Darrell, 158, 182, 326
Gold Rush, Ltd., 238
Gordon Tech High School, 98
Gotti, John, 278, 317
Grammels (couple), 96
Grant (general), 34
Grath, John, 117
Great Depression, 73, 80
Grieco, Donald, 86, 109-10, 113
Grieco, Joey, 86, 110-13
Grieco, Mike, 110
Grisafe, Joseph, 325
Gunnoe, Mark, 10, 61
Gusenberg, Frank, 71
Guzzino, Sam, 159, 233

H

Haggerty, Paul, 142, 204, 223-24,
  307, 319, 328
Hallam, Kathryn, 78
Halprin, Rick, 57, 60, 67, 148, 150,
  168, 182, 259, 267, 270, 275,
  281-82, 284, 288, 300, 303
Hancock Center, 258
Hanhardt, William, 57, 62, 162
Hanley, Delores, 188

Hanley, Ed, 199
Hansen, Joey, 194, 234
Hansen, Kenneth, 99-100
Healy, Edward F., 123
Hilde (little girl), 96-97
Hill Street Blues, 96
Hinkel, Richard "Dick," 118
Hoffa, James Riddle "Jimmy," 146,
  261, 263, 265, 276, 278
Hoffa, Jimmy, 14, 146, 261, 263,
  276-77, 284
Hoffa Execution, 278
Hole-in-the-Wall-Gang, 238
Holy Name Cathedral, 45, 83, 136
Hoover, Herbert, 69
Hoover, J. Edgar, 139
Horwarth's Restaurant, 228-29
Howlett, Michael, 88
Hudson, Dick, 243
Humphreys, Muray "The Camel," 122

I

Illinois Association of Chiefs of
  Police, 90
Illinois Enforcement Commission, 58
Infelice, Ernest "Rocky," 129
Infelise, Rocco, 62, 243
Internal Revenue Code, 145
Iovinelli, Cooney, 26
Iovinelli, Patrick, 26
Ivy Lounge, 194-95

J

Jack, James A., 30, 61
  abandonment, 80
  Ben Franklin Awards for Mystery
    and Suspense, 101

Cen-Flo-S.A.C. Club, 84
as detective, 89
Gregory Elementary School, 317
kidnapped, 81
Last Dance, The, 13, 15
orphanage, 83
police school, 89
Three Boys Missing, 13, 18, 89, 101, 201, 281, 300
Tribune Traffic Award of the Month, 97
U.S. Marines, 88
as Walter James Jack, 87
Jackson, William "Action," 290
Jai Jong, 254
Jarrett, Ronald William, 156
Jarrett, Ronnie "Menz," 119, 156-58, 163, 201, 204, 222-24, 227
Jayne, George, 100
Jayne, Silas, 100
Jimmy Jack. *See* Jack, James A., 13-15, 30
Joe the Pelican, 86, 112, 116
Johnson, Dennis, 55, 142
Johnson, Thomas, 55, 142
Joliet State Penitentiary, 77
Jordan, Michael, 35, 74, 283
juices loans, 193
Juzwik, Edmond, 101

K

Kaluchi, George, 271, 273
Kass, Bill, 115
Kearns, Jerry, 99
Kefauver Committee, 75
Kennedy, Bobby, 137, 139, 277-78
Kennedy, Jackie, 14, 134
Kennedy, John F., 66, 76, 130, 137, 261

Kennedy, Joseph, 133, 137
Kennelly, Martin H., 283
Kerner, Otto, 22, 89
King, Michael, 242
Kluczynski Building, 305
Knight, Jake, 10, 61
Kracker, Frank, 134
Krause, Thomas (a.k.a. Lawrence Krone), 78-79
Kumerow, Eric, 140

L

Laborers Local #5, 233
Lace, Paper, 71
Lake, Frankie, 44
Lake County Jail, 46
La Mano Nera, 40
LaMantia, Joseph "Shorty," 101-2
LaMantia, Rocco, 105
Lamonte, Frank, 204
LaMotta, Jake, 95
LaPietra, Angelo "The Hook," 57, 104, 146, 156-57, 194, 202-4, 210, 228, 230-32
LaPietra, Jimmy "Haime," 192, 197, 208, 210, 219, 232
Lara, Blanca, 282
Laren-Maltese, Betty, 160
Last Dance, The (Jack), 13, 15
Lavin, Katherine, 313
Lee, Robert E., 34
Lefty" Rosenthal, 237, 239
Leighton, George, 128
levee, 33-36, 39
Levinson, Harry, 223-24
Levinson's Jewelry, 223-25
Lincolnshire Golf Club, 233
Lindbergh, Charles, 46, 73

Lisallo, Chris, 117
Liston, Sonny, 152
Livingston, Victor, 98
loan sharking, 27-28, 50, 58, 67, 126, 136, 142, 198, 210-12, 221, 255, 267, 323
Lombardo, Joey "The Clown," 15, 29, 32, 51, 57, 119-20, 138, 169, 183, 237, 276, 280, 282
Lombardo, Joey "The Clown"
  on the Danny Seifert murder, 285
  Last Supper photo, 290
  trip to the dentist, 170
Lombardo, Shawanda, 267
Lonergan Die Co., 77
Loop, 42, 56, 97
Lopez, Joseph, 154, 256, 311, 320
Louis, Joe, 95
lounges, 24-25, 79, 114, 126, 135, 190, 195-97
Lucas, James C., 75
Lydon, Matt, 150

M

M & M Entertainment, 55
Mae (Al Capone's wife), 75
Mallul, John, 10, 316
Maloney, Thomas J., 105, 246
Malooly, John, 226
Manno, Carmen, 135
Man Who Shot Liberty Valance, The, 73
Maravecek, Charlene, 307
Marcello, Connie, 165
Marcello, James "Little Jimmy," 29, 62, 119, 138, 159, 323
Marcello, Michael, 55, 142, 144-45
Marino, Louis, 240

Marione, Mike, 88
Marovitz, Abraham Lincoln, 129
Mars, Mitch, 21, 234, 271, 273, 278, 284, 330
Martin, Marc W., 182, 281
Martin, William J.
  Crime of the Century, 10, 281
Marzaho, Charles, 195
McCarthy, Billy, 179, 194, 246
McCarthy, William J., 246
McCluskie, Norma, 128-29
McDaniel, Roy, 150
McDonald, Michael, 38
McDonald, Robert, 104
McDonald Democrats, 39
McDonnell, Bob, 135
McDonnell, Robert, 129
McGuire, Phyllis, 138
McGurn, Jack "Machine Gun," 66, 70, 119, 136, 141, 224
Meczyh, Ralph, 17, 259
Meczyk, Bruce, 325
Medill, Joseph, 38
Mendell, John, 143, 163-64, 179, 204, 223-25
Meo's Norwood House, 121, 189-90
Merchandize Mart, 76
Miami Dolphins, 140
Michigan, Lake, 36-37, 47, 84
Midway Airport, 43
milk bottles, 25-26
Milleri, Albert, 290
Milton Berle Show, 114
Miraglia, James R., 246
Miraglia, Jimmy, 194
Mirro, James "Cowboy," 129
M&M Amusement, 142, 144
Money to Burn (Zagel), 56
Montana's Restaurant, 191

Monteleone, John "Johnny Apes," 54, 119, 156, 158, 197, 202, 207, 219, 249
Moore, John, 135
Moore, Sylvester, 164
Moran, Bugs, 44, 68-70
Morawski, Arthur, 143, 207, 307, 328
Morelli, Blackie, 112
Moretti, Vincent, 143, 204-5, 225
M&R Auto and Truck Repair Service, 131
Muhammad Ali, 152
Murderers' Row Yankees, 46
Murphy, George, 9, 91, 98, 122
Musto, Tony, 86

N

Nadle, Ronnie, 88
Nagal, Joe, 197, 297
Ness, Edna, 72
Ness, Elliot, 31, 68-69
  chief investigator, promoted to, 71
  death, 72
  Diebold Corporation, 72
Nest Lounge, 24, 213
Neuman, Steve, 60, 302
Nevis, Terri, 159
New York Times, 65, 74, 262
Nitti, Frank "The Enforcer," 26, 32, 35, 66-67, 70, 113-14, 119, 136, 141
Nordberg, John, 115
Norgle, Charles, 162

O

O'Banion, Dion, 68
O'Brien, Chuckie, 277-78
O'Connor, Tim, 97
O'Donnell, Klondike, 43, 104
O'Donnell, Miles J., 104
O'Donnell, William Klondike, 104
O'Hare Airport, 62, 164, 249, 291, 325
O'Leary, Patrick, 38
Onesto, John, 117
Operation Family Secrets, 50-51, 141, 154, 254
O'Rourke, Jack, 157, 267
orphanage, 83-84, 90, 286
Ortiz, Anthony, 307, 328
Ortiz, Ellen, 307
Ortiz, Janet, 328
Ortiz, Richard, 143, 207, 307, 319, 328
outfit, 15, 28, 47-49, 52-53, 107-8, 125-26, 136, 143-44, 156-57, 219, 233, 242-43, 263-64, 266-69, 292-93, 311-12

P

Paprocki (Father), 248
Parclyla, Fred, 236
Parse's Hot Dogs, 195
Patrick, Lenny, 125
Pavlich, Fred, 160
Payne, John, 39
Peterson, Bobby, 97, 101
Peterson, Malcom, 98
Petro, Danny, 86
Petrocelli, Wiliam "Butch," 58, 143, 164-65, 206, 227, 230-32, 242, 246
Petz (sergeant), 98
Pilotto, Alfred, 159, 232-33, 290-91, 293
Pilotto, Henry, 233
Pink Clock, 135
Pless, John, 244
Pomeroy, Charles, 93

Pordzany, Clarice, 140
Potenza, Rocky, 190
Preferred Cigarette Vending Company, 123
Prohibition, 24, 29, 32, 36, 40-41, 46, 67-69, 71, 104, 133-35

Q

Queen of Heaven Cemetery, 140, 247

R

Racketeer Influenced Corrupt Organization Act, 164
Rainone, John, 124
Rainone, Mario, 125
Reichard, James, 93
Renno, Donald, 143, 204, 226
Ricci, Michael "The Hotdog Man," 51, 119, 142
Roaring Twenties, 36, 44, 46, 71
Robinson's Woods, 98-99
Rodgers, Johnny, 286
Roemer, Bill, 18
Roemer, William F. Jr., 119, 140, 237
Romano, Sal, 167
Rosa, Peter, 25
Route 66, 77, 81-82, 90
Rovetuso, Sam, 28
Russo, Matthew A. Jr., 131
Rustin, Bayard, 278
Ryan, Buddy, 163
Ryan, George, 89

S

Sadock, Verna, 12, 218
Sage, Anna, 165
Saladino, Frank "Gumba," 51, 119, 142, 223, 225, 229
Santucci, Frank, 85, 120, 127-29, 135, 194, 204, 232
Sarillo, Nicholas, 63
Scaglione, Johnny "The Nose," 86
Scaglione, Theresa, 86
Scalise, Jerry, 124-25, 176, 227
Scalise, John, 45
Scarpelli, Gerald, 163, 165
Schatz, Susan, 60, 148, 301
Schira, Frank, 78, 90
Schira, Gary J., 90
Schiro, Paul "The Indian," 29, 51, 57, 63, 142-43, 147, 162, 168, 234, 303-4, 306, 311, 317-18
Schuessler, Anton Sr., 99
Schuessler, John, 97
Schuessler, Tony, 97
Scully, John, 11, 62-63, 147, 185, 209, 212, 256, 303
Searby, Edmund, 164
Seifert, Daniel, 142, 147-48, 150-51, 259, 285, 287, 306, 308, 311-12, 321
Seifert, Emma, 12, 147, 282, 321-23
Seifert, Joseph, 147, 308, 321
Seifert, Ronald, 149
Severino, Ernest, 164
Shallow, Gerry "Gene," 18
Shapiro, Gary, 9, 304, 327
Shenker, Morris, 261, 263, 284
Sherwin Lisner, 238
shy business, 132
Shylocks, 132
Siegel, Bobby "The Beak," 119, 161
Sinatra, Frank, 66, 114, 130, 137-38, 225, 293
Skar, Mandel "Manny," 114

Solano, Vince, 254, 290, 293
Spano, Michael Sr., 29, 160
Spano, Paul, 160
Spilotro, Anthony "The Ant," 62, 108, 119, 138, 141, 146, 167, 169-70, 194, 224, 234, 236, 238-44, 247, 250, 267-69
Spilotro, Michael, 62-63, 143, 207
Spilotro, Patrick, 10, 170, 274, 306, 308, 324
Sporadic, Bob "Crazy Bob," 194
Spry, Roger, 99
S.S. Rosenthal, 87
Stardust Casino and Hotel, 57, 235, 267
St. Joseph's Cemetery, 123-24
Stolfe, James, 153
Stubitsch, Larry, 189, 192-98
St. Valentine's Day Massacre, 44, 70, 72, 136, 236
Sullivan, John L., 39
Swanson, Connie, 165-66
Szarat, William, 102

T

Tangled Web, The, 10, 18
Tarnabene, Al "The Pizza Man," 119
Tarpenian, Parse, 195
Teamsters Union, 266, 278
Tennes, Monte, 39
Terrell, Ernie, 152
Terrell, Jean, 152
Terrible Genna Brothers, 43, 46
Teutonico, Frank "The Calico Kid," 162
Theis, John, 327
Thompson, James R., 14, 18, 22, 58, 88
Thompson, William Hale "Big Bill," 31, 35, 41

Three Boys Missing (Jack), 13, 18, 89, 101, 201, 281, 300
Tocco, Albert, 232
Tolomeo, Phillip "Philly Beans," 14, 90, 121, 161, 194, 196
Toman, Andrew, 246
Tom's Steakhouse, 228
Torello, James "Turk," 197
Torrio, Johnny, 40, 45, 66-67, 75, 135
Touhy, Roger, 43
Tricario, Salvatore, 233
Tully, Larry, 93-94, 96
Tully, Strong, 93

U

Unione Siciliana, 44-45
Untouchables, The, 44, 68, 72, 93, 137

V

Vaci, Emil, 63, 143, 178, 234-36, 239, 249, 311, 318
Vagabond Lounge, 159
Valley Gang, 44
Vandermark, Jay, 235
Vandermark, Jeff, 235
Venezia, Joe, 54
Vic Damone Pizza Corporation, 113
Vivirito, Gus V., 104
Volpe, Angelo, 162
Volstead Act, 31, 69

W

Wacks, Peter, 282
Wagner, James, 147
Walker, Don, 304
Warsaw Polish Restaurant, 121

Weiler, Felice, 11, 318, 328
Weiner, Irwin, 149, 262
Weiss, Earl "Hymie," 44, 46, 68, 136, 141
Wenger, Margaret, 160
White Hand Society, 45
White Slave Traffic Committee, 34
Whiting, Robert, 288
Willens, Eugene, 87, 115
Wiszowaty, Ted, 11, 58, 61, 218, 317
Wolf, Anne, 58, 221, 302, 317
Wolfson, Dean, 115, 168
Wolfson, Warren, 87, 168

Y

Yale, Frankie, 41
Young, Mel, 164

Z

Zaccagnini, Vito, 85, 117
  childhood, 115-17
  as a government witness, 118
  indicted for murder, 117
Zagel, James, 23, 54, 56, 58, 146, 153, 183, 187, 189, 208, 221, 259, 276, 280, 320-21, 327
  Money to Burn, 56
Zizzo, Anthony "Little Tony," 119

Weiler, Felice, 11, 318, 328
Weiner, Irwin, 149, 262
Weiss, Earl "Hymie," 44, 46, 68, 136, 141
Wenger, Margaret, 160
White Hand Society, 45
White Slave Traffic Committee, 34
Whiting, Robert, 288
Willens, Eugene, 87, 115
Wiszowaty, Ted, 11, 58, 61, 218, 317
Wolf, Anne, 58, 221, 302, 317
Wolfson, Dean, 115, 168
Wolfson, Warren, 87, 168

Y

Yale, Frankie, 41
Young, Mel, 164

Z

Zaccagnini, Vito, 85, 117
  childhood, 115-17
  as a government witness, 118
  indicted for murder, 117
Zagel, James, 23, 54, 56, 58, 146, 153, 183, 187, 189, 208, 221, 259, 276, 280, 320-21, 327
  Money to Burn, 56
Zizzo, Anthony "Little Tony," 119